W9-CHO-073

DATE DUE

SEP 04 73			
JUN 08			

172107   952
                         Pa

Packard

Sons of heaven

MEDIA SERVICES
EVANSTON TOWNSHIP HIGH SCHOOL
EVANSTON, ILLINOIS 60204

SONS OF HEAVEN

Also by the author:

The Queen & Her Court: A Guide to the British Monarchy Today

American Monarchy: A Social Guide to the Presidency

Peter's Kingdom: Inside the Papal City

SONS

JERROLD M. PACKARD

OF HEAVEN,

A Portrait of the
Japanese Monarchy

CHARLES SCRIBNER'S SONS
NEW YORK

MEDIA SERVICES
EVANSTON TOWNSHIP HIGH SCHOOL
EVANSTON, ILLINOIS 60204

Copyright © 1987 by Jerrold M. Packard

All rights reserved. No part of this book may be reproduced or transmitted in any form or by any means, electronic or mechanical, including photocopying, recording or by any information storage and retrieval system, without permission in writing from the Publisher.

Charles Scribner's Sons
Macmillan Publishing Company
866 Third Avenue, New York, NY 10022
Collier Macmillan Canada, Inc.

Library of Congress Cataloging-in-Publication Data

Packard, Jerrold M.
  Sons of heaven.

  Bibliography: p.
  Includes index.
  1. Japan—Emperors—History. 2. Monarchy—Japan—
History. 3. Hirohito, Emperor of Japan, 1901–
I. Title.
JQ1641.P33   1987   354.5203'12'09   87-20752
ISBN 0-684-18633-0

Macmillan books are available at special discounts for bulk purchases for sales promotions, premiums, fund-raising, or educational use. For details, contact:

Special Sales Director
Macmillan Publishing Company
866 Third Avenue
New York, NY 10022

10 9 8 7 6 5 4 3 2 1

Book Design by Debby Jay

Printed in the United States of America

952
Pa

Contents

172107

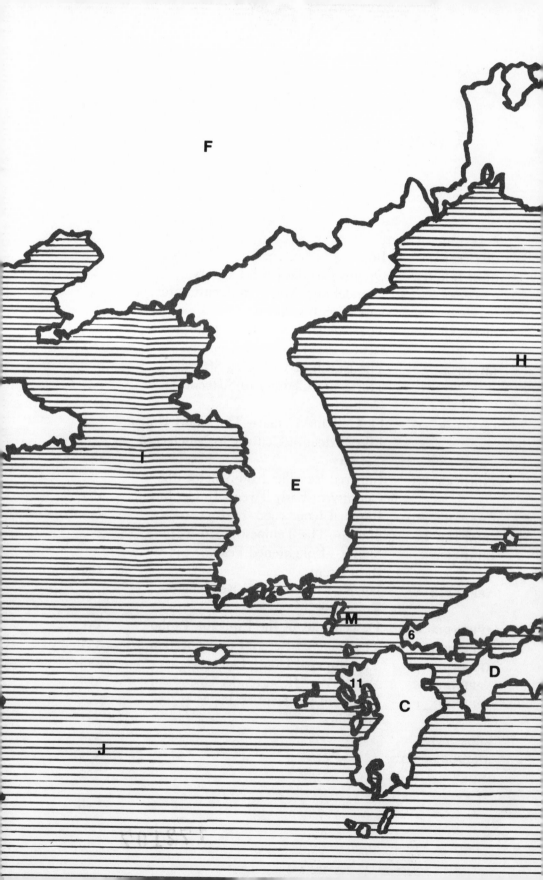

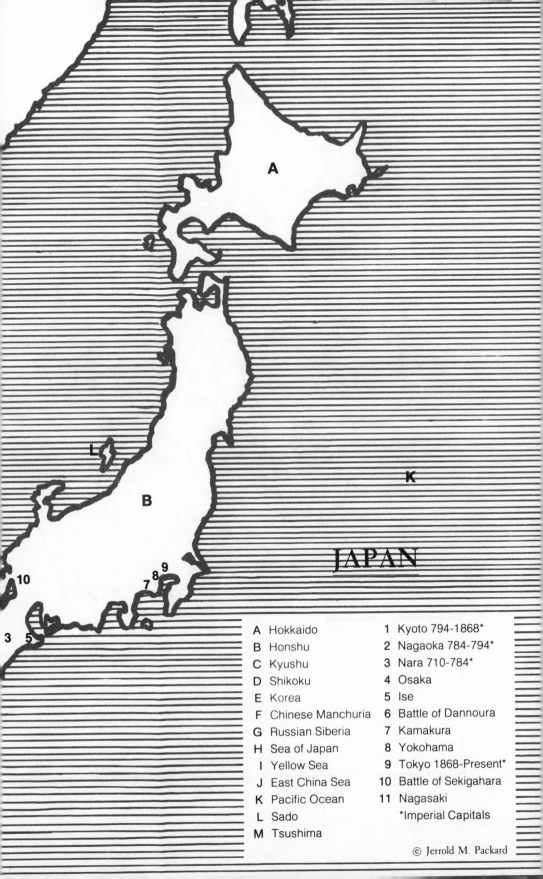

JAPAN

A	Hokkaido	1 Kyoto 794-1868*
B	Honshu	2 Nagaoka 784-794*
C	Kyushu	3 Nara 710-784*
D	Shikoku	4 Osaka
E	Korea	5 Ise
F	Chinese Manchuria	6 Battle of Dannoura
G	Russian Siberia	7 Kamakura
H	Sea of Japan	8 Yokohama
I	Yellow Sea	9 Tokyo 1868-Present*
J	East China Sea	10 Battle of Sekigahara
K	Pacific Ocean	11 Nagasaki
L	Sado	*Imperial Capitals
M	Tsushima	

© Jerrold M. Packard

1	Imperial Palace Plaza		
2	Uchiboridori (Avenue)	5	Imperial Household Agency
3	Private Imperial Palace Grounds	6	Double Bridge
3a	Fukiage Garden	7	Kitanomaru Park
3b	Fukiage Imperial Residence	7a	Science & Technology Museum
3c	Kashikodokoro Shrine	7b	Bukodan
3d	Biology Laboratory	8	Imperial Palace East Garden
4	Imperial Palace	8a	Imperial Guard Headquarters

© Jerrold M.

IMPERIAL PALACE GROUNDS—TOKYO

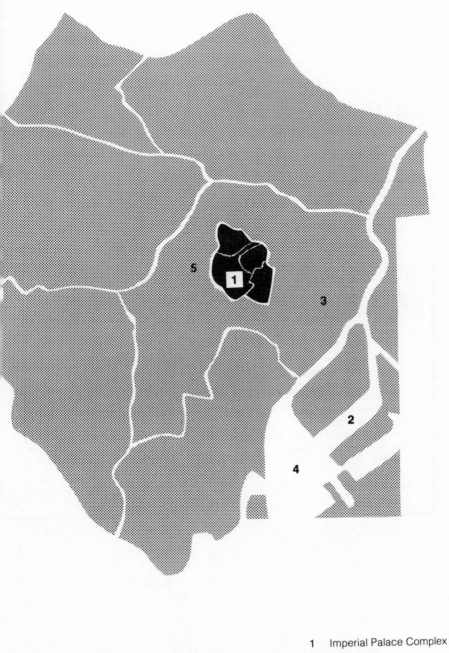

1	Imperial Palace Complex
2	Sumida River
3	Ginza
4	Tokyo Bay
5	Yasukuni Shrine

© Jerrold M. Packard

RELATIONSHIP OF IMPERIAL PALACE GROUNDS TO CENTRAL TOKYO

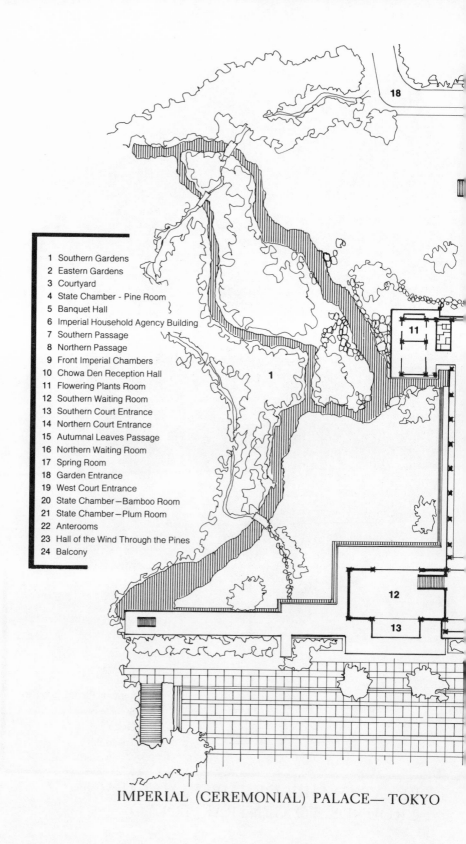

1 Southern Gardens
2 Eastern Gardens
3 Courtyard
4 State Chamber - Pine Room
5 Banquet Hall
6 Imperial Household Agency Building
7 Southern Passage
8 Northern Passage
9 Front Imperial Chambers
10 Chowa Den Reception Hall
11 Flowering Plants Room
12 Southern Waiting Room
13 Southern Court Entrance
14 Northern Court Entrance
15 Autumnal Leaves Passage
16 Northern Waiting Room
17 Spring Room
18 Garden Entrance
19 West Court Entrance
20 State Chamber—Bamboo Room
21 State Chamber—Plum Room
22 Anterooms
23 Hall of the Wind Through the Pines
24 Balcony

IMPERIAL (CEREMONIAL) PALACE— TOKYO

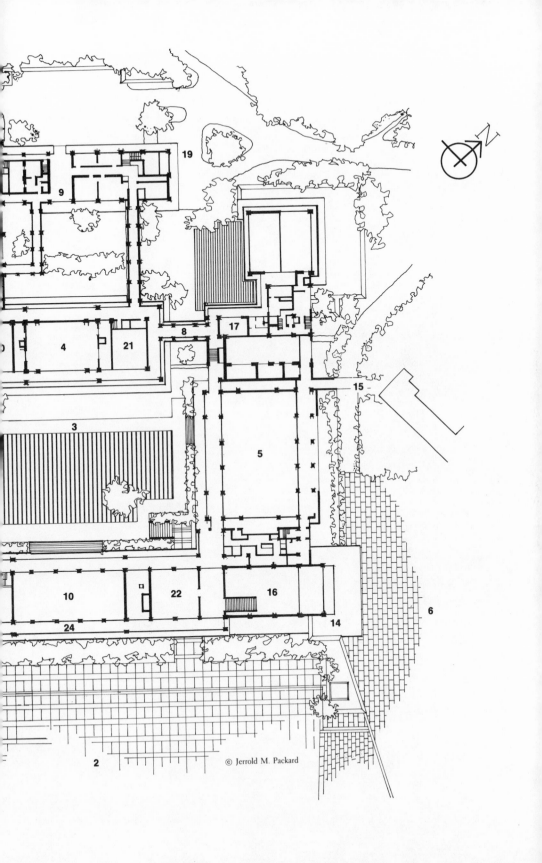

© Jerrold M. Packard

Sons of Heaven

In Japan, given names follow family names, but in this book they are rendered in the Western-style reverse order.

Introduction

Until 1945, he was inviolate, immortal. His person and his actions were clouded and clothed in the ethereality of divinity. When he moved outside his palaces, every eye lowered respectfully to avoid despoilment of his sacred majesty. When he spoke formally outside the closed circle of family and court, his privileged listeners heard virtually indecipherable abstractions delivered in a falsetto voice speaking the cadences of the ancient language of his court. He was the emperor of Japan, and prior to his empire's ignominious and total defeat at the end of the Great Pacific War, his mantle of sanctity came as a consequence and right of occupying the world's most ancient throne.

Hirohito is the 124th "official" inheritor of the title of *tenno,* literally "Son of Heaven," the primary designation used by the Japanese to denote their hereditary symbol of state, their king, or, as the title has customarily been rendered in English, their emperor. To the West, Japan's monarchy is all but unknown, its image almost completely tied to the present emperor, an image distorted by the bitterness of the Pacific War and kept at arm's length in the years since by a lack of the approachability today associated with Europe's monarchies. Even to the Japanese themselves, the throne that has been democratized to an astonishing degree since 1945 nonetheless remains murky in the half-light it allows to have played on it.

The goal of this book is to bring the two thousand years of Japanese monarchy into focus, to trace its development and explain the extraordinary lasting power of a dynasty that had reached the

1

height of its refinement when Europe was still struggling with near-universal ignorance. It is not intended to be a detailed study of the political role of the emperors of Japan; in fact, it would be difficult to find another reigning house that has, over such a large part of its history, been so excluded from any substantive role in the shaping of secular policies of state.

In the end, I will have succeeded in my endeavor if the reader comes to better understand Japan's imperial institution, an enterprise that continues to preside quietly but deeply felt over that confounding land. With the dynamism that grew out of military defeat more than four decades ago ever more distancing modern Japan from its ancient traditions, the monarchy continues to connect, as does no other element in the nation, the people with their past, their traditions, and their origins.

CHAPTER I

Imperial Noon
1928

The last grand salvo was fired so long ago that only a small fraction of the people in today's Japan have any firsthand recollection of the experience. When the next emperor is enthroned, the few remembrances of the enthronement of November 1928 will be so remote, will have become so much a part of the unreachable past, that there will almost certainly be a sense of newfound curiosity in the imperial institution.

But six decades ago, the people of an almost inconceivably different Japan had just cause for profound national joy. The majestic drums of their monarchy, which pealed only with carefully rationed rarity, were, that November, to sound as a carillon. Their emperor, loved from a respectful distance with an institutionalized veneration decreed more by the state than the heart, was, after almost two years since his accession, to be formally enthroned as the godhead of a Japanese nation of 65 million people.

The new emperor was Hirohito, although his subjects never called him by that sacred name.[1] Instead, the monarch was obliquely referred to as tenno heika, "Lord Son of Heaven"—*heika* the equivalent of "Lord" or "Majesty."[2] The young man—not yet

[1] If they had, it would have sounded something like "Hee-roish-toe."

[2] There are numerous additional euphemisms applicable to the emperor, including *tenshi*, "Heavenly King," and *kotei*, "Sovereign Ruler of Nations," which is also the term by which the Japanese refer to all foreign emperors and kings. The ancient *mikado*, "Honorable Gate," is today used primarily in a poetic sense; its

3

thirty—was only the third monarch to occupy the nation's throne since Japan's quick-time retreat from its feudal era, an epoch in which it was completely cut off from the Western world. For Hirohito's empire, the modern age began only with the reign of his grandfather, Emperor Mutsohito, who's period in power became known, after his death in 1912, as the Meiji years.[3] Only the intervening regnancy of Mutsohito's son, the tragically incapacitated Yoshihito, for whom Crown Prince Hirohito had been deputized as regent since 1922, separated the rule of the precedent-breaking grandfather from that of his quiet and scholarly grandson.

Rarely in history has a nation left its feudal ways to enter the industrialized world with quite so sharp a break and concentrated a will as had Japan under the Meiji emperor. It was now 1928, only six decades after the beginning of the social revolution carried out in Meiji's name, and Hirohito was formally being anointed as sovereign of a nation that was already nearly the equal of the world's strongest, one that had since Meiji's imperial "restoration" militarily humiliated both the Russian and Chinese empires with something very nearly approaching impunity.

In Western imaginations, Tokyo, the empire's capital, was, in the late 1920s, still popularly conceived of as a city of delicate paper houses, framed with exquisite pocket-sized gardens, and shaded by the artfully twisted branches of perennially blossoming cherry trees. In reality, it was already an ugly sprawl, its 5.5 million people putting it well on its destined way to becoming the world's largest conurbation. Tokyo covered—many would have said despoiled—Japan's only substantial plain, its countless "towns" just beginning to meld into a great artificial whole whose only real focus, and the magnet holding it together from its lopsided center, was the massive and forbidding Imperial Palace enclosure. Still frenetically rebuilding only five years after the 1923 earthquake and the resulting fires that destroyed most of the city's flimsiest districts on its eastern side,

---

meaning equates almost exactly with "Sublime Porte," the historic designation of the Ottoman emperor's government.

[3]Japanese emperors traditionally choose the posthumous names by which their reigns will be known. Mutsohito's is Meiji, its two ideographic characters signifying the "Enlightened Government" by which he had hoped to be remembered.

Tokyo revealed a newly hewn rawness, a coarseness even the most lavish of the official municipal enthronement decorations stood little hope of effectively masking. Though the occasion was only a respite, the capital still bravely exuded, however transparently, a festive mantle common to all royal venues that mark illustrious events in the lives and times of their dynastic seed.

The emperor's enthronement activities were to be divided, unequally, between two sites. Tokyo would host many of the corollary ceremonies—those primarily involving the reception of official foreign guests—but the most sacred and ancient rites were to be celebrated in Kyoto, until 1868 the proud and formal city that had been the nation's official capital and seat of the imperial court for more than a thousand years. Four hundred miles to the west, Tokyo had, until then, been merely the *shogun*'s capital—the headquarters of Japan's uniquely constituted military government.

Since there is no actual crowning in the rites Japan employs for confirming its monarch's accession to the throne, nor indeed did the Japanese court even utilize the symbol of a crown, the ceremonies could not technically be called a coronation, a term derived from the word for the royal insignia. But like coronations elsewhere in a world then still liberally dotted with kings and sovereign princes, its Japanese equivalent, called the *Go-Tairei*, was essentially an opportunity for the nation to relive the perceived glories of its accumulated history. In addition to being the head of state, the emperor was the nation's priest-king, and it was his duty to appear before the altars of his ancestors, there to worship in the name of all his subjects as though they formed one extended family. Furthermore, and this is a crucial point in understanding Hirohito's role in 1928, the vast majority of the members of this great family believed him to be the *only* intermediary between the living world and the world of spirits that protected the nation; no other mortal could relieve him of any part of this critically vital burden.

The complex round of ceremonies surrounding the enthronement, the oldest state rites in the world, officially began on January 17, 1928, when an imperial messenger reported to the gods the intricately scheduled agenda for the many solemnities. This first cere-

5

mony on the court calendar for that momentous year reflected
Hirohito's all-important obligation to keep the spirits completely
informed and up to date on events bearing on the imperial line. The
messenger's report was delivered at the Three Shrines, a grouping of
temples on the grounds of the Imperial Palace only a short walk from
the Fukiage Garden, Hirohito's private park and one of the lushest
and most beautiful of the many such secluded oases available to the
imperial family. On this same January day, while the pantheon of
Shinto and Buddhist gods who populated the nation's two primary
faiths were being apprised of the impending imperial events, a
quintet of official messengers was dispatched to personally inform the
enshrined souls of Hirohito's four immediate predecessors, as well as
that of the emperor Jimmu, the first of Hirohito's line, of what was
about to happen to the latest heir to their patrimony.

Fourteen months earlier, on Christmas Day, 1926, when
Hirohito's father died and the son succeeded to the throne, the first
duty of the court's chief ritualist had been to announce before the
shrines of the imperial ancestors that possession of the Mirror, the
most sacred of the three ancient items comprising Japan's imperial
regalia, had been officially transferred from the dead emperor to his
heir. Together with the other two sacred totems, the Sword and the
Jewels, it was the nearest equivalent of the crown jewels of Europe's
royal families. Shortly after the accession, the latter two treasures
were also formally placed in Hirohito's custody, an act specifically
mandated by the Imperial House Law to validate the successor's
claim to the throne. Of the three, only the so-called Jewels, in reality
a primitive necklace of tooth-shaped stones, is believed to possess
any great degree of antiquity. The Sword was a replacement for the
original weapon, which had been lost in a feudal battle centuries
earlier, and the Mirror, which would play the most important role
in the upcoming rites, was a replica of the "real" mirror that was
never allowed out of the safety of the imperial shrine at Ise, 200
miles southwest of Tokyo, its depository and considered the holiest
place in Japan.

On January 20, three days after the gods were informed of the
coming events, the new monarch issued what was called in formal
court terminology a "rescript," a rare and generally portentous im-

perial proclamation. The document affirmed his sacred pledge to "observe the fundamental rules of the State, to cultivate the inherited virtues, and to maintain intact the glorious traditions of Our Ancestors"; it also informed Hirohito's subjects that his succession came about by virtue of "lineal succession unbroken for ages eternal." It should be noted that the latter remark shouldn't be taken in a strictly literal sense, but Hirohito's concluding observation that "Our Ancestors looked upon the State as their own household and the people as their very children . . ." accurately summarized the role the sovereign believed he should play, the notion having been impressed upon the young prince since his earliest training that such was his proper role and ultimate purpose. The doctrine by which the Japanese people placed the imperial family at the peak of the nation's social structure was based on a conviction, shared by each of Hirohito's subjects, that the prerogatives of the sovereign, which was to say the state, were boundless and supreme.

What distinguished Hirohito's enthronement from those of his predessesor was the relatively open attitude of the ruling government and the Imperial Household Ministry (the semiautonomous government department that acted as the emperor's handlers) toward the press and its "right" to report the more personal details of the rites. In an attempt to improve the international image Japan was trying hard to cultivate, the government and the Imperial Household wanted to make sure that the hoopla surrounding the ceremonies received the widest possible news coverage. To glamorize the imperial family, money was freely spent in amounts unprecedented in the monarchy's history. The Household Ministry went so far as to issue to the press and public a flood of full-color brochures and booklets describing and analyzing the imperial institution, setting out in gingerly worded detail the history and significance of the esoteric events swirling around the hitherto shielded throne. Reporters were even to be allowed to witness some of the enthronement rites, a situation many of the court's more conservative defenders condemned as barely disguised lèse-majesté. A few political observers dampened the fun by acidly suggesting that the officially sanctioned policy of relative openness was in reality only a government smokescreen covering its embarrassment over having been caught

7

in some minor but nasty military adventurism in China. But the majority of the press, together with its vast audience, regarded the enthronement festivities as a fitting expression of thanksgiving for the nation's and the dynasty's greatness, and the national attitude was one of unabashed joy.

The accession rites of a Japanese emperor have been likened to a symphony in three movements; the *Senso,* or "Tread Throne" (the accession itself), and the *Sokui-rei,* or "Ascend Throne Ceremony" (the actual enthronement) constitute the first two movements. In February, the initial preparation for the third and most esoteric part of the symphony began. The *Daijo-sai,* literally the "Great New Food Festival," was a kind of solemn harvest sacrament ritually tying the sovereign to the nation's traditions of cultivation, a ceremony related to the enthronement that historians have traced back to nearly the beginning of the dynasty. From the Shinto viewpoint, it was the most important part of the accession celebrations, just as its several parts—all interspersed with the other enthronement activities—were the most mysterious, primitive, and intensely *Japanese* rites in this ceremony-filled imperial year.

The Daijo-sai ceremony, whose climax would be deceptively simple, was made up of an elaborate, multifaceted set of rituals, the whole of which involved enormous expense and thousands of indispensable participants both major and minor. Crucial to its success was a hoped-for measure of luck to ensure that the crops planted expressly for these rites would not come to grief in the wake of one of the unpredictable natural calamities that periodically and with devastating effect strike the islands. Accordingly, on a ritualistically reckoned "lucky" February day, two plots of ground were chosen for the rice planting. This was done by "reading" the cracks forming a "map" on the shoulder blade taken from a stag and then scorched, the choice of the gods thereby mysteriously made manifest to the palace priests. The fields in which the sacred grain would be planted were called the Yuki field and the Suki field, one on the shores of Lake Biwa near Kyoto, the other outside the city of Fukuoka in Kyushu, Japan's southern main island; they actually served as backup to each other if one should fail. Small replicas of the plots were concurrently laid out on the grounds of the Imperial Palace in Tokyo, thus allowing the emperor to participate symbolically in each of the series of steps in a parallel harvesting.

Once selected, the sites immediately became the centers of intense ceremonial preparations and purifications. In June, tiny new rice shoots were sowed with precision and solemnity in the knee-deep waters of the twin fields. Three months later, the nearly ripened ears of the sacred grain were purified and harvested. These preparatory tasks reached their culmination in October, when farmers, filled with pride at having been chosen for this once-in-a-reign honor, solemnly brought the rice to Tokyo. Dressed in white robes and marching in a great processional befitting the uniqueness of their burden, these honored sons of the soil delivered the grain to the capital, where it was stored for the last few weeks before the enthronement, when it would be converted into the emperor's holy feast at the culmination of the Daijo-sai.

The enthronement year began to build toward its climax on the morning of November 6, 1928. Hirohito and Nagako, his diminutive consort of five years, left their Tokyo palace for the first leg of the state procession to Kyoto, Their Majesties' early departure coming while a dark gray sky still covered Tokyo. Precisely at seven, the first elements of the magnificently ostentatious procession left the palace compound through its heavy iron-studded main gate, the *Seimon,* and across the *Nijubashi,* the famous Double Bridge reserved solely for imperial use on state occasions. As the procession passed, the edge of the just-rising sun, glinting through the low clouds on the horizon, was beginning to paint the scene with the pearly glow typical of a November morning in the capital. Khaki-colored squares of massed imperial troops decorated the sandy plaza fronting the stone walls encircling the former shogunal castle grounds, a complex that had been transformed into an imperial residence only during the reign of Hirohito's grandfather. Those people standing in the back of the enormous crowd strained to catch glimpses of the procession, peeping through the perfectly aligned bayonets bristling above the ranks of the emperor's soldiers.

Six caparisoned horses pulled Hirohito's coach down the broad thoroughfare that bisected the evenly spaced blocks of the Marunouchi district, Tokyo's newly built business and banking center; the European-style carriage, decorated with overlaid symbols emblematic of Japan's dynastic splendor, was topped by a Chinese golden phoenix bird, reflecting the cultural influence of the nation's enormous continental neighbor. Hirohito's empress, the eldest daughter of Prince Kuniyoshi Kuni, chieftain of the powerful Satsuma clan, traveled just behind in her own coach. Despite the worrisome fact that half a decade of married life had passed without Nagako giving her husband an heir, this was to be the first imperial enthronement formally recognizing an empress consort, a token of the greatly expanded symbolic role she was to play in the modern nation.

When the carriages arrived at their destination, the couple stepped out into the plaza fronting the red-brick facade of the Tokyo Station, an architectural curiosity modeled, a few years earlier, on a rail station in Amsterdam; more than any other place, it was the modern city's commercial epicenter. Following a short distance behind the imperial conveyance was an indispensable part of the procession, although it was more felt than seen because every eye was respectfully lowered at its passing: the holiest of holies and the Japanese symbolic equivalent of the Ark of the Covenant, the *Kashikodokoro,* the portable sanctuary containing the replica of the sacred Mirror. Unfailingly kept near the emperor's person wherever he traveled throughout his realm, the Mirror would closely accompany him through most of the arduous rites to come.

Leaving the station, the imperial train traveled at a solemn, unhurried pace in order to give the public along the route the rare opportunity of a moment in their monarch's presence. It made one stop on the journey when it pulled into Nagoya, the country's third-largest city, where Hirohito and Nagako spent the night at the local imperial villa, one of their several dozen residences liberally dotting the country. After another day of slow travel they finally reached Kyoto. Upon arrival, Their Majesties boarded carriages to be driven down Karasuma Avenue, the city's central thoroughfare, to their destination at the opposite end of the ancient capital's axis in the Imperial Palace, each of whose private apartments in the imperial suite was a modest twelve-*tatami* chamber, measured by the traditional Japanese standard whether occupied by monarch or peasant;[4] the magnificence of the accommodations lie more in their symbolism and breadth of history than in their architecture or furnishings. Meanwhile, the Kashikodokoro, which had accompanied the monarch on the train in its own carriage, was carefully borne atop the muscular shoulders of a band of youth, the icon resting in a colorful boxlike palanquin called the Feather Carriage; the solemn procession's goal was a temple specially built on the palace's grounds to receive the sanctuary and its precious relic.

Kyoto, the most history-charged of any place in the emperor's islands, was, in 1928, a timeworn shadow of the imperial entrepôt it had been in its glory days, an era that had passed long before the new Eastern Capital appropriated much of what was left of its once-splendid thunder. The grandeur that ancient emperors had built into Kyoto's geometric, Chinese-style regularity was now reduced to a provincial reminder of the centuries when it had ranked among the largest and most civilized metropolises on earth. Its streets could perhaps still claim greater width than those of Tokyo, but even their gracious amplitude had been pared down thanks to the reality of modern population pressures. The spectacular imperial park, where one of the strangest, most remote and dazzling courts in history played out its artifices in days of gilded meaninglessness, was now reduced to little more than a mere "must-see" stop on the tourist agenda, its princely villas, which had been set in gardens of exquisite dignity, demolished on the orders of Hirohito's grandfather, his motive to prevent their erstwhile occupants from becoming the nucleus of an opposition against the modernizations deemed necessary for a new Japan. The Kyoto Hirohito entered for his enthronement was, like Versailles and Potsdam and Tsarskoe Selo, full of memory but stripped of consequence.

The couple's schedule allowed only three days in which to complete the laborious fittings needed for the intricate enthronement robes and to practice the final rehearsals for the complex rites in

---

[4]Japanese rooms are still measured in terms of tatami mats; each is six feet by three feet.

which they would play the leading roles. Throughout the remainder of this first day, the city continued to fill with the junior members of the imperial clan—siblings, aunts, uncles, cousins of the emperor—as well as with the nation's nobility, its highest-ranking politicians and court officials, foreign guests representing heads of state and the diplomatic corps down from Tokyo, and finally, the uppermost layers of the Japanese aristocracy. Those who were assigned walk-on parts in the enthronement and the harvest rite busied themselves practicing their roles and learning the craft of moving gracefully while encumbered in the antique ceremonial finery that would be worn only once and then put away for another reign. Kyoto's humbler districts were also packed to bursting with visitors, the residents reminded for these brief days of the lost import of their historic city.

Saturday, November 10—enthronement day—dawned with clear skies over the valley that the ancient capital carpeted. Yet before the enthronement rites could be solemnized that afternoon the emperor had one final preparatory burden to fulfill. Hirohito was personally obliged to make an announcement before the Kashikodokoro that he would within a few hours ascend the throne that had been passed on to him by his 123 predecessors.[5] Observing the monarch in the performance of this ritual duty were some two thousand dignitaries, at whose head the several dozen imperial princes and princesses served as chief witnesses. The hall in which the ceremony was performed was arranged in three separate chambers, with the spectators in the larger, outermost apartment, beyond which the emperor and empress sat isolated in their own anteroom. In the innermost recess was the Kashikodokoro, safeguarding the sacred Mirror from all impurities. In the imperial couple's chamber, two platforms—finely crafted of many thicknesses of velvet-smooth straw mats and bound in brocade—occupied the otherwise bare surroundings.

[5]Hirohito's father was, at his 1912 accession, considered the 122nd sovereign; but in 1926, the disputed fourteenth-century emperor Chokei was officially judged by the court to have legally occupied the throne, thereby making Hirohito number 124 when he succeeded.

At precisely nine-thirty, the drapery separating the ark from the emperor's anteroom was drawn back, and the Son of Heaven prayed in earnest devotion before the precious relic, held by countless generations of his subjects to be a gift from the Sun Goddess herself. For the first time since this same ceremony was performed immediately prior to his father's enthronement fourteen years earlier, priests brought the other two sacred items of the regalia into the presence of the Mirror, the only occasion all three would be together until this emperor would in turn be succeeded by his own heir. Robed in pure white garments, the two Majesties were purified by attendants pouring water over their hands. A white curtain was lowered around the couple, and they had this single brief time to commune with Japan's holiest objects. Hirohito first read the report to his ancestors, and then finally prostrated himself before the regalia. In a few moments drums and bells sounded three times and his duty was done. The company retreated in order of precedence, their leave-taking marked only by the rustling of the priests' ancient silk court costumes. Now the necessary preliminaries were completed; the rites of enthronement could begin.

The extraordinary robes in which Hirohito was arrayed at his enthronement were both the most sacred and the most ornate he would wear at any time in his entire reign; they would be used only on this single afternoon, never to be worn by him again. The set of vestments, together called the *korozen,* was modeled on the Heian-period court dress of a thousand years earlier, during the years when the Kyoto-based imperial culture was nearly unique in the world for its graceful way of life. Woven of silk, they were primarily of a dark yellow-red color signifying the earliest hue of the morning sun as it rises over the eastern ocean, a metaphor standing for the monarchy itself. Intertwined throughout were the emblems of good luck of the paulownia and bamboo, and the magical kirin and phoenix—fabled animals of good omen—their numbers precisely calculated by priests in the most auspicious combination to ensure good fortune for the new reign. Heavy, wide, red damask trousers and high platform slippers of scarlet brocade were copies of those worn by Hirohito's predecessors stretching back to the emperor Saga in the ninth century. The monarch's cap, the *kammuri,* was similar to

13

those worn by all princes and high officials on ceremonial occasions, but the sovereign's model differed uniquely in that its long silk gauze tail—the *ei*—was stiffened to stand straight up behind the head, rather than droop like the kammuri of the lesser princes and officials or curve into a circular loop as did those of military officers. In his hand, Hirohito held the flat, paddlelike wooden scepter of his exalted rank.

If the emperor's robes were cumbersome, the empress's were very nearly unmanageable; indeed, the wearer's inability to move about freely in them was an artful and deliberate indication of the loftiness of her position. The main elements of Nagako's five-layered costume, which together weighed nearly as much as the wearer, were five heavy silk court *kimono*—one inside the next, the longest about nine feet from neck to hem. Five inner folds of different colored fabrics peeked through at the neckline, sleeves, and skirts. The layers of sleeves slightly overlapped each other, as did the skirts, the hems of which were filled and rolled like quilts and drawn up in front with a complicated cinch—looking something like a partially raised venetian blind; a loose white train, embroidered with a bower of flowers and birds, fell behind. The empress's glistening black hair was set in a wide, heart-shaped mound to frame and contrast her powder-whitened face; a curious ornamental gold lacquered comb with three spikes rising from it, resembling a small crown or tiara, a Western ornament not known in traditional Japan, decorated the ancient coiffeur above her forehead. The counterpart emblem to her husband's scepter was a folding fan made of cypress and tied with multicolored silk cords. So enrobed, the empress was, for practical purposes, very nearly immobile.

The enthronement ceremony would take place in the spectacularly polychromatic *Shishinden,* the Secret Purple Hall, a ponderous structure based on Chinese architectural themes and used only for the most important functions of state. Burned and reconstructed many times over the centuries, this open-fronted hall was most visibly distinguished by its roof crafted in the ancient fashion of layer upon layer of cypress bark covered with a final blanket of moss. The structure had served as the decorative centerpiece of Kyoto's imperial complex since its latest rebuilding in 1855. The range of court buildings lay in the center of a larger park that once constituted a virtually self-sufficient city, its high-ranking courtiers occupying the villas enclosed by the walls around the evergreen-embellished grounds.

The palatial park in which Hirohito's formal installation as sovereign was to take place was a short distance east of the earlier imperial buildings, the seminal complex that rose in this city nearly twelve centuries earlier. Strikingly different in tone from the nearby shogunal palace, where the representatives of the empire's military rulers once held court in an atmosphere gaudily decorated even by the standards of European monarchs, the imperial compound and its buildings exuded an austere spiritual symbolism that represented the sovereigns' lineal purity, which was, in fact, the chief reason for the throne's continued existence. Although quiet richness was imparted with the obvious costliness of the compound's details—the rare and flawless Japanese cypress and *keyaki* woods crafted with masterful carpentry and joinery techniques, richly landscaped gardens the equal of which could be found nowhere else in the empire—the palace enclosure appeared to Western eyes an extraordinarily modest setting for a monarchy that claimed more than two and a half millennia of history.

The cynosure of the rites in the Shishinden was the pair of throne enclosures in which the imperial couple would sit, or, more precisely, be encased. The ornate objects resembled miniature temples, hexagonal in shape, perched on elaborately decorated square stepped-up boxes; Hirohito's was about twenty feet high and precisely 10 percent larger than his wife's appropriately less majestic model. The emperor's throne structure, called the *Takamikura*, the "High August Seat," contained within its canopied and curtained temple a throne chair of red sandalwood inlaid with mother-of-pearl that was flanked by two small regalia stands, one for the Sword, the other for the Jewels. Under the canopy, reflecting light down on the throne chair, was a mirror, symbolizing the third element of the sacred regalia.

To the east of the Takamikura sat the nearly matching *Michodai*, the "Curtained Throne" of the empress. Slightly less ornamented, as well as mirrorless, it was making only its second appearance at an enthronement, the first time being fourteen years earlier for Nagako's mother-in-law, the dowager empress Sadako. Affixed to both structures was the golden sixteen-petaled chrysanthemum blossom, the imperial family's symbol. Sometimes called the *enmeiso*, "Plant of Longevity," the flower was believed to have the virtue of confirming great age on those who ate it. Like the sun disk that was the emblem of the state itself, the imperial crest also symbolized the source of the world's light—from which both emperor and nation had so long ago descended.

Early in the afternoon, the first of the guards of honor took up their places in the courtyard facing the Shishinden and its long, open-air gallery, a feature that happily facilitated the audience being able to clearly see the pair of imperial thrones. The broad, gravel-covered granite space—each pebble individually bleached and polished so as to brighten the courtyard with reflected sunlight—was decorated conspicuously by tall banners, each emblazoned with a golden chrysanthemum. Grouped around the banners were most of the same two thousand people who had witnessed the first rites earlier that morning. Closer to the thrones in the Shishinden, but not as close as the immediate members of the imperial family, sat the empire's two highest-ranking civil servants: the prime minister, Baron Giichi Tanaka, Hirohito's foremost constitutional adviser, and Baron Kitokuro Ikki, the head of the Imperial Household Ministry and the monarch's chief courtier and closest personal adviser. Immediately after the "Princes of the Blood"—Hirohito's uncles and brothers—took their places, the dramatic hush that had thus far prevailed was sharply broken by the master of ceremonies' piercing yell, which gave notice of the unseen approach of the emperor. The two principals—the emperor, attended by his retinue of honor guards, and the empress, with her ladies-in-waiting—entered their respective throne platforms from the rear. As a court ritualist intoned the ancient warning cry of *keihi*, "Stand back!," chamberlains threw open the curtains, exposing the fantastically robed couple to the throng for its first breathtaking view.

In absolute silence, Their Majesties rose, the emperor first, holding before him his simple scepter, then the empress with her fan fully opened in front of her. Before the deeply bowing crowd in the courtyard, the pair waited while the prime minister descended the steps toward the throng, leaving them in the solitary splendor of their adjacent thrones.

The Japanese equivalent of a coronation reaches its zenith of solemnity when the emperor formally proclaims to his subjects that he has assumed the highest position in the empire, in effect affirming his own authority to claim the throne. No second party's participation is required to make the enthronement official, no equivalent of an Archbishop of Canterbury's attendance is necessary to ensure ecclesiastical approval—the emperor of Japan is himself the supreme religious figure in the land. This moment arrived: Invoking not a disconnected God but the spirits of his own ancestors, Hirohito read a statement declaring that he was occupying the throne of his imperial predecessors and beseeching success so that "We may with good conscience face the Heavenly Spirits of Our Ancestors," adding a "wish to preserve world peace and benefit the welfare of the human race."

After a short congratulatory address, Baron Tanaka, as the head of the emperor's government and representing the people of Japan, led the crowd, at the full strength of his voice, three times in the ancient Japanese cry of exaltation: *Tenno Heika, Banzai!*, "Lord Emperor, [May You Live] Ten Thousand Years." Each cry was precisely timed to a rigid schedule so that the entire nation could join in at the exact same moment, echoing their feelings as one across an empire that included not only 65 million Japanese but also the combined populations of Korea and Taiwan, people who were then—unhappily and much against their will—the emperor's subjects.

As the echo of the third banzai died against the walls flanking the meticulously sanded and raked courtyard, the solemn strains of the national hymn, the *Kimigayo*, [6] were played by a military band just outside. The curtains were slowly lowered around the thrones—the

---

[6]The entire lyrics: "May our Sovereign reign for thousands of ages until pebbles become rocks overgrown with moss."

17

Takamikura and Michodai—and the newly anointed emperor and his now-recognized empress retired to their private apartments. The "Representative of the Unbroken Line" was enthroned.

The final major element of this national celebration was the austere and deeply religious climax of the Daijo-sai, which, paired with the enthronement ceremony, would officially complete the accession rites of Hirohito's reign. If in other countries an intimate personal relationship between gods and men had long since ceased to exist, in the Japan of 1928 such an unseen bond was still very much a part of the reality of life. It was from this reality that these final solemnities derived their importance.

The day following the enthronement—November 11—saw the emperor again visiting the shrine housing the Mirror, there to report to the Sun Goddess that the enthronement had been successfully accomplished, thus permitting her ever-vigilant spirit to be put at ease. For the next two days, Hirohito would prepare for the arduous Daijo-sai. First, on the twelfth, he was ritually purified to make him as one with the gods for whom he was now the living representative on earth. This physical purification—the Body-Cleansing—was a ceremony symbolic of ancient rites in which priests took the monarch to Kyoto's riverbank and completely immersed him in the manner of a Christian fundamentalist baptism. Hirohito's purification simply involved his outer clothing being cast by celebrants onto the river's current. Parallel ceremonies were performed on the other members of the imperial family as well as the courtiers and clerics who would be participating in the Daijo-sai.

On the following night, the last before the ceremony itself, Hirohito was taken to the *Kogosho,* an elegantly diminutive structure overlooking a small pond on the palace grounds, where the monarch was required to undergo the Soul Quieting ritual, a devotion to prepare him for the ultimate to come the next night. The object of this magico-religious soul pacification was to tranquilize the emperor's spirit, enabling him to pass safely through the momentous mental rigors of the mystical Daijo-sai. Said to have originated with the earliest emperors, this ritual was performed in the hoped-for expectation that it would put Hirohito's rough spirits at ease and prepare him for his encounter with his gods. Although essentially the same ceremony was conducted annually at the palace in Tokyo, the special symbolic importance of this enthronement year's Soul Quieting was unparalleled to both monarch and nation.

The Daijo-sai would take place in the *Daijo-gu*, the temporary shrine compound that was especially set up on the grounds of the Omiya Palace, one of the several major villas still standing in the palace park. In the purposely primitive architecture and furnishings of this compound, built to resemble a Shinto temple from the earliest days of Japanese civilization, modern Japan relived her ancient past. The objects in the compound, especially those near the person of the emperor, were so sanctified by the passage of centuries and their association with the nation's monarchs that they were deeply imbued with an aura of mystery and awe, utterly divorced from the common and unclean that cluttered the world outside.

Two of the three principal structures in the thatch-walled Daijo-gu were the *Yuki-den*, literally the "Consecrated-Purified Food Hall," and the *Suki-den*, the "Next Consecrated-Purified Food Hall"—each had its own ceremonial cook house where Hirohito's sacred meals would be prepared. A variety of smaller huts designed for the imperial retinue were all oriented toward the central and most important structure, the *Kairyu-den*, the "Emperor's Ablution Hall," and were connected by parallel covered corridors with the Yuki and Suki halls. Four *torii*, "god gates," of unbarked pine were set in the thatched wall running around the compound perimeter to give access to the gods. For rites so awesomely sacred, the whole ensemble appeared almost crudely simple.

A nocturnal pageant, the Daijo-sai formally began in the late afternoon of November 14 when the emperor left his palace apartments to walk to the Daijo-gu. In a state procession, Hirohito passed by troops that lined the route to a temporary receiving palace called the *Tongu*; here he was joined by the empress and the members of his family and all were marshaled into their final places for the last bit of the processional journey. A retinue of a thousand high-ranking military and civil officials was in attendance, but these people were to be seated outside the enclosure, from where they would see nothing of the sacred ceremonies conducted within the compound itself.

Eight fires were set around the Daijo-gu enclosure, two on either side of the four god gates, their entrances guarded by archers dressed like apparitions from Japan's most ancient days. Fires were also lit in the Yuki-den and Suki-den as the emperor arrived and entered the Kairyu-den, there to begin the night's ceremony in which, once in an imperial lifetime, a dynasty's distant past is symbolically brought into the present.

The first formality Hirohito underwent was another purification ritual, this time involving an actual immersion. Set in the center of the hut's bamboo floor was a bathtub resembling an oversized flower box and unlike any used in Japan for hundreds of years. The emperor's outer garment, called the Heavenly Feather Robe, was removed to reveal a simple white mantle made of hemp; stepping into the tub, the monarch folded his arms and stooped while ritualists gingerly poured water over him. With the sacred bath completed, he changed into a fresh white silk wrap to dry himself. Finally, he was helped into a third robe, this one also of white silk and closed with a black leather belt set with onyx. By now night had completely blanketed the city, and only a faint glow from the ancient oil lights illuminated the historic events. After one final ritualistic washing of the hands, the emperor was joined by his wife to begin the act whose preparations had begun nearly a year before.

Court musicians stationed near the Yuki cook house struck up the "Song of the Pounding of the Rice," and the central course of the offertory meal was put on to cook. Together with the rice, the majority of which had been gathered from the Yuki and Suki fields, with added bits brought in from every province in the country as well as the small paddy on the Tokyo palace grounds, the masslike feast included delicacies representing the bounty of the empire, such as barley from Tokyo and wheat from Kanagawa, beans from Hokkaido and fish from Sakhalin, lily roots from Osaka and chestnuts from Kyoto, persimmons from Nara and bananas from Taiwan. When all was ready, the emperor proceeded, in bare feet, to the Yuki Hall along a carpet that was unrolled before him and immediately rerolled behind him—a precaution precluding the possibility that other mortals' feet would defile this sacred path to the place of the gods. To symbolically keep the air around the imperial head from becoming permanently taboo by his passing through it, a huge phoenix-topped white sedge canopy in the shape of an umbrella, the symbol of royalty throughout much of Asia, was held over Hirohito's head. The Sword and the Jewels were carried before him.

When Hirohito reached the Yuki-den, the procession of dishes, each of which was borne in state by a scarlet-skirted female attendant, began from the Yuki cook house; even the chopsticks that accompanied each plate were of the ancient kind, looking more like sugar tongs, the style of eating utensil used by his earliest imperial predecessors. As the emperor received a dish, he offered it to the unseen goddess Amaterasu, his immortal ancestress and founder of the imperial line. After seeing that the goddess was offered each of these delicacies, far simpler food was brought for Hirohito's own consumption—boiled rice, millet, and *sake*. By midnight the ceremony was completed and the monarch returned to the Kairyu-den. At 2:00 A.M., the exact same exhausting ritual was carried out at the opposing Suki-den, its final act ending only as the sun rose on the morning of the fifteenth. Within hours after the completion of this mass of communion, the entire compound holding the temples of the Great New Food Festival was put to the torch; no trace was to remain nor would it be rebuilt until a new emperor would once again observe these rites for a new reign.

After this supreme religious pageant, the ceremonies in the wake of Hirohito's accession dwindled down to the last few state banquets and concluding acts of worship by the emperor at the shrines of his immediate predecessors, most importantly including a reportorial trip to the Grand Shrine at Ise. Finally, on the twenty-sixth, the couple returned to Tokyo, again spending one intervening night at the imperial villa in Nagoya. As their homeward-bound train passed through Yokohama, Tokyo's eminent port sister-city, a twenty-one-gun salute was fired from the enormous guns of the massed Imperial Fleet. The last kilometer of the emperor's journey was the reverse of that which had occurred twenty days earlier: from Tokyo's central station, through the heart of the city's financial center, across the broad palace plaza and the photogenic Double Bridge before his fortress home. As his carriage entered the imperial precincts, the first ear-shattering report of a 101-gun salute boomed across the heart of the city.

The people of Tokyo, and the thousands from the provinces who joined them that night, abandoned themselves to noisy joy lit by fireworks and the new electrical lights so recently put up in the reconstructed city. Their empire, their emperor, their existence as a nation were all secure, and nothing could change that comforting reality. That this world would, in less than a generation, be purged almost to total destruction was, of course, unimaginable on that happy, cold, brightly lit night.

CHAPTER II

Origins

TO THE FIFTH CENTURY

In 1928, when these splendid enthronement events were taking place, every schoolchild in Hirohito's empire was being taught a fantastical and complex tale of the origins of the Japanese nation and its imperial dynasty. Assimilating religious mythology in the garb of history wasn't, of course, unique to Japan; in most parts of the Western world educators of that era were teaching and, for the most part, children were uncritically accepting the notion that the Bible accurately described the origins of mankind. In fact, myths or legends or folklore, however highly colored, rarely fail to incorporate at least a germ of historical truth, at the same time serving to perpetuate for later generations a spiritual outlook on the past. But few of the legendary accounts that societies have invented to embellish the homeliness of the reality of history rival the splendor of Japan's cosmogony. In order to understand the vitally central role the emperor system has played in Japanese history one must see how the mythical origins of both nation and sovereign spouted simultaneously from the same wellspring.

Japan's chronology began a very long time ago, and it came to be without the intercession of any Creator, without any prefatory First Cause. Like the changing patterns in a kaleidoscope, the heaven and the earth in that impossibly distant time formed a shifting chaotic mass, its elements not yet separate, each containing bits of all the others. But as the eons passed, the purer, clearer particles gradually became distinct and rose to form the heaven, and later the heavier, grosser residuum left over from this miraculous winnowing sank to ripen into the water-covered world. In this Japanese genesis, the heaven and the earth thus formed, still a largely disorderly and inchoate jumble. It had arisen not out of a divine plan but from the natural elemental evolution of the universe itself.

While the separate realms of heaven and earth were still evolving from their embryonic rawness, three gods sprang miraculously and spontaneously into being; they were—called in the ponderous trans- literation of their Japanese names—Master of the August Center of Heaven, Divine Wondrous Producing Deity, and High August Pro- ducing Wondrous Deity. These pioneering spirits disappeared shortly after seeing the completion of this great work of cosmic division, but, fortunately, successors quickly followed. The first two, Pleasant Reed Shoot Prince Elder Deity and Heavenly Externally Standing Deity, emerged from a reed shoot that sprouted up out of the earth; they, like their three predecessors, died—as gods uniquely do in Japanese terms—without having extended their own line with issue. After two more unfruitful divinities—Earthly Eternally Standing Deity and Luxuriant Integrating Master Deity—came and went, five more pairs of gods appeared, the last of whom would finally bring an enduring continuity to the newly hardened land. This auspicious duo, The Male Who Invites and The Female Who Invites, would become known in the annals of Japanese mythology by their familiar names: Izanagi, the he of the pair, and Izanami, the she. They were the direct progenitors of all the generations that were to follow.

Izanagi and Izanami's four fellow heavenly twosomes issued their most junior colleagues a commandment, one whose results were happily auspicious. They—Izanagi and Izanami—were ordered to turn the still disorderly earth into something relatively neat and tidy, a place where the little band of ten gods could all feel at home. The pair was provided with a divinely empowered jeweled spear to help them accomplish their task. Together, standing on the floating bridge of heaven, they bent over and dipped the end of this magic lance into the briny waters of the ocean that still covered the earth. After a bit of careful stirring, they raised the spear from the sea, and the droplets of pure brine that fell from the tip massed together to form an island, Onogoro, "The Self-Coagulated Isle," the first of the many that became the Everlasting Great Japan.

Now that they had a firm setting under their feet, Izanagi and Izanami began building a palace. Because the fruit of their first labor—the creation of Japan itself—did not involve a physical sexual union, it was only now that the wonderful and secret knowledge of lovemaking was revealed to them; just as Adam and Eve's progeny ignored it, so, too, for them was the issue of siblinghood immaterial. A pair of magpies instructed the lovers in the art of intimate congress, and, once learned, they began to enjoy themselves immensely and often. They even got married. Sadly, the first baby was a leech, which understandably upset the Pair Who Invites, so they set it adrift in a reed boat, like a baby Moses on an oriental Nile. The next offspring was another little island, this one called Awaji, "foam." But Awaji didn't prosper, and soon died. The parents returned to heaven to report their failure; the other gods were sympathetic and suggested they try again.

Number three was the charm. This healthy and cherubic little darling was Iyo, held by later generations of Japanese to be Shikoku, one of the four main islands of the present-day nation. More islands joined Iyo in quick succession, and before long their family—Japan—had grown beyond belief. Now they set about increasing its size even further; first the Rivers and Mountains were born, followed in rapid succession by the Herbs and Trees. Perhaps weakened by such fecundity, the last child, Fire, finally killed the overly imposed-on mother: Izanami departed to the Land of Darkness. Dumb with grief, Izanagi unsheathed his mighty sword and sliced Fire into thirds, but all three parts instantly became new gods. As Fire's blood was falling from the sharp blade, the cascading droplets themselves became gods.

Izanagi then went into the Land of Darkness to look for his beloved sister-wife. Upon finding her—actually, she met him halfway—he implored her to return to their palace where they had known such joy together. Remaining in the shadows so Izanagi couldn't see her, she refused, offering the excuse that since she had already eaten of the food of the Land of Darkness, she felt obliged to remain where she was. But after Izanagi's mournful pleas, Izanami said she'd ask the gods what they thought she should do.

As husbands will, Izanagi became impatient when Izanami didn't return as quickly as he thought she should have. Breaking the end tooth off his comb to make a torch, he went looking for her. When he finally found her, the sight of her putrefying body was so horrible that he fled in terror. (Remember, she'd been dead for some time.) To make matters worse, the eight gods of Thunder had taken up residence in her decaying flesh.

Izanami was furious with Izanagi for finding her this way, and in a blinding rage she sent the eight Thunder gods, backed by fifteen hundred Thunder warriors, after him. He managed to keep one step ahead of this horde, but to cleanse himself after his encounter with the underworld he stopped to take a bath in a nearby river, at which point twelve new divinities were born out of the dirty clothes and ornaments he discarded on the riverbank: one each from his girdle and his skirt, hat, and necklace; one each from his shirt and trousers; and six from the bracelets he wore on his arms. The birthing evidently aroused his libido: After testing the waters, he decided the newborn godlets in the river's middle reach were the most to his liking, so he plunged in after them. Fourteen more gods were thus born, apparently from his skin, but it's only the last three that need concern us here.

When Izanagi rubbed his face, Heaven Shining Great August Deity—later called Amaterasu, the Sun Goddess, and the seminal figure of the entire Japanese cosmogony—fell from his left eye. A moment later, His Augustness Moon Night Possessor—the Moon God—dripped from the right eye, and finally Brave Swift Impetuous Male Augustness—the Ocean God—came forth from his nose (out of which nostril we can only guess). It is with these three that events build to their exciting culmination.

Izanagi was so pleased with these final three that he gave them command of the whole universe: the Sun Goddess was assigned the Plain of High Heaven, and it was to her that he gave the sacred jeweled necklace from around his own neck; the Moon God was given dominion of the night; and the Ocean God all the world's seas. But true to his name of Impetuous Male Augustness, the little

Ocean deity cried and carried on; he wailed for such a long time that his beard eventually grew down to the bottom of his abdomen. (All the gods were evidently born postpubescent, so this didn't take as long as it might otherwise have.) Izanagi wanted to know why Impetuous wasn't pleased with his gift, and was told, "I want to go to my mother [in hell]." Which is where Izanagi sent him. Izanagi's earthly mission thus completed, he retired to heaven and lived in the Smaller Palace of the Sun forever after.

On his way to visit his mother, Impetuous stopped to see his sister, Amaterasu, née Heaven Shining. For a variety of reasons too interruptive of our main story to detail, the pair got into a shouting match, which developed into a frightful row. Amaterasu became terribly angry and retreated into a nearby cave, effectively shutting off the world's supply of sun and leaving the entire firmament enshrouded in darkness.

Wanting to return everything to its prior state of contentment, the gods decided to play a trick on the pouting Amaterasu to get her to come out of her cave. They engaged the seductive goddess Amenouzume to dance a little shimmy around the cave entrance, with the whole pantheon laughing and carrying on at these antics. Amaterasu, curious at the sound of laughter coming through the rock she had placed in front of the cave entrance, peeked out to see what was going on. Immediately she was handed a little gift of a mirror. As she mused on the reflected image, she was led out the rest of the way by one of the male gods, while another quickly sealed off the cave opening behind her. The world was filled with light again, and, fortunately for the future of Japan, Amaterasu forgave the trickery and decided to stay out.

Not forgotten for having been the cause of all this misery—after all, he had started the fight—Impetuous was divinely punished. After having his hands and toes cut off, he was ordered to recite the Great Purification liturgy as an additional penance, and finally was forbidden from ever entering heaven again.

These events had caused a great turmoil across the land, and the gods had to decide how best to pacify everyone so the world would again dwell in order and harmony. Sent to assess matters, a heavenly envoy returned to report that the world was too violent for him to continue his survey, so a second envoy was dispatched. The gods waited eight years for the envoy's report, and after not hearing anything, sent a pheasant down to earth to see what was keeping him. Heaven's envoy, staying in the special palace established for these godly representatives, shot the bird with an arrow. The wounded beast flew back to heaven, where the arrow was extracted and shot back down to earth, killing the envoy. (We don't know whether the pheasant recovered.) Two more agents from heaven were sent out, and they finally managed to make the Central Land of Reed Plains—Honshu, the main island of Japan—peaceful once again.

To rule over this pacified land, the celestial administrators sent a new god, their Heavenly Grandchild and a spirit who figures critically in this tale: His Augustness Heaven Plenty Earth Plenty Heaven's Sun Height Prince Rice Ear Ruddy Plenty, which is usually and mercifully shortened to Ninigi. Ninigi was the Sun Goddess's grandson, which gave him quite a headstart in terms of relative prestige. His grandmother bestowed on him her Mirror and Jewels, and threw in an herb-quelling Sword made from the tail of a dragon, adding that the Mirror was to be thought of as if it were Amaterasu herself. After Ninigi settled in at his palace on Mount Takachiho (now held to be located on the present island of Kyushu), he married and had three sons; Prince Fire Shine, Prince Fire Climax, and Prince Fire Subside.

Young Fire Subside was soon to find himself in great difficulty over, of all things, a misplaced fishhook. As the prince was sitting by the shore bemoaning this minor but nettlesome turn of events, the Ocean God came by, listened with sympathy to the story of Fire Subside's loss, and offered to help out as best he could. The substance of his help was that he would ask his daughter to come tell Fire Subside what she thought he should do about the missing fishhook. Well, when the daughter got one look at the handsome prince it was love at first sight, with no more thought given to lost fishing equipment. A wedding shortly followed.

After taking a bride, Fire Subside and his new princess settled down and lived together peacefully for 580 years in their palace on Mount Takachiho. They were blessed with a boy, who after reaching manhood married his maternal aunt, a daughter of his grandfather the Sea God. They, in turn, had four boys of their own. It is the youngest who brings this legend to its close. Prince Kami Yamato Iwarebiko, known to history as Jimmu Tenno—the "Divinely Brave Heavenly King"—the first emperor of Japan, and the ancestor, seventy-one generations removed in direct order of succession, of Hirohito. The story concludes with the notation that Jimmu lived his first forty-five years at his birthplace at the base of Takachiho; after the deaths of his three brothers, he set out to conquer worlds of his own. In a hinoki-shaded glen called Kashiwabara, about midway between present-day Nara and Osaka in the anciently named land of Yamato, Jimmu settled down, and on February 11, 660 B.C., enthroned himself as emperor, thereby establishing an empire that would come to be called Japan.

As charmingly fantastical as this tale is,[1] there are probably at least some elements of historical truth in it—truth, at any rate, disguised in allegory. For example, historians speculate that the mythical Izanami and Izanagi stand for chieftains of fierce bands of ancient invading foreigners, and that the jeweled sword they dipped into a briny sea is simply symbolic of the weapons used to subdue the earliest aboriginal inhabitants anthropologists have placed in the Japanese archipelago. The misleadingly precise date of Jimmu's accession, 660 B.C., was believed unquestioningly by the masses in prewar Japan—the Japanese people and their leaders considered it a "duty" to accept it as fact in much the same way conservative Christians feel it is their duty to regard the events in the Bible as having occurred precisely as Scripture describes them. Even English-language histories of Japan—presumably not so rigorously subjected to official censorship—unfailingly repeated the 660 B.C. date. Ironically, it was only in the late-nineteenth-century Meiji era, when the authority of the throne was being deliberately reinforced, that this mythical calculation became official state propaganda. The au-

---

[1]There are, by the way, nearly endless variants on the story; ours cleaves to the most commonly held notions as described in Japan's ancient Chronicles and Records.

thors of Japan's first semiaccurate historical records—the *Kojiki*, "Record of Ancient Matters," which was compiled in A.D. 712, and the *Nihongi* (or *Nihonshoki*), "Chronicles of Japan," assembled eight years later in A.D. 720—used Chinese astrological and genealogical tables as the basis of their computations.[2] These tables calculated that 1,260 lunar years had elapsed since the earliest known emperors reigned, and using A.D. 600 as their starting point, subtracting 1,260 from it gave them 660 B.C. This remarkably unscientific extrapolation gained such currency that the Meiji authorities could declare it "infallible" (for their own political purposes, of course) and it still serves as the basis for dating imperial history in not a few post–World War II histories.

As with Western biblical traditions, authentic but exaggerated and reformulated stories about the lives of Japan's rulers were passed down from generation to generation, gaining both currency and embroidery through familiarity, while at the same time strengthening the legitimacy of the imperial institution itself. But even though the actual existence of Jimmu is at best problematical, it is with him—or with an unknown leader or leaders responsible for the deeds and characteristics credited to him—that Japan's prehistory ends and the earliest snippets of the historically verifiable imperial story begin to emerge.

A fairly solid hypothesis[3] traces the series of events that led from the first signs of human settlement in the Japanese islands to the founding of what became the imperial line, though not unsurprisingly the historical evidence theorizes a story far less romantic than that of the Sun Goddess legend. In real life, it took nearly 100,000

[2]The *Kojiki* is also called the "Book of Ancient Traditions"; there are, confusingly, numerous variant English transliterations for nearly all Japanese titles and phrases. *Nihongi* is "Chronicles of Japan"; *Nihonshoki* literally "Written Chronicles of Japan." The *Kojiki* consists of records of pre-fifth-century narrative based mostly on oral tradition. The *Nihongi* often conflicts with its companion volume, but nonetheless encompasses fascinating bits of Chinese observations and conjecture about the court.

[3]It must be stressed that this is only a hypothesis; the exact sequence and nature of events of the peopling of Japan is still not known with certainty.

years to complete the journey that connected Jimmu to his earliest antecedents on the land that came to be Japan.

The four main islands making up Japan include, in a scimitar-shaped curve from north to south and bending to the west, Hokkaido (formerly called Yedo), Honshu (the largest, once known as Hondo), Shikoku (the smallest), and Kyushu. Before the retreat of the last great ice floes ten thousand years ago, the land that became Japan was linked to the continent by land "bridges," and the earliest people were able to wander onto this pre-island Japan, arriving about a thousand centuries ago, give or take a few millennia. Thought to have descended to the warmer southern part of the archipelago through the northernmost island of Hokkaido, these earliest inhabitants probably resembled the Aborigines of modern Australia, nomadic, heavily bearded Asiatics who were hunters and gatherers, people who spent their lifetimes wandering from place to place in a ceaseless search for food. Because of the land bridges to Asia and the chains of closely spaced islets, the tribal groups accomplished their widespread migrations with relative ease. There existed both a northern route connecting Hokkaido with Siberia and a southern route linking Kyushu and Taiwan—and southeast Asia beyond. The early wanderers split, and two predominant cultures gradually developed: a society of Siberians of the Caucasian type in the north, and one of southeast Asians in the southern, more temperate islands. The former, the white-skinned Ainu, were isolated in Hokkaido and developed independently from the peoples centered on the three southerly islands.[4] The latter group, from whom elements of the modern Japanese language descended, is believed by Japanese historians to be that of which Ninigi—or at least of the people Ninigi mythologically represents—was a member in the area of Mount Takachiho. When the great floes of the Ice Age melted and raised the levels of the planet's seas, the land bridges and small island chains disappeared, isolating these peoples in their virgin land and creating the circumstances under which, for thousands of years, a

[4]The word *Ainu* may derive from the pejorative *ai no ko*, "offspring of the middle"—that is, a breed between man and beast, the purported "missing link."

unique prehistoric civilization developed all but independent of influences from the Asian mainland.

In the last half millennium before the beginning of the West's Christian era, the Polynesian-derived peoples in the south began to be replaced by pure Mongolian-Koreans, a group that would eventually displace all the others as the overwhelmingly predominant racial group in Japan. These pugnacious wanderers had tried without success to move onto China's fertile Yellow River plains, kept out only by its fortified Great Wall. Thwarted, they turned back to Korea, and eventually crossed the 122-mile-wide, island-dotted Tsushima Strait to Kyushu. The Mongoloids did not come as a single group of invaders; they trickled into the islands slowly, adapting themselves to the language spoken by the peoples already settled there. In fact, the most significant heritage bequeathed by the original Polynesians of Japan is their language, a few of whose elements took precedence over the Central Asian tongue spoken by the Mongolian-Korean immigrants; this linguistic absorption was inversely comparable to the assimilation of the language of the French invaders by Britain's native Anglo-Saxons.

Language aside, the greatly superior talents and knowledge gained by the Mongolians in the larger continental world they had left behind enabled them eventually to dominate and finally control the Polynesians, and the earlier South Pacific culture ultimately disappeared without establishing any vital continuity with the later inhabitants. Paradoxically, some of the Korean immigrants set up a reverse migration, apparently dissatisfied with the more difficult conditions they encountered in Kyushu, but even these returnees were to leave their historic mark when, with the cooperation of the Chinese court, they later captured political control in parts of the Korean peninsula.

In the last century before both Christ and the purported emperor Jimmu would appear, in roughly the same era though on opposite sides of the globe, one particular group of the Mongolian-Koreans managed, by both sheer force of their rapidly multiplying population and their undeniably superior talents, to appropriate most of the arable parts of the southern island of Kyushu and settle into a static routine. Forced to retreat to the mountains, the natives they displaced continued to wage irritating raids against the new agricultural settlers.

The character of Jimmu, or the early warrior-kings he represents, comes into the picture with these new Mongolian-via-Korea overlords of the southern island. Keep in mind that affixing dates for this early period of Japanese history is even today a highly conjectural undertaking: Jimmu certainly did not live, if he ever lived at all, anywhere near the period around the traditionally mandated 660 B.C.; instead, he probably appeared some six to eight hundred years later. In fact, he may simply represent the amorphous beginning of the nation's "historical" period, the time when individually recognizable events started taking place, episodes later writers would try to recollect and piece together.

Bearing this important caveat in mind, one of the more plausible of the historical theories surrounding his life makes the putative Jimmu the grandson of a pirate-trader from Korea. Other historians have assigned all sorts of circumstances to his existence: Many, it should be strongly stated, dismiss him as so fanciful as to be totally discountable in any kind of historical context. Furthermore, the thought of Korean provenance for their imperial house is especially unappetizing to many modern Japanese, who, as a result, resist historical research into the dynasty's origins. But, for the sake of rendering a framework that explains many of the known elements of the imperial chronology, the Korean thread is worth following.

Distantly of Malayan or South Pacific island descent, the man from whom Japan's imperial dynasty would flow sailed to his destiny from his home port of Karak—a buccaneer's enclave near what is today Pusan—his intention to seek out his fellow Koreans across the straits in the settled area of Kyushu. There he took up with the granddaughter of one of the Kyushu colonies' sun priestesses, Pimeko, the head of a company of shamans whose power depended on possession of the community's "magic" tokens: a mirror, a sword, and a necklace of shells. The union of the adventurer and the priestess's granddaughter produced a son, who, upon reaching maturity, set about exploring the Inland Sea that acted as a lake between the three main southern islands. Eventually, he included his own son in these activities; this latter child—the fourth generation descended from the colony's sun priestess—was Jimmu, the "Divinely Brave."[5]

Jimmu, being the son and grandson of adventuresome men, naturally wanted to make his own mark in the world, and, with the single-mindedness of those who become great leaders, reasoned the best way would be to bring the whole of his known universe under his own rule. Leaving Kyushu, he and a band of followers that included his three older brothers and his son moved across the Inland Sea to the big island, Honshu. After traveling for three years, making only brief forage stops along the way, they eventually landed at the westerly entrance of what is today Osaka Bay, 350 miles east of their starting point. Expecting to find armed resisters, the adventurers sailed into the anchorage in a militarily defensible formation, a line in which the prow of one "ship"—the vessels were probably hollowed-out logs—touched the stern of the one behind. The place where the expedition settled, on the plain encompassing the region of today's Osaka and Kyoto, came to be called Yamato,[6] a name still today used in a poetic sense by the Japanese for their islands, as the English use Albion or the Irish Hibernia. This flatland, Japan's second largest after the Kanto plain around Tokyo Bay, appeared to be ideal for rice cultivation, very likely Jimmu's major consideration in deciding that this was where he would make his mark.

The local defenders they expected to find didn't take long in

---

[5]Names for the early "emperors" were not assigned until the Japanese chronicles were written around the time of the fiftieth (eighth-century) emperor, Kammu. He had directed a scholar named Mifune to select the uniform set of canonical reign names, called *okurina,* to be applied to his predecessors; many are taken from sites associated with the particular ruler. Although it is logically incorrect to refer to these names in a contemporary sense, the alternative would be unwieldy and difficult to follow. Jimmu's supposed "real" name was Sanu-no-mikoto; in his youth, he was said also to be known as Wakamikenu, Kan Yamato Iware Hiko no-Mikoto, and Toyomikenu—"Jimmu" being invented posthumously. The term *mikoto,* applied during their lifetimes to the first fifty or so monarchs, was a title of respect equivalent to "Augustness." Mikoto generally followed long names that eventually gave way to abbreviated Chinese-derived equivalents; the term was dropped after Chinese writing became fashionable at court.

[6]Today the Nara prefecture and its environs.

making their presence known, and Jimmu's little band expended considerable energy fighting to increase its foothold on the contested plain. Other settlements had already been established in the area, and those pioneers, threatened by the latest upstarts from Kyushu, annoyingly refused to acquiesce while Jimmu and his toughs took over, thus creating an impasse that resulted in ceaseless bloody combat between the contending groups. Legend has it that three years were needed to "pacify" the area, and that such pacification was accomplished at least in part by "miraculous aid." But what Jimmu had that his adversaries didn't was an abundant sense of mission, of nation-building, regardless of the puniness of its scale. Instilling a rigid discipline in his followers, he was able to become by far the most powerful contender for supreme authority in the area, eventually subjugating the entire competition in the Yamato plain and even beyond to the fertile mountains that ringed Osaka Bay. With his victory secured, he pronounced himself "emperor," a declaration that would still be recognized almost two thousand years later as the establishment of the historical Japanese state.

It is now clear that both the name Jimmu and the concept of a sovereign king were the fabrications of later Japanese historians in an understandable, if misleading, attempt to equate the origins of their nation with "superior" Chinese dynastic traditions while, at the same time, serving to portray a unified country that certainly did not exist in Jimmu's time. But what is also clear is that *something* approximating the major elements of the Jimmu story *did* happen. A group of warrior families who worshiped a sun goddess *did* put together the first general political and military hegemony over large areas of Japan, their fief generally referred to as the Yamato court. But Jimmu wasn't an emperor; it is far more likely that he was what could be called a tribal chief, albeit one holding power over a number of tribes or communities. The encampment over which he presided wouldn't have been anything like a settled town; it would have far more closely resembled the kind of impermanent tent grounds associated with the aboriginal natives of North America. Interestingly, an important taboo of Jimmu's society involved ritual cleanliness, with an absolute mandate requiring bathing before and after any of life's most central tasks—eating, copulating, doing battle. This stylized fastidiousness, which became a primary and deeply ingrained characteristic of Japanese people, remains today a special mark of the modern court: The emperor's bath still constitutes one of the most sanctified places in the Imperial Palace.

Most significant for the later nation, and perhaps even the primary reason he was chosen to represent the birth of the state, is that the Jimmu king is tied to the origins of what would become Japan's first national religion, Shinto. Adding his continental practice of ancestor worship to the local aboriginal spirit worship, Jimmu decreed that the central position in his culture's pantheon would be occupied by his own family's priestess, the Sun Goddess, a place from which her embellished provenance would grow into mythical fantasies and dominate the country during the reign of every one of his successors.

A remarkable feature of Jimmu's state was the rigid separation of the ruler's own tribesmen from those over whom they held sway. The Koreans were encouraged to think of themselves as masters, a people apart, and intermarriage with the lesser, conquered communities was strongly discouraged. The upper classes, the rapidly multiplying original clan descended from Jimmu and his lieutenants, were granted surnames and titles, attributes denied even the lesser beings of Jimmu's own community. The loyalty of these superior beings was based on inherited perquisites and directed solely to their chief, whose bequeathed authority became both priestly and rigidly hereditary, two attributes common to authoritarian leadership throughout both oriental and occidental history. Racially similar groups were slowly accepted into the Yamato social structure, but, initially at least, at a lower social level. Racial aliens— the native aboriginals—were either enslaved or exterminated.

A point might be made here concerning the country's name during the era in which these protohistoric occurrences were taking place. Evidence suggests that the country we now call Japan was, in the earliest years after its initial unification—an event whose precise date is unknown—called Yamato. The term, which can be thought of as the country's aboriginal name, predating Chinese influence, subsequently came to mean only the province around the seat of government—the protoimperial court—in the area of the

Osaka-Kyoto-Nara triangle. One version of the word's origin has Chinese geographers, who first took cognizance of the land lying to their east, calling the place *Wado,* which was pronounced "Yamato" by the islands' Japanese inhabitants. The ideographs used by the Chinese to write the word conveyed the contempt they felt for the heathens off their shores, so, not unnaturally, the Japanese eventually changed these ideographs to ones with the same sounds but having the rather more pleasing meaning of "Great Peace." Another version of the name's origin has the Japanese themselves inventing it, which they pronounced *Dai Wa*—still signifying "Great Peace." Some centuries later, when they adopted the Chinese writing system, the Chinese characters spelling the name were given a double meaning, retaining the Dai Wa pronunciation when talking to Chinese, but when spoken at home being pronounced Yamato, which really meant "mountain road." A thinly disguised euphemism for "paths to new conquests," "mountain road" was a title that would have been considered cheeky to the ears of the powerful and touchy Chinese emperor, thus the reason for the double pronunciation.

The name used today for the country came centuries later, but it's as well to stop here to see how it developed. Like so many things Japanese, the word *Japan* comes from China (though some historians say Korea). The Chinese ideographic symbols for Japan literally mean "Sun-Rise Islands," a name that would have logically been assigned to a place located in the direction from which the sun rose on China each morning. The pronunciation the Chinese gave the two characters used to spell the word was roughly "Jih-pen," whence, of course, *Japan,* the fifteenth-century Dutch corruption used by Westerners (or one of its several variants, to account for differing letter and sound values among the various European languages). The Japanese pronounced these same characters "Ni-hon," and it is from this distinction that modern complications emerge. The Chinese sound system didn't permit one to say "Ni-hon," preferring instead the smoother—to a Chinese ear, at any rate— "Nip-pon." Over the succeeding centuries, the Japanese-y *Nihon* and the Chinese-y *Nippon* were used interchangeably by the Japanese themselves to denote their own country; Yamato had long since

37

been discarded except for either poetic or jingoistic purposes. Shortly before World War II, the Japanese government formally decided that the characters for the country's name could *only* be pronounced as "Nippon," ironically discarding the Japanized pronunciation that had taken so many centuries to develop. Today, "Nippon" is still official, but contrarily the Japanese people themselves invariably speak the characters as "Nihon."

Returning to the imperial story, it is well to understand that just as it is questionable to give flesh and blood status to Jimmu, the same holds for any attempt to assign actual personal traits to the first several generations of Jimmu's descendants. But the connecting thread of this hypothetical account would be lost if we ignored the chieftains-cum-emperors who certainly tied the imperial line's founder—whoever he was—to those monarchs who *are* indisputably historic figures. The primary source for the lives of this roughly half-millennium's worth of rulers comes from the research of the lifelong Japan scholar, Richard Ponsonby-Fane, whose late-nineteenth-century book, *The Imperial Family of Japan,* contains a wealth of scholarly information on the early Yamato court. Ponsonby-Fane's writing was in turn predicated, as are modern Japanese works on the subject, on material from the Kojiki and the Nihongi.

The assumptions and conjecture on the lives of the early emperors is analogous to that on the ancient popes: Peter, the first man accounted as pope, is written about rather heavily, but his first several dozen successors are little more than historical shadows. A disproportionate part of the story of the very early papacy begins and ends with reference to Peter, and so it goes with the Japanese imperial line in its first generations: Jimmu is so outstanding in representing the Yamato period that his successors, the men listed in the official (which is to say, court-approved) roster of Japanese sovereigns, are nearly lost. As with Jimmu himself, their very existence as individuals before the fourth century is highly dubious, perhaps figments of later storytellers' collective conjecturings in their attempts to fill in lost centuries. This is also undeniably the case as regards the given names associated with them in accounts of their lives. But to eliminate all reference to these earliest occupants of Hirohito's throne would be to ignore an important part of the traditions of the imperial line, traditions that were central to and highly formative of the Japanese national psyche until the end of World War II, and which color the country's outlook even today.

Jimmu's first successor was said to have been called Kamanunakahamimi, or possibly Kamununakahamimi, or Kami-nunagahamimi, or maybe Kamu-yamoto-iwarebiko-hohodemi-no-mikoto. Regardless of what his contemporaries called him, he is referred to in Japanese histories by his posthumous reign name of Suizei. (Since these supposed given names don't get much shorter, this narrative will be considerably less difficult to follow if hereafter we stick to the posthumous reign names, the okurina.) Suizei is thought to have been the younger of two offspring of Jimmu's marriage to a princess of Izumo, a village near the coast on the Sea of Japan side (that facing Asia) of Honshu. Named Himetataraizu-hime, the princess is said to have been declared empress, which probably means Suizei raised her to the position of senior consort among the many women he would have claimed the right to bed. Custom was established from earliest times that the Yamato chieftains were entitled to take several recognized consorts in addition to as many concubines as needed; the latter did not, incidentally, constitute a position corresponding to its Western, prostitutelike connotation. As court traditions coalesced, there came to be various designations for the "empresses," of which *kogo,* reserved solely for consorts who were themselves "imperial" by birth,[7] was the highest, followed by the slightly less regal *chugu.* In either case, the distinction brought great honor on the bearer's family. A primary distinction between consort and concubine in early times was that offspring of recognized consorts were eligible to inherit the throne, while those of concubines generally were not. The bearing of many children to the chieftain in an age when infant mortality rates were appallingly high was the primary consideration for the numerous imperial consorts, but maintaining a fully sated libido was fully as honorable and unremarkable to these Japanese as were dynastic considerations.

[7]Kogo is the title used for the current empress-consort of Japan.

The principle most central to the budding dynasty was the laying down of the foundations of hereditary succession. The emperor's blood heir by his highest-ranking domestic partner would inherit the tribe's chieftaincy, thus keeping dangerous uncertainty over the group's leadership at bay. This principle, whether or not it was actually firmly established in the very earliest inheritors of the imperial mantle, is nonetheless crucial to the ironclad principle of unbroken legitimacy of the Japanese monarchy—although, as we shall see, that principle was altered in ways peculiar to Japan.

Even at this seminal point in the establishment of the monarchy, this absence of certainty created difficulties. Specifically, it seems that Suizei had an older half brother, Tagishimimi, the son of Jimmu's ladyfriend of his pre–Yamato Kyushu days. The discarded "natural" son of this liaison felt, with some justice, that he had a strong "natural" claim to his father's position. The latter had been dead for four years while the concerned elders debated the issue of inheritance. Finally, Suizei is supposed to have asked his older full brother, Kamuyaemimi, to do away with their mutual half brother, but the nervous full brother refused to involve himself in an assassination. Suizei therefore carried out the deed himself. His lack of resolve apparently caused the faint-hearted Kamuyaemimi to recognize his own unworthiness to succeed Jimmu. During its accounts of the early reigns, the Chronicles (Nihongi) make passing mention of the desirability of primogeniture—the principle of the right of the eldest son to inherit—but, like the circumstances surrounding Suizei's accession, numerous instances allude to younger brothers superseding older siblings to the throne. A still gelling principle was easy to overlook when a younger claimant possessed obviously superior capabilities, assets sorely needed to safeguard the emerging society's still vulnerable security.

Suizei established his own headquarters camp at Kazuraki, in Yamato, but not for about seven centuries would the court permanently settle in a "capital," a situation that prevailed for several reasons. Most importantly, Jimmu and his successors held sedentary life in contempt, fearing that to succumb to what they thought of as sloth would bring an end to their hegemony. In their violent world such a fear was justifiable. Only the strong and the mobile survived to father new generations in a time when enemies struck mercilessly from any quarter. Furthermore, the ritual cleanliness that these Spartan-like warriors placed at the center of their rude philosophy dictated that when a member of the group died, his dwelling structure—tent, lean-to, whatever—had to be destroyed. The principle spilled over to the encampment as a whole: When the leader died, everyone packed up and moved on to something clean and uncontaminated. The defilement caused by the deaths of the early emperors was considered so grave and so long-lasting that, to appease the gods and purify his own regime, the new monarch would inevitably make such a move the first major task of his reign. This situation resulted in the imperial "capitals" never becoming much more than crude encampments. The monarchy was seven hundred years old before the difficulties inherent in moving the growing population, especially the top-heavy bureaucracy that supported the court, finally forced later emperors to discard taboo and settle on a permanent capital.

What is known, or surmised, of Suizei is deduced mostly from the Chronicles, but it is difficult to reconcile its account with real life because of the highly unlikely lifespans this account hypothesizes. To fill out the period between 660 B.C. and the time when something resembling authenticated history begins—about A.D. 500— the average reign of these two dozen or so emperors makes them into Methuselahs. Using calculations derived from the Chronicles, the median age of the first seventeen emperors from Jimmu onward is 117 years, and the average reign about sixty years, obviously impossible in an era when reaching thirty was a considerable achievement. The account of Suizei's succession appears to contain at least a germ of truth, however allegorical, but the rest of the "facts" of his life in the *Nihongi* are totally fabricated, details that would be impossible to reconstruct without some concrete historical evidence or records. It should be emphasized, however, that the tenth-century courtiers who wrote the two records of the early emperors did so in a conscientious attempt to explain history in terms not deliberately fallacious, but bound by the requirement to please their sovereigns about matters concerning those sovereigns' own ancestors. Flatteringly exaggerated imperial exploits and achievements paid the bills, as it were.

Suizei was succeeded by his only son, Annei—of whom the Chronicles' accounts are wholly unverifiable. He was followed by his second son, Itoku, who for reasons unknown was preferred to his passed-over older brother. The often-abused principle of inheritance by the eldest son did not become an absolute legal requirement in the Japanese monarchy until 1889; prior to that, the succession had been left to the choice—often appearing to be little more than caprice—of the emperor, or, more generally, of his advisers. Before the Meiji era's constitutional requirement in the Imperial House Law mandating primogeniture, the succession had, according to Ponsonby-Fane's history, passed in remarkably varied paths of familial descent: sixty-six times from father to son, four times from father to daughter, twenty-six times from brother to brother, once from brother to sister, three times from sister to brother, five times from uncle to nephew, once from an aunt to a nephew, three times from nephew to uncle, once from a great-nephew to a great-uncle, three times from grandfather to grandson, once from a grandmother to a grandson, twice from husband to wife (on both occasions also his niece), once from son to mother, and seventeen times from cousin to cousin. Unless a crown prince, which is to say a legally designated heir, had been named, there was often very little certainty as to who the successor would be.

Kosho, Itoku's heir, was the first to claim the distinction of being named crown prince during his father's lifetime, which although far from becoming the rule proved a useful practice in the early monarchy. Kosho's four immediate successors—the alliterative Koan, Korei, Kogen, and Kaika—are as shadowy as their predecessors back to Jimmu. Most importantly, though, these rulers must certainly have had sufficient talent and singleness of purpose to keep the budding dynasty firmly enough on track to deliver it intact to those later sovereigns of whom undisputed historical knowledge exists. Kogen achieved a measure of posterity for ordering the construction of a burial mound to house his remains, in the manner of the early Egyptian kings. This sovereign's relatively modest tomb—the key-hole-shaped tumulus measured about 180 feet from one end to the other—inspired his successors to try to overshadow him until, as was perhaps inevitable, the imperial vaults assumed gigantic proportions as each successive monarch strove to outbuild and out-glorify his predecessors.

The dynasty began to gain some substantial note with Sujin, its tenth monarch, toward the end of this nebulous first half-millennium of the Christian era. This reign constituted the first truly memorable period since the death of Jimmu, and both the Records and the Chronicles refer to him as "the Emperor, August Founder of the Country." The most significant of Sujin's accomplishments was bringing under the dynasty's control vast new territories that had stubbornly resisted the authority of the Sun Goddess's kings; it was during this reign that the Kanto plain—the area around the present city of Tokyo—was subjugated under the jurisdiction of the imperial clan. Except for the northern island of Hokkaido, which wouldn't be considered an integral part of the Japanese state until the sixteenth century, the area comprising the modern country was at last substantially united. It was also Sujin who founded the great temple at Ise—still considered the most holy place in Japan—as the repository for the imperial regalia, putting his personal virgin-priestess in charge as its first keeper.

Sujin came up with a novel way of settling his own succession question: Unable to decide between his two sons, whom he apparently loved and esteemed dearly but equally, the monarch ordered them to recite him a dream from which he would draw an augury to decide the matter. The elder recounted that in his dream he "climbed up a mountain, and, facing the east, I cut with the sword and thrust with the spear eight times." The younger's reverie was gentler: "I climbed the same mountain, and stretching snares of cord on every side, tried to catch the sparrows that destroy the grain." Reckoning their individual characters from this, Sujin said to the older, "You, my son, looked in one direction; you will go to the east and become its governor." To the younger, evidently wiser boy, he said, "You looked in every direction. You will govern on all sides. You will become my heir." Apocryphal perhaps, but in any event the heir, named Suinin, was said to have established a peaceful and successful rule, while his elder brother, true to Sujin's reputed premonition, developed into little more than a fractious warrior-governor in some unnamed and long-forgotten province to the east.

In the fourth-century reigns following that of Sujin, the Yamato court assiduously managed to increase its political strength many times over. Somber mention is made in the Chronicles that this was a "time of taxes," described as "tributes of bow-notches and of finger-tips," the latter interpreted as probably signifying slaughtered game. Also written of was a census, whose findings were lost, and a prototype national navy—probably more by way of a "coast guard"—said to have been ordered by the emperor Sujin. Suinin, Sujin's successor, is credited with placing for the first time the sacred regalia in the shrine built by his father at Ise; the original of the Mirror, only a replica of which is used at the enthronement ceremonies, is still there. Suinin also seems to have had a tender streak to his nature. When a king or a prince died, custom had long decreed that a handful of his chief retainers should be buried alive right alongside, a gruesome rite not unknown to many societies throughout history. But Suinin was said to have been much distressed when this ritual was performed at the death of his younger brother; the prolonged and agonized cries of the prince's very much alive advisers rising from their entombment distressed the royal ears. The practice, called *junshi,* was mercifully forbidden, replaced with the novel idea, advanced by a courtier named Nomi-no-sukune, of burying dolls, little clay figures, instead of living people.[8]

During Suinin's reign, the first references to Japan began to appear in Chinese accounts. A Chinese historian writing in the first century A.D., by which time his country's records are accepted by historians as substantially reliable, noted that "the Japanese [whom he called the *Wa* people] dwell southwest of Korea [*Han*] on a mountainous island in mid-ocean." Already the paramount importance of the Sun Goddess's dynasty had made itself felt on the mainland world from which it had been conceived. "Their country is divided into more than 100 provinces . . . there are 32 provinces

---

[8]A sort of "voluntary" junshi persisted, like its kindred spirit *suttee* in India, down to fairly modern times.

which style their rulers 'kings,' which are hereditary. The sovereign of Great Wa resides in Yamato."

This Great Wa's new sovereign, Keiko, Suinin's successor and the purported father of seventy-two sons, is described by the Chronicles as having been so secure in his power that he personally led his armies against the rebellious and savage aboriginal Kamusu of Kyushu. Keiko's exploit represented the first instance since Jimmu that a sovereign risked his own life to take the field against anyone, an indication of how greatly ceremonialized and raised in totem value had the position of the sovereign become. Today, Keiko's militarily inclined exploits are looked upon with a considerable measure of historical éclat in the eyes of modern Japanese, making him one of the country's earliest hero-kings. But far more important to the development of the monarchy and the sovereign's role in it were the extraordinary administrative abilities of Takenouchi-no-Sukune, one of Keiko's imperial advisers, whose role earned him the distinction of being the first figure in Japanese history to be accounted "prime minister." Eventually, those men who would hold this office would come to completely overshadow the sovereign in terms of both power and administrative authority.

The custom peculiarly indigenous to the Yamato court of taking well-bred local girls into virtual slavery was inaugurated during the reign of Keiko. Daughters of the local magnates found themselves drafted into the imperial encampment and assigned to the culinary department; called *makura-ko*, "pillow-children," all evidence points to their being primarily intended as back-up concubines.

For the record, monarch number fourteen was the first emperor who was *not* the offspring of his predecessor. Until now, the crown had passed down from father to son, although not necessarily to the firstborn son. But Seimu, who followed Keiko, outlived his only legitimate son, and was therefore succeeded by a nephew, the emperor Chuai. Chuai was also the first to leave the familiar surroundings of Yamato, temporarily returning the Sun Goddess's central headquarters camp back to its birthplace in Kyushu.

The yet-untested issue of imperial succession by females arose with Chuai's demise. In its history, Japan has experienced twelve regnant empresses, women who have reigned not as the wives of emperors but as empresses in their own right. Not until the late nineteenth century would the "salic" principle—the rule mandating male-only inheritance to the throne—become the governing dynastic law, although by that time a century and a half had passed since a regnant empress had actually occupied the throne. Chuai declared that the unborn child that was being carried by his chief consort would be designated his own heir on its birth, but, messily, he died before the child was born. During the interval between her husband's death and the birth, this consort—afterward popularly but unofficially called Jingo Kogo, "Queen Jingo"—comported herself in the manner of a sovereign. The baby she was carrying—a male—was born with full sovereign powers in light of its father's declaration, but by that time Jingo wasn't about to give up the very rewarding position she felt fully entitled to keep for herself. To give weight to this contention, legend contends that during her pregnancy she personally led the army and "conquered the country of Shiragi," delaying her imminent laying-in by means of "stones in the girdle." (The Records leave it to the reader's imagination to fathom this.)

But back in Yamato, Keiko had left two ambitious older sons by another, less-favored consort, and directly on hearing of the situation, the pair attempted to seize the throne. Jingo's able spies kept her one step ahead of these spurned princes, and she rushed back to Yamato where soldiers loyal to her made quick work of the would-be usurpers. Though Jingo may have actually ruled and been accepted as such by her dominated subjects, the official modern Order of Emperors omits this ancient feminist role-model. However, by her actions, the stage was being set for the day when legitimate inheritance of the throne by females would become an accepted compromise to ensure the dynasty's survival.

Emperor Nintoku, monarch during most of the last half of the still very dark fourth century, brought to its climax the tomb-building monomania that had been initiated by Kogen. His eighty-acre tombsite, at more than a half mile long, was in reality a moated artificial mountain, rivaling in its building skills and grandeur most of the sepulchers the pharoahs had constructed in Egypt. Nintoku's memorial ranks today as the world's largest funerary monument, and, in common with the Egyptian tombs, it, too, cost the lives of thousands of peasants conscripted to build it. The tomb still exists, in the suburbs of modern Osaka, and the emperor's body is still believed to be enclosed. Although of justifiably intense interest to both Western and Japanese archaeologists, the site, as the personal property through inheritance of the present emperor, remains totally off-limits to modern pursuers of ancient secrets.

An issue of considerably greater impact than funeral architecture is historically tied to Nintoku's reign, one that set a precedent leaving a permanent mark on the ensuing history of Japan's imperial house. Nintoku had not been the choice of his father, Emperor Ojin, to succeed to the throne; in an act perhaps of caprice, perhaps of well-intentioned judgment, a younger son, Waki, had been designated heir. But the designee himself declined the honor on Ojin's death, and Nintoku refused all court-sponsored attempts to involve himself in what he considered to be a "usurpation" of the throne while his younger brother, whom he held to be the legal claimant, remained alive. In consequence of the brothers' stalemate, the throne remained vacant for three years while the imperial counselors tried to solve the contretemps.

Meanwhile, Prince Nintoku fell under the sway of a powerful clan of courtiers, the highly placed Takenouchi family, even marrying a granddaughter of that house. Inevitably, these imperial mentors gained powerful positions of influence with both princes. The clan head, acting as prime minister, badgered the legal younger heir so badly to give up his claim that the by-now half-unhinged prince committed suicide to find relief. Nintoku at last came to the throne, but he was completely under the sway of his Takenouchi "advisers." The principle of the relegation of administrative authority into the hands of the great nobles had taken root, thereafter growing mightily and prevailing until the middle of the nineteenth century.

This early, just-short-of-historical era was approaching its end. With the reign of Nintoku's grandson Yuryaku, Japanese history—the certain knowledge of its past—opened as the country was swept by the influence, especially religious, of the great continental landmass off whose shores the nation had thus far remained largely free to develop on its own. The emperor Yuryaku's reign spanned two decades near the end of the fifth century, when Yamato court life degenerated into a spectacle of demented cruelty thanks to the unbalanced mind of the sovereign, a man who, because of the bestialities he perpetrated, was called "Emperor of the Great Wickedness." Inbred to an obviously overdone degree, Yuryaku took great pleasure in shooting trussed courtiers out of trees in a sort of perverted target practice; shocked attendants testified that peasant women were made available to the emperor so he could enjoy what to him was the heady sensation of tearing them apart, bare-handed. Some of these recordings sound a bit overcolored, but courtiers who survived the emperor's games nonetheless saw to it that potential heirs to the throne no longer bedded with relatives quite so near in consanguinity.

In the era of the emperor Yuryaku, China corresponded to Japan in a way comparable to the relationship then existing between the highly refined classical culture of Rome and its colonies and the rough-and-tumble, semisettled civilizations of northern Europe. In the matter of dress, for example, at the same time Roman aristocrats and courtiers disported in finely tailored linen togas and the untamed Gaullish and Norse warrior chiefs wrapped themselves in the skins of animals, the Chinese mandarin class were the sumptuary spectacle of east Asia in their multicolored silk while the Yamato imperial clan ruled over their domains wrapped in rudimentary fabrics made from the threads of cotton, mulberry bark, and hemp, the lot of which was spun, woven, and dyed in ancient techniques that had been handed down from the times that preceded the dynasty of the Sun Goddess. A Japanese sovereign was distinguished by his long, loose tuniclike garment, which was worn over a loincloth, and straw sandals. His subjects dressed themselves in fabrics made from the same materials but of coarser quality, with decoration achieved mainly through the use of color, an important element of dress irrespective of the wearer's rank. White was reserved for the clothing of the top stratum of society, with red, blue, and black indicating descending rank within the community. A primitive kind of coarse silk was woven during the early reigns, but was used more for the making of sleeping cushions than for clothing; so, too, were furs employed primarily as rugs and coverings. Since its earliest recorded times, elaborate hairstyles have played a major role in Japan; at the primitive Yamato court, young girls dressed their hair in a loose cascade down the back, tied at the nape of the neck, with a sort of topknot added at marriage. Men, just as style conscious, affected a style parted in the center and tied up in two little bunches, one over each ear. All classes wore the high, platformlike *geta,* clogs that had been developed for the soft mud of swampy fields in days long before Jimmu's clan came to dominate the land.

For both highborn and low, the common dwelling was a rude hut, the oblong shelter constructed of tree poles and bark walls lashed together with rush or vine ropes. Developed from the Polynesian models brought into the islands centuries earlier, it proved singularly inappropriate for Japan's harsher winters but persisted nonetheless. The floors were of packed earth, with a fire pit for cooking and heat in the center of the room; the doors and the rare windows were simply holes covered by bark matting. The larger rafters at the roof ends projected and crossed each other, like drawn swords, the primitive model for what would later evolve into the classic Shinto temple. The rank of the occupants was designated not so much in the few amenities as in the relative size of the dwellings.

There were as yet no meadows or hedges or neat rice paddies lending the land the familiar look it would one day acquire. Only thatched huts grouped in tiny villages gave unmistakable evidence of the presence of higher order, but as the people gained the attributes of civilization, the land gradually took on a more tamed look.

Of the many social transgressions that threatened this fragile society, one of the gravest involved damaging a rice field. As it is today, rice—then still brown since polishing was not yet practiced—was in these earliest imperial centuries the central dietary staple of Japanese life. Later ages would see its position usurped by millet, but the less arduous cultivation of the coarser grain had not yet developed. Meat—meaning game, food animals weren't kept—was a fairly common part of the diet, more common at court than at the peasant's table, to be sure, but not yet prohibited by the religion that would one day flow from the Asian continent and impact itself so deeply on Japanese society. Bearmeat and venison were occasionally eaten, horses and oxen less so—the latter being simply too indispensable as beasts of burden to be wasted as a food source. Along with the fish, roots, and edible wild vegetables common to both the rich and poor was a seemingly mild native liquor that was much appreciated for its miraculous ability to take the chill off the night. Until other potables were introduced by Westerners, sake was the only stimulant drink known to the Japanese—the secret for brewing this potent rice drink was probably imported from China. Chopsticks were used for eating utensils, the instruments then still commonly joined at the top end, like tongs. The fires used for cooking were lit by rubbing together two pieces of cypress, a method that continued to be used down through the centuries in the ceremonial lighting of the fires in the Yuki and Suki halls at enthronement ceremonies of the nation's monarchs.

Life, even—perhaps especially—at the top, was still overwhelmingly an arduous and dangerous condition, with menace coming in the form of raids from unpacified and generally nasty neighboring tribes, draconian punishments for infractions of taboos and laws, and, most insidiously, the rudimentary state of knowledge of the body, its illnesses and its complexities. Punishment for breaking the primitive rules of the community were uncompromisingly severe: The practice, relished in Europe at the same time, of determining guilt or innocence by whether one acquires or avoids a scald burn upon placing his or her hand into boiling water was still held valid. Also, as it was in so many other cultures during the first half of the first millennium, the institution of slavery was a normal part of Japanese life. A slave owed his condition either to having been taken prisoner in the almost endless intertribal struggles, or to having been condemned to that condition for breaking the community's laws. Even a member of the Takenouchi family found himself condemned to slavery, in his case for slandering the family patriarch. Not only was a culprit degraded, but his entire family was made to share the disgrace. Paradoxically, evidence suggests that slaves were not really much worse off than the common, noncourtier (which is to say, nonadministrative) class.

The class structure at the time of Yuryaku separated his tribal society into three great primary divisions: the imperial caste; the *shimbetsu* ("descendants of the gods"), the bulk of freeborn society;

and the aboriginal, or native, class. The first, both the highest and by far the smallest, was made up of the families of emperors from Jimmu down as well as their sons, the imperial princes. The heads of the highest families within this class were automatically entitled, as a matter of birthright, to the rank and titular surname of *omi*, those who traced their lineage back through one or another of the emperors to the all-important Sun Goddess herself. Lesser families constituted the *muraji*, those whose lineages were traceable through other deities in the evolving Shinto pantheon. Both omi and muraji clans were under the authority of supreme leaders, who through the fifth and sixth centuries vied with each other and with the emperor for control of the fledgling central government.

Those below the imperial class, the shimbetsu were subdivided into three ranks: the less direct descendants of Jimmu, which is to say the imperial family as it became more diluted through succeeding generations; the descendants of Jimmu's ancestors; and the tribal chiefs and their descendants vanquished by the Yamato emperors, considered shimbetsu so long as they came of the same racial stock as their conquerors. This latter group, though deprived of the power they once wielded, were vested with considerable prestige within the Yamato community. As the sovereigns' descendants increased in number, the nobility found them useful material for enlarging the shimbetsu. Their ritualized exaltation of the emperor and the attendant pride that sprang from it was the basis for many of the traditions that would grow within this noble class.

The aboriginal class was so far below the other two that its members differed little from actual slaves. It was made up of native tribes alien to the Yamato race and included foreigners who had lately come into the country from China or Korea.

Overlaying—not always precisely or neatly—these ranks were the familial divisions into which the budding nation was organized. Called the *uji*, these clans represented Yamato society's largest kinship units, among whom power struggles were constantly being waged. At the top of Yamato society, the court was a federation of the most powerful of the uji chieftains, under the authority of the chief of the imperial uji, the emperor.

A convenient way of describing the meaning of Yamato families is to compare them to the Scottish clans, groups that existed within the national rank structure but were nonetheless virtual tribes within themselves; the Japanese nation was at this time a loosely united federation of uji, each of which controlled specific territories of ricelands. Within each family, households formed the structure we now associate with the concept of family: husband, wife, children, possibly grandparents, and servants for the more fortunate. Primogeniture was strictly followed, with the first sons of first sons inheriting the headship and title to all of the family's property. The families from Japan's protohistoric imperial age established a tradition to which many societies both earlier and later also adhered: Nearly everyone followed a fixed, hereditary occupation, from provincial governorships to herdsmen and farmers. From these pursuits, names were affixed to family members that described their work, designations that were sometimes modified or changed by some particularly praiseworthy or meritorious deed credited to one of the members. For example, Nomi-no-sukune, the courtier who mercifully suggested substituting clay dolls for human sacrifices in burial rites, was, after his famous deed, called Hashi-no-omi, "the Pottery Grandee."

As for the day-to-day role of the sovereign himself, in the time of Yuryaku, three primary tasks constituted his principal prerogatives and duties. The first, and even in this early era incomparably the highest, was the role that every emperor down to and including Hirohito has seen as his chief obligation and the primary reason for his existence: leader, as the supreme head of the Japanese nation-family, in the worshiping of the spiritual pantheon, primarily his own ancestors. The emperor, and the emperor alone, possessed the authority to go straight to the gods for succor in times of famine and other national emergencies, and the Japanese people grew accustomed to the idea of the absolute preeminence of the monarch in all matters pertaining to religion. This factor embodied the single most important distinction in the way in which Japan's monarchy developed when compared to its Western counterparts. From the beginning, European monarchs were expected to yield to the central demands of the Christian church, to admit subservience to the Church's sacerdotal prerogatives; in matters of moral and religious judgment, Christian kings were under the sway of a central authority in the person of the pope. But in Japan, the temporal and, theoretically, the secular were combined in the emperor. As the imperial institution developed and settled into a permanent shape, the throne came gradually to be accorded the role of a state church.

The second role was of the declarer of wars, the instigator of peace. This duty would in time be delegated to, and finally usurped by, the military class, but in the earliest centuries the sovereign's responsibility for war and peace remained undiluted. The third role, and this was critical to the way in which the nation itself developed, was to establish and alter the hierarchy of family groups, nominating new family heads when for whatever political or social reason headships needed rejuggling. Significantly, for reasons we shall soon see, the important role of senior administrator, which was a responsibility of the contemporary Chinese sovereigns, was not one Japan's society expected its monarchs to take.

Waiting to blow over this still rudimentary society's horizon was a great wind, one in whose eddies and whorls the whole of Japan's society would be reshaped. This approaching typhoon grew out of a simple reverie dreamed under a faraway fig tree.

CHAPTER III

Foundations

MID-FIFTH CENTURY TO LATE EIGHTH
CENTURY

The half dozen or so monarchs who followed in the century-long
wake of the demented Yuryaku continue as shadowy figures, men
whose lives and personalities are reconstructed more from legendary
fragments than from unambiguous historical evidence. Vestiges of
passed-on fame cling to one or two, such as the purported debauch-
ery of Buretsu, said to have been nearly as depraved as the great
Yuryaku, though many scholars attribute Buretsu's imputed crimes
to political motives on the part of later chroniclers. But fact and
myth finally began to coalesce as the epochal sixth century lightened
the still rough-hewn society. The Japanese court found itself on the
threshold of acquiring a veneer of refinements whose depths would
soon reach astonishing proportions and contrast sharply to life—
even noble life—on the far side of the globe. Except for a single
flickering beacon in Byzantium, the lights were going out in Europe,
leaving little more than China to keep alive man's intermittent
efforts to rise appreciably above his origins.

A remarkable characteristic of the Japanese people since their
earliest origins has been their capacity to intelligently winnow foreign ideas and cultural influences, take what was needed and discard
that which ill-suited their purposes—the resulting synthesis dis-
tinctly and usefully Japanese. But it was on account of such borrowing that what historian Edwin Reischauer has called "probably the
greatest tragedy of Japan's history" occurred during the early-fifth-

century reign of the emperor Richu. Yamato had to that time managed to develop only a primitive form of writing, a crude system incapable of being applied with any sophistication to the spoken language. But in a historical happenstance for which the nation still pays dearly, a party of visiting Korean scholars sent by the king of Paekche, one of the three kingdoms into which their peninsula was then divided, introduced Richu's court to the writing system of China.

Spoken Chinese and Japanese are utterly unrelated languages. Chinese is a monosyllabic tonal tongue, uninflected (without case endings), and fairly well suited to the pictorial symbols, or ideographs, used to write it. The ideographs themselves originally had no sound values, each standing instead for a whole word, in the same way the numeral "1" stands for the English word *one*; the numeral can be equally understood by Germans who might pronounce it *"ein,"* or *"un,"* as do the French, or the *"bir"* of the Turks. Japanese, conversely, is a polysyllabic, highly inflected, nontonal language, to which the application of pictographs was enormously *in*appropriate. But so high was the esteem in which the Japanese scholars and court held China's advanced culture, and so much were they in need of something to replace their existing and plainly deficient writing system, that the complex Chinese system was adopted whole. Though the use of the new writing method remained for many years pretty much restricted to the elevated confines of the court, it still enabled the writers of the period to become true historians, at last recording with accuracy the curricula vitae of the individual emperors—although we must still treat with some suspicion the earliest records.

From the late fourth century to early in the fifth, the cohesion and simplicity of purpose that had propelled the court into an increasingly powerful position began to fade, leading to destructive power struggles within the imperial family and a subsequent decline in the dynasty. When Buretsu died, no successor could be decided upon, forcing the ministers of state to make a convoluted twist in the imperial line to find a suitable candidate. Settling on a fifth-generation descendant of Ojin, emperor number twenty-six reigned under the name of Keitai.[1] The remarkable point in Keitai's succession is that any one of the most senior ministers was certainly powerful enough to grab the momentarily wobbly throne for himself, but already the principle of succession through the legitimate blood line from the Sun Goddess was so thoroughly respected that no subject, however high, ever attempted such an act. Even when the rare imperial assassination unexpectedly required a quick replacement on the throne, some dynastically legitimate imperial prince was invariably found to ensure that the Sun Goddess's direct descendants remained sovereign.

Of all the forces that would play on the Yamato court and the Japanese nation, the most pivotal was yet another act of assimilation—this time of an utterly foreign philosophy, but one that would have an effect on Japan directly proportionate to that of Christianity on the Western world. Portending great changes for the monarchy, the imperial system, and the nation itself, in A.D. 552 the faith of Buddha arrived on the emperor's shores.

It was in the reign of the twenty-ninth emperor, Kimmei, that the ancient philosophy of the Indian subcontinent, Buddhism, reached Japan after centuries of leavening in China. And in a remarkably short time, this "new" religion profoundly changed the country's social structure. Japan's own belief system, that which had existed in the island-nation prior to Buddhism's arrival, hadn't truly constituted a religion, at least not a structured creed in the sense of a Christianity or an Islam. *Shinto,* meaning "The Way of the Gods," a word not coined until Buddhism started to give it competition, had developed more as a sort of supernatural shamanistic philosophy, one in which the natural elements of the land and the distant ancestors of the inhabitants of that land were all considered to possess divine attributes, some, of course, in considerably greater

---

[1]Some historians consider Keitai's connection to the imperial line to be spurious, reasoning that his succession constitutes a break in the dynasty. Keitai did, however, marry a princess more closely related to the prior emperors, and the line descended through their offspring.

measure than others. The emperors became the leaders in the worship of these ancestral and natural deities, called *kami*, but the divine forces were not bound up in an elaborate system of metaphysics, no dogma was associated with this primitive early form of Shinto, nor was it even held to be universal; the Japanese reckoned Shinto as applying uniquely to themselves, other places and peoples having religious systems both separate and valid as their own requirements dictated.

Like much of value from China that had already been and would yet be appropriated by Japan, the new creed was transshipped via Korea. Buddhism had first been introduced into China from India in the Christian year 65, when the emperor Ming of the Hou-Han dynasty sent a mission to India to obtain both its fabled Buddhist *sutras*—the sacred scriptures held to be the words of Buddha himself—and teachers who could clarify the then-exclusively Indian faith that posited ideals of spiritual harmony and serenity. More than three centuries later, the creed found a firm footing in Paekche, one of the Korean kingdoms, from where, a century and a half later, it leapt to the Japanese archipelago.

A foretaste of Buddhism had actually first been introduced into Japan in 522, when a temple was erected in the Sakata plain in Yamato to glorify Buddha. For reasons now obscure, the creed didn't take hold, most likely because it hadn't come to the notice of the court and therefore failed to gain popular acceptance. But thirty years later, in an act that would immeasurably alter Japan's culture, a small bundle of presents was sent over from the king of Paekche to the court of the Sun Goddess kings. Along with some sutras, a copper image of Buddha, plated in pure gold, was offered as a gift from the Korean potentate to his Japanese counterpart. The memorial that accompanied the statuette informed the emperor Kimmei that "this doctrine is, among all, most excellent. But it is difficult to explain and difficult to understand. Even . . . Confucius did not attain comprehension. Imagine a treasure capable of satisfying all desires in proportion as it is used. Such a treasure is this wonderful doctrine." Excited with anticipation at such a fabulous promise, Kimmei called a hurried session of his top-ranking courtiers to help him decide what should be done with this gift, pregnant as it was with the seed of seemingly unlimited wonders. The counselors were cautious and divided with their advice, but the impatient emperor, whose interest in the foreign doctrine gave Buddhism its entrée, was anxious to see what this Buddhist faith could do and permitted a limited worship of the image by the court. In short order, a clergy sprung up to take charge of the obeisances paid to the creed. That a pestilence—probably a drought or some such— soon came along was unfortunate; that it was ascribed to the anger of the native gods over the introduction of an alien faith was predictable. The statue was thrown into a canal, thus interrupting the first experiment with court-sanctioned Buddhism.

The observation that the Korean gift was motivated far less by selfless generosity than by the donors' hopes that a grateful Japanese court would assist them in their ongoing political struggle against powerful Chinese neighbors is probably not terribly important at this late remove. The central point here is that Buddhism had indeed been given its opening at court, and despite a temporary setback, a soon reestablished clergy anxious to maintain its new privileges wouldn't again fail. Splitting into sects, the growing court-controlled clergy gained new and useful knowledge from study of the faith, ideological notions of kingship that Kimmei and his successors realized could be applied to strengthen their position. For this knowledge, the priests gradually strengthened their invaluable court sponsorship and protection, enabling the clerical ranks to grow until they came to resemble monarchies-writ-small in their own well-defended little religious fiefdoms dotted throughout Yamato.

When Kimmei died, he was followed on the throne by three of his sons in succession, during which time the issue of Buddhism grew in intensity and seriously vexed the court. Whether or not to accept the foreign faith—a previously unknown philosophy and set of elaborate rituals that fascinated the Japanese, especially the court—was heatedly debated in the councils of the imperial family and among the leaders of the most powerful clan families. One such family, the Soga, who claimed close relationship to every emperor since Jimmu, favored the adoption; another, their chief competitors, the Mononobe clan, the family controlling the court's arms supplies and holding critical duties in the nation's Shinto cult, opposed it as alien. In reality, a large part of the Mononobe resistance was probably founded in their realization that the form of Buddhism imported from China had in it the seeds to destroy the established imperial system, on which their high and jealously guarded positions in society were based.

The almost atheistic early Buddhism held that earthly position, no matter how lofty, even imperial, could not be used as an automatic ticket to heaven. To reach Nirvana, Buddhism's supreme heavenly state of blessed nonexistence, individualism must be merged into the godliness of meditation. This sort of thinking obviously presented some fairly ominous problems for the kind of personality-centered imperial system the Japanese had developed, but, fortunately for the future of Japanese Buddhism, the Soga gained the political upperhand over the Mononobe, which is to say they monopolized, in one way or another, the imperial ear. It didn't mean—yet—that the new faith would be allowed to co-exist equally with the native spiritual belief, but this opening represented the wedge in the door leading directly to Buddhism's eventual unambiguous triumph.

The first of Kimmei's heirs to follow him to the throne was his son Bidatsu. When, soon after his accession, a new plague broke out, the Mononobe regarded it as another god-given chance to lay the blame at Buddha's door, and they talked the emperor into the extreme measure of allowing them to destroy all the new temples built to honor the imported faith. When the plague still didn't subside, the bet-hedging Bidatsu immediately ordered the structures reerected, which naturally tended to further erode the already badly weakened Mononobe family's influence at court. Bidatsu did put a condition on the rebuilding, however: The temple priests must not proselytize, a prohibition the clerics were intelligent enough to understand would be fatal to the still struggling Buddhism.

Bidatsu fathered seventeen children, eight of whom were borne by his half sister—the lesson from Yuryaku's day evidently forgotten—but none succeeded him at his death, the funeral obsequies for which were badly marred by near-physical violence between the pro- and anti-Buddhist forces at court. Instead, Bidatsu's brother Yomei,

Kimmei's son by a highborn concubine named Kitashi-hime, "Princess Kitashi," came to the throne. The Chronicles affirm that Yomei "believed in the laws of Buddhism [while at the same time] believing in Shinto," and accordingly the new sovereign finally accepted Buddhism as the official faith of the court and, lifting the proscription on proselytization, allowed the priests to freely spread their teachings. For himself, he begged to be commended for Nirvana, and like the famous example of Constantine and Christianity, this scene, too, was played on a deathbed. Buddha had at last and against tough opposition gained an unshakable footing at the Yamato court.

Sushun was the last of the three sons of Kimmei to inherit the throne. Immediately on Yomei's demise, Sushun was fiercely lobbied by the Mononobe to abjure what his late brother had recognized, but by that time Buddhism was rapidly gaining widespread acceptance among the ordinary subjects, the faceless masses from whom the sovereign and his court had already become impossibly remote. Although Buddhism still carried the potential to destroy the emperor system, it nevertheless acted as a worthy vehicle for maintaining the status quo in society. Like Christianity, Buddhism taught the acceptance of suffering in this life in exchange for the greater rewards sure to come in the next, a concept reinforced with the usual rubrics: gorgeous paraphernalia and impressive rites, elements much in contrast to the gray, morose gloom of Shintoistic practice. The Buddhist priesthood became a goal for men who otherwise would have passed lives of drab colorlessness, and the taking of the veil one of the few escapes for the overworked and underfulfilled women of the community.

Infinitely the most auspicious event of the reign that had preceded Sushun's was the appearance, not of a future emperor, but of a prince, a child prodigy of extraordinary ability and a man whose cumulative effect on the subsequent path of his nation's history would be greater than that of any sovereign until Meiji. Born the second son to the emperor Yomei, the prince was called Umayado, so-named because his mother, while walking in the palace grounds one day late in her term of confinement, was suddenly seized with the pains of childbirth and delivered the son in the nearby stable, the *umaya.* However, the name by which he came to be known to history was Shotoku-Taishi—Prince Shotoku, of "Sagacious-Virtue."

In early adulthood, Shotoku was appointed a court counselor to his nephew, the emperor Sushun, and when the monarch bitterly complained to his new adviser that he was losing power to the increasingly hard-to-control priest-abbots of the growing Buddhist craze, Shotoku counseled his sovereign to follow the path of patience. As it happened, a member of the Soga family had quietly taken over the leadership of the new faith, an act that was construed—not unreasonably—by the sensitive monarch as a direct and ominous threat to the preeminence of the emperor as the country's chief priest over *all* its religious activities. Fearing that imperial wrath might lead to the clan's own destruction, the Soga made arrangements to have the emperor done away with. The hired killer, a naturalized Chinese named Koma, was introduced into the imperial surroundings as a textile salesman from the eastern provinces; once he was past the guard and free to roam the palace grounds, Koma was able to carry out his murderous deed, the act constituting the sole undisputed case of regicide by a subject in Japan's imperial history.

To further aggravate their family's already grievous perfidy, the Soga leaders saw to it that the imperial corpse was buried the same day of the murder—and *without* the usual rites that, in a simplified form, would have been accorded even the least of Sushun's subjects. It was an unforgettable insult to the monarch's memory. As for the assassin, Koma was silenced by his employers; after charging him with regicide (Koma screamed, "I didn't know it was the Emperor!"), he was dragged to the nearest tree, strung up, and used for archery practice—recalling the long-ago sport developed by the demented Yuryaku.

The fact that Prince Shotoku—only nineteen when these events took place—knew of this planned act and thus played a part in the assassination, however secondhand, must be acknowledged. But when his options are taken into account, it is possible to understand why he helped carry out the Soga coup: First of all, although he was an imperial adviser to Sushun, he was married to a Soga lady and sympathetic to her family's ambitions. Second, not only did he support Buddhism's victory as the new national religion, but he also wanted to get rid of the clan system on which the Yamato court was based and which he now saw as an impediment to the nation's progress. And third, had he, at nineteen, attempted to thwart the powerful Soga, the relatively inexperienced junior adviser would probably have fallen victim to that family's great capacity at intrigue, forfeiting any hope he harbored of influencing the country's political direction. One historian described Shotoku's motives as "building the edifice of a great reform," an understatement in light of what he eventually bequeathed to Japan's posterity. Motives such as those credited to the prince have, of course, been the rationale for regicides and renegades for centuries before and after the time of Shotoku, but rarely can a people count an assassination as a positive event. Luckily, as far as this one was concerned, the Japanese could.

Interestingly, Sushun's successor was Japan's first true female emperor. The monarch in question was the empress Suiko, a woman who had already been an empress-consort as the wife (as well as the half sister) of the emperor Bidatsu, Sushun's brother. Known during her consort days as Toyomike Kashikiya-hime, roughly translated as, "The Princess Who Cooks Splendid Food," she became the first woman not only to reign as sovereign over Japan, but anywhere else in the Far East. Suiko did not inherit the throne because of her earlier royal marriage connection, which would have in no way in itself qualified her for sovereignty. Rather, it was her all-important blood ties to the imperial line that led the great ministers to install her on the throne as a sort of compromise to keep the more obviously eligible male candidates from warring on each other, which would have brought no end of problems to the ministers.

Suiko was a daughter of Kimmei, and thus a direct descendant of the Sun Goddess, the sole requirement for sovereignty. Her maternal uncle was the great Umaka Soga, the most powerful minister at court, and her succession was very likely the result of his having personally picked her for the job. Nonetheless, because of her sex, Suiko was never considered capable of handling any substantive administrative duties, and although the supreme role of head of state remained legally vested in her person, a kind of regency was established under Prince Shotoku[2] to carry out the day-to-day job of steering the ship of state. It was during this supervisorship that Shotoku came to the fore and earned his uniquely important and honorable place in Japan's history.

In truth, few of Shotoku's deeds have the documentation necessary to qualify as concrete historical facts, though the Japanese have credited him with nearly everything good and decent that transpired in this era. What Shotoku seems beyond doubt to have given Japan was a constitution—at least a kind of rudimentary protoconstitution. Even though it did not contain any kind of enforcement or penal provisions commonly thought of by today's standards as essential in even a minimal legal code, nor was it officially promulgated by the emperor, the prince's legacy nevertheless stands as Japan's first comprehensive set of written laws. Of extreme importance, Shotoku's constitution attempted to reconcile the still bitter differences between the ancient Shinto practices and beliefs and the new Buddhism. In this endeavor, the prince was wholeheartedly supported by the empress Suiko—herself an ardent adherent to the new faith. Shotoku's drive to ground the court in Buddhism and the orderliness of the continental imperial system represented a positive legacy rare to any society in mankind's checkered history.

The document credited to Shotoku's authorship was called the *Jushichi Kempo*, the "Seventeen Article Constitution." Derived in essence from Chinese sources, its moral maxims were an admixture of the teachings of Buddhism with those of Confucianism, the latter the ancient Chinese philosophy of conscience embodying the principles of an orderly society. Though Japan's powerful clans were immediately suspicious of Shotoku's motives, their leaders saw in the prince's precepts a valuable model of the successful Chinese "imperial state." In such a state, a sovereign monarch—then a nearly universal element of governments in East and West and one without which "civilization" was virtually inconceivable—would be

[2]There really wasn't a function by this name in Japan at the time, but Shotoku acted in Suiko's name, who either was content to assume a retiring role or wasn't given enough freedom to successfully thwart her managers.

served by loyal subjects, who would in turn be amply rewarded with high positions in the life of the state. While Shotoku delineated the relationship between emperor and subject as that existing between heaven and earth, an extra bone was thrown to the jealous dominant families in the form of a dazzling new system of court ranks, twelve formal grades whose auspicious and grand-sounding titles he based on the six cardinal moral qualities of virtue, benevolence, propriety, faith, justice, and knowledge. Each of these was in turn divided into "greater" and "lesser" degrees in a range that ran from Greater Virtue to Lesser Knowledge, with the imperial clan safely and carefully kept above and thus well out of these classifications. Understanding the value of sumptuary distinctions, Shotoku bestowed on these ranks ice-bag-like caps made of a kind of cushy silk called sarcenet (and what became the chief identifying mark of the court costume) that was dyed in a variety of colors, depending on rank, that permitted each to immediately judge the other fellow's relative placement like a new corporal sniffing at a private. The whole system allowed the monarch to weigh and grade his courtiers, and it was the first intimation that the Japanese emperor would forthwith prefer to rank the court on the merits of its individual members rather than on strictly hereditary principles, the first coloration of a Chinese-style central bureaucratic government. Significantly, the new arrangement also made a deep dent in what had been a virtually closed structure of society, permitting for the first time a systematic route for climbing the social ladder.

Of the seventeen articles contained in the document[3] the most important was the twelfth. This paragraph was an exhortation that the people not be double-taxed; specifically, that no government official should tax the citizenry in his own name in addition to that of the central government. By the key phrase, "in a country there are not two lords; the people have not two masters . . . the sovereign is the master of the people of the whole country," the prince attempted to move away from the old Yamato vision of the monarch as essentially only the paramount chief among lesser chiefs and

[3]The original was lost in a fire soon after the writer's death; it was reconstructed shortly afterward from memory by courtiers who had assisted in its drafting.

toward the Chinese model of government as a pyramid, the emperor occupying its peak free from any other mortal's company.

The constitution, which Shotoku, acting as regent for the empress, issued to government officials in the form of "instructions," admitted that "men are swayed by class feelings and few are intelligent," asserting this to be the reason for disobedience, but he added that when the "high are harmonious and the low friendly," almost any problem could be resolved. Another article exhorted citizens not to fail to "scrupulously obey" the Imperial Command, for to obey brings harmony, and to fail to obey is equally sure to cause a "catastrophe to ensue."

The rest of the articles were in the nature of commonsensical advice (i.e., "Chastise that which is evil," "Good faith is the foundation of right," "Let all persons entrusted with office attend equally to their functions"). Nothing earthshaking—except the notable absence of any kind of ratification of the Shinto-based hereditary principle in the monarchy—but they were the sort of things that if a society were to follow closely, something akin to true justice just might result. The world had seen few such documents up to the time of the eighth century, nor would it for many centuries thereafter, which is what accounts for the Shotoku constitution being so conspicuously remarkable.

Other Chinese cultural norms were adopted by the Japanese court when, in 607, the prince sent the first official embassy to China in the name of a Japanese ruler. The ambassador took with him an official letter from "the sovereign of the Sunrise Country to the sovereign of the Sunset Country," the choice of words judged in retrospect to be a bit uppity in light of China's imperial sensibilities. The wording was toned down when the next ambassador adopted a style more befitting a vassal. As it turned out, the honeyed approach seemed to work better, and the ambassador returned to Shotoku with the precious Chinese books that had been the real object of his mission, not to mention the even more important assurance from an all-powerful Chinese monarch that an official relationship was now considered to exist between the two countries.

Shotoku was wise enough not to overlook his own sovereign's personal considerations during this exciting period of wheeling and dealing: The prince made it clear that *his* vision of Buddhism quite unmistakably saw Suiko skipping all the Buddhist transmigration difficulties at her own death, being permitted entry to Nirvana straightaway. Great wisdom often amounts to the dispensation of small but crucial exceptions in important places.

Many modern students of Japanese history believe that Prince Shotoku may have been more a symbol of the introduction of a refined Chinese culture than an active innovator in the affairs of state, a view abetted by the fact that the prince himself actually saw few real reforms in the Yamato court's affairs. Furthermore, skeptics add, little originality is evidenced by the actual content of the Shotoku precepts; an intelligent study and application of the chief moral precepts of Buddhism and Confucianism might be accounted for the true source of the document. But if his "constitution" does in fact simply add up to only a set of moral guidelines and preachments on the way public officials should deport themselves, it put the behavior of the country's governing officials on a path that would be increasingly adhered to in the coming centuries, a path toward the rational and workable Chinese example of the hierarchical, centralized, nontribal state in which the customs, etiquette, and language of the enormous neighbor to the west would rapidly supplant that which had been built up in Japan over the preceding millennia. An entire new foundation of Japanese learning had been laid, not the least of which was the renaming of the imperial office itself. *Okimi,* "Great King," had, until Suiko's ascension to the throne, been the usual title for the emperor. However, the appellation tenno, "Emperor [or Son] of Heaven," henceforth came into style. Besides reinvigorating the drooping image of the monarch, it tended to place the holder of the office at parity with the Sui dynasty sovereigns of China, the cultural ideal the Japanese avidly wished to emulate in this great "borrowing" period of their history.

The loss of Shotoku's steadying hand on the court was immediately felt at his death in 621, as the country was soon swept by a civil war that tested the strength of the Soga clan against its many rivals jealous of the stranglehold this family held over both monarch and government. The Soga princes won the contest and they set themselves up as virtual dictators, their unassailable admiration for all things Chinese permitting the Sinicization of Japan to proceed unabated. The empress had hoped to be succeeded by Shotoku's son, Prince Yamashiro, but her wishes were ignored. At her death in 628, seven years after that of the regent who had ruled in her name, she was followed on the throne by a grandson of Bidatsu, one Prince Jomei, a character far more malleable to the Soga clan's wishes than Yamashiro was envisioned to be.

When the colorless Jomei died, his designated heir, Prince Naka, was only sixteen and thus deemed too young to reign. Because the only other eligible candidates were ready to claw each other to death to prevent the other's succession, Jomei was followed by yet another outright Soga puppet, his own widow, Kogyoku, who, like himself, was a descendant of the Sun Goddess. Being a woman, she was naturally regarded as only a stand-in until her and Jomei's son was old enough to take control of the increasingly fractious government.

At this dangerously unsettled point there occurred another of the handful of truly watershed events that have shaped Japan. Into the story of the monarchy now enters the family that would dominate the court—for a time directly, for a far longer time indirectly—until the end of World War II. The Fujiwara would, simply stated, be the greatest family of subjects *ever* in Japanese history, overshadowed in importance only by the imperial dynasty itself.

The genesis of this unparalleled family hails back to the very earliest roots of the Sun Goddess's throne. Legend has it that three lieutenants helped Jimmu establish the imperial office: on Otomo, "Mighty Friend," the emperor bestowed the duty and privilege of protecting the imperial person and palace; to Mononobe, "Swordsmith," he entrusted the duty to provision the court with weapons and to act as the enforcer of imperial decisions; and to the clan of Nakatomi, "Inner Companion," he gave the responsibility of administration.[4] It was the seed of the third of Jimmu's three lieutenants who, in 645, moved decisively to the helm of state. Here his family would remain, their name many centuries before changed to Fujiwara, until 1945, when the last noble head of the house, Japan's

---

[4]Even in modern Japan, no dearth of prominent citizens proudly claim descent from one of these three noble families.

wartime prime minister Prince Konoye, dramatically ended both his own life and his clan's service to the reigning sovereign, Hirohito.

The events that brought the family to preeminence were, not surprisingly, composed in violence, the overthrow of the Soga hegemony involving a slaughter of hitherto quite unimagined proportions. The act that precipitated the violence was the placing of Jomei's widow on the throne, an act of such arrogance on the part of the Soga clan that it raised the fury of the diminished but still powerful Nakatomi family, at the time under the leadership of Kamatari, which then resolved to overturn the government. Allied with the imperial prince Naka, Empress Kogyoku's own son, Kamatari Nakatomi carried out a carefully crafted strike against the despised Soga.

On the twelfth day of the sixth month in the year 645, the Soga-controlled empress happened to be holding a court reception in the great Taigoku Hall of the imperial palace, there majestically receiving tribute from envoys representing the three kingdoms of Korea. The emissaries were reportedly aware that some kind of a coup against the Soga was to be attempted that afternoon. As a guest at the affair, one of the high-ranking Soga princes had laid down his sword temporarily, it being etiquette to do so when approaching the throne. The appointed assassins quickly seized this moment to begin the coup and attempted to cut down the Soga clansman. They bungled it though, succeeding in only wounding him; immediately they lost their nerve and quickly sprang for a getaway. In the midst of the suddenly hushed gathering, the badly cut-up aristocrat fell at the feet of the startled empress, begging his sovereign to help him. When the near-speechless and quite stupified monarch demanded to know what was going on, Prince Naka boldly spoke up, asserting that he meant to put an end to the odious Soga usurpation of sovereign authority. Seeing that her son was in on the plot, the empress wisely concluded that it would be best to accept the loss of her trusted Soga adviser. Sweeping out of the room, she left the bleeding man to keel over on the floor. Taking this as a signal to continue their work, Nakatomi's men immediately hacked the nearly dead courtier to bits and unceremoniously threw his body into the courtyard, there to be covered rudely with a few odd pieces of straw matting. The outraged but now checkmated leader of the Soga clan retired to his villa, there to immolate himself in a self-set fire. A sad irony in his act is that many of the records and writings of Shotoku, stored in his family's stronghold, went up in flames along with the defeated clan chieftain.

The Soga allies quickly withdrew their support from an obviously lost cause, and in the first such act in Japanese imperial history the empress abdicated in favor of her brother, the new emperor Kotoku. Rather quickly the nobility and high officials saw where their duty lie, expediently rushing to take up the Nakatomi banner. Having been persuaded to stand aside in favor of his uncle's succession (Kotoku had been less conspicuously involved in the Soga overthrow and thus was considered less controversial), Prince Naka became crown prince to his uncle the emperor, and Kamatari Nakatomi was installed as Minister of the Household, the real power in the shadow of the throne.

Sadly, a lack of trust—both political and private—soon caused a serious rift between the new monarch and his headstrong heir. The political factors had to do with Naka being denied what he considered a major role in government, a prize he sincerely felt he deserved after helping oust his mother and her Soga advisers. But Kotoku resisted Naka's attempts to gain more power, precipitating an eventual confrontation with the talented but dangerously thwarted young prince. The personal reasons for the rift were based on considerably more unconventional foundations. It seems that Kotoku's consort was Naka's full sister, Princess Hashihito, and the siblings had, to the full knowledge of the court, embarked on an incestuous relationship, a situation that even Naka understood would probably dash any hope he might harbor of succeeding to his uncle's throne. Carnal knowledge between full siblings was condemned by Japanese custom, and adultery with the emperor's consort added considerable insult to the injury. Later, when Kotoku died in 654, Naka knew that he could never effectively rule while breaking ancient taboo by cohabitating with his own sister, so he arranged for his mother, the former empress Kogyoku, to reascend the throne, which she did in 655, and for this six-year-long second reign she was known to history as the empress Saimei. This constituted, by the way, the first time in the nation's history that a tenno ruled in broken terms.

Although still involved in his disabling love affair, Naka formally succeeded his mother as sovereign in 661, reigning as the great emperor Tenji, "Heavenly Intelligence."[5] An interesting glitch in the imperial succession occurred with Naka's ascendence. Instead of taking the throne, Naka gave his brother, Oama (like Hashihito, Oama was Naka's full sibling),[6] administrative control at court, claiming that he wanted to continue the reforms he had initiated as crown prince and that his own services were more urgently needed to supervise the Imperial Fleet in aiding its then-beleaguered Korean ally, the kingdom of Paekche. Besides wishing to be dissociated with the throne while his reforms were being tested, Naka's reasons for not claiming the succession probably had as much to do with his tangled relationship with his sister. When his lover-sister Hashihito died, Naka finally permitted himself to take over the government from Oama and, in 668, assumed actual power as Tenji.

The effect of this succession on the social and political life of the nation was to be profound and lasting. Naka and Kamatari's first significant act after their coup in 645 had been the Taika (literally "Great Change") Reforms, elaborating on what Shotoku had initiated a generation earlier with an attempt to impose the Chinese bureaucratic system on Japan's government. Now these reforms could finally be promulgated. The Japanese political order was reorganized in a way comparable in its sweeping importance to the Meiji revolution at the end of the nineteenth century. Among the epoch-making changes, the Reforms asserted the crown's—in effect, the state's—ownership of Japan's rice-growing lands at the expense of private landholders. This edict for centuries made the emperor the theoretical proprietor of the country's croplands, at the same time barring private ownership of land. In addition, a census was ordered;

---

[5]Again a reminder to the reader that these imperial names were awarded posthumously many centuries later.

[6]Oama later became emperor himself; he and Tenji were the only two monarchs in Japanese history whose mother *and* father had been ruling sovereigns.

taxes, until then a haphazard and disorderly thing, were systematically imposed; the assignment of official administrative and court positions to the nobility was initiated; and the political divisions of the country, until Tenji's day ill-defined, were formally reorganized into provinces, districts, and villages. A major part of the Taika Reforms involved the compiling of civil and criminal statutes that came to be known as the Ritsu-ryo ("penal and civil") codes, a set of laws that underscored the nation's governance for the next six centuries, and which continued for another seven centuries to be the theoretical basis for Japan's legal system. And, finally and most memorably, a permanent capital was ordered.

Although some historians question whether these changes were imposed in quite so systematic a fashion, and despite the fact that they admittedly ebbed and flooded over a period of two centuries, the Taika Reforms—whether literally devised as a legal code in conjunction with the Shotoku "constitution" or, more probably, merely a straightforward and pragmatic reaction to existing problems—pushed forward with more vigor than ever the country's emulation of all that was Chinese.

While China's cultural, legal, and intellectual influences were to prove lasting, its political system wasn't. Several factors share the blame for the ultimate failure in the political realm: Japan's geography; the country's already deeply entrenched clan system; and the importance placed on the desirability of a long and prestigious traceable ancestry for its leaders. The mountainous islands with their steep and sharply indented coastal edges hindered easy communication between parts of the country, making political control a difficult proposition. This situation enabled the second factor, the strong system of clans, to maintain close autonomy within their own areas of dominance. And despite the Shotoku precepts, Japanese tradition stubbornly continued to call for aspirants to high secular office to hold personal pedigrees of unimpeachable nobility—instead of undisputed ability, which is the primary qualification in the Chinese model—with the resulting bureaucracy overrepresented with noble but dull-witted nonentities.

During the decades in which the imperial family was stiffening its resurrected political authority, the jealous guardianship of its right to supervise the nation's religious rites was the most important element in its strategy. Before the Taika Reforms, leaders of the nation's several dozen family clans retained rights that mirrored those of the imperial clan: A clan chieftain could, for instance, insist on the perquisite of representing his own kin in high religious rites, ceremonies that had a political significance far outstripping their spiritual weight.[7] To remedy this threat to the throne, the Ritsu-ryo Codes gave precedence to the government bureau administering religious ceremonies over those governing secular affairs. But with the confirmation of the leader of the imperial clan as the sole intercessor with the gods, the temporal position of the emperor became utterly unlike that which his subservient nobility enjoyed. By claiming an exclusive, nonshareable relationship with the Sun Goddess as her direct lineal descendant, and thereby reserving the exclusive right to lead rites worshiping her, the imperial family's political ascendancy was guaranteed. In practice, this power would be short-lived; in theory, it supported the imperial family's claim, down to the present era, to temporal authority.

It is worthwhile to note that at this time—just before and during the turn of the eighth century, when substantial physical evidence revealing the details of the events of the imperial reigns becomes available—the Sun Goddess's clan was the only one whose actual name is not known. Though logic would presuppose that they must have had such a name, as was the case with early Japanese clans, the establishment of a rigid taboo against actually voicing it probably had already been firmly established by the earliest centuries of the family's existence. At the beginning of the eighth century, the emperors referred to themselves in their imperial edicts as *akit-sukami,* "Incarnate Deity," and other even more florid usages existed: the *Manyoshu* ("A Collection for a Myriad of Ages"), a volume of over four thousand poems compiled between the fifth and eighth centuries, used many such euphemisms.

The enigma of Tenji's reign is that while the Taika Reforms formally and incontestably established the emperor at the apex of

---

[7]The ancient Japanese word for "administration"—*matsuri*—originally signified a religious service.

the national triangle, the sovereign himself had in his chief adviser, Kamatari Nakatomi, a man whose own principal aim was to strengthen imperial prestige but who would paradoxically directly bring about the diminution of the monarch's role as the nation's secular ruler. The strength of Kamatari's clan was such that by the close of the seventh century, the practice of selecting from it a maiden as the imperial consort had already become a virtually inflexible rule.[8] The irony of this situation is that the physical progenitor of the most powerful line of the Nakatomi family was none other than the emperor Tenji himself.

In 670, Kamatari Nakatomi was mortally ill. Being childless, his friend the emperor presented him with an unusual bequest. Tenji offered as a gift to his closest adviser an imperial concubine, one who was pregnant with the emperor's own child. Tenji told Nakatomi that if the child were a boy, he could become the heir to his dying friend, which would ensure that the line of Kamatari would not be extinguished. A boy was indeed born to the imperial bedmate, and this natural son of Tenji came to head his own branch of the Nakatomi family under the name bestowed on it by the emperor himself, Fujiwara, in commemoration of the wisteria trees that grew in the valley where Kamatari and the young Prince Naka had first discussed their vision for reforming the weakened monarchy. Although the throne would continue to exert considerable political power for nearly another century, with the individual sovereigns still to some degree in control of events, the seeds for the Fujiwara takeover had been sown. Slowly, without immediate or apparent effects, a golden Fujiwara cocoon was spun around the throne as successive emperors were, with unerring skill, made ever more dependent on this vital new element in the story of the monarchy.

Tenji's immediate successor was his twenty-four-year-old son, Kobun. However, Kobun's reign lasted less than a year. In what

[8]Since the wives and concubines of Japan's sovereigns came not from foreign courts in furtherance of military alliances, as in the European model, but from the native aristocracy, the Japanese imperial family has remained thoroughly native. Of the two primary factors that went into the development of this practice, the country's remoteness from foreign lands and its racial exclusivity and disdain of non-Japanese, the latter was probably the more critical determinant.

came to be known as the Jishin War, a vicious and bloody power struggle, Tenji's brother Oama wrested the throne from the legal heir and newly elevated emperor. Though Kobun himself escaped with his life, he had no safe refuge where he could permanently escape Temmu's fast-pursuing army, and in desperation strangled himself in a temporary hiding place at Yamazaki.[9] Following custom, the head of the vanquished was presented to the new emperor, where it was soon joined by those of eight of Kobun's ministers. Oama's power play over his nephew resulted in complete victory. Posthumously known as the emperor Temmu, Oama, the fortieth sovereign, was the only historic monarch to wrest the monarchy from an already-enthroned emperor and the last to struggle for that throne by force of arms.

Very often in history, a triumphant reign tends to sublimate the bloody circumstances of a sovereign's accession, and so it is with this monarch. Thanks to Temmu, the immediate hand of the monarch became far more visible than it had ever been in the administration of the emerging nation's affairs, reviving the sputtering Taika Reforms whose vigor Tenji had allowed to slip. Temmu's achievements were remarkable: He required that all officials appointed to positions of public trust give promises of accountability and competence; by taking away their control over the unfree classes of the population, the emperor siphoned off much of the strength of the great clans to the enrichment of the central government; he initiated a new order of titles of nobility, something along the lines of the modern British rankings of duke, marquess, earl, viscount, and baron in their relative standings, with the lowly place given the ancient and heretofore revered title of omi, almost at the end of the rankings, a clear indication of the emperor's efforts to supplant and discredit the old peerage;[10] and he ordered the writing of the country's first history, with its goal the enhancement of a glorious emperor-centered past, a project eventually resulting in the *Kojiki* and the *Nihongi*, (Records and Chronicles), Japan's historical equivalents of Western civi-

[9]It was only in 1870 that Kobun was added to the official roster of emperors.
[10]Some ranks were made nonhereditary, requiring imperial ratification of successors.

lization's biblical scriptures. The net effect of Temmu's revival of the reforms begun by his brother was again to push forward for centralization of the state along Chinese lines, as well as to stabilize the succession laws—always critical to the dynasty—through lineal primogeniture (succession through first sons) in a paradoxical attempt to avoid the kind of internecine bloodshed that accompanied his own rough-and-tumble road to the throne.

Wishing that the reforms he made be consolidated by the obvious genius of his wife before the throne passed to his son, Temmu's queen (who, as his brother Tenji's daughter, was also his own niece) succeeded him as sovereign. The reign of the empress Jito was most notable for the legislation enacted regulating slavery. A pestilence that has since the beginning of recorded history attached itself to countless societies around the globe, slavery was also a shadow over Japan at the end of the seventh century and one that would not be totally swept away for almost another thousand years. The number of slaves was huge since slavery was a common punishment for even minor criminal infractions, and such slave-prisoners were routinely traded like any other chattel—the usual price for an able-bodied slave hovered around fifty *koku,* [11] the common currency of the time. To keep track of all the slaves, the state had long ago decreed that they were to wear black garments, to distinguish them from the usual yellow-tinted clothing of the free-peasant class. Jito ameliorated the system with an edict that effectively canceled interest on the debt for which people sold themselves or their dependents into slavery. Debt slavery was a frequent practice at the time, and most persons thus in servitude were unable to repay the debt that caused their condition. The empress's edict in effect forbade adding interest to the debt, the major factor that kept the people in their slave status and the slave population swollen.

Jito abdicated in 697, primarily to ensure the political future of her grandson, the emperor Mommu, and secondarily in the expectation of freedom from further ceremonial cares of state. She retired with great honor and was given the title of *dajo tenno,* "Great

---

[11]A measure of rice and a unit of value; about 180 liters of the grain, or forty gallons, filled one koku.

Abdicated Sovereign," the first to bear this honorific reserved for retired monarchs. Later, it became automatic for a new emperor to offer the title to an abdicated predecessor.

The Taika Reforms were revised during Mommu's reign with yet another constitution. Called the Taiho Code, or Laws, which—pertinent to the story of the monarchy—even more strongly reinforced the sacrosanct religious position and hereditary inviolability of the emperor, it represented a major fine-tuning in the borrowed Chinese state system that had itself been the imperial clan's attempt to reform the old and failing Yamato system. Perhaps more central to Japanese society as a whole was the beginning of the legally sanctioned relegation of women to a grossly inferior position vis-à-vis men, a condition that the Japanese people are only in recent decades beginning to undo.

The Chinese rationale implicit in both the Taika Reforms and the subsequent Taiho Code had one more effect on Japan, and it was an enormous one. Jito's successor, Mommu, would be, in effect, the last itinerant emperor. From that point on the country would possess a vital element of nationhood heretofore missing: a permanent capital city, an essential element for a state becoming increasingly sedentary, complex, and, as a result of the changes emanating from the great reforms of the prior decades, bureaucratic.

As explained earlier, Japan's native religious beliefs always held that death contaminated the place in which dying occurred, serving as the rationale for moving the imperial court with each new sovereign. In 710, the empress Gemmei—Mommu's mother and successor[12]—established what was to be a permanent capital, the first of only three cities that have functioned as the seat of the emperors of Japan. A shortage of funds had for some time been as much responsible for the lack of a permanent capital as were Shinto notions of ritual impurity, but the economic boom fueled by the fortuitous discoveries of silver and copper in the provinces made a new capital an economic possibility. The new seat of the court

[12]When Mommu died, his will stipulated that his mother, a daughter of Tenji and therefore eligible to occupy the throne, should serve as monarch in a sort of temporary trust for his infant son.

would be the first *real* city of any kind in Japan, as previous "permanent" settlements had been little more than encampmentlike collections of rude huts around the somewhat fancier huts of the higher-ranking members of society.

The city the empress ordered was to become Nara, often called the most beautiful in modern Japan, though today even its historic central district bears a sadly uncomfortable resemblance to Japan's other McDonald's-cluttered metropolises. Set southwest of Tokyo, not far from Osaka and Kyoto, in a beautiful and blessedly fertile plain ringed by the coastal hills of Honshu, the large island, Nara is today primarily a tourist attraction, a magnet drawing millions of people each year to its shrines and temples and the famed giant Buddha set in the magnificent twelve hundred acres of pond-dotted woods, a sylvan paradise populated with a thousand quasi-sacred fallow deer who benignly poke their cold noses into strangers' pockets in a constant forage for rice crackers. Over these modern streets and reconstructed temples and neatly pruned pine trees of the deer park, the truly settled age of Japanese history had its birth.

Before Gemmei established her court in roughly what was the center of the old Yamato kingdom, the notion of a permanent capital had been only an unfulfilled promise. But with the passing of one reign into another, it became clear that the onerous burden of building a fresh site for each new regnancy was exacting an insupportable burden on the country's financial resources. Although earlier emperors had built temples in the vicinity of Nara, there is no record of why Mommu selected this particular site. It probably wouldn't be too far off to surmise that, in addition to whatever military defense considerations were involved, a significant reason had to be the area's graceful beauty. There is evidence, too, that the choice was made in accordance with geomantic principles, the antique Chinese art of divination. In Nara's case, priests would have approved the site after throwing an amulet skyward, the views of the gods carefully divined in the chance direction of the charm's landing.

The model pattern for Nara[13]—a great rectangle about two and

---

[13]Which was officially known as Heijo during the years it served as the capital.

two-thirds miles on the short side by about three miles on the long—was the fabled T'ang Chinese capital, Ch'ang-an. The Japanese builders assiduously copied the Chinese city's severely rectilinear street plan, reserving the most auspicious site for the Imperial Palace—the planners knowing full well that the more magnificent the emperor's residence, the greater would be the prestige emanating from both the country generally and the monarchy specifically. A notable difference marked the city from other world capitals of the time: Nara was built without outer walls, an indication of the lack of domestic enemies of any consequence as well as Japan's status as an island-fortress lending it immunity from foreign invasion. Unhappily, absolutely nothing that can be dated with certainty survives from the seventy-four years Nara housed the court, primarily because, in sharp contrast to the stone that made up much of Europe's built-for-the-ages cities, wood and paper were Japan's primary building tools. Though only a vague image can be conjured of the long-vanished buildings that formed Gemmei's city, evidence suggests that red-lacquered walls were the chief characteristics of the imperial quarters, their roofs tiled in the distinctively upturned Chinese fashion that the court slavishly admired and copied. What lavishness there was could be found in the sovereign's quarters; the mansions of the nobles—that of the Fujiwara not surprisingly the finest—and the increasingly powerful Buddhist monasteries filled out the second tier of splendor. The country's entire supply of bronze, incidentally, was exhausted in the thousands of gilt-covered images of the Universal God that piety caused to be erected.

Early on, the city began to fill with these Buddhist temples, as well as Shinto shrines, many denoted by their lovely up-curving roofs. But especially prominent were the proliferating monasteries, places where the power of the haughty priests began to strongly assert itself in imperial affairs. As is true with royal capitals all over the world, a grossly disproportionate part of the national wealth was spent achieving a properly magnificent setting for the court. The country's wealth derived from the land, which technically belonged to the state, its fruits seized in heavy crop levies, its workers' sweat-wrung labor pressed into building projects and military service. Besides the "free" peasants, some 6 million propertyless slaves

served as an additional labor pool for the massive government building projects. Although all land holdings were in theory subject to
equal taxation, in actual practice personal exemptions freed many
monasteries and noble families with court ties from paying their
share. The increased burden this placed on the small peasant holdings drove many farmers from their fields. Their fertile, vacated land
was quickly seized by nobles or by the ever-growing monasteries.
The emperor's court as well as the nobility and the religious organizations with their armies of parasitic priests were all supported by
the taxes squeezed from the masses to whom the new splendors of
Nara might as well have been on the moon.

A bureaucracy centered on the court quickly grew, and as with
most bureaucracies, it lost little time spreading its tentacles wherever they could be spread: It was in Nara that the brilliantly engineered Fujiwara transformation of the monarchs from rulers into
figureheads began to be locked into place. But to the Nara court also
came learned men who brought great erudition, anxious to partake
of the Chinese learning that was concentrated in the city. During
the reign of Gemmei, the *Kojiki*—Records—was written, and
under the daughter who followed her, the empress Gensho (this
representing the single instance in the dynasty's history when a
regnant empress was succeeded by another regnant empress), the
equally famous *Nihongi*—Chronicles—was compiled.

Both Gemmei and Gensho had followed their predecessors by
acts of abdication: Gemmei, who became the first abdicated sovereign to take Buddhist religious vows, allowed her daughter Gensho
to follow her because her son, the "rightful" heir, was still too young
to rule effectively. After Gensho's abdication in 724, a male tenno,
Gensho's nephew Shomu,[14] again ascended the throne. Shomu's
twenty-four-year reign saw court etiquette begin to stiffen into the
almost unimaginably florid liturgy that would be its distinguishing
mark until the time of Meiji. One noteworthy and long-lived addition to the Japanese scene during Shomu's reign was the introduc-

---

[14]Shomu is most noted for raising his nonroyal Fujiwara wife to the rank of
empress-consort, the first time a person not born to the imperial family had been
so honored.

tion, via its Chinese origins, of *go,* the oriental board game rivaling chess in intellectual difficulty.

A striking development emanating from the Nara period involves the status of women, specifically those who populated the court. At the time that Gemmei and Gensho reigned, women of high rank enjoyed a social standing that approached (but never quite achieved) parity with men. During the seventy-four-year-long Nara period, half the sovereigns were women, a fact that by itself doesn't "prove" equality between the sexes—in many societies women have ruled as monarchs without their sex in the general population enjoying anything like true equality, England's Queen Elizabeth I and Russia's Catherine the Great coming rapidly to mind—but it does indicate an acceptance by the nation that sex wouldn't of itself disbar a woman from high position. However, the injudicious actions of Shomu's successor, Koken, the last empress of the Nara court, coupled with the recent Taiho Codes, paved the way for an abrupt end to this situation. Perhaps the male courtiers of the court were just waiting for an excuse to effectively disenfranchise women; if so, they certainly found a strong one in Koken's unwise actions, for she would be Japan's last regnant empress for nine centuries, a tenno who foolishly compromised the sacred principles of succession to the imperial throne through the passion of illicit love.

After a twenty-four-year reign, Shomu abdicated the throne, shaved his head, and retired to a Buddhist monastery. The second sovereign—his mother was the first—to take advantage of this peculiarly Japanese expedient, he probably retired to ensure an orderly succession for his heir. That heir was the empress Koken, who was designated her father's official successor after Shomu's only son died. But after nine years as tenno, Koken herself retired to a cloistered religious life, the reasons quite unlike her father's dynastic altruism: Koken had been entangled in a steamy affair with her chief adviser and prime minister, Nakamaro Fujiwara, a grandson of the great Kamatari, who had founded this most powerful line of the family. Nakamaro may have held high rank in his sovereign's government, but the alliance nonetheless represented a completely unacceptable mésalliance—Nakamaro's rank was simply too far below his lover's to make the relationship acceptable. The affair between sovereign and prime minister, the latter generally conceded to be an able and learned administrator, was carried out at the Fujiwara mansion to which the empress would quietly repair of an evening. Wiser heads at court, on watching this situation develop, tried to convince both parties to put an end to the liaison, but the well-meant counsel of several was repaid with exile from court.

Finally, in 758, pressured on all sides, Koken abdicated to become a nun, though still thoroughly besotted with her lover. Her abdication appears not to have decreased either her passion *or* her power one whit—her abdication message stated forthrightly: "In regard to matters of government, the emperor shall carry out regular ceremonies and minor affairs . . . I will deal with important affairs of state and rewards and punishments"—and, hand in hand, she and her lover continued to run the government unabated. After bestowing every available title and honor on Nakamaro, Koken did one of those things that, though they pepper history with their arbitrariness, aren't easily explainable. The now ex-empress took up with a handsome and ambitious Buddhist monk by the name of Dokyo, suddenly discarding Nakamaro. Furious at being spurned, Nakamaro began a brief and ultimately failed rebellion against his ex-lover. For his pains, he lost his head, which, together with those of his wife (adultery, too, was an element of this steamy brew), children, and followers, was sent to Nara for general public exhibition. Koken's retribution, probably egged on by her feelings of guilt, was massive and merciless.

The emperor who acceded when Koken stepped down—a cheerful nonentity named Junnin—owed his position entirely to the influence of Nakamaro, and, naturally, was contemptuous of the priest with whom the ex-empress-now-nun—who was now styling herself "Dowager Empress"—had taken up so flagrantly. Knowing of the new emperor's feelings, and not about to permit the faintest possibility of a Junnin-led plot against her, Koken dispatched her still considerable private army against the palace. Junnin was forced to abdicate and was exiled to the island of Awaji, from which he tried to flee the following year and was killed—strangled, to be precise—in the attempt.

Koken was back on the throne, this time with the name Shotoku (this posthumously assigned name is not to be confused with the earlier imperial adviser, the great Prince Shotoku). The reconstituted empress not unexpectedly promoted her main-monk Dokyo to the all-powerful position of chief adviser. Now Chancellor of the Realm, the empress's adviser soon starting getting grandiose ideas far beyond his station—ideas of claiming sovereignty for himself. One junior counselor tried to apprise the monarch of the danger in allowing Dokyo to position himself to take over the throne; this loyal courtier, named Kiyomaro, urgently warned his sovereign that "since the foundation of Our Empire, the State has *never* been ruled by a subject!" His troubles earned him a thrashing from the monk— a beating that left him mutilated—and an exile from court.

The empress's death resolved the situation before any further bloodletting took place, and before Dokyo could make an overt move on the throne itself. The Fujiwara, who were strangly acquiescent to these imperial shenanigans—some said because Koken-Shotoku was herself a Fujiwara—finally drew up their considerable indignation and banished the miscreant Dokyo into ignominious disgrace, averting a threatened civil war by placing an indisputably eligible member of the imperial clan—the sixty-two-year-old Konin, a grandson of the emperor Tenji—on the throne.

This new emperor wasn't without assets, having served some years as an able and proven administrator. But in his own choice of a successor—his daughter—he was thwarted by a wary court. Konin's advanced age in an era when sixty-two was almost freakishly old required that a crown prince should be named without hesitation. After the problems a woman on the throne caused in the preceding reign, Konin was leaned upon by his Fujiwara adviser to name his youngest son, Kammu, to the role in place of his favored daughter, a course the emperor at first resisted because the boy's mother had been deficient in qualifications of lineage. Only twice more would Japan be ruled by women—two unexceptional empresses in the seventeenth century—the matter of female succession being controlled by nearly implacable custom until the end of the nineteenth century, and thereafter by the imposition of a Salic law in Meiji's imperial constitution that barred their succession.

Its waters muddied, the Nara monarchy was reaching an end. But it wasn't only its personnel problems that were giving it trouble: A great part of the court's and state's decline was caused by the country's imported religion. Buddhism brought with it esthetic qualities comparable to the florid excesses of feudal Roman Catholicism; however, of more significance, it also set in motion forces that caused the nation to lose the fine balance between opposing social forces that all successful states must maintain. During the last years of the Nara court, the government found itself spending fully half its income on what amounted to religious frippery—temples, statues, works of art glorifying Buddha. The nation's currency—then copper coins—was debased because the coins were being melted into countless images of Buddha, a practice that inevitably resulted in disastrous inflation when the government issued new currency. Money was spent in profligate amounts by all strata of society in an attempt to honor the new faith with bigger and better temples and works of piety. At the palace, religion-inspired sumptuary display became the primary consideration of the emperor and his courtiers, producing the sort of effete uselessness that would many centuries later be mirrored in the same kind of politically motivated grandeur at Louis XIV's court at Versailles. After so much turmoil with the Koken-Shotoku affair and now the over-Buddhization of the government, the need for a change in the monarchy's bearings was all too apparent.

That change came in the person of one of the most famous sovereigns in the dynasty's history, the man whose reign coincided with imperial prestige achieving its pinnacle. Kammu, the fiftieth sovereign in succession from Jimmu, had been his father's choice— albeit a reluctant choice, as we've seen—as crown prince, lending Konin a measure of greatness if for nothing more than his recognition of and grooming as heir a gifted son. On his succession, Kammu immediately acted on his realization that Nara had become a city where effective and efficient government had degenerated into near-religious anarchy. The capital's by now almost hysterical Buddhism put absurd emphasis on the outward manifestations of that faith, with the great monasteries engorging themselves with riches, most of which was diverted from the public treasury, leaving little money for the needs of governing an increasingly complex state.

Three years after he ascended the throne, Kammu decided that the corruption of the principles of the ritsu-ryo system by the parasitical priests had made Nara such an undesirable place from which to govern that a fresh start at a new site was necessary. This time there were no Shinto considerations of ritual cleanliness. The move was unapologetically an effort to revitalize the system that had increased the nation's strength under the previous emperors and to extricate management of the state from the influences and pretensions of the temples. The site Kammu chose to build anew was a place called Nagaoka, a short distance north of Nara on the navigable river Yodogawa in the province of Yamashiro. It was an area inhabited by Koreans, and the fact that the emperor's mother, Takano Niigasa, was descended from the Korean royal house of Paekche perhaps played a part in Kammu's choice.

There was an ancient legend in Japan, strongly held in Kammu's day, that said when a man leaves life peaceably and naturally, he continues to keep an eye on the world as a friendly spirit, but the man who leaves bearing a grudge or who has met his end in a violent fashion returns as a strife-prone ghost. Unhappily, such an angry ghost within the imperial family itself returned to cause Kammu to abandon the ten years of effort and expense he poured into his slowly rising capital at Nagaoka, and finally to move the entire court and apparatus of government yet again.

The trouble arose over the murder of the emperor's senior adviser and the man he had placed in charge of the Nagaoka construction, Tanetsugu Fujiwara. On a September night in 785, the forty-eight-year-old Tanetsugu was shot to death by two arrows that passed cleanly through his body. One of the suspects who were rounded up and interrogated testified that the emperor's brother, the crown prince Sawara, was a participant in the plot. The brother's motive, according to his accuser, was anger over an official rebuke by Tanetsugu that resulted in the humiliating loss of his princely title. At first, Kammu could not believe Sawara could be involved in anything so low as murder, but the weight of evidence was apparently sufficient to convince the monarch that the accuser was telling the truth. The angry emperor stripped Sawara of his remaining offices and sentenced him into exile on the lonely island of Awaji, where the outcast emperor Junnin had languished so cruelly. The ex-prince vowed to starve himself to protest his innocence.

Because the dead victim in the case had been a close friend and an irreplaceable adviser, the emperor closed his mind to his brother's protestations of innocence, officially reaffirming the punishment he believed his brother's criminal act merited. But the fasting Sawara died while en route to his ignominious destination, his body thrown into a crude grave—an act of such spectacular desecration for a member of the imperial family, even one in disgrace, that all who heard of it were stunned.

The equally horrified and now perhaps even unhinged Kammu threw himself into the reform of his government, convinced that the Buddhist leaders had irreversibly turned the philosophy of their imported religion into mere power- and land-grubbing venality. Further upsetting the sovereign was an impertinent rebellion by the northern Ezo, "barbarians," then in full cry, not to mention a smallpox epidemic spreading like a spring weed over the land, killing many people in the district of Nagaoka itself. And finally, the emperor's son and newly appointed crown prince was showing signs of unmanageable mental illness. These Job-like afflictions, combined with the early deaths of first his mother and then his wife, convinced Kammu beyond any doubt that the curse of a grudge-bearing ghost, specifically the spirit of his younger brother Sawara, was out to get him.

To lift the curse, the monarch dispatched a high-ranking imperial household official to the grave of Sawara, recently reburied with honor in a fitting manner at Kammu's order, there to beg forgiveness from the spirit of his late sibling. But the whole affair was so unnerving to the emperor that his health gradually eroded with concern over Sarawa's malicious ghost. Kammu finally began to realize that the only effective way to relieve the whole wretched business was to move the capital itself, a site now so diseased by Sawara's spite that to stay would be to invite disaster upon disaster. Kammu's somewhat more fiscally prudent advisers opposed their sovereign's intentions, as the capital had been in Nagaoka for only ten years and a huge amount of money had already been lavished to turn the place into a city worthy of the sun dynasty's greatness.

But imperial superstition won out and plans were begun to find a new site for Japan's court and government.

The place Kammu chose would endure as the capital for an astonishing 1,074 years. It was the village of Uda, in Kadono County, and, first in January and then in May of 792, Kammu went to inspect what his surveyors had chosen, a place that seemed at first to have as its only asset its extraordinary beauty. Six months later the decision was ratified, and in January 793, Kammu's court began its mass journey to Uda. The forsaken Nagaoka was razed utterly, leaving not a single scrap of evidence of what was for ten years the place from which the nation had been governed. The new capital, which should have been named Uda-kyo—the place name affixed to the word for capital, *kyo*—was instead called Heian-kyo, "Peace and Tranquillity Capital." Later generations were to know it by its common name, Kyoto, and the next seventy-seven emperors would reign from this sometimes raucous, sometimes war-torn, but most often tranquil city. It was, ironically, to be in this place so closely and for so long associated with the monarchy where the throne would steadily lose its power.

CHAPTER IV

The Golden Epoch

LATE EIGHTH CENTURY TO THIRTEENTH
CENTURY

More than a century before Kammu first set eyes on his tranquil valley, the great Prince Shotoku is said to have climbed one of the mountains that overlooks the place. Gazing eastward from the slopes of Mount Hachioka, he reportedly observed to a companion that this was where "the gods of the four directions are in harmony," adding the prediction that the "imperial seat will be moved [here] and remain forever." This honeyed tale savors rather too much of the legendary to ring of literal truth, but the valley Shotoku is credited with seeing did as a matter of historical fact prove to be eminently suitable to the establishment of Japan's greatest and most splendor-filled imperial city.

The reader must keep in mind that such attributes of "splendor" need be taken in the sense that they would have been understood in the ninth century—splendor relative to the mean conditions then almost universally prevailing outside the rigidly closed microcosm of court and aristocracy. There are not today nor have there ever been in Japan the kind of majestic architectural compositions that are associated with European and Islamic civilization. It had neither marble palaces nor towering forums framed in the majesty of great stone cities. The beauty that surrounded the Japanese monarchy of the Heian era[1] seems, at the least, restrained, perhaps even crude to an eye accustomed to the monumental usages of the West. But

[1]The period from the establishment of the capital until the founding of the first nationwide shogunate at the beginning of the thirteenth century.

in that long-ago Japan, beauty was measured in extraordinarily precise degrees of social refinement, in subtle nuances of life that was lived, at its height, in an unimaginably studied punctilio of observed niceties. And it was such splendor that was in large part responsible for causing the monarchy as a political force to fall, almost as if on a schedule, in a nearly unbroken cascade from the heights to which Kammu had restored it.

The place Kammu selected for the court after the decade at Nagaoka encompassed qualities beyond mere beauty, it being so perfectly suited for his purposes as to have seemed a gift from the Sun Goddess herself. As geomancy had eight decades earlier played the primary role in Gemmei's selection of Nara as her capital, so again did this art of divination determine the choice of the valley bottom that would over the next four centuries become one of the most sophisticated cities on earth. The sole breech in the otherwise closed ring of surrounding hills and mountains rising above Kyoto's horizon opened to the south. The valley's northeast side, from which direction the court priests deduced evil spirits were likely to swoop, was protected by the soaring, basaltic hump of Mount Hiei. The many streams emptying their runoff into the valley generously provided fresh water, and a major river, the Yodo, connected the plain to the Inland Sea, the body of water that protected Japan from the unknown terrors of the infinitely greater Eastern Sea. In careful accordance with geomantic principles, the priests came to the conclusion that the site was more than adequately safeguarded by the influence of the four spirits whose protection counted heavily. To the east, the Azure Dragon stood guard, whereas to the west the White Tiger would keep the sovereign safe, with the Red Bird on the south and the Dark Warrior to the north completing the mythological *cordon sanitaire*. It was, all in all, a site in which the forces of nature fused perfectly in a heaven-imposed harmony.

With the preliminaries completed, the city itself was planned along lines nearly identical to those of Nara. Larger than its predecessor by about a third, Kyoto[2] followed the same mathematically

---

[2]From the very beginning, the city was popularly called Kyoto or Miyako; the words mean "metropolis"—Kyoto in the Japanese reading, Miyako in the Chinese.

precise right-angled lines that emulated the much-admired Chinese Ch'ang-an—the continental city then housing a million inhabitants, which made it the largest populated place in the world.[3] But there was to be one major difference between Nara and Kyoto, and, to no one's surprise, it had to do with the monasteries whose presence had prompted the court to abandon the older capital in the first place.

Kammu's most dramatic act as monarch, the abandonment of Nara as the seat of his court, was a telling indication of the force the sovereign was willing to exert to reclaim the imperial government's singular authority from the invidious encroachment of the haughty and powerful Buddhist monks. To prevent the same abuses from reoccurring on settling in Kyoto, one of his first moves was to issue an imperial command absolutely forbidding monasteries from moving their headquarters to the new capital. Kammu clearly understood that to return affairs to the condition that led to the abandonment of Nara would be a lesson stupidly left unlearned. The monks were forbidden to place any but branches of their orders in the capital, and even these were to be strictly limited. Most importantly, the few that were permitted were kept at a safe remove from the new palace precincts. If the meddling monks had to be in the city, Kammu reasoned, at least they would be denied any access whatsoever to court, an arrangement whereby their influence could be kept tightly under the throne's control. Such, at least, was the theory, and during Kammu's lifetime it was rigorously adhered to; when he left the scene, alas, less careful successors weakly permitted the situation to degenerate pretty much to the way things had been in Nara.

As to the appearance of Kammu's city, Kyoto was generously laid out and arranged in the middle of the valley in an even rectangular form, one in which a perfectly balanced symmetry was a primary, if not overriding, design consideration. The north-south axis stretched for about three and a half miles, the east-west about half a mile less, the northern end of the rectangular grid of streets being crowned with the palace compound set like a keystone on a great portal. Had Kammu been able to see his capital through the eyes

---

[3]Chang'an was soon thereafter to disappear when a successor regime supplanted the T'ang dynasty; its site is the modern city of Xi'an.

of the birds that populated the valley, the whole composition would have looked very much like the lines of a *go*-board, only slightly jiggered by a notch representing the palace grounds skewing the northern edge.

That notch cut from the top was, of course, the reason for the whole of the rest. At the spiritual heart of a vast complex of assembly and audience halls and government buildings representing the various administrative departments of state, the emperor's red-lacquered palace reigned with its green-tiled roof above all lesser structures. The wooden palace was graced by open verandalike porches running the course of the main fronts. In the adjacent gardens, verdant weeping willows, pines, and flowering plum and peach trees were artfully placed to take the greatest advantage of the artificial hills that had been constructed to give substance and character to the emperor's precincts in the flat Heian valley bottom. Rocks carved to resemble whales and stones cut to imitate fantastical dragons guarded the tranquil ponds on whose silvered surfaces Chinese ducks swept dreamily past the inhabitants of this world created solely for the pleasure of a fortunate few.

Twelve portals pierced the city's walls, the magnificent and famous *Rasho-Mon*, the "Rasho Gate,"[4] being designated the main entrance from the south. A central ceremonial boulevard called Suzaku Avenue, which led from the Rasho Gate to the palace grounds, was wider than any street in the world at that time—at two hundred feet, it was even wider than modern Paris's Champs Elysées.[5] Plans for the city called for houses to be built in the narrow side streets that cut through most of the rectangle, with the grand mansions of the aristocracy prominently framing the main thoroughfares, the nearer the house to the palace grounds the more prominent the family dwelling within.

In December 804, while still personally supervising construction of his capital, the emperor fell sick, an illness he ascribed to the

---

[4]This gate, immortalized in the Kurosawa film, fell apart in the tenth-century reign of Enyu and was not rebuilt.

[5]The primary justification for its great width was to serve as an emergency firebreak.

continuing influence of the bad ghosts from the ill-used Prince Sawara. After going slowly downhill for a year and a half, and while listening to the joined voices of the chanting priests praying for his recovery, Kammu died, his spirit at last free of Sawara's revenge. In spite of his aversion to the excesses of the monasteries, the monarch had ordered that following his death Buddhist sutras be chanted twice a year for eternity, once in spring and again in autumn, in propitiation for the soul of his dead and martyred brother.

In the reigns of those who followed Kammu—a sovereign who was in every sense the head of his government—the emphasis at court began a permanent drift from the political to the cultural, finally gelling into a world that would have been incomprehensible to a contemporary observer from the West. While Europe stewed in the low brew of the darkest of the Dark Ages, its somnolent Greco-Latin culture lit feebly by isolated bridgeheads of the Roman Church, the court world of Heian Japan was embarking on an age that would be dominated by razor-sharp canons of etiquette, its inhabitants suffocatingly, archly conscious of the thinnest, most minute gradations of rank and privilege, a kind of civilization such as the world had never known nor would ever again experience.

Control of the affairs of the early post-Kammu Heian state accrued almost exclusively to the Fujiwara. This remarkable clan, as complex in its branches and family units, both major and minor, as the imperial house, acquitted itself with honor in the execution of what it saw as its sacred duty to emperor and dynasty. Historians have compared the Fujiwara to the Frankish Mayors of the Palace, but the comparison falls short: While Pepin aspired to actual kingship, no Fujiwara ever attempted to usurp the throne from the rightful imperial line, no Fujiwara was ever illegally installed on that throne, and no Fujiwara ever permitted an interloper to endanger the legitimacy of the Sun Goddess's bloodline.

The family employed a single, overwhelmingly important tool to retain control over the Heian-era monarchy: the expediency of abdication. Abdication was, as has been noted, a common practice in the imperial line for some centuries, but under Fujiwara tutelage it became routine, a ritualistic formula that was expected of nearly every sovereign who ascended the throne. While it unquestionably

172107

MEDIA SERVICES
EVANSTON TOWNSHIP HIGH SCHOOL
EVANSTON, ILLINOIS 60204

helped the Fujiwara keep their capable thumbs on the political situation, it paradoxically never threatened the legitimacy of the imperial line itself.

The usual route taken in imperial abdications was a cycle in which mere boys were vested with sovereignty and allowed to serve until they were old enough to marry—importantly and almost inevitably to a Fujiwara princess, often the bridegroom's first cousin or aunt— and, as quickly as possible, beget an heir. As soon as that heir was in turn old enough to accede—say, at the age of eight or there- about—the Fujiwara chancellors (the nearest equivalent in modern terms to the rank they bore) forced the still-young (thirty-one, on average) emperor to abdicate so his son could succeed, starting a whole new cycle. There were often three or four generations of retired emperors, each with his own mini-court, all still available to serve the country as the Fujiwara saw fit. The incredibly esoteric system was neat, nearly foolproof, and lasted for centuries. The Fujiwara stayed in control, the occasional uppity sovereign was dealt with, and all the while the office of monarch politically atrophied into stupefied impotence.

The first period of Japanese history of which we have primary documentary evidence of the intimate details of life, albeit primarily of court life, begins about the middle of the tenth century and lasts to the middle of the eleventh. It is mostly to two extraordinary documents—one a diary, the other a novel—to which we owe this authentic glimpse of the Heian world. The earlier of the two volumes (by a small margin) was the masterful *Pillow Book of Sei Shonagon,* the journal of a court lady in the service of the emperor's consort during the last decade of the tenth century, the very peak of the Heian cultural epoch. By far the best factual source of how life was actually lived in this impossibly remote civilization, Lady Shonagon's penetrating and sagacious book is among the greatest works of nonfiction prose in the entire history of Japanese literature, with few, if any, equals in its genre until the seventeenth- and eighteenth-century works of the European writers Pepys, Boswell, and de Staël.

When Shonagon so tartly captured her hothouse world, now

regarded as the mid-Heian period, two quite distinct languages were used at court, their division split on sexual lines. The stilted and solemn Chinese-based speech of the court, rarefied and remote from day-to-day experiences, was exclusively employed by male courtiers. The language in which Shonagon wrote and all women used was the vernacular Japanese, which was far more colorful and capable of expressing the homely details of domestic life in a way Chinese cadences could not.

All but a tiny fraction of Shonagon's writings chronicled upper-class court life, and she was much criticized for ignoring the dull lives of the peasants and even of the small urban merchant class. The fact is that to this lady of the court, and to others of her elitist kind, the lower classes simply didn't impinge on their consciousness. So unbreachable a wall existed between the two worlds that to conceptualize life other than that lived in the emperor's bosom would not have crossed her mind or that of any of her fellow scriveners.

Born about 966, Shonagon was the daughter of Kiyowara Moto-suke, a provincial official and therefore a member of a fairly lowly class of civil servant all but ignored by the chirping ladies of the Heian court. But Shonagon's future was tied to a lucky star: Marriage to a government official led to her presentation at court. In addition, besides being a bureaucrat, her father was also a poet and scholar of merit, and evidently endowed his daughter with the requisite intellect to describe with exquisite wit and pungent allusions the silken world she took so much to heart.

Her world of a thousand years ago was one of mind-boggling insubstantiality. Not a single branch of science or of the learned world pressed itself on the brow of the court. Instead, the intricate meanings inherent in the different ways of folding a letter absorbed vast amounts of what concentration the gentlemen and ladies of the court were able to muster. The highborn players in the etiquette-besotted rituals of Shonagon and her milieu cared not a bit for either their heritage or their country beyond Kyoto—yesterday was already dismissed as "old-fashioned," a term of venomous opprobrium. Even the short distance to the capital's outskirts was considered to be on the other side of the moon, socially speaking that is.

More substantial, and far more serious in tone than Shonagon's diary, *The Tale of the Genji* was the second masterpiece of Japan's early literature, the world's first novel and still adjudged one of the best. Although the archaic language of the book is as foreign to modern Japanese readers as is the saga of Beowulf to twentieth-century English-speaking people, the novel is still held to be the single greatest work of literature ever produced by a Japanese. A modern *Tale of the Genji Encyclopedia* is only one of the latest tomes analyzing it. In the thirteenth century, a fifty-four-volume Japanese commentary was published dissecting this chronicle of passions, commenting on every nuance buried in its exquisitely wrought relationships.

Written soon after Shonagon's work, the romance was begun at the turn of the eleventh century by Lady Shikibu Murasaki, occupying her for the next fifteen or twenty years until its completion. This enormously talented writer was a Kyoto-bred member of a minor branch of the Fujiwara clan. When her father was appointed governor of Echizen, a post requiring a geographical parting from the "civilizing" atmosphere of the court, he arranged for his daughter to become a lady of the court to the empress-consort Akiko; Prince Genji, the "Shining Prince" and hero of the book Murasaki would write, was the son of the emperor.

The power of the *Tale* lies in the reflection of the minutiae of court life, of which Lady Murasaki was such a wonderfully astute observer: the enduring of long and dreamily torpid periods of time suddenly punctuated by a white-hot moment of sexual passion; the endless concern with rank and precedence and the finest shades of etiquette. Genji's love affairs took on a cloak of tragedy with the death of a beloved mistress, the vicissitudes of his life painted in shaded strokes of remarkable psychological depth. Nature in all its colorations and moods is almost as much the protagonist of the work as is the prince, nearly every page describing the wonders of the natural world that so delighted the indolent but observant aristocrats who populated the author's scenes.

At court, real life closely reflected the thinly disguised fiction of Lady Murasaki's writings. The etiquette restrictions that enveloped the Heian-era imperial person in inviolable taboos continued to increase unabated. Completely cut off from the world outside his cossetted compound, his face rarely seen by any but his wives, bed partners, and the highest ministers of state, the monarch was literally hidden behind a gauzy curtain, his feet never being allowed to touch the bare ground lest defilement occur. Steeped in sensuality and growing effeminacy, gun-shy, nearly mute, the emperor came to be regarded by his subjects at an ever more mythical, otherworldly remove. Gilded artifice and deliberate deification led him on an irreversible road away from the ability to be a creative, potent individual, opening a path for those who would use the imperial demigod for their own purposes, either benign or ill.

The secular concerns of the Heian state were controlled directly—in the name of the emperor, of course—by four chief officers of state: the great ministers of the left, right, and center (titles based on Chinese usage), and the prime minister. Since two of these offices—the prime ministry and that of Great Minister of the Center—were generally left unfilled, in practice the imperial government was headed by only two officials, nearly always Fujiwara. Later in this period, an additional high office of state would develop, an extralegal station that eventually came to supplant the others by controlling singlehandedly the entire apparatus of the state.

Under these highest offices radiated ever-widening tiers of authority. First came the major, middle, and minor counselors; these, together with eight imperial advisers, comprised the Great Council, the offices of which would degenerate into empty formalities long before the end of the Heian era, although the major counselors managed to retain some considerable authority through succeeding centuries. A number of ministries were assigned to report to the Council, those most relevant to the imperial family being the Ministry of Central Affairs—the most important since it controlled palace ceremonials—and the Office of the Empress's Household; the Ministry of the Imperial Household, which acted as overseer of the palace; and the Ministry of the Treasury, guarding disbursements from the monarch's own purse.

An area of vital interest to the entire world of courtly Kyoto, one that Lady Murasaki would have been able and undoubtedly happy to discourse on at endless length, was rank, the daily bread of the court. Questions pertaining to precedence and etiquette were what most feverishly occupied the ordinary work of the massive bureaucracy then growing like a thick moss and slowly strangling the imperial machinery.

The rank system was an evolutionary product of the Great Taika Reforms and was central to the structure of the government itself; it was specifically designed to centralize the court along Chinese lines while at the same time holding the powers of the clan hierarchy in check. Immediately below the emperor in precedence came four grades of imperial princes, each category delineated by nearness in degree of familial relationship to the sovereign. Thirty established ranks—composed of upper and lower, senior and junior, first and second gradients—were established for the rest of society. These ranks applied only to the minutest fraction of the population, the part called the *yoki hito,* "persons of quality"; these lucky few numbered probably less than one-tenth of one percent of the total population of the some 5 million people who inhabited the country during the Heian period. Even within Kyoto itself, easily the largest settled place in the country with about one percent of all the people of Japan, the tradesmen and ordinary citizens outside the impermeable walls of the palaces and villas were socially invisible. The overwhelming mass of the people—the *tadabito,* "mere persons" —simply didn't count in the imperial order of affairs, existing so far outside the consciousness of the small nobility as to be reckoned with only for the indispensable fruits of their labor. The concept of a national entity was still an undeveloped theme in Heian Kyoto; the entire world for the court *was* the court. Communications with the rest of Japan were primitive almost to the point of nonexistence. Highways were little more than dirt paths, and to travel anywhere beyond Kyoto involved agonizing difficulties; even water journeys were dangerous, long-term affairs in the primitive boats of the time. In short, everything outside the capital was so remote, and everybody else so comparatively primitive, that the Heian court understandably but with disastrous results turned its collective back on the world beyond its gilded walls.

But inside those walls! In a dark world, aristocratic Kyoto was among the pathetically few places on earth at the turn of the first millennium where life was lived for physical pleasure. Europe remained a menacing place, stalked everywhere by ignorance and religious hysteria; its scattered towns more filthy collections of hovels than civilized cities, security thus only being found in sturdy castles and monasteries, the sanctuaries of nobles and priests. Tormented by marauding Asiatics spilling out of the east, marauding Norsemen out of the north, and marauding Mohammedans out of the south, the common people of Europe endured lives void of anything remotely resembling grace, or—God forbid—fleshly pleasure. The continent was truly, in the words of historian Ivan Morris, experiencing "a time of great leanness." Neighboring Byzantium and its adjacent Arab world did harbor substantial islands of learning and culture, but even those civilizations were on the cusp of decline. China, since the fall of Rome the world's brightest beacon of learning—the factor most important to the meaning of civilization—had shortly before endured the turmoil of passing from the end of one dynasty to the birth of another, inevitably a time of trial. And in the Western Hemisphere, only the Mayan civilization was undergoing anything similar to the late settled culture of the classical Mediterranean world. But it must be stressed again that in tenth-century Kyoto the life of grace and delicacy and sophistication was not shared even in the smallest degree with the "mere persons" who made possible those comforts enjoyed by their betters. No middle tier of society approached the relatively comfortable middle class of ancient Rome, no honorably bourgeois merchant class was born on which the court's merits might attach and grow into a balanced order.

But the peak of Heian society was undeniably a world vividly memorable, one in which, for example, the exquisite court robe of the emperor, a fantastically engineered thing, had its fabric ingeniously ground with the weft threads delicately floated to create a raised motif of imperial symbols—a garment that would be considered more valuable than the combined goods of every peasant of an entire province. On the highest occasions of state, the emperor might wear this robe over his scarlet kimono and its pleated overapron, the whole held together with a jeweled girdle, under which was worn two pairs of trousers, a red pair contrasting with a white, one over the other. Silk stockings, black lacquered shoes, a scepter, and his phallus-topped kammuri cap completed this state finery. As with the ceremonial kits of rulers and princes all over the world, a large part of the reasoning behind this incapacitating plumage was to symbolically demonstrate the wearer's exemption from any effort so common as mere movement, a function it capably fulfilled. The imperial robes formed such an important part of the mystique of the throne that an Office for Court Dress was established, its primary responsibility being the storing and caring for these fabulous costumes.

The dress worn by the women of the court made them closely resemble Empress Nagako at her 1928 enthronement, the primary difference between the Heian example and the modern empress being the cosmetic peculiarities affected by women in that distant world. Eyebrows shaved and replaced with inch-thick black rising strokes almost to the hairline, teeth blotted out with inky dyes—white teeth were considered glaring and ugly—and never-cut waves of loosely bound hair were their distinguishing marks. A minor error in judgment in choosing one's kimono or any of its accessories would brand the offender aesthetically "insensitive," lowering her social standing or even, if the error was egregious enough, her official position at court. Men, too, were just as concerned with this attention to cosmetic detail: To be really correct, one's white-powdered face had to be punctuated by a tiny patch of assiduously groomed chin beard.

Artifice for artifice's sake even extended to the food of the highest courtly classes: Rather than taking an interest in either its quality or flavor, far greater stress was laid on the careful arrangement of the various dishes of esoteric dainties and on the simple but costly lacquerware and ceramics in which it was presented.

Heian-era Japan was a culture in which the exclusive rituals of the court made up the most sacrosanct dates on the social calendar of the yoki hito. For instance, the annual New Year's Day ceremony, when the emperor, traveling in a closed palanquin, visited the palace of the ex-emperor, invariably drew out not only acknowledged society but the entire city to gape at the spectacle. It was a world where the sovereign magnanimously lent his august presence to the annual

Chrysanthemum Festival, a tribute to what was even then recognized as the empire's noblest flower; after inspecting the freshly opened blooms in the gardens of the imperial enclosure, a banquet was held at which the wine had been slowly steeped with the buds of the honored blossom, the resulting brew confidently believed to promote longevity. It was a world in which the ritual purification ceremonies at the bank of the capital's bisecting river shared nature's role as the unmistakable harbinger of the Fourth Month's warming weather. It was a society in which the perfect man, the equivalent of Europe's knight in shining armor, was elegantly understated in his learned accomplishments, sensitive to the infinite beauties of nature, easily roused by pathos—all the attributes, in sum, of Lady Murasaki's impossibly immaculate hero.

After the era of the emperor Kammu, real power in Heian Japan rested almost exclusively with the Fujiwara "advisers." The rare periods when the monarchs showed even the vaguest signs of independence and desire to personally rule happened to be the infrequent times when one was born to a non-Fujiwara mother, thereby crimping the family's leash on the court. But the emperors nonetheless remained at the theoretical apex of the governing apparatus of the state, the pyramid of control spreading out below their all-highest authority. The primary split in the organization chart divided the religious functions of state from the secular concerns of government—the emperors' role as head of the national religious apparatus was never disputed, but as their real political power decreased, eventually to nothingness, their nominal importance was conversely increased to a level safely beyond any criticism, however muted.

The sovereigns of considerably less prominent place in the story of the monarchy who succeeded the great Kammu included his sons, the fraternal emperors Heizei, Saga, and Junna. The court that their father bequeathed continued without apparent diminishment, the T'ang Chinese culture still serving as the ideal model for Heian society's upper stratum. Saga and Junna both fancied themselves accomplished poets, an inordinately large part of their otherwise somnolent days being passed in the heat of poetic composition, thus initiating a verse-writing fashion that became the rage among the pampered courtiers.

Through the seed of Junna's successor, the mid-ninth-century emperor Nimmyo, the Fujiwara blossomed into the height of their powers. To further Fujiwara plans to appropriate for themselves more administrative power, Nimmyo's grandson, the reputedly handsome Seiwa, reigned as the first child-emperor to be manipulated onto the throne in place of his half brother, the legitimate heir, whose mother was a daughter of a powerful rival to Yoshifusa, the then-head of the Fujiwara family. Since the time of the Taiho Codes' enactment, the office of regent had nearly always been confined to princes of the blood or to dowager empresses serving in that capacity while waiting for young sons to attain sufficient maturity. But the ambitious Yoshifusa, acting as regent for the nine-year-old monarch, did away with that tradition, possessing the necessary power to declare himself regent for the child-emperor. (Along with his new dignity, Yoshifusa also claimed a bounty of three thousand houses, the right to a constant escort of Guards of Honor, and the same honors ordinarily perquisites only of an empress-consort.) The monarch was eventually compelled to abdicate at the age of twenty-seven by Yoshifusa's nephew and adopted son, Mototsune Fujiwara, Seiwa's imperial duty of siring an heir safely fulfilled. What the episode represented was a hefty dent being pounded in the Taiho statutes with this flagrant abuse of the throne's tradition of legitimacy.

Seiwa's heir, Yozei, whose mother was Mototsune's sister, was only ten years old when raised to the imperial dignity of sovereignty. Furthermore, he was completely crazy, most likely the result of Fujiwara inbreeding, which was spinning the royal circle into a narrowing series of incestuous relationships. Yozei's lunacy was expressed in peculiarly sanguinary forms, like setting half-starved monkeys and dogs at each other after which he would gleefully finish off the bedraggled survivors. The removal of a sovereign was an act requiring very serious consideration even for the Fujiwara, but the clan's power was so great that they were able to force the unfortunate Yozei to step down, at which the now ex-emperor is said to have gone into a fit. A much needed expansion of the Fujiwara gene pool came with Yozei's replacement.

In an interruption of the Fujiwara-placed boy-emperors, the deposed Yozei was succeeded by the fifty-five-year-old Koko, the son of Nimmyo who had originally been designated his heir until Fujiwara machinations prevented it in favor of Seiwa. Happily, from the outset, Koko showed signs of restoring a measure of much-needed sanity into imperial affairs, marked by such acts as his immediate confirmation of the capable Mototsune Fujiwara as chancellor. Mototsune, by now head of the clan and the official who had suggested to his uncle Yoshifusa that crazy Yozei be removed from the throne, became Koko's chief adviser and the first man ever to be granted the title of *kampaku,* "Civil Dictator," the highest formal dignity a subject would ever be capable of achieving in the Heian state. Henceforth, it became the recognized rule that the current head of the Fujiwara would serve as kampaku for adult sovereigns, while the slightly less honorific *sessho,* signifying "regent" and much the same thing as kampaku, would serve those monarchs still legally underage. Later codifications added that both officers could only be chosen from one of the five senior branches of the Fujiwara family, namely the Konoye, Kujo, Ichijo, Nijo, and Takatsukasa, together thereafter known as the Five Regency Houses.

The combined offices of kampaku/sessho, called the *sekkanke,* would attain an extraordinarily long pedigree in Japanese imperial history, its incumbents serving, in its early years, as the forerunner of the later, more powerful office of shogun. From this first granting of the title to Mototsune Fujiwara in 882 by the emperor Koko, it would continue to be the foremost dignity bestowed at the imperial court for almost a thousand years, until 1868 and the advent of Meiji's revolutionary monarchy, by which time the office's authority had for centuries been limited to the Kyoto court's inner workings. The office amounted to a sort of extralegal station, technically outside the formal structure of government, but nonetheless holding precedence—a matter of incalculable importance in the rank-conscious palace—over all other court offices. The kampaku was essentially both prime minister and regent in one, acting as executive intermediary between the emperor and his highest officers of state. The position has often been compared to the Frankish "Mayor of the Palace," but "civil dictator" is more to the point since the kampaku not only represented the sovereign but even assumed his place and powers (but never his authority) in important councils of state.

Koko's reign lasted only two years, after which he was succeeded by his twenty-two-year-old son, Uda, who presided over the cessation of Japan's formal diplomatic relations with China, a strife-ridden empire whose collapsing T'ang dynasty retained little of value from which Japan felt it could benefit. In a seeming self-contradiction, the relative stability of Japan's political affairs during this period, with the throne dominated by the Fujiwara, was a significant factor in that clan's ability to lull the emperors away from any vestiges of vigor or sense of responsibility for the state. The success of Fujiwara power in keeping the country secure from enemies both external and internal had the effect of enervating the sovereigns to a point where they simply lost the will to govern.

Uda's heir was the emperor Daigo. Thanks to the power of his abdicated father (who managed to keep the Fujiwara away from his son and the court), Daigo reigned with neither a regent nor a kampaku. The new emperor governed in accordance with the letter of the Taiho Code, and was remembered primarily for this last short burst of imperial independence before the Fujiwara righted their only temporary decline and reclaimed all power from a monarchy they now turned into a ceremonial sideshow.

Government structured on the ritsu-ryo system floundered when the land tenure system on which it was in turn based faltered. According to the ritsu-ryo ideal, the entirety of the country's productive land belonged, in theory, to the state; when a proprietor-farmer died, his parcel was assigned to another tenant. But gradually the intricate bureaucratic mechanisms designed to ensure the smooth operation of this system weakened as the Fujiwara governors, obsessed with power plays at court, ignored provincial affairs, the land coming into and remaining in private hands, hands very often belonging to members of noble families who resented the

Fujiwara family's monopoly on power. With virtually no chance of making their own marks in the capital, the increasingly land-rich nobles drifted back to their distant estates and slowly built their own local power bases. This, in essence, became the basis for the feudal system, a system that would eventually overturn the sekkanke-dominated Kyoto governments. The shortsighted contempt the high officials felt for almost everything beyond the capital's brilliant but shallow court life eventually doomed both them *and* their pampered world.

Most of the monarchs who reigned during the later Heian period blur into anonymity, but the aforementioned Daigo, ruler for the first three decades of the tenth century, is honored in Japanese history as the last sovereign to run the state in accordance with at least the spirit of the Chinese-derived ritsu-ryo code. Daigo's thirty-three-year reign was inaugurated with political fireworks when Michizane Sugawara daringly attempted to usurp Fujiwara power. A brilliant scholar, Sugawara achieved prominence in the court of Daigo's father, the retired and cloistered ex-emperor Uda. The Sugawara family had long harbored a jealous rivalry with the Fujiwara, considering themselves the most ancient rivals of that all-highest clan of subjects. When Uda abdicated, he tried to ensure that his son would be dependent on neither the suave courtier Michizane nor the collectively ruthless Fujiwara. But the latter now had their tails up and, imputing treason, managed to remove their capable adversary to a distant governorship in Kyushu—the near-equivalent of banishment for a man of such rank. The ex-emperor generously pleaded Michizane's case, but Fujiwara hearts were hopelessly hardened by the threat to their predominance. After being followed by his twenty-three children into banishment, Michizane died of what his enemies at court reported to be a "broken heart," a fate even his patron the ex-emperor Uda had been powerless to change. The hapless Michizane went down in Japanese history as a figure of considerable sympathy, having been both unjustly denigrated by his rivals and then suffering greatly for his thwarted counsel to his sovereign.

When shortly after Michizane's death, three of the highest-ranking Fujiwara counselors mysteriously died, word was put about at court that Michizane's spirit was taking its revenge on its enemies. Wasting little time, Daigo ignored the anticipated Fujiwara wrath and posthumously restored Michizane's titles, and for good measure raised him a healthy degree in the peerage—specifically to the first grade of the second rank, a high position indeed for any of the sovereign's subjects. But the Fujiwara learned their lesson from this affair, and not for very many years would they allow their control to be so dangerously compromised.

Though some historians credit Daigo with an effort to put down the piracy and brigandage epidemic to tenth-century Japan, and others even ascribe to him a degree of ordinary human sympathy because of his concern for the humbler of his subjects, an attribute that if true was a laudable distinction for a man so carefully guarded from worldly realities, his fulfillment of the broader requirements of sovereign office was notably deficient. Perhaps the monarch's greatest failing was in allowing the display of lavishness at court to rise, unchecked, to a critically dangerous point. So concerned with appearances were the nobles that affairs of state were completely overshadowed by self-destructive spending on expensive frivolities: A banquet might cost a nobleman's entire annual income, while another courtier would heedlessly spend an inheritance on a single suit of clothes that would be worn once, and then solely to impress or outshine his fellow idlers at court. Equally disturbing was the corruption of Buddhism, where aristocratic priests engaged in the same boundless displays of extravagance as their lay brethren.

Into this increasingly unreal world came the next monarch, Daigo's son Suzaku, whose reign was memorable only because a subject pretended to sovereignty, the only time such a calumny occurred in the dynasty's history. The individual concerned—one Masakado Taira—was, however, hardly a peasant, being directly descended in the fifth generation from the emperor Kammu. Masakado, a well-intentioned sort, apparently concluded that the government, in its decreasing virility, wasn't really concerning itself sufficiently with the threat he posed. He declared himself tenno, and in all seriousness established a mirror of the real court at his encampment in Shimosa. Well-meant or not, this was still an outrageous impertinence and it roused the real emperor's armies to rush to suppress the impostor. Hidesato Fujiwara, the kampaku of the day, ordered Masakado put to death, after which his head was carried to the capital on a tray in a manner reflecting that in which Salome served up the Baptist. The whole affair evoked little more than a snicker from the Kyoto courtiers, but if anyone had paid attention he would have seen the danger the slow but ominous growth of local strength posed to the emperor's centralized government.

Japan's monarchy entered into one of the brightest episodes in its history with the appearance of the most powerful and famous of all the Fujiwara, the scion in whom the clan's power and hubris reached its fiery climax. Born in 966, the last full year of the emperor Murakami's reign, Michinaga Fujiwara enjoyed talents that made him the acknowledged ruler of Japan during the era when Lady Murasaki was writing her novel of court life. At the age of twenty-nine, as Minister of the Left, Michinaga succeeded in a power struggle with his ambitious nephew Korechika and won the coveted office of civil examiner, which had much of the same power as the vacant office of kampaku. In his path to the regency, he showed typical Fujiwara skill in achieving his ends. Banking on his rival's jealousy, Michinaga let it be known that Korechika's own lover was having an affair with the retired emperor, Kazan, who was ensconced in a monastery because of earlier Fujiwara chicanery. When Korechika went to his paramour's garden seeking to prove or disprove her faithlessness, he observed Kazan enjoying the woman's intimate favors. Korechika then fired an arrow at the former emperor. Though he only grazed the imperial sleeve, this act of lèse-majesté, however justified, earned him instant banishment from court by the victorious and now supreme Michinaga.

Over the next five reigns—from 995 to 1028—Michinaga ruled Japan from his sumptuous palace—a copy of the almost equally luxurious hideaway he kept at nearby Lake Biwa; both mansions tactlessly overshadowed the emperor's dwelling in grandeur. Consolidating his power, he married four of his daughters to monarchs (the last two were so related to their grooms as to be marrying their own nephews), with the result that four future emperors were his own grandsons, a triumph that was the crowning glory of the Fujiwara clan's prestige. In alliance with another clan of high-ranking courtiers, the Minamoto, Michinaga reestablished in the capital an atmosphere of law and order that had been eroding for years prior to his stewardship of the government. The Minamoto warriors, called the "nails and teeth" of the Michinaga administration, ensured that no sovereign, however independent-minded, had any hope of overturning Fujiwara control to rule personally. So adroit and clever was Michinaga, and so enamored of the splendid existence his position enabled him to enjoy, Lady Murasaki took the virtual dictator as the model for the famous Shining Prince in her *Tales of the Genji*. It was at this time that the Heian culture, like the Fujiwara family itself, reached its peak in the sharp curve of its uniquely and exquisitely bright existence, the time when the microworld of the Shining Prince sparkled more brilliantly than anywhere else on the benighted planet.

The throne was about to embark on a new phase: *insei*, the era of the so-called cloister government, in which the monarchy would flare brightly for the last time before dimming into a seven-century-long sleep. Insei would involve an even more labyrinthine relationship, burying the Fujiwara family and the throne in complex layers and multigenerational courts of "active" and "retired" emperors, the latter with their own well-engineered apparatuses of power. The reigning emperors themselves would assume for the most part a colorless, watery quality that highlighted more than ever their growing separation from the actual governing of their country or the reality of life outside their tightly sealed palace walls. But if the emperors themselves finally faded into insignificance by the end of the insei era, the imperial clan would for a time benefit greatly under the new order.

Insei, in reality a misnomer, was given its name centuries later by scholars of Heian history; it neither necessarily involved retirement to a religious life, as is implied by the word *cloister*, nor did it see the supplanting of the legal government's authority under the sovereignty of the reigning emperors and their noble—usually

Fujiwara—advisers. The system, unique to Japan, was reckoned to have begun officially with the abdication of Go-Sanjo's[6] son Shirakawa in 1086. As discussed, since the late tenth century it had become the custom for every emperor to have a regent, a sessho, during his minority and a chancellor, or kampaku, after coming of age, the offices inevitably Fujiwara sinecures. But Go-Sanjo, recognizing the danger of a permanent Fujiwara usurpation of power, made a final attempt to return ruling power to the sovereign and in doing so brought memorable reforms to his reign. Some of the changes even survived him, including a fairer system for the enormously important assessment of rice contributions, which was the basis of the country's monetary system and constituted, in effect, the empire's income tax. To ensure that he would be succeeded by Shirakawa—who shared his father's desire to displace the sekkanke as the court's real political power—Go-Sanjo retired after only four years as monarch, permitting his son to take over. With this new sovereign, the practice of insei was to become a ritualized formality, one that would last nearly a century.[7] Essentially a stopgap measure to shore up the declining post-Michinaga central Heian government, a government eroded by both the frivolousness of the officials at court and, more ominously, by the growing power of local magnates, many of them Fujiwara relatives, insei represented the last real attempt by the imperial family to take into its own hands, at the expense of the Fujiwara, control of the state. Perversely, the local noble landowners (the ritsu-ryo principles of state ownership of the land had been significantly eroded by the insei era), in an act seemingly running counter to their best interests, helped the dynasty in this limiting of Fujiwara power. Their motivation came from jealousy of this great clan as the country's premier landholders, a situation brought about because of the estates handed over to the Fujiwara for centuries as imperial favorites.

Insei seems a curious oddity to those who are accustomed to Western governmental experience. A variation on the long-

---

[6]The prefix "Go" means, in effect, "the second"—in other words, Sanjo II.

[7]When a tenno retired under the insei system, his new title became *ho-o*, which is, by the way, the same word used by the Japanese today for the pope.

established imperial prerogative of abdication, it became, instead of a mere expedient to ensure succession of the sovereign's choice, a political device for the reenfranchisement of the dangerously weakened imperial clan. Insei involved an emperor abdicating—always, in theory, a purely voluntary act—in favor of his designated heir, usually his son or grandson. The abdicatee would then generally withdraw to a nearby retirement palace, called an *in* and suitably fitted out for its prestigious occupant (who would also be known as an in), from whence under the protection of his own cohort of warriors he would set about furthering the imperial clan's fortunes, primarily the acquisition of political authority and estates, both of which were historically proscribed to the sovereign because of his (or her) sacred role as the nation's temporal totem. The "retired" emperor, no longer bound by the maze of precedence and etiquette designed to hold the sovereign in check—restraints that could only legally be applied to the real "emperor"—was able to function as a "civilian." By controlling the malleable boy-emperor on the throne, the ex-sovereign was also free to more effectively check the hitherto all-powerful Fujiwara courtiers. Since the Fujiwara family's single aim had for centuries been to make itself indispensable to the accepted order, suddenly finding it had to thwart an "unofficial" emperor, one who was also sheltered by and under the protection of the Buddhist priesthood, constituted a blow to its carefully laid plans. As a result, for the few decades of Shirakawa's effective kind of insei government, the imperial house's political influence was raised high as the dominant factor in Japanese politics.

Insei also figured as another major factor in Japanese statecraft by steering the state away from a matriarchal and toward a patriarchal order of affairs. Not a small part of Fujiwara control emanated from the system that ensured that the wives and mothers of Japan's monarchs were women of the Fujiwara clan, with the young emperors still being subjected—exactly as planned—to strong maternal influences. With insei, the most intimate control of the boy-emperors was paternal, from their "retired" fathers. By some biological quirk, following Michinaga, Fujiwara princesses either entered a period of abnormal infertility or else just happened to give birth mostly to girls—who long ago had been barred from succeeding to the throne—and this shift added another fillip of strength.

Though Shirakawa was unarguably a shrewd manipulator of his dynasty's fortunes, and the man responsible for devising government-by-ex-emperors as a means to restore lost imperial power, he didn't regard his own retirement as a cynical maneuver. The ex-emperor spent a considerable portion of the Treasury—to which he retained free access from his retirement quarters—on the construction of lavish temples, including the famous Sanjusangendo, still standing in Kyoto with its 33,333 images of Kannon, the Buddhist goddess of mercy. Shirakawa's respect for Buddhism was soon carried to untenable lengths, however: His imperial interdiction against the taking of any form of life logically but tragicomically resulted in the enforced destruction of eight thousand fishing nets and with them the subsequent loss of their owners' means of earning a living. His devoutness sank eventually to insanity; on one occasion, when rain forced a cancellation of a planned religious procession, Shirakawa sentenced the errant downpour to imprisonment, confining a quantity in a barrel.

Japan's period of effective insei government lasted exactly seventy years, from the abdication in 1086 of Shirakawa (who continued to govern from the retirement palace until his death in 1129) to the death of the equally capable retired emperor Toba in 1156—a period of time during which five sovereigns occupied the throne. However, by the second half of the twelfth century, the military class, which had, under the leadership of the Minamoto clan, been marshaling its strength, began to transform itself into a new major power. While the ultimate control of the state was irretrievably passing to the backbiting, quarreling clans in their provincial strongholds, the relative peace and gentleness of the Kyoto-controlled Heian civilization was speeding to its annihilation.

The last quarter of the twelfth century witnessed the final disintegration of the imperial Heian system as the source of power in Japan and its replacement with a government ruled by naked military power. When the court, dominated by either Fujiwara or retired emperor, came ultimately to regard social refinement as an end in itself, the tragic decay of its hard-won order was foreordained. But the event that finally set this enormously portentous transformation into motion was a deathly serious struggle between two great rival clans, extended families around whom the fratricidal local military lords polarized. They would ultimately fight each other without quarter for control of Japan's destiny.

The first of the two were the Taira, a family that proudly claimed its wellspring in imperial loins. The Taiho Code specified that after six generations of descent from an emperor a family would cease to rank as princes and members of the imperial family, and would instead descend to the rank of commoners. The family would acquire a family name and a genesis as a clan unto itself. The Taira began in this way, from a second son of the emperor Kammu, a prince who had been appointed governor of Hitachi, one of the fifteen provinces of the Tokaido running along Honshu's Pacific underbelly. Gaining a power base in the eastern provinces around this governorate, the family rendered many and important services to the state, particularly the suppression of the dangerously out-of-control piracy in the Eastern Sea. Eventually, the Taira came to Kyoto to serve as court advisers, and in the capital their rough skills as administrators were tempered by the cleverness they soon learned in the soft and torpid atmosphere surrounding the imperial seat.

The Taira archrivals, the Minamoto, likewise arose via descent as a cadet branch of the imperial tree; they were, in fact, connected by blood to *several* sovereigns, the most powerful Minamoto branch descending specifically from the ninth-century emperor Seiwa. Achieving prominence through alliance with the Fujiwara, the Minamoto assisted that highest clan in the administration of the state, services that earned them the contemptuous sobriquet of "running dogs of the Fujiwara."

In the middle of the twelfth century two significant civil disturbances flared briefly, both arising out of conflicting claims to the throne; these events would lead directly to the final collapse of the Heian-era court and an abrupt, cataclysmic change in Japan's history. The first of these was the bloody succession dispute known as the Hogen Insurrection, named for the imperial era in which it occurred. When the seventeen-year-old emperor Konoe died in

1155—according to his mother he was killed by his half brother, the ex-emperor Sutoku (the allegation was never proven)—Yorinaga Fujiwara, the head of the clan, wanted to see the Fujiwara-controlled Sutoku returned to the throne. Sutoku had been forced to abdicate in Konoe's favor in one of the many countless imperial power plays. The Minamoto faction also backed Sutoku, but the powerful Kiyomori Taira wanted *his* candidate, Go-Shirakawa. Kiyomori finally won the day. Yorinaga wouldn't, however, concede gracefully; together with his failed candidate, Sutoku, Yorinaga the following year occupied the ex-emperor's palace in proclamation of Sutoku's legitimacy. The palace was surrounded and burned by the Taira forces supporting Go-Shirakawa, but Yorinaga Fujiwara escaped through suicide. The capital suffered horribly in the conflict, the city that had for centuries been an island of grace and elegance transformed into a scene of heinous cruelties perpetrated by the contending forces. Palaces of the nobility on both sides were set to the torch and their occupants beheaded after enduring all manner of depravities at the hands of ill-disciplined troops, the ominous strength of the aroused clans only too apparent to the stunned courtiers who watched this bloody test of wills. This insurrection's duration and scope were limited. Neither force was wiped out, but the conflict portended far more evil tidings to come.

After the Hogen Insurrection ended in a Taira/Go-Shirakawa victory, the second and vastly more alarming incident took place: the Heiji Rising of 1160, a decisive clash between the Taira and the Minamoto. Taking advantage of Kiyomori Taira's short absence from Kyoto, a Minamoto and Fujiwara together abducted the Taira-backed emperor. On Kiyomori's return to the capital, the quick-witted Taira leader thwarted the coup by helping the captive emperor escape, dressed as a lady-in-waiting, to the Taira stronghold. Following a spirited but doomed defense, the Minamoto conspirators were defeated, due in large part to the help given the Taira by local soldier-monks of the monasteries on Mount Hiei. The Minamoto survivors fled to safety in the eastern provinces, a frontier area out of the reach of the Kyoto government, where they regrouped their forces for an eventual repeat try at power. But the tired clan had been brought low, and—an ominous fact that could not be ignored—the central issue, that of deciding who would occupy the throne, was resolved not through civilian machinations but by armed military might. The Taira momentarily controlled the government with Go-Shirakawa their puppet, but a strange error in Taira tactics now opened the way for the deluge that would follow.

The Heian leadership's philosophy, regardless of the faction in control, had for centuries abhorred and generally avoided capital punishment, a violation, as they saw it, of revered and inviolable Buddhist principles regarding the supreme sanctity of life. Executions were, as a consequence, a rare punishment in the capital, even for treason. Perhaps because of this tradition, Kiyomori Taira had been persuaded not to sentence to death two highly important young captives, Yoritomo and Yoshitsune, the exceedingly talented sons of the Minamoto clan's chieftain Yorimasa, who had killed himself after being injured in a minor skirmish with his Taira enemies. This error in judgment, which in hindsight it surely represented, eventually destroyed the house of Taira. Taira leaders would continue to hang on to power in the capital for a while longer, but the burning desire for revenge that kept the Minamoto rage alive represented a passion that wouldn't be sated until their mortal enemies lay before them in final defeat.

Either foolishly or blindly, Kiyomori Taira proceeded to immerse himself in the pleasures of the patched-up Heian court life, giving the appearance that the deadly danger to this fragile world had ended, a goal seemingly in emulation of his Fujiwara predecessors. More importantly, he wanted to make the emperors instruments of and intimately related to his own Taira clan, in pursuit of which Kiyomori even married his daughter to the emperor. The resulting issue, his grandson, the emperor Antoku, was ridiculously elevated to the throne in 1180 at the age of two. That this shoddy imitation of Fujiwara-inspired policy failed to recognize the reality of a vastly changed Japan—that the real strength now came from military prowess forged in the provincial clans—was the primary cause of its failure.

After the boy-emperor Antoku acceded to sovereignty, his Taira managers decided to abandon Kyoto. Reasoning that they and the emperor would be safer in their own stronghold, Fukuhara in Settsu province, an appropriately impressive imperial procession left the Heian capital in June to establish a new seat for the court. Not only was Antoku himself taken to Fukuhara by the Taira, but two ex-emperors, Go-Shirakawa and Takakura, were also brought along for good measure. (The move was, incidentally, carried out in the same month Kiyomori had defeated Yorimasa in the minor skirmish and generously but unwisely decided to let Yorimasa's sons live.)

The residents of Kyoto found themselves in much the same straits as did those of Rome when Pope Clement V packed up the papacy and moved it to Avignon in 1309. In no time Kyoto fell into a state of misery. The absence of the imperial government and its protective troops allowed the still-titular capital to degenerate into an extremely dangerous place. So loud were the protests of its residents, and—fortunately for the city—so little did the climate of Fukuhara suit the sickly young monarch's health, that by the end of the year Kiyomori Taira moved everything and everybody back to Kyoto. Soon after, the smoldering sparks of Taira-Minamoto rivalry erupted into true general warfare.

The Gempei War can be envisioned as Japan's just-as-bloody version of England's War of the Roses, the conflict that would three centuries later turn that far distant people into bitter enemies of themselves. Gempei is a compound word of the two Chinese versions of the names of the major antagonists: the character for Gen is pronounced "Minamoto" in Japanese, that for Hei is "Taira"; the compound phonetically alters to "Gempei." The first skirmishes of the conflict were fought in the last months of 1180, but following the death by natural causes of Kiyomori Taira in the spring of the following year, the main struggle was joined in earnest. Lasting for five years, the war became the inspiration for countless Japanese dramas and works of heroic literature down to the present day. Filled with colorful acts of rousing valor and derring-do, it gave the martial arts—particularly its samurai practitioners, of whom more later—an irresistible edge over the soft feminism of what was becoming the thoroughly discredited Heian aristocracy.

In a seesaw struggle of orgies, bloody destruction, and no-holds-barred cruelty, the precarious lead in the war swung back and forth between the two main antagonists and their complex network of allies. A breather was forced after famine and disease swept the country in 1182, but when the Minamoto forces threatened the capital itself in the summer of 1183, the Taira leadership abandoned the city, taking the emperor Antoku and the critical imperial regalia with them. In the void, the ex-emperor Go-Shirakawa shifted his symbolically still-important allegiance—probably because he expected a Minamoto victory and envisioned better treatment for himself by supporting their cause while he could still reasonably claim such support was voluntary. He refused to join the Taira exodus, throwing his support to the opposing forces, an act that lent them a newfound legitimacy. Though no longer emperor, Go-Shirakawa's aura of one-time imperial divinity swayed many undecideds to the Minamoto camp. The former sovereign then used the substantial strength of his official blessing to persuade Minamoto to even more tenaciously pursue Taira.

The end came in 1185 in a battle in the Inland Sea, one of the most auspicious naval encounters in world history. The Taira purposely chose to make their stand against their enemies in the waters off Dannoura, a fishing village just east of modern Shimonoseki, on the country's main island of Honshu, presumably to gain from what they misjudged to be Minamoto deficiencies in this form of warfare. Five hundred Taira craft and 840 of their enemy's ships faced each other across the riverlike strait. But the Taira's morning advantage in the disposition of their naval forces vanished with the afternoon's lengthening shadows: Wind and tide turned in favor of the Minamoto, and under the leadership of brilliant Yoshitsune Minamoto—one of the two boys whose lives had been spared by Taira magnanimity—the Taira clan's fleet went down to final defeat.

The most poignant casualty of the battle was the young sovereign, Antoku. Having fled the rush of the Minamoto in the custody of his grandmother and mother, Kiyomori's widow and daughter, the three, together with many Taira court ladies, found refuge on one of the Taira ships anchored at Dannoura. Their fate was decided when the vessel's captain betrayed them and treacherously sold out to the enemy. The Minamoto wished desperately to capture the imperial craft intact so as to be able to obtain possession of the regalia—sure to be near the ship's most illustrious passenger—and pass it to their own emperor-of-choice.

As the blazing vessel started to take on water and sink under them, the grand dowager empress gathered the six-year-old boy in her arms and jumped into the sea amid the flaming hulks of opposing warships still wildly careening around the imperial barque—the old lady knew the alternative to be a life of serfdom under the "Eastern criminals." Whether suicide or not, neither grandmother nor grandson was ever seen again. With this last living symbol of the splendors of Heian civilization went the regalia that had been handed down to Japan's monarchs since the first still half-wild kings had claimed sovereignty over the land. The Mirror and the Jewels were eventually recovered, but the Sword, the inexpressibly sacred token of continuity with the Sun Goddess, was lost forever.

The keepers of the past were completely defeated. A new ethic and a new era dawned on the country. Amid the changes, one great institution of state alone remained: Japan's monarchy and court would, although now greatly altered, continue into the new times.

CHAPTER V

The Epoch of Unending Struggle

THIRTEENTH CENTURY TO SIXTEENTH CENTURY

With its dark ages now enveloping the fractious islands—the thirteenth century by Christian reckoning—the Japanese throne and the position of its central character took a final plunge into impotence. The old-style monarchy would never resurface, not even—in the sense of direct rule—under Meiji. Furthermore, the locus of the country's power would shift unstoppably eastward, to the Kanto and its riverine plain that became Tokyo. Kammu's now tattered and wartorn capital withered into political irrelevance—except for the great paradoxical fact that the city continued without interruption to house the imperial authority that legitimized all political life in Japan. The country would for century upon century be at war, both with waves of slavering invaders and with itself, but through it all the emperors *reigned*, their civil power virtually extinguished but their role as the successors of God and validators of authority never, ever seriously challenged. The role now undertaken by the monarchs was almost completely a symbolic one, serving the single important duty, aside from chief priesthood, of legitimating the country's military rulers, the sovereigns' existence having become a sort of religious iconship far removed from participation in government. The world had never before nor has it since experienced a legally reigning monarchy so politically emasculated over so long a period.

One of the two great institutions that came to dominate the saga of Japanese life at the opening of its feudal period was the shogun-ate. Etymologically, the term originated from the eighth-century *sei-i-shi,* loosely meaning "Sent Against the Barbarians," a title signifying the general staff of an army sent by the emperor to fight a border war. At the end of that century, the emperor Kammu first bestowed on one of his generals the enhanced title *sei-i-taishogun,* "Commander-in-Chief Against the Barbarians," generally short-ened to shogun ("general" or "generalissimo")—the word *barbari-ans* referring to the indigenous Ainu peoples of eastern Japan who did indeed seem wildly barbaric compared to the more sophisticated Japanese. A few years later, the emperor Go-Toba issued a decree making the high-sounding title permanent and hereditary. Under the Minamoto the shogunate would gain profound new importance, its holders becoming in terms of actual power the emperors' masters, even one day becoming confused, at least in European minds, with the office of the monarchy itself.

The second institution was the caste known as samurai, which, almost precisely coincidental with the shogunate, officially lasted until the dawn of the Meiji era at the end of the nineteenth century. The rise of the samurai—men who lived by and for the sword—had been a major cause of the downfall of the court factions as the arbiters of Japanese government and society. The destructive strug-gle between the great Taira and Minamoto families ushered in the nation's millennium, the beginning of a militaristic philosophy of government and society that rolled over everything in its path until its own final destruction in 1945. Split as it was into four great divisions, Japanese society fell under the complete dominion of this highest caste, followed at a great divide by peasants, artisans, and merchants, in that order,[1] all far below the samurai in the slowly gelling order of social affairs.

The first samurai were, in effect, imperial castoffs, warriors related to the imperial house but whose birthright as princes was canceled when the monarchy, finding itself with too many relations to main-

[1]Contrary to European views of society, in Japan peasants were always held to rank higher than those who didn't till the soil.

tain in princely splendor, relegated those past the fifth generation descendant from the throne to the status of commoners. These princely descendants gradually dispersed to the northern and eastern provinces, where their own descendants became of necessity toughened frontiersmen living in the harsh climates and fighting the aborigines of those border regions. (Both the Taira and Minamoto clans come directly from such princely roots.)

The word *samurai* means "military man," or "man of arms." Originating in the verb *saburau,* or *samurau,* it first meant "to be on one's guard," later evolving into a noun, "one who serves." Finally, it came to specifically signify those guarding the Imperial Palace together with its sacred occupant. The samurai's loyalty rested with his chief, his clan, and his emperor—in strict descending order. As the shogunate developed, a host of important privileges and distinctions accrued to this new warrior class: authority to wear the famous double swords, state pensions, and, most importantly, the legal perpetuation through inheritance of their status as a separate and superior class, a perquisite established by the head of the Minamoto, the great Yoritomo himself.

Like their contemporaries, the knights of feudal Europe, Japan's budding samurai received their training through an elaborate military education whose sole purpose was to turn each man into a weapon to be used at his master's discretion and always at his master's disposal. Cosmic social overtones aimed at sanctifying their existence were predictably invented, but in reality military service was their chief raison d'être. Boys—little more than toddlers, really—were taught to handle wooden swords smoothly and lethally, a skill that was expected to pay dividends when real blades became extensions of their arms; the samurai's astonishing mastery of swordsmanship generally overshadowed that of his occidental counterpart. Vigilance was inculcated when the sleeping trainees were struck by their teachers with blunted clubs, enabling the fledgling warriors to develop a state of awareness that even sleep wouldn't entirely dull. Each was required to swear an oath to ignore the Buddhist injunction against the taking of life. Killing was a bloody chore that many were required to carry out often during careers in the service of powerful lords. Conversely, the samurai was expected to show willingness, even eagerness, to forfeit his own life through suicide, without hesitation, to atone for any failure to his master or stain on his own honor.

After his decisive victory over the Taira at the Battle of Dannoura, Yoritomo, now the Minamoto clan's chief, emerged as the undisputed overlord of Japan. Understanding that the permanent consolidation of his power depended upon establishing an orderly military dictatorship, Yoritomo made his first priority the destruction of any opposition from within his own family—meaning his brother Yoshitsune, the real architect of the Dannoura triumph. The younger sibling had become the lionized hero of the capital's smart set, that narrow wedge of court society now headed by the Minamoto ally, the ex-emperor Go-Shirakawa. It hadn't taken the sophisticated denizens of this upper crust milieu very long to figure out whose favor needed currying, and licking Minamoto boots could pay large dividends. But news of Yoshitsune's lionization soon reached Yoritomo at his camp in Kamakura, a small village on the peninsula that guarded the mouth of Tokyo Bay. The site had been carefully chosen as a place where Yoritomo could safely remain aloof from and uncontaminated by the temptations of Kyoto's fabled softness. When the dashing Yoshitsune heard of his elder brother's anger at his popularity—which ire probably amounted to the elder's jealousy of the far more dashing Yoshitsune—he wrote a saddened letter asking forgiveness for any sins of which he was thought to be guilty. Yoritomo's response—a reaction prompted by rumors that Yoshitsune was planning a revolt—was to send an execution party to dispatch the hero of the Gempei War. The unjustly accused brother fled, but when he and his loyal followers were eventually surrounded by Yoritomo's Kamakura troops, the thirty-one-year-old Yoshitsune decided *seppuku* was his only option; he slew himself together with his entire family, and his head was ceremonially sent to Kamakura.

After ridding himself of a few more suspect lieutenants, Yoritomo at last felt able to rule in solitary, unthreatened splendor. Though careful to show respect for the emperor—evidence of the awe in which even this most audacious of dictators still held the concept of a legitimate sovereign—he made it clear to the monarch (then his hand-picked incumbent, the boy-emperor Go-Toba) that imperial power was to be limited to those matters pertaining to God, while everything else was to be entirely in the keeping of the Minamoto, firmly entrenched in the military fastness of Kamakura.

Yoritomo lost little time in consolidating his hard-won preeminence, an effort helped enormously by his judicious distribution of the estates seized from the vanquished Taira. The primary beneficiaries of this largesse were his top lieutenants, and as these soldiers assumed the status of vassals bound inextricably to Yoritomo, they in turn became profoundly and understandably interested in the care and maintenance of this tidy new system of military rule. The culmination of Yoritomo's rise to the top came in 1192 when he was named shogun by thirteen-year-old Go-Toba, a near-prisoner whose main pleasure in life was his sword collection, a few of which he supposedly forged himself. Even as the fullness of power was seemingly being irreversibly shifted from Kyoto to Yoritomo's so-called Kamakura tent government—known as the *bakufu* [2] in Japanese—fate intervened to write an early end to the story of the first great Commander-in-Chief Against the Barbarians.

One day in the last year of the twelfth century, while riding in procession at the dedication of a new bridge, Yoritomo fell from his horse and died. There was no apparent reason for the inexplicable fall other than happenstance—whether the fall caused the death or death caused the fall is unknown—but the superstitions of the time ascribed it to a swoon over the guilt he "should" have felt at the treatment he had handed out to his heroic young brother. The consequences of the timing of his passing were manifold.

To its credit, Yoritomo's bakufu had managed to create a stable civilian administration in the country,[3] but Yoritomo himself was followed in power by one of the most convoluted ruling combinations Japan has ever experienced. The Minamoto overlord's immedi-

---

[2] The term *bakufu* came to stand generically for the shogunal administration until its demise seven centuries later.

[3] Which the emperor himself fully recognized when bestowing the shogun title on his preeminent general.

ate successor was his eldest son, Yoriiye, but inexperience crippled the youth's ability to follow effectively in the larger-than-life wake his father had cut. Instead, it was Masako, Yoritomo's strong-willed widow, who seized the reins of power into her uniquely capable hands. Theoretically, it was still possible at this time for a clever and capable woman to control the state, but only if the woman concerned was, first, of unimpeachably august position and, second, managed to make it appear that the strings were in fact being pulled by someone else—specifically by a male, in this case her son, Yoriiye, Yoritomo's legal heir. Masako's talents were such that she was able to maneuver her own family, the Hojo clan, into a regency over the shogun, thereafter replacing the Minamoto as the wellspring of real power in the Kamakura shogunate. The so-called Hojo regency thus became, for the next century and a half, the nation's controlling political factor. Masako became known in Japanese history as Ama-shogun, "Mother Shogun," an honorific richly deserved.

The anomaly of this situation was the incredible organizational hierarchy of the country's top leadership. The emperor was still the titular ruler of Japan, but his immediate venue—the court—was controlled by the imperial regents, who were still chosen from the now-ineffectual Fujiwara family, a clan that, though possessing considerably less power than in previous generations, nonetheless remained at the side of the monarch. On the other hand, while the Kamakura bakufu acted as Japan's true government, the effective leader of the shogunate was no longer the shogun himself—that office, for the next several decades at least, was usually filled by mere boys, as was the imperial throne itself. Instead, the country was ruled by shogunal regents. Fortunately for Japan, these regents, in the persons of successive Hojo clan leaders, bestowed remarkably capable government on the nation during this pivotal thirteenth century. And because of a new and potentially lethal threat arising out of the continental landmass lying beyond the empire's western horizon, every bit of good government would be needed to save the civilization Japan had so doggedly built since the time of Jimmu.

Meanwhile, back at the Kyoto court, the activities of the emperors and their still-lavish court continued to spiral on a downhill plunge to immateriality. In 1198, the emperor Go-Toba voluntarily abdicated in favor of his young son, the emperor Tsuchimikado. Though to all appearances still the bakufu's man, Go-Toba wanted to attempt real governing. He thought he might have a better chance from the position of retired sovereign. Had Yoritomo, himself still a year from his own death at the time of the abdication, sensed Go-Toba was harboring such ambitious notions, the dictator would either have forbidden the abdication or else barred Go-Toba from interfering in any substantive way with the bakufu's political preeminence. But Go-Toba kept his ideas to himself, and the reverent trust Yoritomo reposed in the throne caused him to let the ex-monarch go his own way. Over the next two decades, the cloistered Go-Toba bided his time in the the Sento Goshen, "Retired Emperor's Palace," staying aloof from political intrigue but becoming increasingly irritated at real or imagined slights from Kamakura's new masters. By 1221, his still unsated ambition led him finally to act and thereby bring about his own downfall in what became known as the Shokyu War.

Go-Toba issued an imperial edict urging the destruction of the Kamakura shogunate and its Hojo masters by any means available. The edict was lent a degree of credibility by the fact that he was still able to muster a motley army in Kyoto with which to threaten Kamakura's military dictatorship. In response, a shogunal army of 190,000 cavalrymen immediately descended on the capital to put an end to Go-Toba's absurd insolence. The very model of seasoned military spirit, the Kamakura army easily overwhelmed the imperial forces, bursting into Kyoto "as though tidal waves were surging toward a rough, rocky shore," as a contemporary poet phrased the bloody event. Meeting total defeat, Go-Toba was exiled to the desolate Oki Island in the Sea of Japan, there to spend the last eighteen years of his life in poverty amid decidedly nonregal environs. The cloistered ex-emperor Juntoku, equally involved in Go-Toba's plans, was exiled to the correspondingly desolate Sado Island. The imperial pair's principal samurai followers were beheaded or banished, depending on how seriously the Hojo regents assessed their individual guilt. An imperial candidate disposed to peaceful (that is, subservient) relations with the bakufu was installed on the throne as the emperor Go-Horikawa, and the imperial lands belonging to the members of the families who had supported the losing side were redistributed, yet another factor in the drearily endless emasculization of an imperial presence outside the confines of Kyoto's palace walls.

This one heady bit of spiritedness did, to its credit, teach the Kyoto monarchs a valuable lesson in self-preservation. The swift action of the Hojo demonstrated beyond any doubt that the change in the structure and reality of Japanese power from courtiers to military-backed warlords was not to be reversed. Most significantly, Kamakura's strength was the primary factor that later saved Japan from occupation and an indeterminable future under the ruthless heel of the Mongol hordes of the marauder called Kublai Khan. The relatively tranquil years of domination by the Hojo regents were about to be replaced with a whirlwind.

In the early part of the thirteenth century, the Mongolian tribes of central Asia had been united into a nation under the brutal but effective leadership of a chief, or *khan,* called Genghis. This astonishingly aggressive potentate decided early in his terror-filled career to expand his insignificant desert state as rapidly and as widely as possible, the results being that within a few years he amassed an empire stretching from eastern Europe—bands of his warriors reached as far as the Tigris and Euphrates rivers in what had once been the heart of the Babylonian empire—to eastern Asia, sowing little culture but inflicting massive destruction throughout the entirety of his new dominions. The predatory Mongol first smashed through China's Great Wall to overthrow the Chin empire in the north in 1234, but it was his grandson Kublai[4] rather than Genghis who brought the Mongols to the zenith of their glory by establishing rule over China under the name by which the clan was known to history, the Yuan dynasty. Immediately on subjugating the continent to its Pacific edge, Kublai turned his attention to the great archipelago lying so tantalizingly close to its shores.

It was a Korean named Cho who suggested to the Great Kublai

[4]Known as Kopitsu-retsu to the Japanese.

that he now demand Japan's vaselage. The khan's first thought was to attempt to subjugate the offshore prey by the relatively peaceful means of turning Japan into a vassal state, and then to bleed by taxation the country's treasure to finance his own Yuan court. The island empire would be left to govern itself under local overlords, a privilege by no means universal to the many less fortunate territories the khan had already brought under the Mongol boot. Japan, however, didn't appreciate this subtle distinction, and had no intention of acquiescing to the khan's view of the inevitable.

The first Mongol overture to Japan came in 1268, via the kingdom of Koryo, one of its vassal states on the Korean peninsula. The invitation to the "King of Japan"—snidely characterized in the smaller print at the bottom of the khan's petition as a "ruler of a small country"—sought "friendly intercourse" with China, but threatened war against the "king's" subjects if he didn't accede. After consulting with the court in Kyoto, which had been quite prepared to negotiate with the khan's fiercesome-looking envoys and would probably have submitted to the foreign demands, the Hojo government (by now the shogun was of course powerless, the shogunal regent the real power) rejected the thinly disguised threat. The envoys were sent back without an answer or even an acknowledgment that they and their invitation had been received, a diplomatic snub that added a dangerous insult to the injury of a negative reply to Kublai.

After floating additional entreaties to the defiant Japanese, the outraged Kublai finally ordered his military to subdue these cheeky Japanese nonentities. Sensing such a reaction, the Hojo leadership began preparing for the inevitable. Reasoning that the mainlanders' attack would arrive at the southernmost island of Kyushu, nearest the China coast and a convenient jumping-off place for a further killing blow on the main island of Honshu, the Hojo regent urgently initiated a massive buildup of defense fortifications in the southern sector. Not only did he instruct the samurai of the area to keep themselves especially vigilant, but the regent also sent spies to Korea, the probable embarcation site of any Mongol invasion fleet. Having eschewed the usual luxurious trappings of rule that still characterized the free-spending ways of the Kyoto court, the Kamakura bakufu was, fortunately for Japan, in a financial position to put its emergency plans into action.

The inevitable came six years later. Kublai had indeed used Korea as his staging site, ordering one of its captive regional kings to build a thousand junks and amass forty thousand troops for his invasion. In November 1274, an armada of 450 of these ships carrying the mixed Mongol and Korean troops, one of the most fear-inspiring invasion forces that had ever been assembled, landed at Hakozaki Bay on the north coast of Kyushu—directly in the maw of the defenses that the Hojo bakufu had wisely prepared. Nonetheless, the terrifying techniques used by the troops of the Mongol khan— especially the catapults flinging horrifying bombs—caused the Japanese defenders, armed only with their swords and bows and arrows, to wisely withdraw to a fortified line of defense.

Nature, in the form of a typhoon, came to the aid of the Japanese. Afraid of being caught on the high seas it raised in their own escape route, the Mongols withdrew all the way back to Korea. The exhausted defenders were, fortunately unbeknown to the attackers, on the verge of defeat. For the time being, the Japanese were given a truly miraculous respite.

Taking full advantage of the situation, the Kamakura government again ordered massive new defense preparations, the central feature of which was a stone wall running all the way around the shoreline of Hakozaki Bay, where it was reckoned that a second invasion force would try to overcome already probed and weakened Japanese defenses; the works were built by and at the expense of the landowners who dominated the area. A new fleet of small ships was rapidly constructed, a manpower draft put into effect, and stores of weapons stockpiled. Even the court made its own small but undoubtedly appreciated contribution: temporary abstinence from certain minor luxuries, the funds thus "saved" diverted to the military buildup. In truth, the nation had rarely shown such unity and never was it more needed than in the face of the great trial that was to come. Much to everyone's surprise, even the local pirates, the buccaneers who normally terrorized the Inland Sea, threw their support to the government, the defense of the greater economic interests evidently taking precedence over their normal felonious activities.

Shortly, the Great Khan sent another, even more demanding mission to the "King of Japan." This time the ultimatum borne by the five emissaries bid the sovereign to come directly to the khan's court in Peking, there to do obeisance and ask forgiveness for the trouble that had already been suffered by the patient but by now long-tormented Mongol state. Overcome by fear on hearing the new demand, the imperial court in Kyoto awaited word from Kamakura, which to its credit resolutely rejected the ultimatum. Looking for a way to convince the khan that they didn't wish even to have the matter *raised* again, the shogunal regent ordered that the heads of the members of the Mongol diplomatic party be severed from their shoulders and stuck on pillories outside the city. Kublai was understandably annoyed when told of this supreme impertinence. The man whose warriors had ravaged territory stretching from Hungary in the west to the China Sea in the east soon initiated the process he *knew* would finally subdue the intolerably insolent islanders.

This time the Japanese respite lasted just five years, until 1281. The largest amphibious invasion force ever to be assembled until D-Day in World War II—100,000 men borne by 3,500 vessels—sailed as had its predecessor up the Inland Sea into the waiting Japanese defenses, a fortuitous strategem from the Japanese viewpoint. The Mongols tried desperately to outflank the wall around the bay, the intense samurai courageously thwarting them with a contemptuousness for death that would mark their fighting spirit down to the twentieth century. Neither side could gain the upper hand. The fighting raged for seven weeks, from June into the typhoon season of August. In Kyoto, the emperor attempted intercession with his divine ancestors by writing imploring letters in his own hand, missives that begged divine assistance to throw off the hideous and subhuman invaders. The monarch was assisted with his priestly chores by a large number of monks who didn't hesitate to assert that they had seen portentous signs of heaven's assistance while praying with their usual fervid intensity, for which work the emperor generously gave out handsome emoluments. In sad contrast, the legions of gallant soldiers even then risking and gladly giving their lives in the name of their sovereign did so without any matching prospects of such fiscal compensation.

The elements of nature again proved the Mongol undoing when divine assistance arrived in the form of yet another "divine wind" whose churning dark clouds descended over the ungainly Mongol invasion craft. Over the next two days the tempest blew the Mongol flotilla into little more than kindling, destroying along with it the smaller Japanese ships that had been struggling against them with some small success. The Mongols caught on the shore were, along with those forced to shore from their sinking ships, quickly slaughtered by the superior Japanese land troops. Some three thousand prisoners were executed by the Japanese, while a spared trio was put on a boat to take their admonitory tale back to Peking. The continental threat was repelled (Kublai's death twenty years later permanently ended the Mongol danger to Japan), Japan was safe from foreign military invasion for another seven centuries, and the Hojo regency shone at its brightest. But the Kamakura government would bask in this peak of its ascendancy for only a short time more before it, too, started a slide that would end in ignominious destruction.

Wary of a repeat of the khan's adventurism, Kamakura's tent government rationalized the necessity to continue the extraordinary defense measures that had represented so large and burdensome a part of the nation's spending during the years of the Mongol threat. But contrary to the Kamakura victories against the Taira and against the court in the Shokyu incident, this victory brought with it no new fresh supply of booty—either land or treasure—with which to reward a triumphant army. As happens when a hard-used military force goes unrewarded, resentment quickly dissipates whatever euphoria accompanied success. What should have been a threshold of glorious consequences for the bakufu turned into the precursor of an irremediable weakening of its grip over the nation.

After the Mongol danger was repulsed, and while a new drama of the seemingly unstoppable crumbling of the Hojo government and birth of its successor regime unfolded in Kamakura, the imperial court in Kyoto continued its placid play-acting, the monarch carrying out his sacerdotal functions meant to invoke the protection of the gods on Japan. The energy once derived from active participation in national affairs had been all but entirely drained from the imperial establishment, its now-reduced entourage carrying on only by the momentum gained in thirteen centuries of existence. Still, no government and no dictator envisioned the monarchy's actual extinction.

Pastimes both exquisite and ephemeral occupied these still self-infatuated and peacockish courtiers, men and women who played at titillating games and gigglingly crafted precious bits of poetry, worrying themselves sick over some minute question of sumptuary consequentiality—whether an official's skirt was a mite too long for his rank or its fabric slightly too rich for his station, whether his eyebrows were shaved cleanly or his cheeks rouged just so. The preparation of the courtier's queue, long and bound in handmade paper, might consume the better part of a day, leaving almost no time to do justice to an unfinished billet-doux destined for some exquisite lady made achingly desirable by her delightfully blackened teeth. While his less fortunate countrymen were still existing on the millet that had become the culinary mainstay of all classes below the ruling one, those in Kyoto's court stratum enjoyed dainty dishes based on Chinese models, exotic concoctions all but unknown to the masses. Bereft of the tools to regain power, let alone the spirit, the monarchy as an institution of political consequence just about gave up.

While it is true that Japan's fourteenth century saw the fears of the Great Khan and his predatory armies fade away, two new upheavals occurred in the country's mutually suspicious national institutions: the monarchy and the shogunate. While the former was sundered into competing courts, both claiming the legitimacy that only one could legally possess, the tired shogunate shuffled itself with new personalities into a reconstituted regime. To recount first the imperial machinations that led to the throne's being split for nearly a century, we start with the single strong monarch to arise from the catalog of faceless sovereigns who populated the monarchy in this era. It was 1318, and Go-Daigo, the ninety-sixth emperor and a man resolved to rid himself and his court of the domination of the Kamakura usurpers, came to the throne.

Age was the crucial factor setting the emperor Go-Daigo apart from the succession of nonentities who had preceded him in the 125 years since Go-Toba's departure from the throne. In the era of boy-emperors, Go-Daigo was a mature man of thirty-one when he mounted the throne, a sovereign possessing both the vigor and will to try to return his office to its former powerful station, a dream he had harbored since his installation as crown prince a decade earlier. The conditions that followed in the wake of the Mongol defeat formed the basis for Go-Daigo's optimism at his enthronement. As stated earlier, after Japan's victory the shogunate was left without spoils with which to placate its restless forces, dangerously thwarting samurai expectations of gratitude that had been the accepted custom for many years. Petitioning the shogun with righteous pleas for something to show for their efforts, the soldiers weren't long in becoming first disgruntled and soon openly angry with the Kamakura government. Loyalty was the glue that held the feudal system together, and its going unrewarded meant the system was in danger of coming undone.

Go-Daigo carefully watched and measured the samurai's changing attitudes toward the shogunate, waiting to strike against the institution when he thought the balance of the warrior class's sympathy had sufficiently shifted to his point of view. Though the suspicious shogunal regent—at the time the vicious and debauched Takatoki Hojo, a man whose habit it was to leave most affairs of state to unworthy favorites—tried to force Go-Daigo's abdication so as to place a more malleable substitute on the throne, the emperor courageously refused to step down. And because the regent in Kamakura no longer had the wherewithal to enforce his will, the emperor was realistically able to ignore the bakufu, all the while picking up ever-increasing numbers of samurai adherents to his cause. These factors, together with the monarch's ambition and sense of wounded imperial pride, combined into a heady brew, and Go-Daigo continued to build his power base and position himself to eventually regain what he considered to be his rightful patrimony.

The emperor first attempted to assert himself over the Hojo-dominated bakufu in 1331, but the clumsy and premature revolt was put down; Kamakura prevailed and the captured sovereign was exiled to Oki Island for two years, during which time a substitute emperor named Kogon was placed on the throne. But in 1333, following his escape from the island prison, Go-Daigo's renewed audaciousness nearly paid off. The shogunal army sent to thwart the emperor, now returned to Kyoto, was led by one Takauji Ashikaga, who halfway from Kamakura to Kyoto suddenly switched his allegiance to that of the imperial cause—probably due to some old grievance against the Hojo and after a careful reading of each side's prospects. Ashikaga's about-face had a salutary effect on other disgruntled local lords and their samurai, a number of whom seized the moment to march on Kamakura and burn the shogunal headquarters to the ground. When Ashikaga entered Kyoto, he came as Go-Daigo's ally and defender, and it appeared as if the emperor's vision of restored imperial power and rule through court-appointed bureaucrats might indeed come to pass.

Tragically for the imperial cause, Go-Daigo now repeated the Hojo mistake. Rather than immediately rewarding his new ally and his army with rich prizes, readily available in the form of appropriated Hojo possessions, the emperor ignored them. So instead of restoring a Kammu-style monarchy, Go-Daigo's vision evaporated in the smoke of a righteously wounded Ashikaga, who simply took what he wanted, namely those same ripe-for-the-picking Hojo possessions. What's more, Go-Daigo's plans to resuscitate imperial rule through a revival of all the former ministries and official positions and a reform of the country's financial and judicial system were stillborn. His attempt to recall the past was not only ill-conceived, but the imperial system that he envisioned had in reality lost its credibility centuries earlier. The now-anachronistic fiscal and judicial reforms he attempted to impose from Kyoto were met with fury from the strong warrior class. The latter, though now applauding the hazy concept of a strong throne, nonetheless had no desire to see their hard-won perquisites and prerogatives in any way circumscribed by Go-Daigo's renewed imperial pretensions. When the emperor, expecting to be able to control the military, personally granted the title of shogun to his own son, the samurai finally had enough.

The powerful and powerfully backed Takauji Ashikaga endured Go-Daigo's policies for a scant three years before he simply replaced him, in 1336, with a puppet, a malleable sort named Komyo who was cravenly amenable to the new strongman's point of view. At the same time, Takauji created a new shogunal regime of his own. Having escaped[5] with his consort to the Yoshino hills south of the city, in what is today the Nara prefecture, Go-Daigo naturally did not view these rump proceedings as constituting a legal deposition of his own sovereignty. Instead, he declared that he remained the *real* sovereign, and proceeded to reign in opposition to that *other* court back in the capital. For the next fifty-six years, from 1336 to 1392, Japan had, like Roman Catholicism with its rival papacies during a portion of this exact same period, two courts. Each claimed total sovereignty, each called the other false and illegal, and, as we will see, the consequences of all this can still be felt, albeit faintly, in Japanese affairs and questions of imperial legitimacy to this day. Because the schism went on for more than half a century after Go-Daigo's death, the matter of ascertaining which of the two lines had the superior claim to the throne grew to pose some fairly thorny difficulties.

In order to understand how both courts were able to claim legitimacy—each with some measure of well-grounded historical evidence to back up its own passionate assertions—we have to backtrack to the time of the emperor Go-Saga, who reigned a century before Go-Daigo. Because of a dispute regarding the succession, the imperial house at that time was split into senior and junior branches—the senior line descending from Go-Saga's successor, the emperor Go-Fukakusa; the junior from Go-Fukakusa's younger brother and successor, Kameyama. The shogunate in Kamakura imposed a formula whereby each branch would reign alternately, and with the short terms in office caused by the remnants of the system of boy-emperors, each branch had the opportunity to see

[5]In an ominous sign for its future economic health, the imperial family's lands were appropriated by Ashikaga when the monarch fled.

several incumbents succeed to the throne. The inevitable impasse occurred when both dizzily convoluted branches made a claim at the same time. So when Ashikaga threw the junior branch emperor Go-Daigo (who had, incidentally, made it quite clear on his accession that he intended to keep the succession in his own line forever) off the throne to put in Komyo,[6] his own senior branch candidate— a maneuver that placed a genuine prince on the throne and thus caused no insult as such to the imperial house—the junior branch incumbent's refusal to accept the move's legality meant that two "emperors" were now claiming the throne when, of course, only one could be the "real" monarch.

A quick interruption in this complicated issue of imperial succession is needed to recount what was coincidentally happening to the shogunal government. The Hojo bakufu of boy shoguns, kept in power by regents since the early days of the Kamakura tent government when the Hojo family succeeded through the machinations of Yoritomo's widow, had by Go-Daigo's day collapsed of terminal incompetence. A new military government was set up by Takauji Ashikaga in Kyoto,[7] and became known to history as the Ashikaga Shogunate; its latter part is often called the Muromachi period, after the luxurious section of Kyoto of that name, a district in which the highest-ranking officials of the new order built their palaces and villas.

This move from the rigors of Kamakura to the comparative luxury of Kyoto had a markedly deleterious effect on the Ashikaga leadership. In fact, from the outset the new regime would be a disaster for the country. Lacking clear-cut authority from the throne, the talent of either a Yoritomo or the early regents who guided the puppet shoguns following him, or even the ability to hold at bay the ever more troublesome and independent-minded provincial barons—the *daimyo,* or "great names"—real Ashikaga authority quickly dissipated. In reality, the clan never controlled the entirety

[6]Who as a "schismatic pretender" is, of course, not in the official roster of Japanese sovereigns.

[7]Kamakura was not fully rebuilt after its destruction, and only a relatively unimportant branch of the new shogunal government was maintained at the site.

of the country as Yoritomo had; only the eight easternmost provinces were firmly under its authority, with the daimyo who lorded over the remainder constantly having to be bargained with for either tribute or military assistance. Ironically, while the shogunal government's effective power rapidly decreased to a shadow of that exercised by Yoritomo—and that of the imperial court virtually disappeared—Japan herself actually prospered, the respite from war allowing the citizenry to get on with long-neglected business.

A solution still had to be found to the imperial succession conundrum that had come with the Hojo fall and the attendant Ashikaga rise. In the first place, the monarchy had become so irrelevant to the nation's life that there was a very real danger it might be entirely swept away if it didn't get its house in order. But the resolution of the problem was a poor one: In 1292—decades after Go-Daigo's death—the shogunate finally convinced the more precarious of the two competing emperors, the southern one—who was bereft of the legitimacy that residence in the capital gave his opponent—that he should call it a day. The northern emperor, Go-Komatsu, would reign as sole sovereign, there would be an equable division of property, and the two branches would again take turns at rule in direct violation of whatever legitimacy the already much-violated concept of primogeniture still retained. The plan proved as unworkable and susceptible to treachery this time as it had when first initiated during Go-Toba's time—the shogun cheated on the deal and refused to allow Go-Daigo's southern line, now without its powerful supporters, the right to supply any emperors at all. The branch consequently left the active stage of Japanese history, its real legacy the strong spiritual influence its ideal of single-minded devotion to a great and worthy cause would exert on later generations.

The imperial schism lasted but a relatively short time, and it happened many centuries ago. But its impact on Japanese history and society was nearly as great and traumatic as the papal split and the restructuring of Europe's political institutions that followed in its wake. The steady loss of the lands held by Japan's court aristocracy had been progressing unchecked for generations, but the affair of the two monarchial camps symbolized most succinctly that class's almost total loss of power in both the central government and in the provinces. The new land tenure system that took hold during the Muromachi age following the court schism put an end to the long-crumbling system that had for so long provided recruits for the prefeudal civil aristocracy. The court class would be permitted to survive as a legacy from and spiritual link to the past, but from now on *raw power*—the strong sword arm in service to the feudal warlord—was the preeminent factor affecting political events in Japan.

The schism's effects were to be felt by the throne itself for centuries, the lingering questions of legitimacy that sprang from the lineage problems it raised visited even upon the present emperor. From the days when each of the two courts was still exhorting the sole right to reign, learned scholars found merit in the claims of both, and succeeding centuries of scholastic research into the question leave no absolute answers as to one or the other's rights. The adherents of the losing southern court's side usually put their emphasis on the matter of *taigi meibun,* a Confucian principle espousing a subject's absolute loyalty to his sovereign, loyalty that the "traitorous" Takauji Ashikaga obviously did not show when he removed Go-Daigo and thus precipitated the ensuing mess. During the remainder of the shogunal centuries, the bakufu-backed northern court was considered "official"; with the Meiji restoration, the southern emperors became the "legitimate" line backed by the state, and today remains the official line. At the middle Meiji period, school textbooks began ignoring the whole question with the intention of avoiding giving offense to what had become a deeply entrenched emperor-state in which questions of imperial legitimacy were not considered proper to public discussion.

Most recently, a Nagoya shopkeeper named Hiromichi Kumazawa petitioned the supreme allied commander of occupied Japan, General Douglas MacArthur, to recognize his claim to the throne, supposedly "superior" to that of Emperor Hirohito, claiming he was a direct descendant of the southern lineage of sovereigns (Hirohito was in direct line from the northern, Kyoto, branch). The whole matter, though perhaps an absurd abstraction by the 1940s, still had the power to arouse considerable popular passion, not only because of the insult done to the reigning emperor by having the matter brought up at all, but also because of the still nagging possibility that descendants of the southern emperors *could* conceivably have the superior "genetic" claim on the throne. That this ruckus was raised after six hundred years speaks volumes about the feelings of the Japanese people concerning any matter related to their dynasty's legitimacy.

With the freshly reenfranchised Kyoto court finally rid of the southern thorn in its side, life in the capital could try to find its way back to normality, a "normality" that verged on the moribund. One of the world's great historical curiosities is that for the next five hundred years, until the advent of the Meiji era, the Japanese who lived outside the tiny court circles in Kyoto—meaning more than 99.9 percent of the population—very nearly lost sight of the fact that the emperors even existed! There would remain the fragment of realization that somewhere there dwelled a living God connected with the deities who protected the nation's well-being, but the samurai governments and the feuding warlords became, in all but the finality of narrow legal definition, the empire's political sources of last resort.

Of most pressing day-to-day concern to the post–Go-Daigo emperors and their courts was the now extremely serious issue of finances. The Ashikaga shogunate—which had become a hereditary office like the Hojo shogunate that preceded it, and was equally contemptuous of the court since the Go-Daigo affair—was occupied with struggling for political control in the face of fast-growing provincial power. Internecine warfare wrecked the country as one provincial daimyo beat on another for the most minute advantage. On top of everything else, the new Ashikaga shogun, Yoshimitsu, Takauji's successor, every so often took it upon himself to insult the person of the emperor in a demonstration of the reality of the new relationship between monarchy and shogunate.

In March of 1408, Yoshimitsu "invited"—in effect, commanded—the emperor Go-Komatsu to his splendidly accoutered villa in Kyoto's Kitayama district for a small ceremonial soirée he was throwing;[8] imperial attendance at such an affair was still considered quite an honor, a demonstration of the host's status not easily outshone by his less powerful allies. In these rare but not unknown imperial visits to subjects, standard etiquette had heretofore required that the host send an honor guard to the palace to escort the sovereign to his destination. When none showed up to guide Go-Komatsu, the emperor nonetheless proceeded to the Ashikaga mansion in the sole company of his kampaku. After such an inauspicious start, the rest of the evening was all downhill, Yoshimitsu subtly twisting the knife ever deeper as the evening's banquet progressed. First, the ex-shogun had arranged the places so that both he and the emperor were seated on cushions of equal honor: Not only were the pillows the same, but their brocaded pattern was fashioned in a design supposedly reserved solely for imperial use. Furthermore, Yoshimitsu's fifteen-year-old second son, Yoshitsugu, was seated *above* the emperor's kampaku, another breathtaking snub. There's more. Young Yoshitsugu then personally toasted the emperor; a boy, shogun's son or not, simply did *not* toast his sovereign as an equal. The banquet was said to be saved only by the inborn grace with which the sovereign carried these sad events to a finish. Four years later, the exhausted Go-Komatsu abdicated in favor of his eleven-year-old son, Shoko.

With the influx of the Ashikaga and their retainers and camp followers into the capital, such refined life as remained among the ruins of the city's now poverty-stricken exquisites came to a thunderous halt. Even the imperial family was not immune to the insults of the oafish bullies who had attached themselves to the Ashikaga star. A retired emperor—who we've seen was referred to as an *in*—ran into this new force one day. Addressed rudely by a drunken warrior, a shocked courtier belonging to the personal retinue of the emperor reproved him. The soldier insolently responded, "Who is

[8]He had already technically handed the office of shogun over to his son Yoshimochi, but still controlled affairs as prime minister, or dajo daijin, and did so, by the by, in a luxurious setting in the belief that the embellishment of the capital and his honored place in it was a fitting way to dispose of the nation's cash resources.

this *in* [emperor] you speak of? If you mean an *inu* [dog], I'll shoot it!" Instantly, a volley of arrows was fired at the imperial oxen carriage, cutting the harnesses and releasing the animals. The former sovereign sat there in his motionless carriage, eyes filling with tears at having to endure such unprecedented indignity.

At least back at the palace the sovereign enjoyed some protection against this kind of thing. Go-Komatsu's heir, Shoko, stuck it out for sixteen years, actually managing to retain the throne until he died at the age of twenty-eight. But for the first time a shogun actually tried to interlope his way directly into the bosom of the imperial family itself, a deed that, if successful, would obviously have had grave effects on the vaunted inviolability of the monarchy, legitimate descent through the Sun Goddess's line being the one indispensable element that permitted it to survive, powerless but at least intact, into the twentieth century. Yoshimitsu Ashikaga, the third shogun of his family line, coveted the title dajo tenno, the honorific normally bestowed only on retired emperors but also sometimes given to princes who themselves had not reigned but had sired heirs who did ascend the throne. Yoshimitsu's attempt to gain the title was mired in symbolic adoptions and assumption of honorary parental status in the imperial family, but his death prevented the title being granted. Go-Komatsu, who had realized the necessity of staying on good terms with Yoshimitsu's heir, offered to grant the title posthumously, but that successor, Yoshimochi Ashikaga, surprisingly refused the now-empty honor for his dead father. The new shogun evidently pridefully reasoned that the shogunate didn't need the imperial title, having quite enough honor without it.

Although the court and its occupants were forced to live a penurious existence through these years, the term must be understood in its relative sense. Economies were great when compared to the sybaritic indulgences of past imperial life, but examined side by side with the precarious existence of the vast majority of their subjects, monarchs of the early fifteenth century weren't that badly off. Even this situation deteriorated though, when, in the seventh decade of the century, the imperial palace was set ablaze in the disastrous conflict called the Onin War, a time of horrendous suffering in which all of Japan sank into anarchy and murderous civil strife. Even the court's sole justification for its existence, the proper performance of ceremonies of state, had to be foregone in the name of economy, funds simply not being available to carry out these symbolic rites, the monarchs themselves silently retrenching into whatever inner resources the gods may have given them.

Ashikaga control over the country had been steadily evaporating, and with it went the financial crutch on which the emperors had become accustomed to leaning. The fiscal managers that earlier shoguns installed in provincial positions of authority lost their ability to control and extract tribute from the daimyo. After simply appropriating their own lands, these managers came themselves to heed shogunal orders with far less circumspection than had their loyal predecessors. Minor local authorities began to erect barriers on roads within their control, sometimes as closely spaced as every mile or so, each charging high toll fees, and because of these levies, its representatives now were forced to pay to travel from one place to another, adding further to the central government's financial woes. Halfway through the fifteenth century, shogunal authority took a disastrous nosedive when assassinations of the successive Ashikaga incumbents weakened the family almost beyond its ability to maintain its tenuous hold over the capital. The bakufu tried to buy its way out of these troubles by issuing what were called Edicts of Good Government, documents that erased the debts of hard-pressed samurai and peasants, who threatened to turn to anarchy if they weren't helped out of their problems. The economy was collapsing, plague and famine were scourging the countryside, and the harried monarch, Go-Hanazono at midcentury, did his best by writing pleading poems to the shogun asking if *something* couldn't be done?

It was at this already low point that the Onin War began, bringing the horrors of near-total devastation once again to the imperial-shogunal city. For seven years Kyoto succumbed to the ravages of the general civil strife blowing across the entire archipelago. Its genesis came when Yoshimasa Ashikaga, the lightweight eighth shogun of his line, became tired of his duties at the age of twenty-nine and retired in his brother's favor. Unfortunately, Yoshimasa's wife objected to the move on the grounds that she wanted her son to inherit her husband's mantle, with the result that wife and brother wasted little time in enlisting their own armies of supporting daimyo warlords, all anxious to settle long-standing grudges. Each side soon had enormous armies parked opposite each other across the capital, aching to be let loose. When they finally engaged each other in 1467, the city was demolished, and the eleven-year Onin War was launched.

The principal effect of the war was to put an end, finally, to the shogunate's national authority. Neither side won. Thousands were slaughtered by massive gangs of marauding mercenaries who fought for the booty they could capture in their butchery. The end came only when neither side was able to continue the carnage. The provincial lords, though shuffled around a bit in their loyalties, remained the force that kept the country from tumbling into a final anarchic spin.

Yoshimasa survived the slaughter, but it was not because the warring parties particularly feared or respected him; he was simply an irrelevancy and so was by-passed. In the midst of all the horrors that surrounded him, Yoshimasa quite unshamefacedly took the opportunity to build himself a splendid villa in Kyoto, called the Silver Pavilion, an earthly paradise from which he watched the remaining crumbs of his authority vanish in the dust and heat of opposing mobs of grunting, blood-crazed combatants.

No such luxury for the sovereign, who deserved that appellation in only the most legalistic sense. Because of Go-Daigo's actions against the shogunate, very few estates still existed from which the imperial family could draw an assured income. The sovereign's finances were now almost entirely dependent on the generosity of the bakufu, which was itself in terrible fiscal shape. Successive sovereigns in the dark years during and following the war reached ever-greater depths of penury. The emperor Go-Tsuchimikado, who for the greater part of his reign saw the cessation of all court ceremonies because of the throne's dire financial straits, had looked on as his palace burned out from under him in the Onin ravages. When shelter was at last again provided, the building turned out to be a cheap affair surrounded by a spindly bamboo fence that didn't even bar the rats that scrounged through the city's burned-out streets. When Go-Tsuchimikado died in the first year of the sixteenth century, his body lay for six weeks putrefying in a darkened storage room of the palace because there was no money for a coffin; furthermore, this happened in summer, when even the weather conspired against efforts to keep the corpse reasonably intact. After enough money was at last found, the imperial family was so happy that in appreciation the shogunal official responsible for the release of the burial money—one thousand hiki (about $5,000)—was granted the coveted right to personally display the imperial crest of chrysanthemum and paulownia.

Thirty-seven-year-old Go-Kashiwabara, the 104th sovereign, ascended the throne of his circuitously descended dynasty in October 1500. With the single exception of Go-Daigo, no incumbent who had passed the age of thirty had become emperor since 1073, but with the court now so impoverished, the cause of the boy-emperor syndrome—imperial abdication—became impractical: Funds were simply no longer available to pay for the ceremonies involved in abdication, and as a result monarchs from now on would routinely stay on the throne into their mature years.

Go-Kashiwabara's first item of business as emperor was to request of the shogun sufficient funds to stage an appropriate enthronement ceremony, an event still considered so sacrosanct that not even the nearly broke shogunate could refuse to allot the necessary pieces of gold from its own depleted treasury. Only a small portion of the funds needed for the ceremonies was forthcoming though, and when Go-Kashiwabara heard the Barbarian-Subduing Generalissimo's official explanation, he was dumbfounded: The shogun's deputy, reflecting his master, informed the monarch that "in my opinion, there is no reason to hold a grand enthronement ceremony. If the man being crowned were not worthy to become an emperor, no degree of pomp and splendor would make people revere him. If, on the other hand, he were a worthy man [an attribute the shogun evidently granted the emperor] there is no need of an enthronement ceremony for he would naturally be regarded as the sovereign majesty over the land. A ceremony as grand as you are petitioning is not suitable for these turbulent times." The closing statement of this sassy epistle indeed may have accurately reflected circumstances, but the idea of an enthronement service on the cheap was unprecedented. When, after twenty years (Go-Kashiwabara reigned for twenty-six years), the Lord Abbot of Hongwanji donated the necessary money—ten thousand pieces of gold—from his well-to-do monastery's funds (a story that is generally accepted, although some sources say the shogun actually supplied it), a grateful emperor raised his benefactor to appropriately high ecclesiastical rank. Truly, few monarchies have reached such depths and survived.

The sixteenth century is with ample and undoubted justification known in Japan as the Epoch of Wars, the *Sengoku Jidai*. After the Onin War of the late fifteenth century, the country's whole fabric would continuously be rent by unceasing civil strife and near-universal lawlessness, a situation lasting until the period was finally brought to an end at the close of the sixteenth century by the greatest trio of figures in Japan's history. That the monarchy got through these times without simply disappearing from uselessness was, with paramount irony, due in large part to the low condition into which it had sunk—in effect, it played possum for a century. By letting the flame of the throne die down to a flicker, it consumed very little oxygen, and it survived.

During the Epoch of Wars, the dynasty lost its few remaining estates, the lands falling to the avaricious military magnates who coveted the taxes that could be wrung from the already overburdened tenant peasants, drones who bore on their backs the entire weight of Japan's economy. Court officials who still managed to retain their outlying estates were forced to leave the capital and return to these properties to protect them from raids; the sovereigns, of course, were unable to take any such actions themselves. The exodus of Kyoto's officials was just one more burden for the emperors of this period to bear, being left without even the minimal support their courtiers might be able to give.

When Go-Kashiwabara died in 1526, his ashes were taken from the crematorium in a box slung around the neck of a general. The imperial funeral procession consisted of a paltry twenty-six officials, a meager little parade presenting a sad scene to the few citizens of the city who ventured out of their barricaded homes to witness it. During the reign of his successor, Go-Nara, war again ravaged the city, and the few courtiers who were left crowded into the dilapidated imperial palace, which stood completely defenseless now that its flimsy fence—the sole barrier between it and the real world—had been pushed down.

Go-Nara's primary personal fame comes from having experienced the absolute deepest relative poverty in the recorded history of Japan's throne. The palace was little more than a ruin, the emperor openly earned his daily bread through sale of his autograph, and no enthronement ceremony was even contemplated until ten years into his long reign of over three decades. In 1542 came the epochal landing of the Portuguese in Japan, and in 1557 (St.) Francis Xavier arrived and requested an audience with Go-Nara to plead for the right to proselytize. Besides being short-circuited by officials who wanted to keep the existence of the emperor hidden from this new foreign menace, so sorry a spectacle was presented by both the ruined city and the broken-down palace, and so obviously was the emperor bereft of power or even influence, that Francis left the capital without attempting to fulfill his mission. Three hundred years would pass before a Westerner was actually privileged to see a Japanese monarch, and during that time the very existence of the emperor was first disputed and then forgotten in the West.

Go-Nara's thirty-one-year reign was coincidentally matched by that of his successor, Ogimachi, the latter's reign extending nearly to the end of the horrible sixteenth century. Although the turmoil in the capital subsided to a pitiable but manageable state, Ogimachi's early years on the throne were marred by more of the same anarchy that his recent predecessors had had to endure. Both emperor and shogun remained without power, the many fighting daimyo warlords still running the Balkanized country uncontested except by each other. Life was made even more dangerous for everyone from first-rank courtier to untouchable gravedigger when Western firearms were introduced by the Portuguese. Employing the innate skills that have stood their industry in good stead through the ensuing centuries, the Japanese first copied and then considerably improved the imported product. Battles henceforth took on an even grislier visage with these new and indiscriminately lethal weapons of war.

If Japan were to have any future—especially if it were to defend itself against the greed of the Western tyrants, religion-crazed fanatics who regarded the non-Caucasian world's inhabitants and cultures as being without value and in need of salvation in the name of the European version of God—anarchic chaos *simply had to end.* That it did is in great measure due to three men who appeared in the last half of the sixteenth century, men whose motives were to redeem and preserve what was good in Japanese culture, and to reject—by fire if need be—what was bad. The order they established would survive until the second Western wave of imperialism brought the house they established in on itself.

CHAPTER VI

Of God and Caesar—
The Court Under Edo

SIXTEENTH CENTURY TO NINETEENTH
CENTURY

Nobunaga mixed the dough.
Hideyoshi baked the cake.
Ieyasu ate it.

—JAPANESE PROVERB

The monarchy's doleful tumble from the briefly won ascendancy of
Go-Daigo to the woes of his successors was soon to end. By the
middle of the sixteenth century, the fortunes of the emperors—now
penniless, powerless, and virtually ignored—were such that the observer can only again wonder at the institution's fortitude in carrying
on. Even the shogunate was by now, if perhaps marginally less
pauperized, nearly as impotent as the throne. But in the five decades
preceding the turn of the seventeenth century, a new and transfig-
ured Japan emerged out of this vacuum, the roles of every member
of Japanese society affected, not least that of the sovereign who had
through it all, good and bad, reigned as the supreme symbol of the
nation.

During these years, which closely coincided with Europe's age of
artistic rebirth, three men—Nobunaga Oda, Hideyoshi Toyotomi,

and Ieyasu Tokugawa[1]—would follow in succession as dictators, a trio of personalities possessing such extraordinary political talents as Japan had never seen. Through the regimes they established, the throne would continue, in deepest shadow, to lie nearly dormant for another three centuries. But it survived, its prestige and utility very slowly regaining the lost patina of ancient times, until it eventually reestablished the glory of its Heian-era zenith.

Before we can discuss the reigns of these unique men, we need to briefly depart the court to explain why imperial authority remained so thoroughly eclipsed during this period. An extraordinary series of political events marked the late sixteenth century, the period when Japan finally achieved unification—now known as the Azuchi-Momoyama era. During this time, the monarchy waited patiently, its own reawakening still too far over the horizon to see.

Following the formal conclusion, in 1477, of the bloody and debilitating Onin War, Japan nonetheless continued to suffer its national nightmare: Civil strife, with misery fed by the absence of an effective central government, continued unquelled. The viciously fought wars erased all vestiges of chivalric behavior in combat. The battling warlords built themselves mammoth castles, enormously expensive fortified strongholds from which they kept guard over their fiefdoms. Since both the monarchy and the Ashikaga shogunate were moribund, the country's only effective "government" were these warlords operating out of their semiautonomous provincial domains, constantly jockeying with each other in an ongoing struggle for self-aggrandizement. Japan's lost central authority, if it could be reestablished, was ripe for the first man strong enough to go after it. It was into this vacuum that the initial member of our triumvirate stepped.

The first of the national saviors—all of whom had been born within eight years of each other, from 1534 to 1542—claimed roots that could be traced to one of the principal participants in the Battle of Dannoura, which had seen Taira power crushed four centuries earlier. After that historic naval engagement, a grandson of the

[1]All of whom will hereafter be referred to by their given names rather than family names.

Fujiwara-descended Kiyomori, a member of the vanquished Taira clan, was to escape Minamoto retribution by being secretly taken by his mother to the small village of Tsuda, bordering Omi province's Lake Biwa, a few miles from Kyoto. A Shinto official from Oda adopted the baby, and its name was changed from that given at birth, Chikazane, to one reflecting its new benefactor, Oda. When the child grew into manhood, he was to found his own family, and for generations its members passed unremarkable lives performing Shinto duties at Omi's shrine.

When circumstances rooted in the turmoil of the crumbling Ashikaga bakufu caused the head of this family of shrine attendants to be promoted to the stewardship of the daimyo Shiba family, the clan packed up and moved to Owari province, toward Edo in the east. It was in Owari that the seed of the clan's future greatness was planted. The head of the family at the time of the move, Nobuhide Oda, descendant of Chikazane in the seventeenth generation, acquired sufficient wealth and military power to challenge the family of a rival daimyo, the Imagawa, from assuming control over the immediately adjoining province of Mikawa. At the same time, Nobuhide also took the precaution of pledging cash contributions to the poverty-stricken emperor Ogimachi in Kyoto, funds he specifically earmarked for the repair of the crumbling walls around the Imperial Palace. Ogimachi was much appreciative of this gesture of loyalty, and would repay it handsomely in court favors and strategically useful insider's information when it came time for Nobuhide's brilliant second son[2] to succeed the father.

With that son came the beginning of Japan's long-awaited deliverance from the anarchy to which its gods had relegated it for so long. At fifteen, on the death of his father in 1549, Nobunaga Oda inherited his clan's leadership and was soon recognized as a force with which all the neighboring daimyos would one day have to contend. A wild youth who callously disregarded the established social canons of his time, he cared not at all for the finer points of etiquette or the sort of deportment expected in the upper circles of the local society to which his position entitled him. Vested with a

---

[2]The firstborn son would be killed at the Battle of Nagashima in 1574.

samurai's sword in an age when such a blade was longer than a fifteen-year-old carrier was tall, he would never lose the love of this traditional weapon of the warrior class. Frugal by habit, the youth was capable of lavishness when the occasion called for a generous display of munificence. Far more importantly, he possessed a mind endowed with genius, especially in military affairs, a gift eventually enabling him to become a master of both politics and of men.

All the great provincial lords dreamed of a single overriding goal during the civil wars that continued to ravage the country while Nobunaga grew to manhood. By extending power into neighboring provinces and coming to control the loyalty and resources of the samurai of their defeated opponents, each daimyo envisioned broadening his authority until he reached the capital and, once there, to rule over the entire country, if not as the holder of the still hugely venerated title of shogun, then at least to monopolize the actual governance of the country. When the neighboring Yoshimoto Imagawa actually undertook a drive that might accomplish this grand design, the now-grown Nobunaga Oda, the warlord of Owari province, resolved to beat him to it.

After destroying Imagawa's army in a brilliant attack at Okehazama in Owari province, Nobunaga was himself positioned within striking distance of Kyoto. Knowing it to be only a matter of time before either the local samurai wrecked the city or someone else captured and claimed it, the emperor Ogimachi, in 1568, gave Nobunaga, who had by now taken over his entire home province of Owari, his imperial blessings to try to enter the imperial capital. Remembering with gratitude the generosity of the warrior's father, the sovereign felt he might trust the son to respect the inviolability of the monarchy. Though he himself commanded no power, and frankly didn't expect to be involved in the administration of the country, Ogimachi viewed Nobunaga as the man most capable of assuming the real power that the still breathing but now-enfeebled shogunate had been unable to wield for as long as anyone could remember.

After battling his way past the remaining warlords between his own seat and Kyoto, during which he captured eighteen castles,

Nobunaga finally reached the city. In a token act to preserve at least a symbolic tie with its greater past, Nobunaga confirmed the crumbling Ashikaga shogunate (although he deposed the incumbent generalissimo and put in a new one), for a time even attempting to renovate it so the institution might come to possess at least a shadow of the glory it once held. However, he himself issued orders completely independently of the shogunal administration, an independence it was clear he meant to preserve. In what time the capital's new master could spare from the cares of his complex military administration, Nobunaga ordered lavish new quarters to be built for the emperor, and grew to take childlike delight in the visits he made to his sovereign within the grounds of the elegant new palace.

Unhappily for the Nobunaga-supported shogun, pride and ambition overcame what should have been keener judgment tempered by gratitude. In concert with disgruntled daimyo, using household troops still under his own command, Yoshiaki Ashikaga conspired to bring about the downfall of the upstart warlord from Owari. Perhaps predictably, the dictator could never have shown deference to the shogun, and Nobunaga was finally forced to admit failure and turn Yoshiaki out of office, ending nearly two and a half centuries of the Ashikaga shogunal dynasty.

Sadly, Nobunaga's relations with the emperor deteriorated after the initial sweetness and filial walks in the imperial gardens. Soon after taking control of the capital, Nobunaga started subtly to pressure the emperor into abdicating, the warlord's probable intent being to signal to the rest of the provincial lords the fact that he now reigned supreme over political *and* imperial events. Nobunaga clearly indicated he was willing to pay the considerable expense involved in not only the elaborate abdication rites, but also in the soon-to-follow and even more expensive enthronement ceremonies for Ogimachi's successor. But Ogimachi had a mind of his own. He refused to abdicate and remained firmly on the throne. The sovereign possessed his own still considerable symbolic authority, and used it to mollify the dictator by offering him high court rank and the post of imperial adviser, honorifics that Nobunaga was human enough to jump at. The acquisitive warlord was also awarded a prized piece of sweet-smelling *ranjatai* wood as a token marking his new stations. This particular imperial souvenir became the central highlight of Nobunaga's rapidly growing treasure house.

Having secured his position, Nobunaga now embarked on his real task—and the primary reason he is so firmly enshrined in Japan's pantheon of heroes. What this product of Fujiwara genes envisioned was a nation entirely reformed, cleared of both the feuding daimyo lords and, most particularly, the ever-meddlesome Buddhist priests for whom Nobunaga harbored special contempt and reserved a special fate. So, to have fewer noble warlords with whom to deal, he ordered those who had opposed him on his rise to power to commit mass seppuku—the honorable but grisly self-mortification reserved for the upper classes—an order with which they were obliged by the samurai social code to comply. In reference to the troublesome clerics, the dictator was recorded to have voiced his disgust: "If I do not take them away now, this great trouble will be everlasting . . . how can they [the priests] be vigilant against evil, or maintain the right?" The priests were simply trussed on spits and roasted alive. Christianity and its practitioners, the fast-growing sect introduced into the country by the Jesuit missionaries, found themselves, temporarily at least, exempted from his housecleaning; apparently Nobunaga admired the puritanical streak that distinguished the sect, as well as the fact that it was reported to him that the foreign faith acted as a "tonic" on his troops.

The one burr, albeit an immense one, still under his saddle was the threat from the yet-unbowed northern coastal clans. Gathering up his army of over 100,000 warriors, he put into practice a long-standing admiration for the efficiency of the newfangled firearms. He also used brilliant tactics that more than offset his equally dedicated enemy. Placing his legions in ranks—with the lowest-caste troops in the front as befitted their relative disposability—Nobunaga sent his musketeers to bowl down sixteen thousand of the sword-swinging cream of the north's finest cavalry troops at the Battle of Narashino. To nobody's surprise, the musket permanently became the army's weapon of choice even at the expense of horse and sword. Henceforth, Nobunaga controlled almost the whole of the country, with only a few scattered pockets of local resistance left to nip at his flanks. In 1581, the triumphant dictator presided over a glorious review of what at the time was probably the world's most disciplined and capable army: twenty thousand brilliantly caparisoned troops, riding at full gallop in front of the reviewing stand where the proud and now invincible Nobunaga enjoyed the inestimable honor of the imperial presence at his side.

One year later, at the zenith of this meteoric career and when his generals were laconically mopping up the few remaining hold-out daimyo, Nobunaga was struck down at the age of forty-nine. It was apparently a chance act of bloody treachery by one of his lieutenants, committed for reasons that have never been fully explained but seemed to have involved obscure jealousies and political intrigues. The killing may indeed have been only the solitary act of a deranged minion, but it opened the path for the second of the trio to make his way into Japan's pantheon.

Not only was the still-not-recovered country fortunate in having experienced Nobunaga Oda's steadying grip, but that the man who succeeded him was available immediately to take over the revolution Nobunaga started was a national blessing of the rarest kind. In truth, it is to the dictator's association with Hideyoshi Toyotomi, often called the Japanese Napoleon and regarded today as perhaps the greatest figure in his nation's history, that the awesome achievement of permanently ending five centuries of civil conflict must be credited.

The most surprising fact about Hideyoshi was what he was not: He was *not* born of the nobility, either major or minor, a class that both before and after him was the wellspring of virtually all figures of substance and leadership in Japanese history. His father was a farmer, Yanosuke Nakamura, of Owari, the same province into which the Oda family had settled. Fate had decreed that Nakamura was to serve as a retainer in the Oda family's service. The latter were then only minor aristocrats, but an almost unbridgeable gulf nonetheless separated anyone belonging to the lowly peasant caste from his highborn betters. To escape the inevitable obscurity that his birth mandated, the youthful Hideyoshi left the land and enlisted as a foot soldier, an infantryman, in the Oda militia. Very nearly everything worked against him even in that lowly and brutal

undertaking: his insignificant birthright, his complete lack of education, even his appearance—contemporary accounts of his life almost
unanimously agree that, more than anything else, Hideyoshi looked
like a monkey.

But destiny's spark struck when the teenage soldier was brought
to Nobunaga's attention by being promoted sandal-bearer to his
lordship, a position obtained through the memory of the good reputation of Hideyoshi's hard-working father. Nobunaga soon came to
realize that the uncommonly brash and outspoken soldier-servant
might have military abilities as great as they were rare; that
Nobunaga assigned higher value to these talents than he did to the
social conventions dictating the "proper" role of inferiors was to
have tremendous consequences for the future of Japan. When
Hideyoshi came into Nobunaga's service, the general was on the
verge of the military journey that would take him to Kyoto and the
position of dictator over the country, and Hideyoshi's attachment
to his liege would through a series of steady advancements and
promotions eventually place him at Nobunaga's right hand as ranking heir to the immense authority the dictator possessed at the time
of his assassination.

When his mentor was murdered, Hideyoshi was off in the western part of Honshu leading a campaign against daimyo who had not
yet been neutralized or destroyed. Hurrying back to Kyoto in the
then record time of seven days, he skillfully made an end-run around
Nobunaga's two sons, who little expected their father's lowborn but
decisively successful general to dare usurp what they considered
their birthright. In truth, few Japanese had ever risen so far on the
social ladder from so low, and Hideyoshi's success was a matter of
not inconsiderable stress to courtiers and samurai shocked at the
very thought of this son of peasants—landowners or not—in military command of the nation. But once having captured Nobunaga's
mantle, Hideyoshi's master plan for the future of Japan could be
summed up succinctly: He wished to freeze society into a totally
inflexible state based on the existing (but up to this time still mini-
mally fluid) caste system. The methods the military genius employed
to fulfill this vision ran the gamut from unthreatening reasonable-
ness, where that guise would achieve his ends, to the most wanton,

callous, blood-curdling barbarism the Japanese people had ever seen perpetrated by a legitimate central government.

His edicts bore on the lives of every citizen. The traditional warrior-farmer-artisan-merchant caste structure was set as a hereditary framework, with absolutely no movement allowed between ranks. Vertical mobility had never been easy in pre-Hideyoshi Japan, as was the case with virtually all societies at the time, but it had been possible, Hideyoshi himself the obvious and ironic example that skill and talent were occasionally the ticket to a higher station in life for a lucky few. No more. From now on peasants were prohibited from leaving the land, villagers weren't allowed to migrate to the cities, and anyone caught attempting to thwart these rules was liable to immediate execution in a manner designed not only to punish but more importantly to deter repetition from those witnessing these revolting legalized murders. Hideyoshi also came up with a splendidly effective way to keep the still-uppity daimyo under control: He ingeniously required their periodic presence in Kyoto, theoretically to symbolically renew their vows of allegiance to the throne. Those he considered dangerous he forced to leave their families in the capital as prisoners in gilded cages, hostages who could and would be instantly and bloodily dispatched on the arrival of news that their husbands were up to any antistate, which is to say anti-Hideyoshi, activities.

Opposed, like his predecessor, to Buddhist meddling in state affairs—apparently endemic to the priests ever since the faith arrived on Japan's shores so many centuries before—Hideyoshi nonetheless cultivated the Jesuits and tolerated their Christian converts. The only feature of Christianity at which he publicly snorted was its ridiculous insistence that a man should take only one consort. "If this could be changed," he was reported to have said, "I would convert to Christianity myself." That's as may be.

The immediate results of his draconian social revolution were the opposite of what might be expected: The country prospered mightily, as both rural and urban dwellers got on with their lives in an environment largely rid of the predators who had for so long turned much of the country into a wasteland. Not only were the cities rebuilt when the daily and dangerous nuisance of banditry was finally controlled and the farmers were again able to count on normal planting cycles, but a goodly portion of the money that these safer conditions generated found its way from the newly gerrymandered provinces into Hideyoshi's treasury. The result was a Kyoto that again wore, after so many centuries of neglect, a mantle more beautiful than any with which it had ever been graced, even than at the height of the Heian aristocracy of Lady Murasaki. Meanwhile, off on the horizon stood Hideyoshi's most grandiose dream: the conquest of east Asia to serve as a buffer against the rest of the outside world, whose influences Hideyoshi viewed only as an implacable threat to the essential spirit of Japan.

Life during this time of transformation, while punctuated by many of the horrors with which ignorance and violence always disfigure society, was still marked by progress in many of its corners. Remarkable strides were made in agriculture, manufacturing, and, perhaps most serendipitously, in the arts.

Kyoto remained indisputably the source for and center of Japan's developing new civilization. Aside from its imperial establishment, the capital continued as the heart of the country's peculiarly Japanized but now much subdued Buddhism, as well as the native Shinto faith. The city was home to the largest and richest ecclesiastical institutions, and in and around Kyoto a spectrum of sects took root in the hills. As in the cathedrals of medieval Europe, inviolable shelter could be found within their compound walls, and defeated soldier and retired imperial minister alike sought refuge there to end their days in prayer and piety, days in which simple reflection replaced sword and wine and pleasures of the flesh.

Although the artisan had occupied a low caste for centuries, he had never before been legally immobilized in the despised status, a permanence imposed by Hideyoshi's social engineering. Though lacking in status, craftsmen brought ceramics, lacquerwork, gilding, bronze casting, engraving, swordmaking, and goldsmithing to a stunning level of excellence—the surviving handiworks of the era even today among the artistic wonders of the world. Most such artisans labored anonymously in hidden villages at a single category of objects until, after many generations, the art inherent in the craft seemed almost to be born into the worker's hands. Lacquerware, a technique discovered around the beginning of the ninth century, owed its excellence in large part to the generous yield of the lacquer-tree forests around Echizen and the skill of the local workers in extracting the milk-white virgin sap that flowed from these trees. Eventually, various schools of lacquerware sprang up, one specializing in gold finishes, another in silver, others in reproducing the birds and insects and flowers in the world surrounding the craftsmen's hard lives.

Progress in medical knowledge far outstripped that which had developed in Christian society by the onset of its Age of Reason. In particular, the Chinese-developed practice of acupuncture, the methodical insertion of needles into the body to relieve all manner of ailments, was greatly improved when adopted by the Japanese. This humane and effective treatment, coupled with herbal medicines and the relatively higher degree of emphasis the Japanese put on cleanliness, made many illnesses of the era not quite the inevitable death sentences they were in Europe.

As for the lives of the small wedge at the top of Kyoto's court world, their indulgences and fripperies took that society ever farther from any kind of social utility save the historical preservation of the rarefied pastimes by which their days were rigidly delineated. Among the divertisements engaged in to stave off boredom-induced madness were games involving guessing the provenance of unmarked vials of rare and expensive perfumes. Standing for flirtation in this hothouse court culture was a graceful flick of the kimono sleeve, its message dependent on the precise composition of the infinitely classifiable elements of the flutter. A maid at court might even find herself promoted to maid of honor—even imperial concubine—if her felicitously wrought poem brought a moment's amusement to powerful ears. The ethereality of the court was a universe far removed from the politically charged milieu of the dictators.

In 1586, four years after Nobunaga's death, Ogimachi abdicated the throne at the age of seventy, freely resigning in favor of his grandson, Go-Yozei. The new emperor confirmed Hideyoshi as kampaku, the post Ogimachi had given him a year earlier and which the lowborn warlord probably thought of as merely a stepping-stone to the higher and far more meaningful military office of shogun. The title of kampaku had traditionally only been conferred upon members of the Fujiwara family, a technicality Hideyoshi overcame by having a compliant but authentic Fujiwara formally adopt him. As adoption was common and accepted, the transparent maneuver was recognized by the court as legitimate and the title was thus conferred under an umbrella of legitimacy. To ensure the ascendency of his own adopted son, Hidetsugu, Hideyoshi resigned the title of kampaku in the boy's favor, himself assuming the honorific of *taiko*, the title taken by a kampaku when succeeded in office by his son.[3] As for the shogunate itself, the new taiko decided to bide his time.

Hideyoshi very likely was the richest man in Japanese history up to that time, his ownership of gold and silver mines ensuring the financial wherewithal to support a lavish way of life. The regent built himself a grand palace called the Mansion of Assembled Pleasures, its perimeter wall running some eight miles. The central house was so high that the golden dragons decorating the roof were said to "sing songs among the clouds," and the formal tearoom that was Hideyoshi's special joy was covered in gold leaf from ceiling to floor, the late afternoon sun reflecting off the precious metal suffusing his intimate teas with a mellow light not to be found anywhere else in the islands. The dictator's residence thoroughly and shamelessly outshone the palace he himself had recently restored for the emperor, but the mansion was overpowered by an even grander castle he built in Osaka. It was a golden-towered structure and at the time one of the largest man-made works in the world. Everything in it that would be touched by or come into the personal orbit of its master was crafted from pure gold. Hideyoshi's passion for gold was indulged without any consideration whatsoever for the cost involved, his personal purse a bottomless reservoir providing for the fulfillment of every whim.

Soon the supremely rich warlord was receiving social visits from his sovereign, Go-Yozei probably tactfully refraining from comment on the degree by which the splendor of the palace of his ex-kampaku outshone that of his own. In any event, Hideyoshi, as a dutiful

---

[3] As corrupted in English to "tycoon," the title has historically been associated almost singularly with Hideyoshi himself.

servant of the dynasty, made it his practice to see that the emperor and court were showered with lavish presents, the imperial person unabashedly held in a high degree of awe and reverence by the taiko. The largesse thus parted with made little appreciable dent in Hideyoshi's reserves; his horde of gold and silver was said to be sufficient to fill a courtyard of his palace three hundred yards long, the gold alone estimated to have totaled sixteen thousand pounds, perhaps $100 million in modern currency. Whatever presents he gave his sovereign were more than matched by those he bestowed on his own family. One contemporary called him "a river, an ocean of magnanimity, [one who] strove for magnificence in all things." Surely no Japanese had ever before or since so thoroughly cloaked his low birth in such high raiments.

In 1590, after Hideyoshi completed the military pacification of the home islands with the destruction of the still-powerful army of the Hojo family (a clan distantly related to the Hojo regents of the early feudal era), the country emerged, literally for the first time, as a truly unified nation. Hideyoshi could now begin the realization of his final dream, the conquest of the Orient, and he would start with the relatively unimportant Korean peninsula, considered merely a stepping-stone to eventual conquest of the Celestial Empire— China itself. Like the powerful American general in a war that would come nearly four centuries later, Hideyoshi, too, at last met his match in the bottomless armed might of this behemoth enemy.

Hideyoshi's expeditionary force crossed the Sea of Japan—the Nihon-kai—landing in Pusan in the spring of 1592. The proud China quite understandably felt Korea should be subservient to her will alone, such always having been the case, and when the successful Japanese military forces approached the Yalu (the river that separates Korea and China) after six months of fighting up the peninsula, the million-strong army of the declining but not-quite-moribund Ming empire leapt on it in force. The Ming dynasty may have been mightily sick, and would in fact soon be destroyed by the Manchus, but the Japanese were still not able to match the sheer numbers that could be fielded by China's leaders. Confident when steamrolling over the Koreans, Hideyoshi's 150,000-man expeditionary force was unexpectedly and savagely pushed back down the peninsula. A second Japanese thrust two years later was no more successful than the first. The struggle ended in a stalemate, the chastened taiko temporarily forced to shelve his plans for foreign conquest, it being clear that his army's momentum now lacked the fire with which it began the campaign.

In 1598, peace negotiations were in progress between the two Pacific powers, but Hideyoshi's death intervened.[4] After the dictator's body was entombed—under a solid gold shroud, of course—the Board of Administrators, serving as governing guardian for Hideyoshi's five-year-old son (born to the taiko after his adopted son Hidetsugu's promotion to kampaku), realized an unavoidable power struggle at home was going to require all their energies and craft, and wisely negotiated a face-saving peace with China. From this moment, Japan would turn inward with a passion the world had never before seen in such a powerful state. The third member of the triumvirate, the one whose name would define a nearly three-century-long era in Japanese history, was about to build an invisible but utterly impervious wall around the Sun Goddess's empire.

If Nobunaga can be credited with laying the framework for a centralized Japanese state, and Hideyoshi with making that state, Ieyasu Tokugawa can be said to have carved the basic principles of centralization into a lasting legacy. A popular Japanese saying gives a fair summation of how the three men differed: In comparing the disunited Japan to a voiceless songbird, Nobunaga would say, "I'll make it sing"; Hideyoshi would threaten, "I'll kill it if it doesn't sing"; whereas Ieyasu would promise, "I'll wait until it *does* sing." And because of this ability to wait until the time was right before taking what he wanted, Ieyasu succeeded in dispatching all his foes. In founding the nation's third shogunal dynasty (after the Kamakura [Yoritomo-Hojo] and the Ashikaga), Ieyasu Tokugawa combined Nobunaga's force of personality and strength of character with Hideyoshi's ruthless administrative and military talents, establishing

---

[4]Coincidentally, only a year earlier the last of the hereditary Ashikaga shoguns, the Yoshiaki Ashikaga who had been forced by Nobunaga to resign his office in 1573, had died.

a shogunate that would last for 264 years before an entirely new set of forces on the nation would require his legacy to be supplanted.

The Japan that Ieyasu and his successors would close to the world was one of the strongest nations on earth; when those doors were broken open again in the nineteenth century, it was among the weakest. But even had Japan's new master realized the price his islands would pay in order to keep the nation's essential character unsullied by "barbarian" influences, indications are that the brilliant shogun-to-be wouldn't have done anything differently.

Ieyasu Tokugawa sprang from neither the minor nobility from whence Nobunaga came nor the peasant background of Hideyoshi. He was rooted in the country's highest aristocracy, a member of the Minamoto clan in whose proud ranks all the nation's shoguns had claimed membership, the family that had flourished so spectacularly at the beginning of the feudal period.[5] Ieyasu's twig of the Minamoto family tree had settled in the hamlet of Tokugawa, in Serata village of Kotsuke province in Honshu's eastern Kanto highlands, hence the adopted name for the cadet off-shoot clan of the aristocracy. Ten generations removed from the great eleventh-century military hero, Yoshiie Minamoto, the family lived in Mikawa province, on the east shore of Ise Bay in the vicinity of Nagoya. As generations passed, they managed by alliance and prowess to gain possession over about half of the province's territory.

When in the middle of the sixteenth century their control was challenged by Nobuhide Oda, Nobunaga's father, the threatened Tokugawa sought help from the powerful Imagawa family. In 1547, the youngest member of the family, five-year-old Ieyasu Tokugawa, was sent to the Imagawa stronghold as a kind of earnest money payment to be held in escrow for Imagawa help. Unfortunately, Ieyasu was captured by Nobuhide's troops on his way to hostage-hood, and remained an Oda prisoner for the next twelve years. Only when he persuaded his captors of his harmless intentions was he allowed to return home. The years under Oda control, however,

[5]Like the two earlier shogunal lines, the Tokugawa were also descended from a cadet branch of the house of the ninth-century emperor Seiwa.

apparently convinced the young samurai of that clan's invincibility, evidenced by the fact that, after some initial revenge-taking, he allied himself with this great fighting daimyo family.

Over the years, through his enormous military talents, the freed Ieyasu was able to extend his power—basically at the expense of the Imagawa family—until he was master of the entire Kanto, the great alluvial plain on which the modern city of Tokyo sits. First known to Hideyoshi as a strong proponent of Nobunaga's rule, he eventually became the kampaku's chief lieutenant, trusted so utterly by his master that at one famous meeting the senior gave the junior his sword to hold, in that era a symbolic but rare act of complete trust between one man and another.

But Ieyasu was not expected to be Hideyoshi's heir, at least not in the dynastic sense. Like virtually all larger-than-life leaders in the predemocratic era, Hideyoshi wished to be succeeded by a son. In an age of high infant mortality, Hideyoshi unfortunately found himself without an heir after the death of his firstborn, a son, and appointed his grown nephew and adopted son Hidetsugu, as kampaku. The move was made not only out of consideration of dynastic continuity, but also to ensure against chaos in case of his own unexpected or untimely demise.

But eventually one of Hideyoshi's concubines gave birth to a boy-child, Hideyori, a natural son Hideyoshi quite naturally regarded as his primary heir. At this juncture, evidence suggests that the taiko's final years may have been clouded by at least a degree of madness: He not only ordered Hidetsugu to commit seppuku, but so as to eliminate any possible rivals to Hideyori, Hideyoshi commanded his grandnephews/grandsons—Hidetsugu's sons—stabbed to death along with thirty of their equally innocent consorts. The bodies were all unceremoniously dumped in a mass grave, that of Hidetsugu placed at the very bottom of the victims at the taiko's special order.

When Hideyoshi died in 1598, his five-year-old son and heir obviously wasn't able to wield his father's authority, so to guide Hideyori until he came of age and to act in the boy's stead, Hideyoshi had decreed that a five-man council of regency—the Board of Five Administrators—be established, all of its members taking an oath of loyalty to Hideyori's right of succession. Before his death, the taiko had no reason to suspect that his chief lieutenant and most trusted ally among the five councillors wasn't satisfied with the substantial fief he had carved out for himself in the Kanto, an area vying with the plain around Osaka as the richest in Japan. But within fourteen months of Hideyoshi's passing, Ieyasu did indeed strike decisively to gain the entirety of the empire.

Exploiting political machinations between the five administrator-generals, all of whom were furiously trying to out-maneuver each other for their own aggrandizement at Hideyori's expense, Ieyasu trumped the lot of them. Allying himself with those who freely chose to join him, he slaughtered most of the remainder at the famous Battle of Sekigahara, the seminal contest fought on a plain sixty miles west of the capital. Ieyasu allowed Hideyori to retain the now politically empty title of kampaku while he took the far grander accolade of Barbarian-Suppressing Generalissimo for himself. It was 1603, and the first year of the Tokugawa shogunate had begun.

With this short look at how the top rungs of the government had developed by the beginning of the seventeenth century, we should return to our primary focus, the emperors, seeing how these almost invisible men in the calm of the hurricane's eye fared while such significant events were swirling around, but rarely touching, their lives.

Stated forthrightly, Japan's emperors cannot be said to have had the slightest personal effects on the outcome of the political deeds that had transpired between the rise of Nobunaga Oda and the final victory of Ieyasu Tokugawa. Key to understanding why imperial power in this era was nonexistent is the realization that the institution of the monarchy very simply lacked either the military strength or the resources required to wield great power in Japan's samurai centuries. Indeed, after Nobunaga occupied the capital in 1568, the emperors no longer even possessed the freedom to bestow or withhold their blessings on one military leader as against another. The monarchs instead were sequestered in their palace as if in a cage, leading lives entirely cut off from the world of rough-

and-tumble samurai power plays, their totem value now called on only occasionally to be exercised in the aquatint splash of religious rite.

The bodily needs, at least, of the monarch and his court began early in this era to merit more punctilious attention, if for no other reason than that the three men who in succession commanded the empire believed it beneath national dignity for their sovereign to exist in a disreputable state of physical want. Still, there was never, *never* any question of either abolishing or usurping the throne, the strongest evidence extant that it was still considered even by men of such outsized pride to be the most important source of the political *authority*. The fact still remained that any significant act encompassed by the dictators could be completely legitimized only if it was carried out in the name of the sacred sovereign.

Despite the material irrelevance of the imperial institution, the monarchy nonetheless remained surrounded by the most scrupulously observed ceremony. A distinctive, rarefied court language developed over the centuries of imperial isolation, with a special deification distinguishing all references to the throne: The emperors themselves used a unique personal pronoun, similar in application to the royal and papal "we" of Europe, but reserved solely for the sovereign. Not only was this character—pronounced "chin" and borrowed from the Chinese word meaning "I"—the emperor's alone to use, but when written or printed it was customarily followed with a blank space, symbolizing the unbridgeable gulf between sovereign and subject.

Though today it bears only the memory of the millennium-long status it proudly held as the imperial capital, at the turn of the seventeenth century, Kyoto was still very much the epicenter of the island-nation over which its sovereigns never ceased, at least symbolically, to reign. Edo, later called Tokyo, would start to grow in a significant way only after Ieyasu made the city his shogunal capital in the early 1600s, and Osaka was still more a samurai-dominated camp city huddled around its heavily fortified castle than a truly multifaceted urban center. Though Kammu's Heian capital of imperial consequence was by the sixteenth century only a memory, it was still the closest thing Japan possessed to a first-rank metropolis.

A good starting point in visualizing the Kyoto of the beginning of the Tokugawa shogunate is by stating what it was not. Because of the presence of the imperial institution and its attendant army of courtiers, it was a place unarguably vested with a luxury and dignity—and, most importantly, a past—exceeding that found elsewhere in the country. Still, it was *not* in any sense the equivalent of a Western royal capital of the time, nor did it approach the overwhelming splendor found in the mighty Chinese monarchs' Forbidden City. Kyoto's principal buildings resembled Shinto shrines far more than they did the Western archetypical vision proper to a king's venue. The imperial enclosure, called the *Gosho*, was peppered with structures if not majestic then of infinitely refined taste and understated elegance, but few of its components achieved any immense degree of antiquity for the simple and unavoidable reason that fires periodically razed the notoriously flammable wooden pavilions. Neither did the imperial quarters themselves possess comforts much further in advance of those to which the majority of the Japanese people were heir: paper walls and braziers permitted perhaps even less wintertime comfort in the salons of the sovereign's mansions than they did in the more modest but cozier dwelling spaces of his subjects.

The emperors did possess a modicum of privacy, a coveted rarity in the Japan of both past and present. The walls surrounding the imperial enclosure ensured that the imperial existence was lived free from the *karma*-disrupting gaze of curious eyes, and, even more important than personal privacy, they served to add to the sovereign's security in an age when Kyoto's streets were the open playground of cutthroats and miscreants. The gates piercing these enclosing walls lent their name—*mikado* in Japanese—to the principal inhabitant of the compound, in much the same way as the Sublime Porte of the Ottoman sultan's palace in Constantinople came to stand for the Ottoman court itself.

The Gosho that housed the imperial retinue during the early Edo period had not been built on the site of the emperors' original Heian palace, the Daidairi, or "Great Inner Enclosure," a palace constructed farther to the north on the city's geometric checkerboard. After the Daidairi burned, the whole court was packed up and moved to its new location, a site that had housed a supplementary "detached" palace since earliest times and had also served as a refuge for sovereigns when disaster struck their main quarters. In 1331, the emperor Kogen became the first to use this modern location for parts of his main residence, his palace lasting until 1854 when it, too, burned and was replaced by the set of buildings that are seen today.

Rather than a single palatial structure embracing all the functions of the imperial institution, the twenty-seven acres of the Kyoto palace grounds were set with an abundance of special religious pavilions, free-standing reception halls, audience chambers, and living quarters. Many served purely ceremonial functions, a few housed the Imperial Guard, and still others were built for the great *kuge* families, the hereditary caste of courtiers popularly known as the "public families." Actual living quarters were separated in many cases only by *shoji,* the semitransparent paper sliding screens that acted as walls in the palace's interiors. The higher the occupant's rank, the closer his personal rooms were to those of the godhead emperor at the center of this imperial hive. And that center—the day-to-day residential palace of the emperor, unceremoniously named the "Ordinary Palace"—was the reason for all else's existence. Far less majestic—or less gaudy, as a purist might put it— than the palace Hideyoshi built for himself in another part of the city, it was nonetheless a beautifully rendered structure by any standard, employing the very highest of ancient Japanese skilled arts and crafts in its construction.

Buried deeply within the residential palace was the *yon-no-otodo,* the two-step platform-room that served as the emperor's sleeping space. The monarch himself passed the quiet nights on twenty-one thicknesses of tatami mats, an arrangement theoretically guaranteeing his superior comfort but at the same time forming a pile high enough that he might, if not careful, injure himself in a nocturnal spill. Specially designed floorboards called *naruita* surrounded the sleeping area. When trod upon, the planks emitted a characteristic squeaking sound designed to warn of approaching courtiers or of possible danger; similar naruita announced visitors approaching the imperial audience chamber. Adjoining his quarters, a garden and artificial lake gave the usually underemployed sovereign a pleasant vista upon which to gaze in his plentiful spare time.

When an emperor abdicated, a practice that continued right up to modern times,[6] he was obligated to take leave of the principal palace to make room for its new occupant. This didn't result in any kind of deprivation for the abdicator; on the contrary, he could now escape the grindingly exact round of ceremonies that only a reigning emperor could fulfill as well as the endless audiences begged by courtiers and high officials. If he wished, the abdicator could also pretty much control his heir—or heirs: As during the long-past period of insei, sometimes it happened that several abdicated emperors were simultaneously jockeying for their heirs' attention. The specially designed residence inhabited by these ex-monarchs was called the Sento Gosho, or "Retired Emperors' Palace," whose charms, luxury, and privacy often exceeded those enjoyed by the reigning sovereign.

Though the emperor occupied the center around which all else in the court spun, the lives of the other inhabitants of the imperial establishment were played out quite independently, motivated by the momentum gained through centuries of custom and ceremony. The highest-ranking courtiers resident in the imperial village— representing the officials of the Imperial Household—were the kuge, holding this status by virtue of birth, themselves ranked according to their nearness to the throne and antiquity of family and imperial service. In the Heian period, from which most of them traced their courtly origins, the kuge were the administrators of the state bureaucracy, but as the monarchs came to have less and less to do with the governance of the country, the kuge role changed to that of simple courtier. Still, the relative ranking among the kuge was of utmost importance and it was structured in finely delineated strata. The greatest kuge families, the Fujiwara[7] and the Minamoto, functioned as the nation's highest-ranking nobility, although after the Heian period they were certainly not its most powerful civil or

[6]Specifically, through emperor number 119; Kokaku was in 1816 the last to do so.

[7]At the time of the Meiji Restoration, 96 of the 137 kuge houses claimed descent from the Fujiwara clan.

military figures, roles assumed by the newly empowered military nobility, the provincial daimyo warlords. The five highest branches of the Fujiwara clan were alone allowed to provide candidates for the offices of kampaku, the emperor's principal adviser/servant.

The kuge bloodstrain remained almost undiluted, with virtually no outsiders being allowed to penetrate its closed ranks. Younger sons were encouraged to become Buddhist priests or else to start their own non-kuge families, it being understood that such pruning was necessary to maintain the courtier population within reasonable bounds. As with the British aristocracy, the kuge code of etiquette could only be learned from childhood if one was to be accepted as authentic within the peer group. No adult outsider could hope to master the fantastically complex intricacies and precise manners and mannerisms that were the stuff and lifeblood of the imperial courtier class.

The primary reason for the courtiers' existence (although sometimes such justification must have seemed more theoretical than substantive) was to serve the succession of men who occupied the pinnacle of the nation's sharply defined social pyramid. The emperors of postfeudal Japan, those who reigned during the Tokugawa shogunate, the Edo period, are known in Japan as the *kinsei* sovereigns, the emperors of "modern times." Together they totaled thirteen men and two women and spanned the years from Go-Yozei's accession in 1586 to Komei's death in 1866, the latter bringing with it the ultimate destruction of the Tokugawa ascendancy.

The size of the imperial family also had to be controlled, not only to keep questions of succession relatively tidy but to ensure sufficient sums in the privy purse to meet the sovereign's needs. Just as in ancient times, the mere fact of descent from an emperor did not alone qualify one for membership in the imperial family. At the beginning of the Tokugawa period, the rules for inclusion in the nation's first family were remarkably similar to those that still hold today, with imperial status descending only through the male line, daughters ceasing on marriage to be considered imperial princesses. As with the British monarchy, the families of younger sons, beginning with the third generation removed from the sovereign, de-

scended to mere nobility, forsaking imperial status; grandsons generally remained imperial in case closer offspring to the emperor should
inadvertently predecease them or else not sire their own heirs. In
many cases cadet princes—younger, non-inheriting sons—were
adopted into the kuge, with the result that many of the courtier
families became, biologically speaking, just as royal as the first family
itself. An avenue commonly employed by Japanese cadet princes
(one not often utilized in Western royal families) was the practice
of entering the priesthood, in which case the incumbent was—
officially, at least—celibate and without issue who might muddy the
waters of succession.

Of tremendous impact on keeping the imperial family within
limits during this period was the wretchedly high rate of infant
mortality even in relatively clean Japan; the lack of understanding
of the dangers of infection was just as grave a threat to the highest
as it was to the lowest. Even by the late nineteenth century, only
five of the emperor Meiji's fifteen children survived into adulthood,
and it might be noted that matters affecting child mortality in the
imperial family in the later Tokugawa period appeared to have gone
downhill from the earlier part: Of the thirty-seven children of the
fifteenth-century emperor Go-Mizunoo, fully twenty-three lived
into adulthood.

The question of the role consorts played in Japan's imperial order
of affairs was considerably more complex than that which generally
held in Western royal families, and more complicated, constitutionally speaking, than it is in the present Japanese imperial family. In
the West, a queen or an empress was invariably the sovereign's wife,
unless she herself was a queen-regnant or an empress-regnant, meaning a woman who reigned in her own right. There were, in fact, two
such regnant empresses during the two and a half centuries of the
Tokugawa era, women whom we'll talk more about in a bit, but
suffice it to note here that female sovereigns were at this period a
decided anomaly in the Japanese imperial scheme of things.

As for the rank of empress-consort, the title was bestowed more
to indicate a woman's status and official standing than simply to
denote marriage to the emperor. The emperor's wife (he was allowed only one), called the chugu, may or may not have been given

the title of empress, kogo. An official empress-consort didn't even always exist, but acceptable heirs-designate to the throne were in no way dependent on having been born to such a woman; notably, most were not. Nonwifely consorts, called *ngoyo,* possessed far less status than the kogo, but a boy-child born to a ngoyo could be named heir—the critical factor for eventual sovereignty emanating solely from the imperial status of its father. A child born to the lowest-ranking palace concubine might be "adopted" by the high-ranking Fujiwara empress-consort to preserve the principle that, even though the emperors were indeed highly polygamous, the institution itself was adhering to the normal monogamous nuclear family structure of Japanese society. What mattered, though, was that the child be a valid descendant of the Sun Goddess, descended through the "unbroken" line of her successors. Incidentally, the official title of crown prince, *kotaishi,* wasn't necessarily formally bestowed on the designated heir apparent, nor, indeed, *was* there always such a designated heir named until after the emperor had one foot well into the grave.

The imperial quarters of 1600 were not a model of Western-style domesticity. Empresses did not live with their husbands, but were assigned a separate ceremonial palace called the Higyo-sha. Neither her own children nor those born to concubines (women of sufficient rank that their children were officially placed in the line of succession) would ordinarily live with the empresses in their quarters. Within the Gosho grounds, dormitory-pavilions were set aside to serve as quarters for the older princes and princesses, imperial fledglings who left their mothers' residences around the age of six. All the members of the imperial family would occasionally get together, either for regular religious ceremonies that formed a substantial part of and primary reason for their existence, or for informal familial visits.

What filled the personal lives of these gilded characters—the women decorated with intricately sculpted coiffeurs stiffened with camellia oil, the men whose high shaved foreheads were topped by long queues turned curiously up and fastened to the crowns of their heads—were matters of consequence only to those within their iron-bounded circle, having virtually no effect on the world outside their sanctuary. These daily routines were understandably of quite breathtaking import to people who had little to do but spend inordinate amounts of time worrying about the smallest of the complex code of social obligations and rules circumscribing their existence. Some historians assign a high degree of importance to the daily activities of the court, attaching merit to Kyoto's nobility for having brought forward ancient and graceful Japanese arts that would almost certainly have been forgotten or discarded without imperial patronage. But the fact remains that it is impossible to find another monarchy and court contemporary with Edo-era Japan so occupied with what must, in the final analysis, be called trivial pursuits that are quite unrelated to achieving any larger political purpose. Only those ceremonies of a religious nature or of unseen but still profound spiritual importance to the nation truly justified the existence of this court. Even those few nonreligious powers retained by the throne— powers that affected the court itself rather than the political life of the nation—were not actually carried out by the emperors themselves. What authority remained still in the hands of the monarchy was exercised almost exclusively by kuge officials in the emperors' names. The ultimate personal decision that a sovereign could make—whether or not to abdicate—was itself sometimes thwarted if such desire conflicted with what the shogun considered to be sufficient political reasons against it.

Shortly after the beginning of the Tokugawa era, the emperors would begin a period of almost total immobility—a time of rigid physical seclusion within the palace walls, an incarceration that wouldn't end until 1863. Historian Herschel Webb colorfully described the effective operating area of the emperor's existence at the time to that "about the size of the deck of a large modern aircraft carrier." So complete did the shogun's authority become over even the minutest phases of imperial life that for more than two centuries Japan's monarchs were literally little more than prisoners. They were men ignorant of the practical matters of the world, men whose physical apartness was matched only by that endured by the Roman Catholic pontiffs between the fall of their papal states in 1870 and the establishment of an autonomous Vatican in 1929.

The ceremonial obeisances that occupied the sovereign were in the main Shinto, tasks comprising very nearly the entirety of the official work of the imperial family as well as that of his courtiers, who had served as the primary "keepers" of these rites through centuries of courtly existence. The duties were held to be of profound importance to the nation by the men who arranged them and essentially lived for them, priestly officials typically ascribing a concrete good to justify not only their unproductive but symbolically important rites, but also their very existence. After the unification of Japan through the talents of Nobunaga, Hideyoshi, and Ieyasu, the court was at least no longer quite the pauperized affair it had been under the Ashikaga shoguns, when many of the imperial rituals had been suspended for lack of funds to pay for them, money essential for the elaborate costumes and props that were deemed vital to authenticate and validate the rites.

The grandest of all imperial solemnities, then as now, were the accession and enthronement rites of a reigning monarch and, finally, his funeral. The first two were both necessary for an emperor to be considered truly and well sovereign, but once a man—or woman— was enthroned, an event that usually occurred some years after accession, that person was then held to have been legitimately sovereign since the accession itself. Something analogous to this has been seen in the British system in modern times: The trauma that accompanied the abdication of King Edward VIII in 1936 was judged less painful because he hadn't yet been crowned, the implication being that Edward was somehow *less* a king because he hadn't actually been *ceremonially* crowned. In the Japanese arrangement, accession and enthronement rites were together, in historian Webb's words, a "compact binding the people to a single sovereign, and through him to Heaven's order and morality."

Since the majority of Tokugawa-era monarchs acceded because of the abdication, rather than the death, of their predecessors, the ceremony of abdication of the one was sometimes combined with the ceremony of accession of the other, the two rites together forming a sort of imperial extravaganza called the *juzen*. [8] Because accession didn't instantaneously follow a monarch's death—there

[8]Eleven of the sixteen accessions between 1586 and 1867 followed this order.

was no concept matching the Western notion of "the King is dead, long live the King"—an interregnum, its length mostly dependent on whether or not an official crown prince had been named and how many possible heirs were wrangling for the throne, separated all reigns. During the Edo period, such interregnums lasted anywhere from the sixty-seven days between the death of Go-Komyo and the accession of Gosai, to the six-day span between Momozono's death and Go-Sakuramachi's accession.[9]

Because Japanese custom did not mandate that a empress-consort was the only person eligible to provide an heir, the matter of who would accede to the throne was rarely clear-cut. Ideally, the choice of heir would be decided by the sovereign, in accord with the thinking that as he himself was Heaven's choice, then his choice of successor would also, automatically, have Heaven's vote. But when an emperor died young, or suddenly, or for whatever reason had failed to make manifest his choice of heir, the highest kuge officials, or sometimes even the shogun, had to step in to interpret Heaven's will according to the political requirements of the moment.

In addition to the supremely important rites surrounding the perpetuation of the dynasty, there were scores of other ceremonies and observances that couldn't be validly carried out without the imperial presence. Of those of the secondary rank, the rites observed on an annual basis were considered to be the most auspicious. They were held on a calendrical schedule beginning and ending with the winter solstice, the season that included a disproportionately high percentage of the emperor's chief ritual duties. Among the greatest and most colorful, the New Year's greeting to the court was held in the Purple Dragon Hall of the palace in an atmosphere of great pomp and seriousness of purpose. Following a token delegation of the highest-ranking courtiers making obeisance to their sovereign, the principals progressed for the concluding services to the palace's smaller Clear Cool Hall, named for the small stream that tinkled down a walled sluiceway near its outer steps. Afterward, a small celebration of the emperor's first handwriting of the new year and

---

[9]Since the Meiji Restoration, the Western custom has prevailed. The crown prince is instantly considered to accede at the moment of the emperor's death.

a poetry festival, the latter especially popular among the poetry-loving courtier class, topped off everyone's day.

The line between ceremonial duty and ordinary, everyday activities was blurred where the emperor's life was concerned. Just as the court of France's Louis XIV was specifically designed to institutionalize him and his dynasty's glory, so, too, were the pointedly hallowed rituals that permeated almost everything the Japanese emperors did, from practicing calligraphy to the stylized motions that accompanied their strolls around the gardens of the imperial compound.

For the overwhelming majority of the Japanese people, the shadowy throne was simply too far removed from their lives to be a real, understandable institution. Before Meiji's revolution, perhaps the closest the common people of Kyoto got to splendor was in 1588 when a *dai-chakai*, "Great Tea Ceremony," was performed by the famous tea master, Sen no-Rikyu. Several hundred thousand people, nearly the entire population of the capital, witnessed the ten-day-long ceremony, a rare spectacle to an audience to whom such entertainment was an all-but-alien concept.

Mass communication except among the literate elite did not exist at the time, and consequently there was no "news" of the court in anything like the modern sense. The Japanese were dimly aware that the institution of monarchy sat at the theoretical apex of the nation, but as the emperors had no involvement in the day-to-day running of the country, even the noncourtier provincial elite almost came to forget about the sovereigns in all but a religious sense. The monarch was the nation's living God, but he was otherwise totally divorced from ordinary concepts of reality. Ironically, inside each Japanese home was an emblem of the monarchy that might have reminded even the lowest subject of his emperor's distant existence. A *tokonoma*—a recess built into the wall of practically every inhabited place in the country and in which was displayed some small, usually humble treasure—was in theory the place reserved for a bed for the emperor should he ever decide to pay a visit.

With the ongoing entrenchment of Ieyasu Tokugawa's shogunate, the position of the throne continued its slide to ever deeper detachment from the national polity. Ieyasu's establishment of his own military dynasty was a perfectly straightforward Japanese variant of the nearly universal phenomenon of absolutist monarchies, except that Ieyasu's "dynasty" was, technically at least, only second in the land. Soon after he had consolidated his power with victory at the Battle of Sekigahara in 1600, Ieyasu began, under the ubiquitous crest of the famous Tokugawa hollyhock on his army's banners, his sweeping transformation of Japan, and in 1603 he accepted the title of sei-i-taishogun. To do so he employed the legalistic maneuver of asserting that the last Ashikaga shogun had willingly handed over to him the family office, a novel but effective manner of assumption of shogunal authority. The fact that the Tokugawa bakufu was the nation's largest landholder—in conjunction with its retainers, it owned over a quarter of Japan's land, including ports and cities— became, besides its founder's intellectual gifts, the unassailable basis of Tokugawa power.

The same year he ascended the shogunal throne, Ieyasu moved his administration to his home turf, Edo, or "Rivergate," thus beginning what became known as Japan's storied Edo period, a term very nearly synonymous with the Tokugawa shogunate itself. It should be remembered, however, that the legal capital of the country remained Kyoto, the seat (or the gilded prison, as it more accurately became) of the emperor, and that, theoretically, the shogunate was simply the military arm of the emperor's government. And as with previous shogunal dynasties, while the Tokugawa throttled the imperial voice down to the merest whisper, neither Ieyasu nor his successors ever contemplated seizing imperial authority for themselves.

In 1615, the shogunate issued a formal ordinance entitled "Laws Pertaining to the Nobility," codifying in seventeen carefully crafted articles how courtiers, as well as the emperor, must in future comport themselves. Among the constrictions it placed on the Kyoto imperial establishment was the injunction that "the emperor should devote himself, first and foremost, to study and learning," a convenient tool to discourage political meddling on the part of any future monarch who might forget the laws of political reality. It also removed one of the few remaining imperial privileges, that of granting honors and titles to distinguished ecclesiastical masters. In placing such direct restrictions on the court, the shogunal authorities for the first time made clear that it—the Edo bakufu—was the sole political court of last resort, even where it came to deciding the conduct of religious observances. Although all political organs of government had been removed to Edo, the shogunate set up a new office in Kyoto called the *shoshidai,* "shogunal deputy," ostensibly to guard the imperial interests but in reality to serve as the Tokugawa eyes and ears at court. The shoshidai also, incidentally, took over administration of all land owned by the imperial family, depriving them of even the power to control their estates, a power the bakufu saw fit to leave to even the most minor of clan chieftains.

This was the period when the final bits of political control over the country were still being pocketed by the Tokugawa. The remnants of the Hideyoshi faction, with the young taiko Hideyori as its symbolic rallying point, were finally wiped out by the Tokugawa army in a war fought in 1615 at the Hideyoshi stronghold of Osaka castle. When the immense fortress's defenders were finally overwhelmed by the attacking samurai of the shogun, young Hideyori Toyotomi committed seppuku before the attackers were able to take him prisoner. With the boy-taiko went the last major organized threat to the Tokugawa ascendancy. It also introduced a new ingredient into imperial-shogunal relations: If the new masters couldn't themselves *be* emperors, they could at least, so they figured, be the *progenitor* of emperors.

To this end, Ieyasu proposed that Kazuko, the daughter of his son Hidetada, should marry the emperor Go-Yozei's son, Go-Mizunoo, a marriage history has painted with a conspiratorial provenance. Ieyasu was said to have shocked the emperor with the proposal, a dynastic impertinence of the first order. But as the nation's religious leader was at this time so agitated by the growing threat of Christianity—by the early seventeenth century one out of every fifty Japanese had converted to the alien faith—Go-Yozei struck a deal with Ieyasu. If the shogun would rid the country of the Christian plague, he, the emperor, would agree to the marriage between the shogun's granddaughter and his son. Whether a sovereign and a Tokugawa would have been able to dicker quite so brazenly is historically problematical, especially as Ieyasu was known to be highly respectful if not of the person of the emperor then of the institution of the monarchy. What is clearly demonstrable, though, is that history records the shogun beginning to drive the foreign devils from the land with a single-mindedness of purpose, and that the marriage did eventually take place. Unfortunately, Ieyasu didn't live to see it, dying in 1616, but his son and successor, Hidetada, pressed for the fulfillment of the deal, and Kazuko was eventually brought to the palace for her marriage to Go-Mizunoo, which was, reportedly, a happy one.

Though Hidetada Tokugawa, following in his father's outsize footsteps, unremittingly worked at ridding the country of its foreign element, he nonetheless continued to hear from the palace that the undertaking wasn't progressing fast enough for the impatient and xenophobic Go-Mizunoo, a man who clearly regarded his position as the chief guardian of Japan's native virtues a primary part of the monarchy's much-depleted powers. Even after the shogun sent emissaries to Kyoto to keep the sovereign informed of the gradual re-Japanization of the country and to counsel imperial patience, the still-unsatisfied emperor continued to mutter deprecations against the bakufu. Determined to commit an act that would force the shogunal government to speed up what the sovereign felt should be its holy crusade, in 1629 the surprisingly assertive Go-Mizunoo caught Edo off-guard by abdicating. In his choice of successor his act became transparent as an only slightly veiled insult at what he saw as shogunal dawdling: The new monarch was to be his seven-year-old daughter, Okiko, who, as the empress-regnant Meisho, would be the first female to occupy the throne since the eighth century. There were plenty of sons from whom the abdicated sovereign could have chosen an heir, but his taunt to Iemitsu, the new shogun and the third Tokugawa, was as if to say, "Let's see if you might be more effectively guided in your great work by a *girl* on the throne of our ancestors." Meisho was, of course, bereft of any authority whatsoever, Go-Mizunoo keeping unto himself the few remaining crumbs of imperial influence.

In 1634, Iemitsu and the now-abdicated Go-Mizunoo finally came to a meeting of the minds, and in doing so invoked the little-employed tactic of *burei*, "free and easy impoliteness" or the temporary suspension of court etiquette as a technique to get down to business where time was limited. In Kyoto in 1634, the shogun and his still-assertive ex-sovereign met as equals under the rules of burei. Full of grievances, which he laid out on the mat he shared with the dictator, Go-Mizunoo said that his only desire was for the country to be finally rid of all foreign influences—especially that of the Christians—so the ancient and thoroughly time-tested order of affairs might be reverently protected against any further contamination. In exchange for Iemitsu's tacit agreement to restore Japan to its original, foreign contamination–free purity, Go-Mizunoo tacitly agreed that the monarchy would remain totally withdrawn from affairs of the world and would cease the constant carping that had of late been directed from court to bakufu. And as it came to pass, the ex-emperor's consent was indeed the last peep heard out of Kyoto's Imperial Palace until the middle of the nineteenth century. The visit also represented nearly the last a shogun ever made to the imperial capital.

What came in the wake of this extraordinary compact was the lowering of an impermeable, military-guaranteed curtain around Japan, one that excluded even the outlying islands that had for centuries been subject to Japanese hegemony: From this time on, only the four main islands would be considered "homeland." The people of the now completely isolated nation remained frozen, without any exceptions, into the classes into which they were born. Nobody could aspire to anything other than what his parents had been, the people tilling the soil weren't permitted to move to the towns, the town dwellers couldn't return to the land. No Japanese could leave the four islands, no Japanese who left was permitted reentry, with the penalty for attempting movement in either direction swift, unquestioned, and painful death. In fulfillment of the deal struck between emperor and shogun, Christianity, the faith inexplicably proclaiming the brotherhood of all men, was proscribed, death the penalty for embracing it. To underscore the seriousness of this new national order, tens of thousands of Japanese Christians were gruesomely slaughtered by slow crucifixion, the standard Tokugawa method of execution. With the hated Catholic Portuguese thrown out of the country, only a handful of Dutch traders were permitted to remain, their tiny number restricted to Deshima, a man-made flyspeck of an island in Nagasaki Harbor that wasn't even considered "true" Japanese soil. Presumably, the sacred land of the Son of Heaven was now secure, but as with most draconian social policies that artificially impose barriers against free human intercourse, the price paid would be very high.

The monarchs who followed Go-Mizunoo to the throne in these years of isolation were historically unnotable. What small ripples emanating from Japan to reach foreign shores invariably originated in Edo, the growing city in which hereinafter all political power resided. Within Japan, only members of the courtier class were touched by the dormant monarchy, and the imperial family remained behind an impenetrable wall, a wall that bakufu authorities ensured would remain unbreached in inviolate maintenance of the imperial-shogunal contract.

While Go-Mizunoo lived to a great age in the relatively etiquette-free atmosphere of his Retired Emperor's Palace in Kyoto, four of his children endured in succession what must have been a stiflingly oppressive burden of sovereignty. All of Go-Mizunoo's successors were personal nonentities, but the first must have endured the greatest trial of all. Putting a female on the throne was, as pointed out, a deliberate gesture of belittlement on the part of her father toward the Tokugawa, and as the girl grew into adolescence, she surely came to realize the ludicrousness of her position. Both bakufu and court were anxious to be rid of her, the former because it viewed a female sovereign as belittling to the honor of the nation, the latter in respect of its deeply held antifemale prejudice and the fact that inheritance by her children, if permitted, would throw a wrench into the "normal" line of succession. As it happened, Meisho was never allowed to marry, undoubtedly because of the messy effect it would have had on the succession, not to mention the anomalous position of any male consort to the sovereign. She remained on the throne because, first, the court saw her continuing presence as an act of independence from Edo, and, second and more to the point, Edo simply didn't choose to push the matter. In time, Meisho's abdication would be arranged by the kuge to make it appear as though it were purely routine and voluntary. With the ascension, in 1643, of the empress's brother Go-Komyo to the throne, even the small undercurrent of tension caused by a female emperor disappeared from the court.

Go-Komyo was a scholar by inclination and experienced little discomfort with the bakufu's injunction that sovereigns restrict their nonceremonial endeavors to academic pursuits. He rose a fraction above dead-zero status because of such scholarship, becoming a patron of Japanese neo-Confucianism—he considered Buddhism useless because of its teaching that man couldn't control events, personally declaring that "no sovereign should ever study a useless branch of learning"—and thus achieved some stature in the history of Japanese thought of the period. He also exhibited a streak of spirit: When, after having decided to learn fencing as a personal accomplishment, he was told by his resident bakufu keeper that such an activity might "upset the shogun" on the basis that martial arts were not an appropriate pursuit for the imperial person, Go-Komyo still refused to give up his lessons. The shogunal representative, not being able to fulfill his duties, was put into the position of having to get ready to commit seppuku should the emperor continue in this vein of obstinacy. "I have never seen a military man kill himself, and the spectacle will be interesting" was the monarch's sanguine reply. The shogunal representative kept his dirk sheathed, and before the matter could come to a head, Go-Komyo conveniently died of smallpox, in 1654, at the age of twenty-two. In the end, Go-Komyo's only accomplishment to have any lasting effect on the management of the court was to order that cremation be abandoned in the case of imperial family members.

Sibling number three, Gosai, unexpectedly ascended the throne when Go-Komyo died suddenly, leaving only a daughter. Gosai suffered an amazingly singular humiliation at the hands of the Tokugawa bakufu: When, during his reign, the country was hit by more than the usual numbers of natural disasters—earthquakes, typhoons, and the like—the shogun decided the cause must be a lack of imperial virtue (the exact nature of which was not specified) and ordered an imperial resignation so as to spare the nation any further tribulations. It can be imagined with what disdain this brazen and bizarre demand was received at the palace. But fearing the shogunal wrath that would undoubtedly be forthcoming in the absence of imperial compliance, the court quietly persuaded the monarch to step down, again ostensibly of his own "free will."

The last of Go-Mizunoo's offspring to sit on the throne was Reigen, halfway through whose reign the abdicated ex-emperor and father of the four monarchs finally died, at the age of eighty-four, probably enormously satisfied with the thoroughness by which the Tokugawa had purified his country. Reigen is known for absolutely nothing except that he, too, abdicated so he could move to the far greater freedoms of the Retired Emperors Palace, from where he could, until his death in 1732, in turn pull the strings at the end of which danced the next two sovereigns, the first of whom was his son.

Like Reigen, the next four monarchs—Higashiyama, Nakami-kado, Sakuramachi, and Momozono—were inconsequential as far as any substantive effect on history is concerned. During Higa-shiyama's tenure of the throne the new Tokugawa shogun, Tsunayo-shi, a man generously disposed toward the emperor, raised the annual privy purse by ten thousand koku, the standard measure of wealth, representing almost 2 million liters of rice. Moreover, an additional three thousand koku was provided for the ex-emperor. Nakamikado earned the distinction of becoming the patriarch of the imperial house after the death of his grandfather Reigen, retaining the additional honor that went with the position even after his own abdication. While Nakamikado was serving his quarter-century-long reign, the bakufu, in a further attempt to weaken the imperial household officials' influence on the sovereign, decreed that all imperial princes other than the heir should take vows as Buddhist priests, and furthermore, that all imperial princesses except those specifically chosen to be shogunal consorts likewise enter Buddhist nunneries. Through his courtiers, Nakamikado let the shogun know that he considered the order both unfair and unacceptable, arguing that as any other man wished to see his children prosper, so, too, did the sovereign—the veil or tonsure being obviously mutually incompatible with "prosperity." Sympathizing with this line of reasoning, the shogun Ienobu Tokugawa rescinded the rule and allowed the emperor's children to start their own princely but nonimperial houses. From one such imperial offshoot grew the House of Kanin, which would soon see one of its sons raised to the throne and, in the period before the Great Pacific War, influence Japan's military aims in a direction that would lead directly to its tragic clash of arms with the United States and Britain.

During the reign of the emperor Sakuramachi, a radical doctrine regarding the throne was born, one that constituted the first clouds of the storm that ultimately would sweep away the great Tokugawa shogunate. Ansai Yamazaki, a famous philosophical scholar of the period, asserted that the monarch owned literally everything and everybody in the nation; this concept was a part of his attempt to merge the cults of Confucianism and Shintoism in order to give added credence to his view that the emperors were unequivocally divine and should be regarded by Edo as such. Furthermore, he added, any opposition to the sovereign's will must be regarded as treason and merit the punishment of instant death. When the shogun got wind of this dangerous philosophy, ideas that though perhaps technically unarguable in the abstract sense were nonetheless clearly a political slap at shogunal control over the monarchy, Edo's response was swift and merciless: The proponents were rounded up; most were put to a slow and memorable death, the others were exiled. The idea itself, however, once let loose and having slowly gained a degree of acceptance in influential circles, would not long be suppressed by even the most brutal of bakufu reaction.

The monarch succeeding Momozono is worthy of note primarily because of her sex, reigning as Japan's most recent empress-regnant and legally the last unless the present Imperial House Law barring female succession is changed to again allow such inheritance. As the empress Go-Sakuramachi, the princess Toshiko succeeded to the throne only because her dead brother left sons deemed too young to reign—the oldest was only six at the time of his father's death. Toshiko was put in as a pinch-hitter, as it were, with the intention that she should resign as soon as her eldest nephew, Hidehito, was old enough to carry out the ceremonial duties of sovereignty. This planned scenario was followed to the letter, and Go-Sakuramachi quietly left the stage of monarchy without disturbing in any way the pages of history.

And neither did the nephew, Go-Momozono, unless one counts the fact that he caused a crisis in the imperial house when he suddenly died leaving no male heir. His daughter could have succeeded in the same sort of technical way as had Go-Sakuramachi, but the situation in this instance was different. Go-Sakuramachi had been installed on the throne clearly as an interim sovereign only, a legal reign but one of planned brevity; her nephew was unquestionably in line to replace her as soon as he was old enough to sit up unassisted on a throne platform. Go-Momozono's daughter, on the other hand, had no direct male replacements in line, and because of the firm tradition that the throne should pass through the male line only, it would have served no purpose to install the girl as monarch. And because Go-Momozono's brother was also dead and equally without issue, and Nakamikado's sons were old Buddhist priests unlikely to produce their own heirs, the court was faced with the startling situation of the main branch of the imperial family having run dry. In consequence, a young prince of the Kanin branch of the family—connected by blood to Amaterasu, still the paramount qualification for sovereignty—was chosen to reign, and he came to the throne as the emperor Kokaku.

The first of only four monarchs to reign in the nineteenth century, Kokaku was born in 1771 and enthroned nine years later, getting off to an inauspicious start when Mount Asama, in the Japanese alps northwest of Edo, erupted, killing 25,000 people. The calamity was shortly followed by a disastrous famine and pestilence in the northeast, which was in turn followed by one of the worst of the recurring general famines that periodically swept the country. Finally, in 1788, Kyoto itself was reduced to a giant ash heap in the most destructive fire in its history; not only were the Imperial Palace and the shogun's castle reduced to cinders, but the capital lost 220 Shinto shrines, 128 Buddhist temples, and 183,000 dwelling houses in the conflagration. The 2,600 residents who died were at least spared the misery the city had to endure before it could be rebuilt. The bakufu acquitted itself honorably by sending massive relief aid, funds that were especially appreciated because of the poverty that resulted after the country was closed to trade. Sadanobu Matsudaira, the shogun Iyenari

Tokugawa's chief adviser, personally supervised the reconstruction of the palace, making sure that the new buildings were roomy enough for the grand court ceremonies over which the bakufu liked to see the court frittering away its energies. When the new residence was completed in the record time of two years, Kokaku very kindly invited the ex-empress Go-Sakuramachi to move in with him. And in gratitude to the shogun, the monarch sent Iyenari a personally autographed book of poetry, a gesture that reportedly profoundly pleased the generalissimo in Edo.

It seemed a pity to disturb this budding cordiality between palace and bakufu, but a thorny issue of protocol threatened to undo the goodwill that was slowly being rebuilt between the two camps. The issue involved the emperor Kokaku's father, Prince Kanin, who was head, or patriarch, of his family. The prince wanted to have conferred on himself the honorary title of dajo tenno, "Retired-Emperor," which was not technically his right because he himself had never been monarch, but which he nonetheless felt his due since his son was emperor. He was unhappy at having to endure, because of his "lowly" station, the personal "slights" generated by the strict protocol of the court, namely having to sit below any number of mere ministers of state who outranked him. Not only didn't he like it, but, more to the point, his son didn't like it either, feeling a sovereign's father should certainly merit respect higher than that accorded some piddling minister. What was more, historical precedents were dug up justifying dajo tenno rank for an emperor's father, even one who had never reigned. The shogunal government nevertheless deemed the promotion "inadvisable," for complicated reasons essentially founded in the coincidental fact that the father of the incumbent shogun had also never been shogun and was also expecting, because of his son's rank, to be raised to the more esteemed status of Former Shogun. If the emperor's father were granted the honorific, then the analogous title couldn't very well be refused Iyenari's father, Hitotsubashi, who Iyenari felt didn't deserve any upgrading. One thing led to another, and the result was that Kanin was refused the dajo tenno title in a manner notable for its curt tactlessness. Renewed bad blood between Kyoto and Edo was thus occasioned over a relative triviality, and the warmth that existed at the time of the palace's rebuilding was lost, never to be recovered.

As the years of the nineteenth century became decades, the mystery-enshrouded allure of Japan became unbearable to foreign nations anxious to tap its buying and trading powers. The bakufu of the nineteenth century was not the virile thing it had been in Ieyasu's world two centuries earlier, and the heirs of the first great Tokugawa could no longer fend off the desecration being increasingly wrought by foreign ships on the sacred shores of the emperor's islands. The effect this weakness would have on the monarchy was unseen at the time, but there was slowly building in the land a dangerous resentment that Great Yamato was either deliberately or impotently being allowed to be sullied by the foreign devils. The groundswell of anger was at first barely noticeable, but during the first half of the 1800s, more numerous and more important strata of the country's society were calling for an end to increasing foreign defilement—especially Russian—of the land of the Sun Goddess, and, by extension, of her legitimate heir on the dynasty's throne. The most reactionary among them solemnly believed more strongly than ever that the monarch was the sovereign owner of all that the country contained, *including* its people, and out of such men a movement was born called the *sonno,* or those dedicated to "venerating the emperor."

When Kokaku decided, in 1817, to step down from the throne—most likely because he was tired of the ceremonial onus of kingship and came to the conclusion that he had reigned "long enough"—he had no trouble convincing the courtiers who controlled him and the shogunate who controlled them to let him go. Ninko, Kokaku's successor, occupied the throne until nearly the century's midpoint, and silently witnessed the rapidly escalating decline of the Tokugawa shogunate. Some opening of windows in the emperors' otherwise air-tight imprisonment had lately been allowed by the bakufu, and Ninko must have listened with fascination as the gathering cries for restoration of imperial power and revival of the ancient precepts of emperor-centered Shintoism grew from small ripples at the outset of his reign to something approaching a national mania at its close. Ninko died unknown to the world, but he was the last Japanese monarch who would be invisible to all but the tiny circle of courtiers and bakufu officials who wrote the scripts for these imperial lives.

In 1846, the last emperor of the old, hidden Japan came to the throne. Komei would be the first sovereign in centuries to take a well-illuminated place on the world stage. Unhappily, he would also be the first to be murdered in the almost thirteen hundred years since Sushun had met that fate.

CHAPTER VII

Imperial Reveille

MID-NINETEENTH CENTURY TO EARLY
TWENTIETH CENTURY

> "May everyone come to the aid of the Sovereign's court . . . may everyone hear the Sovereign's command."
>
> —IMPERIAL RESCRIPT ON THE ACCESSION OF THE EMPEROR MEIJI

Komei's Japan was, despite the Tokugawa attempt to stop the clock, a nation far different from that which had gone into seclusion more than two centuries earlier. Hoping to preserve a temperate atmosphere of everlasting peace as well as a clearly delineated national social order that was to its liking, the Tokugawa shogunate thought it had safeguarded for all time an idealized Japan, but there had been one miscalculation: The country had already been seriously infected with a tantalizing knowledge of the outside world. The additional bits and scraps of Westernization that continued to seep in through the tiny Dutch pinhole of Deshima (at Nagasaki) during the era of seclusion both fascinated and frightened the country. In the middle of the eighteenth century, an enlightened shogun had tried to placate increasing popular pressure for changed social conditions by relaxing somewhat the bar against Western learning and allowing Dutch books to enter the country. But now the people were clamoring for the luxuries that a growing population and economy made possible, pleasures that had hitherto been known only to the top levels of the society. And to make matters worse, peace was rapidly rusting the shogunal sword.

Particularly ironic was the way the Tokugawa-guaranteed class structure backfired. As mentioned, the four primary groupings—samurai, peasant, artisan, and merchant—based on the Confucian system of society and class left the urban commercial class at the bottom[1] of the country's class structure, both legally and in terms of social status. The warriors, the highest of the four classes, found themselves with a great deal of time on their hands after the Tokugawa pacification of most of the country's warring landowners, and many embarked on lives notable more for frivolousness, lechery, and sweetmeats than for deeds of chivalry and derring-do. Frivolousness costs money, and to pay for their gaiety and frolicking many samurai borrowed heavily from those with money to lend. Despised though they were at the near-bottom of the national social ladder, the merchants hadn't been idle in the Tokugawa centuries. In an empire whose tranquility encouraged plebeian commerce, the commercial class had enriched itself by thoroughly mastering the art and science of trade, their classrooms the growing cities of which Kyoto, Osaka, and Edo were becoming substantial by even international standards. The despised merchants then served as middlemen for the farmers, and eventually ended up with large cash surpluses as rewards for their applied diligence and single-minded effort. The next step in this logical economic progression was to advance some of these surpluses to the idle warrior class at high interest rates, rates to which the samurai were by now powerless to object. Like the nation's rich rice crops, the surpluses, too, just kept growing, the inevitable result of this fiscal engorgement of the urban merchants being the dominant power and growing status it gave them, even though they remained politically weak since they were not yet organized. The sad reverse of the coin was the growing self-denigration the new realities of Japanese life lent the warrior class.

Not unexpectedly, this evolving situation was not to the liking of

[1]Except for the two virtually hereditary special outcast groups, *eta* and *hinin.*

the samurai. Despising both money and commerce with a lordly haughtiness nurtured by centuries of *bushido* philosophy, the formerly undisputed masters of the nation's tranquility wanted Japan and their role in it to regain the status that had been lost. Resisting what they viewed as the corruption of the nation's virtues by foreigners, who by the middle of the nineteenth century began to clamor ever more loudly and persistently to be allowed access to Japan's ports and markets, the military class saw salvation in a return to the Japan that for centuries operated within sharply defined social parameters.

It became increasingly and more painfully obvious that the shogunate was losing its power to thwart either this unwelcome social change or the foreign tide, much less the ability to return the country to its status quo ante. A cry went out among the disgruntled for what was seen as the salvation of the old ways: the reinstatement of the emperor as the undisputed political leader and the overthrow of the rapidly weakening shogunate. This was music to Komei's ears, for he, too, was as disgusted as any offended samurai at the thought of a Japan contaminated either from within or by the ways of the evil-smelling barbarians from places no Sun Goddess could have ever imagined.

The reality was that a hidden price had been buried in the long-ago imperial arrangement with Edo to freeze Japanese society and close the country to all that wasn't native. While the nation entered its isolation as one of the strongest military powers on earth, it soon became, at least relative to the West, one of the weakest. The Spanish and the Portuguese and the Dutch who dominated Japan's view of occidental society in 1600 had, by the nineteenth century, been replaced by the English and the French and the Russians as the world's most powerful imperialists. And even the United States, a country that was a mere collection of primitive settlements in Ieyasu's time, was by Komei's day a cocky bantam, filled with its sense of "manifest destiny" and determined to demonstrate that it was a force with which the world had best learn to reckon. And it turned out to be this bantam that led the others in finally forcing a showdown, a confrontation that would soon free Japan's monarchs from their lacquered and perfumed prison, bring the throne a measure of genuine sovereign power for the first time since 1185, and strip the Barbarian-Suppressing Generalissimos of seven centuries of hard-won and ironclad authority.

While Komei grew increasingly agitated by the weakening resolve of the shogunate to repulse the foreign pressures to open Japan to international exploitation, the shogunate continued to flounder. What had begun under Ieyasu as an austere and carefully designed military-based institution of government had long been gradually giving itself over to many of the same diversions and profligacies that had for centuries sapped the Kyoto court of its vitality. One such example of this frivolousness was a project of the early-eighteenth-century shogun Tsunayoshi Tokugawa. He had decided to build, on 138 acres of valuable land near the center of Edo, a luxurious "dog city"—kennels designed as a refuge for the stray curs that roamed his capital. Tsunayoshi's whim may have been notable for its charitable impulse, but it was highly questionable in light of the country's chronically short treasury reserves.

Although he couldn't have known it, and he certainly didn't wish it, Komei's agitated displeasure with Edo—he now openly spoke of the bakufu as a "nest of robbers"—was leading directly to the rise of a completely new system of monarchy in Japan. What the emperor wanted was simply for the Tokugawa-in-charge to put an end to all the tranquility-disturbing ruckus caused by the yammering of the foreigners—he referred to them as "unclean beasts"—trying to put an end to Japan's blessed isolation. Komei considered his imperial role to be conservator of the uniquely distinct culture that had been both molded and guarded by every one of his six score of predecessors: let the shogun guard the nation's security, and he, Komei, would see to its soul. The antiforeign sentiment was winning new converts to his "cause" every day, the converts paradoxically becoming far more a threat to what he really wanted than were the smelly ships that were arriving with revolting regularity from God knows where to demand God knows what. The shogun continued to assure the emperor that "something was being done," knowing full well that its long isolation had left Japan hopelessly unable to defend itself should the foreigners with their devilish cannon start doing more than merely *asking* to be let in. Seeing how easily the semibarbarian Chinese court had been cowed by its white-faced tormentors was yet another consideration causing more sleepless nights in Edo than the bakufu cared to admit.

And predictably, it wasn't long before the foreigners started doing more than just asking. The new tack began with a relatively peaceful diplomatic overture, but one that left little question about what kind of an answer it expected from Japan. One morning in the summer of 1853, a ship carrying the unusually ample personage of Commodore Matthew Calbraith Perry steamed into Uraga Bay, the outermost part of what is today Tokyo Bay. This time there would be no divine wind to turn the invader back from the emperor's sacred shores.

The message Perry was carrying had been carefully drafted by Daniel Webster for the president of the United States, Millard Fillmore, and was addressed to "His Imperial Majesty," a personage who as far as Fillmore knew might have been either the emperor or the shogun, the American authorities being confused as to which was which and who did what. It was a misunderstanding on the Americans' part that the bakufu officials found contemptuous, but one of which they purposely did not disabuse the visitors. In any event, Webster/Fillmore's letter, addressed to "the Emperor," took a tone one might employ when writing to a child with a learning disability. "Our steamships can go from California to Japan in eighteen days. It sometimes happens, in stormy weather, that one of our ships is wrecked on Your Imperial Majesty's shores," said the president. "In all such cases we ask, and expect, that our unfortunate people should be treated with kindness. We are very much in earnest in this. We understand there is a great abundance of coal and provisions in the empire of Japan." Perry shared his commander-in-chief's opinion that the addressee was probably little more than an illiterate savage, taking the common Western view that relegated the Orient to backward and "pagan" status.

After the splendidly uniformed Perry made his way to Yokohama, where he was allowed to deliver this disrespectful request to the low-ranking bakufu officials who had been designated to meet with him but who referred to themselves as "princes"—the better to impress the American—he preceded to Edo accompanied by two enormously tall and heavily armed black sailors, all the better, in his opinion, to bully the short-statured Japanese. In point of fact, it wasn't the height of his guardians, much less the gold encrusting Perry's naval uniform, that convinced his hosts that here was something serious. What brought the shogunal officials to that realization were the bristling men-of-war—"four black ships of evil mien"— from which the American party had just disembarked (the *Susquehanna*, a coal-powered sidewheeler, was Perry's flagship), apparitions responsible for putting a newly heightened fear of the West and its infinite powers into the shogunate.

The shogun, given a translation[2] of the American president's letter within hours after Perry had handed it over, sought to buy time. After consulting the emperor by the quickest runners available, and hearing from Komei that it was expected that the shogun would protect the sacred character of Japan from these intruders, he answered Perry, probably with trepidation, that a final reply to Fillmore's requests would have to wait until the following year. Not being entirely ignorant of oriental face-saving measures, Perry agreed to the delay but left Japan with the undisguised impression that there had better be an acceptable answer when he steamed back into the emperor's waters.

It was here that the shogunate effected a major tactical about-face, one that would be seen by its enemies as, in effect, relinquishing its dictatorial power in relation to both the throne and the feudal lords who supported the imperial wish to free the nation of its "invaders." To help the bakufu decide what it should do next in regard to Perry, the shogun solicited the opinions and advice of all the daimyo and even of members of the powerless Kyoto court. In a country in which major decisions of state were decided only from above and participatory government was an unheard-of concept, this action proved a disastrous mistake, contemptuously interpreted by the provincial leaders as unworthy and evidence of weakness. What's more, it was damaging to the bakufu's credibility in the eyes of the upper classes. Almost all those consulted unhesitatingly responded that the foreigners should indeed be removed, by force if

[2]Knowledge of English was one of the skills that seeped in through the Deshima crack in Japan's Wall.

necessary, and that the nation should remain firmly and irrevocably closed to outsiders. But in achieving such ends, few wanted imminent war with the Westerners, counseling the wiser course of appeasement with vague promises of cooperation while at the same time building up the nation's military capabilities in case the "black ships" attempted to use force to bend the country to the Americans' demands.

Hoping the emperor would join in and support this relatively moderate approach, the bakufu officials sought Komei's moral backing. But the intransigent sovereign, who had neither set eyes on a barbarian nor even ventured outside the golden-walled security of his palace, could see only that his patrimony of nineteen centuries was in danger. He wanted the threat ended *now*. Reasoning that a million samurai might give the barbarians pause in any attempt to bring down Japan militarily, Komei informed Edo that the shogunate "should make the country safe for another two thousand years of the reigns of the descendants of the Sun Goddess." Replying to the shogunal decision to proceed slowly and carefully, Komei sent the straightforward and imperially pithy answer, "Strengthen coastal defenses," his uncomplicated reasoning springing from the notion that if shogunal authority were now to require imperial consultation in its formulation, then imperial wishes should be obeyed. As insurance, Komei backed up his authority by ordering that all the principal Shinto shrines and Buddhist temples offer prayers to aid the shogun in the task of stopping the Westerners. The critical point in understanding Komei's role in these momentous affairs was that the sovereign wished *not* to return the monarchy to direct imperial rule, but instead only wanted the shogunate to do the job it was supposed to do. The irony was that Komei's now-widely-disseminated feelings for the nation's physical sanctity encouraged yet more young zealots who saw the shogunate as a dead institution and fervently desired that the imperial court be Japan's new rallying point.

The Edo government and the Kyoto court were essentially at opposite poles at this juncture, as critical as any in the nation's history since the Mongol was turned back. The shogunate became increasingly aware that Komei couldn't be obeyed, having come to realize that seclusion was simply no longer possible—indeed, it was no longer desirable if Japan was to retain her position as a free and independent nation. What's more, Kyoto itself might have been safe from the brutish guns on the brutish black ships, but Edo certainly wasn't. The shogun had no more regard for the foreigners than Komei, but *he* had seen the muzzles of Perry's topsiders. So when Perry returned the following year, a Treaty of Amity and Friendship was signed between the two nations. Almost identical treaties soon followed between Japan and Britain, Russia, the Netherlands, and France. If—a big if—Japan could rebuild herself to the status of an international power, then, reasoned the shogunate, the doors could perhaps be slammed shut again.

Now that it had obtained half the loaf it wanted from Japan, namely the treaty, the United States pressed for the other half: a commercial trade agreement, a document tenaciously sought by the new American consul isolated in the small port of Shimoda, on the Izu peninsula, midway between Edo and Nagoya. Before deciding to give in to the entreaties of the envoy, Townsend Harris, the shogun again consulted with the emperor, knowing that a publicly acknowledged imperial agreement would be essential if the bakufu were to stand any chance of unifying the nation behind its position. The daimyo, earlier consulted by Edo in the matter, responded that no decision was possible without imperial agreement, a new and vastly changed appreciation of imperial authority by the same feudal lords whose predecessors had virtually ignored the palace for the last eight hundred years. After the shogun himself received Harris on December 7, 1857, at his Edo castle to sign the trade agreement— an act of submission unprecedented in its scope in bakufu history— Komei's imperial backing for the treaty was even more urgently sought. The emperor took counsel with eighty of his nobles, mostly antiforeigners like himself, who convinced him he should consult with the spirit of the great Ieyasu. The treaty was laid on the generalissimo's tomb, but no advice issued forth from whatever ghosts it may have contained. Komei therefore flatly refused. "If such developments occur during my reign, I will be regarded as a disgrace to the country by posterity. How can I apologize to Amaterasu? How could I shirk the imperial duty which my predecessors have fulfilled?" Komei's response may have been heartfelt, but it was also the first nail in his coffin.

The treaty went forward, of course, a wiser shogunate knowing its implementation was no longer an option to a Japan militarily unable to stop it. But the imperial wrath had been irrevocably incurred and the shogunal actions crystalized the nation's forces of dissent. The sovereign abstained from meat and wine for six days in propitiation for the monumental insult, after which he decided on abdication, reasoning that the imperial line would fare better if the disgrace of his inability to keep the country hermetically sealed were atoned by his giving up the throne. The court nobles in the end were able to talk him out of this course, but Komei made his acquiescence conditional on his demand that the shogunate do a better job of correcting its deficiencies than it had done so far. The bakufu, however, refused to humor the meddlesome monarch any longer, and all parties were finally forced to take sides. The outcome of this power struggle between Kyoto's interests and those of Edo decided the broad outline of the country's course down to the devastation of its ancien régime and its peoples' trial by fire in the horrendous events of 1945.

A point that should be made at this juncture concerns the nature of the bakufu during these eventful times. The brilliance of the Tokugawa patrimony that Ieyasu left his descendants had clearly long since been played out, the Tokugawa family itself having come to resemble the weak imperial line. What saved the shogunate from complete incompetence were a handful of still capable counselors, advisers who themselves were spaced at intervals too wide to save the institution from its own weakness at the top. Had the bakufu chosen a stronger stance in the face of imperial intransigence and itself forthrightly dismantled the outmoded locked-door policy from above, the revolution that it now faced from below might have been averted. But the four Tokugawa figureheads over these years of Komei's reign produced not a single truly memorable or able incumbent. Japan's system of military government, begun in 1185 and unique in world history, was approaching its expiration.

When the treaties took effect, the newly expanded imperial factions' combined cries of *Sonno* and *Joi*—"Revere the Emperor" and "Expel the Barbarian"—echoed back and forth across the country, primarily voiced by the *ronin,* the masterless samurai most at sea in these unsettled times. Doubly irrelevant—not only was the samurai class by now of little importance, its ronin subclass was of even less moment—and with not much else to fill his time, the samurai's sense of mission lay in striving to regain the perceived glories of the past, with the discredited shogunate enduring the brunt of his hatred. That discarded world in which three hundred daimyo claimed the loyalty over some 2 million samurai who in turn held the power of life and death over 30 million Japanese was one very much to their liking. Though still unseen as such, this criticism of the system by the samurai proved to be the real harbinger of the old order's end.

The increasing flow of foreigners who came to Japan with their despicable treaties were also recipients of the xenophobia that was sweeping the military class. Some of these aliens were even killed, including, in 1862, a young British merchant visiting from Shanghai named Charles Lenox Richardson. Richardson suffered the chance misfortune not to have removed himself in time from the path of a daimyo progression. He received the sharp side of a samurai sword for his insolence. The incident was leapt upon by the British, who by their lights saw it as murder and thus reasoned that it might be a good time to give these "natives" foolish enough to resist the tide of civilizing influences a taste of the consequences of wounded Western sensibilities.

The particular noble whose party young Richardson had run into was a member of the Satsuma clan of the southwestern island of Kyushu, a family that together with the Choshu of the westernmost tip of the main island comprised the two most powerful daimyo clans of feudal Japan. Both were hereditary enemies of the Tokugawa, having been on the wrong—that is, losing—side at the Battle of Sekigahara and therefore excluded from shogunal corridors of power, and their combined force of 38,000 hardened warriors continued to pose an enormous potential threat to Edo. They were also the most arrogant, most volatile, and physically the furthest from shogunal authority. These so-called Sat-Cho needed only a spark to set them off in the tinderbox that the split between imperial and shogunal authority had become. Charles Richardson was the spark.

In June 1863, after the bakufu let pass the day on which the Sat-Cho had demanded the last of the foreigners were to be expelled from the country, Choshu batteries ranged along the shore of their Honshu stronghold fired on an American vessel that had dropped anchor in the narrow Straits of Shimonoseki, the waterway separating Honshu from Kyushu and Satsuma from Choshu. The effect of the guns was to close the important passage to allied craft. Later that same year, when the Great Lord of Satsuma refused to pay the indemnity the British were demanding for the slaying of Richardson, gunboats of the Royal Navy made short work of the Satsuma capital of Kagoshima, shelling the town into rubble. And the following year the Shimonoseki incident was revenged when an allied fleet of sixteen warships attacked the Choshu defenses and captured their guns. Both Choshu and Satsuma leaders were forced to make their peace with the barbarians, hating the bakufu more than the foreigners in this abrupt and unarguable demonstration of the irreversible bankruptcy of any kind of exclusion policy. Together, Choshu and Satsuma aimed their sword at the government in Edo.

Wanting to bring the whole matter to a head, the more excitable Choshu clan decided to "rescue" the emperor in Kyoto from the stupidity and ineptness of the shogunal mire into which the sacred throne had been dragged. A Choshu contingent in Kyoto, permanently stationed in the imperial capital as a peacekeeping force, rebelled against the local bakufu representative only to be put down by a stronger army dispatched from Edo; the latter was backed by a Satsuma division, the Satsuma daimyo clearly displeased with the precipitate action his erstwhile Choshu allies had taken. By executing its enemy's leadership, the Tokugawa authorities decided to get rid of the pesky Choshu once and, it was fervently hoped, for all. But their action only drove the Satsuma right back to their former alliance, and now the Edo shogunate again had to contend with both of these strong military forces. A failure to persuade neutral daimyo to rally to its aid and a slowness on the part of its allied nobles to come to its rescue spelled the imminent military defeat of the shogunate.

The nation was in thrall to the hopelessly deadlocked factions, the hotheaded Satsuma and Choshu warriors leading the campaign against shogunal control, the shogunate paralyzed, the emperor cursing the foreigner but wanting the shogun to remain. Finally, in 1866, Keiki Tokugawa[3] acceded to the head of the military government as its last ruler. Keiki pleaded for unity among the disputants, but was powerless either to appease the daimyo, who had by now made their begrudging peace with an ever-increasing foreign presence, or the emperor, who stubbornly continued to argue for "expulsion of the barbarians." On January 30, 1867, the death of Komei removed the first of the two men who stood in the way of a new Japan.

Most historical sources, those in Japanese and those in Western languages, report merely that Komei "died of smallpox" smack in the middle of this profoundly important turning point in Japanese history. Some gingerly hint that he may have been removed from the scene, by "unnatural" means, to allow a resolution to the crisis to be effected. But in his book *Japan's Imperial Conspiracy,* David Bergamini states with little equivocation that the emperor was in fact assassinated, the assassin not identified but presumed to have been in the employ of the Satsuma-Choshu faction and the murder justified because the monarch stood intransigently in the way of a much-needed Tokugawa overthrow. Other rumors that have seeped through the closed world of the court conversely claim the shogunal government itself engineered a poisoning because the court hadn't compromised sufficiently with the Tokugawa government. Though it isn't likely that the truth of the matter will ever be known with absolute certainty, Komei's death did unquestionably remove one of the two major symbolic obstacles to the eventual resolution of the country's domestic tangle. The emperor's passing left the political situation at court completely transformed. Where the dead sovereign had been the principal moral force in the capital mitigating against a Tokugawa overthrow, the court was now free to join forces with the dominant Satsuma-Choshu in restoring direct rule to the monarchy—under a Sat-Cho controlling interest, of course. At the

[3]Also known as Yoshinobu Tokugawa.

bakufu, a number of feudal lords under the leadership of the daimyo of Tosa, and including even leaders of several branches of the Tokugawa clan, saw the inevitable course of coming events and counseled the shogun to resign in order to avoid a civil war, an almost sure-to-come disaster if the Tokugawa didn't abolish their authority voluntarily.

To the last shogun, the reform-minded Keiki Tokugawa, would fall the obligation of making a gesture of strength as great as any in the history of his family: He would end the office Ieyasu willed to posterity. When Keiki saw the hopelessness of his position, he gave in. On November 9, 1867, the last shogun issued a document announcing the abolishment of his family office, a statement remarkable in its dignity: The fourteenth heir to Ieyasu wrote ". . . if full authority is not vested in the court alone, the foundations of the state will be in jeopardy. If, however, the evil practices of the past are corrected and ruling authority returned to the court, if extensive deliberations are carried out throughout the empire, the imperial judgment secured, and the nation sustained by harmony and cooperation by all, then I believe it is certain the nation will be able to rank with the other countries of the earth." With this act, carried out in the expectation that he would be chosen chief adviser to the emperor under whatever new regime replaced the shogunate, Keiki Tokugawa signed away his patrimony, eight centuries of military government ending with the broad black strokes of his calligrapher's brush. Although not asked to serve as an adviser, Keiki received respect from the victors, and he was allowed to retire to his estate at Mito.

For two more years, the anti-Tokugawa and the pro-Tokugawa forces fought each other as the fledgling government established in Kyoto attempted to assert its authority. Though the downfall of the shogunate was viewed with satisfaction by the new military-court alliance, many of its individuals weren't satisfied that the members of the Tokugawa dynasty were able to escape with lives and property intact. Accurately understanding that the clan's power emanated as much from its vast land holdings and military alliances as it had from directly controlling the Edo bakufu, its enemies resolved to destroy the family.

The Japanese feudal era by no means ended at the stroke of the shogun's formal abdication, and the modern era by no means began with the assumption of power by Komei's heir. Confusion, blood-shed, war, famine, and urban chaos followed in the wake of the old era, with many usages of feudal society continuing well into the new reign. But within an incredibly short time, Japan instituted in her social order a stunning about-face, and a society's modus vivendi that had survived for centuries collapsed before the eyes of the world. And as Japanese history foreordained, the change came from above. The new world was named Meiji.

The second and only healthy son of the emperor Komei, Prince Sachino,[4] entered the world on November 3, 1852. The birth took place at the tree-shaded *Gosanjo*, the lying-in chamber especially erected for the occasion in the compound assigned to the prince's maternal grandfather within the Kyoto Imperial Palace's parklike grounds. Sachino was not the child of Komei's chief consort, the empress Asako, but of a highborn concubine—the emperor's favor-ite—named Yoshiko ("Child of Joy") Nakayama.

Although the boy's comparatively humble birth allowed him a relative freedom in his first years of life, including the right to reside away from the central palace until he turned five, being the son of the emperor by *any* mother meant the child was far from free to live an existence in any way approaching normality. Destined to be the first ruler in a thousand years to appear physically before any sizable portion of his people, Sachino as a child was hidden from view as securely as the dozens of generations of imperial princes who preceded him as far back as the establishment of the military govern-ment. His early youth was spent with Confucian scholars learning the structured view of society as encompassed by Confucianism, with rank and station securely in the forefront of an orderly civiliza-tion. When the boy was seven, his father, an accomplished poet, began personally giving him lessons in *waka* composition. The inter-est thus aroused was so passionate that over his lifetime Meiji would

[4]Meiji's name before being upgraded to crown prince; an earlier son, by another mother, had died at birth.

compose some 93,000 such poems, many still preserved in the Imperial Household archives.

Despite the uniqueness of his existence, the prince who, at the age of fifteen, would become the emperor Meiji spent his young life in far more modest circumstances than those in which he would live his mature years. Komei's palace, which because of its occupant's status was also a shrine, the dwelling of the Son of Heaven, reflected the severity so central to Shinto and to the notion of the correctness of simplicity of divinity in Japanese royalty, although luxury was abundantly evident in the details of the buildings' quality. What elegance there was notwithstanding, economic necessity dictated that the household be conducted along the frugal lines needed to stay within the relatively meager allowance provided by the bakufu. Courtiers—even the emperor—transacted their business affairs on common cotton-padded floor mats, little different from those of any subject and quite unlike the luxurious mats that characterized the shogunal government in Edo, an administration ironically named after the spartan "military tent" of its Kamakura origins. The contemplation of such imperial deprivation quite saddened some loyalists; one, a man named Takayama, sat outside the palace walls with eyes glued to its sloping wooden roofs, tears of unhappiness running down his cheeks over the heavy fate and hard times being endured by his nation's supreme leader.

In truth, Komei's son had so few playthings that the high-ranking guests who visited the palace would leave toys in inconspicuous corners of the rambling building, not wishing to embarrass the apparently impecunious imperial father but nonetheless taking pity on the lonely son. When other scions of the court's highest-ranking members were allowed to keep the prince company, the socially isolated Sachino would lash out at his forced companions if the games weren't proceeding to his liking, but the boys raised in this artificial milieu were trained from their earliest years that striking back at an imperial prince was sacrilege.

Thick curtains of tightly woven bamboo shielded the prince from view of the curious on the rare occasions when he was driven abroad to see the new cherry blossoms of spring, or to gaze on a particularly beautiful moonrise. The attendants who served the meals in the imperial living quarters tied strips of paper around their mouths so their breath would not cause impurity in the food to be eaten by divinities. That Sachino grew into an intellectually curious and virile man was very much in spite of the ancient rubrics that nipped the youthful wing-spreading of his predecessors. Sachino was five years old when the American consul Townsend Harris was attempting to lobby the empire into signing the trade agreement with the United States, and the flurry this event caused at the palace was probably the boy's first awareness of foreigners, the devils whom his father castigated as the ruination of everything that was good in Japan. But the son was very different from the father, fortuitously realizing early in life that both he and his country harbored an immense intellectual void.

At age nine, Prince Sachino underwent the traditional and arduous court ceremonial called the *okufasogi,* a highly ritualized dressing of his long black hair signifying the onset of maturity. Sachino was declared imperial heir in August 1860, and his personal name changed to Mutsohito, meaning something like "Peaceful Gentleman," the name by which he would be known for the remainder of his lifetime to everyone but his own subjects, who would by custom refer to him only in the abstract, as "the Emperor."[5] Three months later, the imperial heir was formally upgraded a notch to crown prince and ceremoniously presented in his new dignity by the Lord Privy Seal to the Supreme Council of State. Until Komei's death, Meiji was kept in a sequestered state, unaware of most of the intrigues eddying around his father's throne, but the boy's intelligence was honed enough for him to understand that the old order was being severely tested. He must have had some realization, too, that it would be his destiny to bring new and unimaginably exciting possibilities to his country—if its doors could be opened to the technological wonders waiting in the distant places beyond its shores.

On February 13, 1867, the heir became the sovereign, the 122nd

---

[5] Japanese sovereigns are even today expected to be less personalities than sacred figureheads, partially accounting for the fact that their people never use the emperor's *imina,* "the name not to be used."

monarch in a line from Jimmu, and only the third back from the present day. The sudden pressures on the new emperor gave him nightmares on his first nights as sovereign, dreams in which he vividly saw monsters at his bedside, a troubled period he would never forget. His maternal grandfather's diary records that "[the new emperor] has mysterious visions troubling his mind. Every night a monkey appears before him and torments him. . . ." The composing of waka poems, forty of which he penned in the two months after his father's death, seems to have helped ease his mind of what today would probably be considered a mild nervous reaction to the enormous changes in his life.

It was a time when Victoria occupied the British throne and her first ministers, Disraeli and Gladstone, were jostling each other to increase British power and prestige; when France was ruled by a second Napoleon not nearly as talented as the first; when Italy and Germany were waiting to become united nations; when Andrew Johnson was facing impeachment as president of the thirty-seven United States; and when Russia was still enslaved by a serf system that mirrored that semicivilized country's society as it had existed for a thousand years. But in the lee of the industrial revolution that had swept Europe and America, Japan itself was without a single industrial company in the entire empire. It had no bank buildings, no printing presses, no insurance policies, no telegraph wires. Though it didn't know it, this dormant and backward nation was about to replace its feudal era with an industrial age, the way of life that had long since transformed the West into a world with which Japan could not then even communicate, much less expect to be treated as an equal.

In November of the year of his accession to the throne, the still-adolescent emperor accepted the Tokugawa shogun's abdication and act of abolishment of the office. It was the beginning of what history would come to call the Meiji Restoration, a far more peaceful Japanese equivalent of the 1789 French Revolution or of Russia's seizure by the Bolsheviks in 1917. In reality, though, even after the "restoration," the emperor himself would remain what his predecessors had been since ancient times: legitimizers of government by others; the monarch would continue to do as he was told, or what tradition demanded. At no time during this era of the repoliticization of the throne did the emperor ever personally act as a Peter the Great or a Prussian Frederick, rising grandly and omnipotently to command great deeds to be wrought at the sovereign's word. The three who have reigned since the restoration have been well-known personalities, certainly in comparison to those sovereigns who went before them. These emperors have symbolized and epitomized Japan to the world outside its borders and have even come to be seen and relatively intimately known by the Japanese people in a way unthinkable before 1868. But the monarch himself—even Meiji—never became more than a constitutional figurehead, a man entirely under the control of the government of the day regardless of being perceived by his subjects as firmly in command of the nation's engines of government. Although Meiji would in time gain undeniable personal influence, what was really "restored" in 1868 was the *symbol* of the sovereign as the sole head of the nation's government.

Who were the men around the throne who made this imperial restoration possible, the men who became Japan's new oligarchy? The leadership of the combined sonno and joi movements drew their members mainly from the military class, with some court officials acting as advisers to and collaborators with the antishogunal, proimperial forces. As stronger personalities emerged to replace the ineffective, basically ceremonially minded courtiers who had continued to control the imperial milieu throughout the Edo period, they attracted an ever-growing number of vigorous younger men of the samurai class and even educated members of the lower divisions of society. Those who eventually rose to the top were called the *dajokan,* the "executive body," early Meiji leaders who lent this name to the whole structure of government between Meiji's accession and the establishment of a constitution two decades later.[6] Faced with the immense task of establishing a new government to replace that which the bakufu had up to 1868 provided, they lost

[6]The dajokan government was divided into ministries, the names and numbers of which floated throughout the period; it was formally superseded by a cabinet system in 1885.

amazingly little time in beginning what was in the end the nation's mind-bogglingly successful transformation.

The first crisis Meiji's advisers were forced to confront was the civil war that flared between the old Tokugawa allies on one side and the clans led by the Sat-Cho on the other. When the Tokugawa realized that the aim of the western clans was the complete annihilation of the former shogunal family, they felt they had little choice but to resort to arms. In the war that followed, the Tokugawa were thoroughly defeated, putting an end to any hope of a reinstallation of the old system. The new leaders, primarily the Sat-Cho revolutionaries, quickly took steps that would institutionalize a powerful new national system of emperor worship as their primary tool in remaking the country, the magic power of the throne serving as the nation's incomparably potent icon.

On December 9, 1867, the Restoration of Imperial Rule was officially announced. Still below the age when he could legally reign alone, the new emperor had been obliged to serve under a regent when he acceded to the throne upon his father's death. His new government, acting in the stead of the old shogunal administration as the nation's ruling body, was made up of thirty-one members: eleven court nobles, five daimyo, and fifteen middle-ranking samurai leaders from the same five provinces as the daimyo. A declaration called the Charter Oath was issued in the emperor's name in 1868, with Meiji announcing its principles from the throne platform in the Shishinden of the Imperial Palace; the document, considered something like a declaration of independence for the newly constituted state, set forth the principles on which imperial rule was to rest, recognizing, formally if somewhat ambiguously, the public's right of free discussion of the political issues confronting the nation. The Oath called for the abandonment of "absurd practices" of the past, meaning essentially anything the new regime wanted to do away with. Clearly intended to serve the old samurai class and not the general interests of the public—in this way it was somewhat analogous to the Magna Charta, its Anglo-Saxon counterpart—the Oath was nonetheless later to be held up by liberals as their promise of imperial acquiescence in the establishment of a true representative democracy in Japan. Its major provisions formally swept away most official class distinctions, and, as an expedience intended to weaken the power of the ever-resourceful Buddhist monasteries, clerics were ordered to marry and raise families—even, to their shock, to eat beef in emulation of the Western custom, a dietary novelty the document's drafters assumed to be one of the reasons for the West's strength. Minor notes declared the teeth blackening and eyebrow shaving of married women and court nobles to be illegal, and men were urged to discard their antique hairdo with its picturesque lacquered topknot, now held as a symbol of backwardness. However, the country's nascent political institutions themselves were to wait another fifteen years before finally being molded into the patterns that would carry the empire forward to the end of World War II.

With the accession of the new emperor, one change was made in the nation's life that greatly eased the job of future historians. Because of a custom going back to the seventh century, Japan marked the passage of time with a series of names given to (usually) short periods within each emperor's reign. The names of the eras were often changed willy-nilly in the middle of reigns after some auspicious event, good or bad, and then changed again (usually) at the beginning of each new reign. The difficulties in actually tallying true calendrical years under such a system are obvious. On October 23, 1868, in a Shinto ceremony recalling centuries of ritualistic court pomp, the young emperor had placed before him slips of paper with two Chinese characters, each standing for the highest of the cardinal virtues. Mutsohito chose the paper bearing the ideographs for "bright" and "rule," which together gave his new reign its name: "Mei Ji." The years of his reign would be numbered, for official purposes, as Meiji 1, Meiji 2, and so on. It was furthermore ordered that the name Meiji would apply to the *entire* reign, and that on his death, Mutsohito himself would be known by this name for posterity's record. Although the new dating system was still undeniably personality-oriented, it would at least have the virtue of measuring the emperor's actual years on the throne.

A far more important change the reformers set about implementing was to bring the emperor out of his physical isolation and turn him into a "true" head of state, visible to the eyes not only of his own subjects, but those of the world as well. And since Kyoto itself had been synonymous for so many centuries with isolation and backwardness, the political desirability of moving the capital to a fresh site was overwhelming. The first candidate seriously considered was Osaka, a burgeoning commercial entrepôt with the advantage of relative nearness to the existing imperial seat. Though Osaka held the court's attention for a time, it was soon discarded in favor of a city whose choice would be within the space of a few decades the major factor in turning it into one of the world's greatest political and commercial metropolises.

When the rule of the Tokugawa ended, that clan's primary seat—the great fortress of Edo castle, covering the heart of the shogunal capital—was ceded as spoils to the imperial government. The luxurious complex of buildings in whose shadow the city grew like rings around the center of a tree's trunk was to Western sensibilities, accustomed to the stolid royal architecture of Europe, far more impressive than the elegant but relatively modest shrinelike buildings that served as the imperial residence in Kyoto. A rudimentary fortress had stood at the site of Edo castle since the fifteenth century, some three centuries after the Edo clan had first settled the place. Its builder, a minor warlord named Ota Dokan, had been influenced in his choice by the goddess Benten, whose shrine stood on the little island of Enoshima, near the old bakufu military town of Kamakura a few miles downbay from the Dokan's staked-out site. Benten was said to have revealed herself in the guise of a fish called the *konoshiro*, a word that, if written with different characters, translated to "this castle"—an indisputable sign to Ota Dokan of heavenly intervention in the matter. To encircle his fortress, the samurai ordered the construction of an immense wall of quarried Izu basalt, the area to be thus enclosed larger than any other castle in the world, then or later. "My dwelling is connected with pine fields, near the sea," he recorded in a poem, and "Mount Fuji is seen just under the eaves." In essence the nucleus of Tokyo, Dokan's completed castle complex covered some 1,150,000 square meters. The founder's declining fortunes weren't long able to maintain such grandeur, and after his death the place fell into ruin, the state in which Ieyasu found it when he chose the still solidly fortified structure in 1590 to be his headquarters.

Fulfilling, in a loose way, the requirements of Chinese geomancy in its siting, the castle's concentric rings of moats, spanned with numerous bridges, more closely resembled the whorls of a fingerprint than the classic right-angled blocks of the Chinese ideal. By the time Ieyasu was finished rebuilding Dokan's fortress, it ranked as incomparably the largest and most magnificent castle in Japan, a country in which during the preceding centuries castle building had been brought to an amazingly high art. Although the Tokugawa buildings burned a number of times in the fires endemic to Japanese wooden structures, each time the destroyed elements were rebuilt it was done more stoutly than in their prior incarnation. The fortress remained the primary home of Ieyasu's descendants throughout the entirety of the Tokugawa shogunate. By the time the dynasty ended, it was one of the most securely fortified places in the world. Though the Tokugawa palace of the 1860s covered only a fraction of the ground area of Dokan's complex, it was to this still-magnificent site that the young emperor now turned his attention.

The city in which his ancestors had for eleven hundred years reigned was, indisputably, now too full of memories of the monarchy's powerlessness for the again-emperor-centered state. To clearly demonstrate to the world its resolve to break with the past, it was irrevocably decided to move the capital and seat of the court to the old shogunal headquarters city, the place reborn as To Kyo, the "Eastern Capital." The new site also had an economic advantage over Kyoto. Nearness to the bustling new foreign trading colony at Yokohama, which fortunately suffered relatively little during the civil war between the Tokugawa and the imperial government, played a major part in the final selection.

At first light on the morning of the twentieth day of the ninth month of Meiji's first year as sovereign, the stunned and saddened people of Kyoto watched the city's historic reason for its existence slowly disappear in the dust of the longest state procession ever marshaled in Japan's history. It took thirteen days for the stream of humanity to wend its way up the three-hundred-mile-long Tokaido, the "Eastern Sea Road," that was Japan's equivalent to what the Boston Post Road had been to colonial America, linking the capital with a string of major population centers. The brilliant-hued uniforms of the thousands of courtiers and soldiers were often drenched in the torrential downpours that made November travel a wretched labor, but the adolescent monarch was securely protected from the elements, enthroned in an ebony and gold-lacquered pavilionlike litter borne by sixty bearers and shielded from the storms by draperies over which perched a golden phoenix bird. On each of the four corners of what resembled a wheel-less coach hung four red silken cords, each pulled taut by a special handler in an attempt to minimize the inevitable jostling and pitching transportation in even this most luxurious of litters necessarily entailed.

The bulk of the procession was made up, appropriately, of samurai of the western provinces who had put Meiji into this new position of prominence. Moving at a pace dictated by the roughness of the primitive road, the three thousand or so participants initially detoured down the Ise peninsula to their first objective: the imperial family shrine at Ise, there to allow Meiji to ask his ancestors to give their blessing to this momentous alteration in the nation's fabric of existence. After four days, the emperor's arrival at Ise occasioned the most solemn reports to his forebears: Among other things, he had to explain exactly why it was deemed necessary to give up the sacredness of Kyoto's time-hallowed soil to move the Son of Heaven to God-knows-what dangers in the eastern wilds of Edo. Apparently, Meiji and his advisers believed the gods were adequately convinced of the correctness of their motives, and the procession was able to lurch back into motion, this time heading up the coast and rejoining the Tokaido Road after crossing Nagoya Bay in ferries. While the traveling court used castles and temples along the route as overnight way stations, imperial messengers conveyed news of the government's victories over still-recalcitrant pro-Tokugawa forces that continued to engage in delaying skirmishes north of Edo. Meiji was reported to be pleased to hear of a particularly decisive victory at Wakamatsu, the tidings bringing unexpected joy to the last half of the grand but arduous progress.

On the eleventh day out of Kyoto, the marchers passed

Kanagawa, near enough to the foreign colony of Yokohama so the melange of weirdly dressed Westerners was able to witness the imperial splendor. A grandstand had been thoughtfully set up for the growing barbarian mercantile community. As it was for the Japanese onlookers, this was the first time the gaijin[7] obtained actual eyewitness proof of the unimaginably exalted One Who Dwelt Above the Cloud, a figure whose existence was by this time known to them but whose person was still entirely a mystery. Although the Japanese subjects who saw the progress bowed low in respectful silence, as was right and proper, the Westerners noticeably treated the occasion as though it were something of a carnival. This show of foreign impertinence was noted by the amazed emperor, who had never before in his entire life encountered an iota of disrespect.

On the thirteenth day, Edo was reached. It was November 26, 1868, twenty-three days after Meiji's sixteenth birthday. During the final miles, three attendants waved fans at the clouds scuttling overhead so as to warn them against approaching too closely to the Exalted Presence. As the centerpiece of the parade passed, the curious but probably terrified citizenry bowed like a wave breaking along a beach, foreheads pressed into the dust of the shogunal city's unpaved streets. One of the newly ensconced sovereign's first edicts would be to forbid such practice of prostration before his person—a new capital and new times clearly required fresh rubrics and the adoption of Western notions of respect. The best place to start was at the top.

The matter of his subjects' obeisances was perhaps emblematic of the Japan that was to come, but it was only a minor thing in the fantastic changes that were about to take place. When Meiji and his court and advisers settled in their strange but fascinating new castle-*cum*-palace, the reforms in Japan's life took off at a numbing pace. At the outset, few obvious signs altered the day-to-day life of the humbler elements of the citizenry. The Russian czar of the day, Alexander II, was reasoning that change is best when it comes from

[7]This Japanese term for "foreigners," literally "outside people," still elicits debate as to whether or not it conveys a pejorative connotation.

the head of the nation. So, too, the new Meiji governors believed. Two overriding principles were inculcated by the government, both with the full and public support of the sovereign. First, the nation must adopt Western technology and its scientific knowledge to bring Japan into the late nineteenth century where it belonged, and, second, the whole structure of government must be rearranged to centralize power under the aegis of the throne and away from the Balkanized authority of the local provincial lords.

As to the implementation of the first, young highborn imperial advisers were dispatched to Europe and America to learn the "secrets" of the West's strength and its economic successes. Meiji understood, as did his advisers, that Japan's only hope of remaining independent from Western imperialism—and, indeed, from actual Western occupation, as China was suffering at the time—was unlocking and either adapting or copying outright these secrets. Already, the relatively minor loss of sovereignty to the foreigners that Japan suffered as a result of the 1858 treaties was galling to the proud Young Turks who controlled the new government. The traveling delegates, a mixture of scholar and reporter, soaked up everything they saw in a dazzling display of aptitude that on their return would redound manifold to the country's advantage. Especially intriguing to the research team was Bismarck's Germany: a nation strong scientifically and technologically, but secure in a firm constitutional monarchism that left little room for other than the anointed top class to direct the government. Perfect! Bismarck took the eminently sensible position that international law and diplomacy was a farce, substituting force as the only effective way to influence events. The Prussian examples brought back to Meiji were to have in the coming years a direct bearing on those nations who would ever again dare to wound Japan's delicate sense of national pride.

On the second goal, that of centralizing the country's power system and administration, even greater speed was achieved. One of the first efforts was an official ordinance separating Shintoism from Buddhism. Since the foreign faith had first come to Japan and joined up with the native Shinto in the sixth century, the two religious/ideological systems had grown together into a body metaphorically resembling Siamese twins. Some of the Shinto temples and Buddhist shrines had merged with joint administration by the nineteenth century, Buddhist priests officiating at ceremonies of both confessions and Shinto shrines built within Buddhist temples. To better utilize Shinto as a locus around which emperor-worship could be encouraged and centered, Shinto needed to be "purified" and stripped of its humanist Buddhist elements, "reviving" it in the form that would have been familiar to Jimmu Tenno two millennia earlier. Shinto and its classic belief in reverence for the emperor thus became, in effect, the new state religion.

Soon after the imperial move to Tokyo, the provincial lords of Satsuma, Choshu, Hizen, and Tosa formally returned their fiefs and the people in them to the emperor, a move based on the concept that they had always "belonged" to the emperor. "The place where we live is the Emperor's land," they reasoned. "The food that we eat is grown by the Emperor's men. How then can we claim any property as our own? . . . Let all the affairs of the Empire, both great and small, be referred to [the Emperor]." The Sat-Cho recognition of the new order may have been partially motivated by a desire to be assigned preeminent roles in the conduct of the new government, but there were reasons involved other than ambition alone. Patriotism now played a large part in the actions of the leading daimyo, and any recalcitrant noble was told in explicit and unmistakable terms that he, too, had better join the parade. Now that the last vestiges of the harrying Tokugawa adherents had mostly been hunted down and destroyed, hold-outs could easily be intimidated by the imperial administration's military forces.

Finally, in 1871, the death knell of the feudal era sounded in the law of the land. Feudal domains were officially abolished and replaced by seventy-five new units,[8] the Japanese equivalent of France's revolutionary restructuring of its provinces into new "departments." Obviously, old feudal associations were deliberately gerrymandered in such a way as to break, permanently, geographical loyalties in the new alignment. The nonhereditary governors and

---

[8]Seventy-two prefectures and three metropolises; today reduced to forty-seven units.

deliberative assemblies that replaced the former hereditary daimyo were beholden only to the central government.

Profound changes in other aspects of the national life soon occurred in this period that became known as the *rokumei-kan*, [9] Japan's period of Westernization coinciding with Britain's late Victorian era.[10] One of the most far-reaching came in 1872 when the feudal learning system was completely overturned with a new Educational Code. Although slightly modernized through the elimination of some of the more fanciful details, the bizarre mythology of the nation's founding and the beginning of the imperial line was taught on a level of equal importance to that of the latest Western knowledge of physics and chemistry. English became a virtually mandatory course of study in the nation's classrooms. A state plan called for the establishment of eight universities, 256 middle schools, and 53,760 elementary schools, all under state control, to be supported by the overhauled national taxation system. And the results were stunning: By the early 1900s, more than 95 percent of schoolage Japanese were attending primary school.

In 1820, in Kyoto, the emperor Kokaku had established a unique school for the children of the nobility, and under Meiji, Kokaku's legacy was transformed into the famous Peers' School. Like Eton or Harrow in England, the new school, relocated in Tokyo, was designed primarily to educate the younger generation of aristocrats who were expected to form a pool from which the nation's leadership would eventually be drawn. In 1877, through the Department of the Imperial Household,[11] Meiji commanded that the Peers' School place especially heavy emphasis on inculcating the cardinal virtue of character building on its mostly wealthy and noble student body. The school proudly bore the unique distinction of being a branch of the Imperial Household, and while all other Japanese institutions of learning were controlled by the Department of Education, the Peers' School remained under imperial aegis through the

[9]Named for a club in Tokyo that was the gathering place for the city's cosmopolitan set; the word literally means "House of the Cry of the Stag," an allusion to a Chinese poem about a convivial gathering place for illustrious persons.

[10]Japan officially adopted the Western calendar on January 1, 1873.

[11]The name would later be changed to Imperial Household Ministry.

end of the Pacific War. In 1877, Empress Haruko, Meiji's wife, sponsored a corollary institution for girls, the Peeresses' School; only in the two establishments' combined kindergarten were the sexes mixed. Both eventually extended their training through the university level, and in time even began to accept a few children from nonaristocratic families, providing the families were of sufficiently high social standing in the still extremely class conscious Japan.

The national military force, formerly restricted to the hereditary warrior class but now raised by universal conscription, began to include commoners alongside the samurai, though the former were restricted primarily to enlisted ranks. When universal service for adult males was mandated in 1873, the government suggested converting the special pensions that had been established for former samurai to half cash, half bonds—a shrewd move since it was anticipated that much of the proud warrior class wouldn't quibble over anything so "demeaning" as money. Three years later, exchanging the pensions was made mandatory. When the wearing of the samurai sword was outlawed—a clear indication that service in the emperor's new armed services would no longer strictly be an aristocratic calling—rebellions by disgruntled samurai who were unhappy with their loss of privilege and prerogative continued to needle the government. The new army experienced its first bloody encounters in the setting down of these uprisings.

A smaller but still telling issue involved national dress. At court, the absolute bastion of old Japan, Western dress became mandatory, the kimono and ancient robes giving way in the greater interests of the modernization of the nation.

With the abolition of feudalism, the old social class system of warrior-peasant-artisan-merchant was legally abandoned, and in 1869, the population was reclassified into five categories. At the top stood one person, the emperor. Below him, on the second rung, was the imperial family, followed by the nobility, who were classified without reference to their former specific place in the intricate structure of court ranks. In fourth position were the former samurai, now to be called the *shizoku*. At the bottom was the *heimin*, the "common people," comprising, of course, the overwhelming majority of Japan's population. Notably included with the heimin were the two former outcast categories, the eta, gravediggers and other holders of "unclean" occupations, and the hinin, paupers. Giving credit where due, under the new Meiji ordering of society these outcasts—about 5 percent of the total population—were assigned truly equal status under the law, although prejudice against them never ceased and exists in remarkably strong measure to this day.

Twenty-five years later, in 1884, another decree from the palace further delineated the status of the nobility, establishing one that fit into the Westernized constitution then in the planning stages. The *kazoku*, the "old nobility," after being forced to renounce their ancient titles, were divided into five new ranks, imitating almost to the letter those of the British peerage. At the top were princes, the equivalent to Britain's dukes; such princes were not members of the imperial family, the latter specifically distinguished as "imperial princes." Next came the marquesses, followed by counts, the equivalent of earls. Viscounts and barons were in the fourth and fifth places.[12] The new peerage came in just at 500 members: 12 princes, 24 marquesses, 74 counts, 321 viscounts, and 69 barons.[13] The top two categories were to be automatically entitled to seats in the planned House of Peers, with a set percentage of the lower three ranks, to be selected by their fellows, also to sit in the envisioned upper chamber. The peerage was initially planned as a continuation of the old daimyo class, but imperial additions to it gradually changed its membership into something resembling a true meritocracy. Interestingly, when the Japanese government in 1875 abruptly and with dubious legality (China lodged a feeble protest) declared as a prefecture of Japan the semiindependent Ryukyu islands— Okinawa was the largest and most important—the former King Tai of the small archipelago was stripped of his royal title and given, together with ¥30,000 and a villa in Tokyo, the substitute rank of marquess in the Japanese peerage.

In 1890 a remarkable document, the Imperial Rescript on Education (see Appendix C), issued in the emperor's name, became a

---

[12]No rank was established corresponding to British baronets.

[13]Why the degree of viscount was so disproportionate was unexplained by the creators of the patents of nobility.

fundamental part of the Japanese political psyche; some authorities call its issuance the single most important cultural event in Japan during the Meiji years. Its writ extended far beyond mere education, and it became the unchallenged source of social and educational policy as well as of a significant portion of the nation's political thinking through the end of World War II. Rescripts were policy statements issued by emperors at infrequent intervals and having something like the force of papal dogma delivered ex cathedra. They were treated as sacred documents, even the paper on which copies were printed being handled with special, painstaking reverence. But this particular rescript actually attained much the aura of Scripture. The Imperial Rescript on Education stated that *all* authority came from the divinely founded imperial line, and then mandated a Confucian-based code of ethics based on social obligations. In the 1930s, the bland and courtly cadences in which it was written lent themselves perfectly to conversion into a tool of ultranationalism: Its language expressed the imperial desire that the emperor's subjects be obedient not only to their elders, but to the state. To do otherwise would be to disappoint the sovereign, and *that* was something every Japanese subject was to avoid.

The life of the emperor Meiji, private as well as public, was vastly different from anything his ancestors could ever have imagined. An article published in the London *Standard* at the time of his funeral described the late emperor: "His height—five feet seven inches—made him conspicuous among a people not generally running to great stature. His eyebrows, heavy and black, had the exact slant to be seen in antique models of manly beauty . . . to European eyes he seemed a little clumsy in foreign clothes, and his gait was marred by a slight halt. But on those rare occasions . . . when he reverted to the old Japanese costume, he assumed without an effort the manners as well as the dress of a long-vanished age. . . . The Emperor's personal tastes were simple, his household free from ostentation, and his table frugal." The sovereign's personal freedom of movement was greater than any monarch had experienced since the earliest days of the warrior-kings. He was fond of horseracing, and frequently attended the small derby in Yokohama. Probably his closest companion was

Hirobumi Ito, with whom he would carouse in the privacy of the imperial bedchamber, sipping their favorite Château LaRose and swapping stories of the greatness of the country's samurai-dominated past. Curiously enough for the head of what was to become in his reign a great seafaring nation, the monarch had a horror of the open ocean, even eschewing the luxury of a private yacht. He never mastered a foreign language, though he once tried to learn a bit of English.

Japan's rapidly increasing wealth was making the Meiji court into one that compared favorably to the settled splendors of Europe's royal venues. The new imperial sense of democracy, still in its infancy but nonetheless already far removed from the absolutism inherent in the old caste system, led Meiji to command that his subjects "should continue their business uninterrupted" when the imperial presence moved around the streets of Tokyo. Thenceforth, whenever he passed, the Japanese crowds he encountered broke the age-old rule of silence in the monarch's presence by shouting "Banzai." Meiji became enamored of collections of small, expensive, and mostly Western objects: clocks, swords, even autographs; he wrote once to the pope for his signature, which the pontiff very kindly dispatched to the emperor by return post. And although he possessed dozens of "detached" palaces all over his empire, Meiji seldom visited any of them, taking breaks from his duties in Tokyo only rarely, even in the worst of the capital's summer heat.

His day was a model of ordered rhythms. Awakened by his manservant at six in the morning, he was bathed and had taken breakfast within an hour; he ate frugal Japanese-style meals, his curiosity for the foreign not extending to its cuisine. A physician would check the sovereign each day to make sure he was fit to begin his daily work, and when the exam was finished the emperor changed from a pure white kimono to the uniform of commanding general in his own Imperial Guards. From ten in the morning to four in the afternoon he concentrated on the administration of affairs of state, receiving and reviewing official papers and reports and other such routine bureaucratic deskwork. Lunch was at one, which was followed by a nap until two. Late afternoons, after the last of the document signing and personal audiences, were his learning times—

enthusiastically delving into Japanese and Chinese classics, he was tutored by his country's leading scholars in the Western legal and political systems. The monarch quickly developed an increasing awareness of and taste for his own honorary role, a *direct* role, as he saw it, in the administration of the state.

The sovereign's interest in all things military was a lifelong passion. Ordinarily garbed in the undress uniform of a field marshal, the emperor nonetheless took pains when in the company of his highest-ranking generals and admirals to vest himself in the full ceremonial regalia of his station and rank. For Meiji, these order-bedecked uniforms were not merely unearned appurtenances due him as monarch. His personal concern for his troops in battle became legendary later in his reign when the imperial armies would go to war against China and Russia.

Dinner, often in the company of the empress, was served at six, husband and wife dressing in Western evening wear even when they dined alone in the palace's sumptuous dining room. Evenings were given over to the emperor's favorite pastime of poetry writing. The physician came for a final check of his sole patient at nine, after which the handkerchief-dropping ritual could commence. This was Meiji's routine for signaling which of the available ladies would share his bed that night, a child by any of these ladies automatically having the necessary pedigree to become the imperial heir. The pair would not, incidentally, retire to a tatami mat, Meiji's preference running to a soundly built Western bedstead.

The emperor's marital life was the first to be lived in a fashion considered at least partially "normal" in Western terms. The monarch's wife—not merely a consort or chief concubine, but a partner in the truest sense of the term who for the first time was granted social parity with her husband—was the former Princess Haruko, third daughter of a high-ranking minister named Tadaka Ichijo, whose family was a branch of the Fujiwara clan from which imperial wives had compulsorily been drawn for centuries. Their wedding was celebrated shortly after Meiji's accession, on February 9, 1869, at the palace in Kyoto when the bride was eighteen, her bridegroom two years younger. Haruko, arriving at the ceremony in the traditional oxen-drawn cart called a *biroge*, entered the rites a commoner and left an empress, but in the first years of her marriage she still clung to the ancient customs of an imperial consort and did not leave the palace except when her confinement was near. Traditionalists objected to her husband's insistence on granting her the style of "majesty" that Meiji had decreed was her due.

In 1873, Haruko stopped blackening her teeth, signaling the direction that the nation and its women should attempt to follow. Coming from a time when a woman of the empress's rank would be attended only by vestals—attendants who had never even seen a man—Haruko would eventually influence and then personally lead Japanese womanhood into a world of freedom it had hitherto only glimpsed secondhand. By the latter part of her husband's reign, she was known affectionately as the "Mother of the Nation."

Meiji's consort ventured out of her traditional role to participate openly in the nation's life, albeit a highly selective sliver of that life. For example, for twenty-five years she paid a yearly visit to the Tokyo Jikuen Hospital, where, with her secretary, Princess Norihiko, the empress would pass out winter clothing to the older patients, toys and candy to the younger. The privileges Mutsohito accorded his consort recognized that the freedom of women in the West was, in his words, "in accordance with the right way between heaven and earth." Of greatest importance was the fact that flowing from the status granted his own wife was to come the eventual legal ending of polygamy in Japan. Sharing her husband's love of poetry, the empress sent him a particularly tender sample of her skill when he was absent on an inspection tour of the north. "I neither seek nor expect an early flight of the wild geese, but I gaze at the northern sky, wondering how He fares." Only one small instance of Haruko's subservience is recorded for history: She was enjoined by her husband not to disturb his Yorkshire terrier when it slept in her lap.

Though fastidiously exhibiting remarkable dignity in public, Haruko still engaged in ways a mite strange, even though peculiarly and idiosyncratically Japanese. One such was her habit of smoking a golden pipe at public receptions, lifting her veil every few minutes to accept from a lady-in-waiting the proffered pipe for three—always exactly three—quick puffs, the instrument quickly to be replenished by a second lady from a special lacquered tobacco box.[14] The befeathered and tightly corsetted Victorian-style clothes that the empress wore did little to enhance her tiny figure, sometimes putting her at a cosmetic disadvantage when seen next to the graceful and traditionally kimono-clad women of the court. In any event, few people ever really got a good, close-up look at her, it being strictly enforced court etiquette never to gaze directly at the Imperial Presence, the notion being that a throne held as an exalted mystery was inevitably a better throne.

If a single characteristic act were to stand for the Meiji era, the promulgation of modern Japan's first constitution would be many historians' choice. In February of the twenty-second year of Meiji—1889 in the newly adopted Western calendrical system—the Constitution of the Empire of Japan was formally granted by the emperor to his people. Modeled on Bismarck's strongly state-centered Prussian constitution, the document was not, of course, even partially devised by Meiji himself. But the sovereign did support it by his presence at each of the constitutional assemblies—called Diets, and the forerunner of the coming national legislature—convened to work out the format and content of the document that would outline the legal nature of the new Japanese state. The major drafters were the now-middle-aged aristocrats who had led the knowledge-gathering expeditions to the West at the beginning of the postfeudal era. Though the constitution borrowed the Prussian format, the document was designed with uniquely Japanese concerns foremost.

Although the constitution was regarded as "transmitting the immutable law according to which the land has been governed" and was not held to have been created by the emperor himself, it was considered to be a "gift from the throne." Therefore, only the sovereign could legally initiate amendments, though actual changes

---

[14]Though the accoutrements she used would have been available to relatively few, the tobacco habit was by no means restricted to the imperial circle. At the time, smoking was a national rage, even among women.

required the consent of both houses of the Diet. Shortly before the first draft was complete, the emperor ordered the highest-ranking members of his ruling oligarchy to form a personal consultative body to the throne—called the *Sumitsu-in*, "the Privy Council"—to work out the final details of the draft.

When the Meiji constitution did appear (the nation's new radical journals were shrewdly muzzled for the occasion), it left absolutely no question that, in theory at least, the sovereign stood indisputably alone at the helm of state. Drawing on the appeal of the popularly perceived uniqueness of Japan's past, the framers sought to legitimate the bloodless nationalist revolution by officially garbing it in the colorful glory of an imperial "restoration," a move of supremely adroit brilliance on the part of the Meiji oligarchs. They reasoned—correctly—that not for many years had the importance of the imperial institution lain in the personal actions of the sovereigns. Rather, the emperor's power rested in the way Japanese society outside the palace walls regarded the monarchy and its unique mystique. The framers frankly set out to make the throne the highest spiritual force fueling the nation, much as Christianity was perceived in the West. Lacking a comparable religious experience, Japan's closest equivalent—the monarchy itself—became the repository in which the nation's sovereignty was forever to lie.

Article One proclaimed that "the Empire of Japan shall be reigned over and governed by a line of emperors unbroken for ages eternal." Articles dealing specifically with the powers of the sovereign followed: Article Three held that "the Emperor is sacred and inviolable"; Article Four declared "the Emperor stands at the head of the Empire, combining in Himself the rights of sovereignty and exercises them"; Article Eleven gave "the Emperor . . . the supreme command of the Army and the Navy." Others richly endowed the monarch with the sole power to convene, open, close, and prorogue the Diet; to give sanction to laws; to determine the organization of all branches of the armed services; to declare war, make peace, and conclude treaties; to confer titles of nobility; and, finally, to order amnesties, pardons, and commutations for criminals. In theory, little was left in Japanese life that was beyond the direct authority of the nation's sovereign.

Though the constitution was beholden to the throne, it was in reality subordinate to the oligarchs who controlled the throne. At the same time, it gave such vast prestige to the emperor that few would dare to challenge his moral authority as the fount from which flowed all power. The document was purposely and carefully crafted not to further any evolutionary liberalization of a modernizing society, but to preserve the status quo. Because the Meiji constitution was hamstrung by its great inherent flaw of trying to contain two irreconcilable concepts—popular government and absolutism—endless compromises on the part of the nation's governors had to be continually worked out. And right up until 1945, compromise was an ever-narrowing one-way street, the democratic parliamentarians giving in to the militarists and those who despised democratic processes.

While the oligarchs were putting this document together, a unique twelve-chapter addendum was also prepared. The Imperial House Law was an all-embracing act explicitly setting out the rights and privileges as well as the definition of membership in Japan's reigning family. It could not legally be affected by legislation, thereby placing it safely beyond the powers of the Diet. Amendments were possible only when proposed at the emperor's personal initiative, his sole advisory group an "Imperial Family Council" in concert with the Privy Council.

Thought to be of supreme significance, and therefore made the first article of the first chapter, the key provision of the House Law stipulated that "the Imperial Throne of Japan shall be succeeded to by male descendants in the male line of Imperial Ancestors." When the monarchy had been without personal power it was all right to install the rare female on the throne, as had happened nine times in the dynasty's history, but now that the monarch again substantively figured in the national limelight, women were no longer allowed to reign. The document continued, precisely clarifying how the throne was to be passed on: It would be inherited by the emperor's eldest son; where the eldest son predeceased the emperor, the throne would go to eldest son's eldest son; in default of sons, the emperor's next eldest brother would succeed; and then the emperor's uncles and their descendants. And so on. What was being clearly indicated was that the Imperial House Law, *not* the constitution, set the rules of succession. Importantly, if the Privy Council determined that a designated heir was mentally unbalanced or otherwise "incurably diseased in mind or body," the order of succession could be changed at the Council's will. The terms of this last provision would eventually be invoked to subject Meiji's own heir to a regency in the last, sad years of his life.

Titles were formally laid down for the various members of the imperial family: the heir apparent was called the *kotaishi* ("Imperial Eldest Son") if the son of the emperor, the *kotaison* ("Imperial Eldest Grandson") if the son of a deceased kotaishi. "Majesty" was declared the form of address for the sovereign, the empress, the empress dowager (the emperor's mother, assuming she had reigned as empress), and the grand empress dowager (the emperor's grandmother, with the same proviso as for the empress dowager). "Highness" was designated for the heir and his consort, the monarch's younger sons and their consorts, and the emperor's daughters; these constituted "imperial" princes and princesses. Official membership as an "imperial" prince or princess extended only through the great-great-grandsons and great-great-granddaughters of the sovereign; further generations downward would remain princes and princesses but without the important "imperial" prefix. Marriages of members of the family were restricted to the extended family circle, or otherwise to a group of qualified noble families, specially designated by imperial order. To make sure this structure was adhered to, the emperor was specifically granted personal control over the entire family, extending as far as those with the prefix "imperial" before their titles. Article 42 prohibited any member of the family adopting a son, with the intent of positively ensuring that the throne devolve through blood relationship only. The entire family was protected against any civil or criminal charges brought against them unless the emperor sanctioned such litigation. Happily for their financial security, Article 46 granted that all expenditures of the family would be met by the national treasury.

Probably the most powerful influence in Japanese government and politics from the middle years of the Meiji era on were the *genro,* the "elder statesmen," an extraconstitutional group of high-ranking advisers without whose consent no important government decision was taken. In actuality, the most important decisions were made by the genro themselves. The most famous of these formidable personalities were Hirobumi Ito, the brilliant maker of the constitution and the man with whom his friend Meiji loved to carouse; Aritomo Yamagata, responsible for modernizing Japan's army; and, best known in this century, Kimmochi Saionji, the last of the genro and a man who remained behind the scenes to advise Hirohito through the early critical phases of his reign. These men's principal contribution to the throne was to protect the emperor from personal responsibility for the exercise of his supposedly absolute powers, a service they rendered by making decisions in his name and being seen to take the burden off the imperial shoulders.

The heart of Tokyo, and certainly its soul, was the castle Meiji inherited from its former Tokugawa owners. The complex had by the middle of the Meiji era changed enormously from the military fortress that it had been in 1868 when the young sovereign arrived. The residential structure Meiji first occupied was destroyed by fire five years after he moved into its honeycomb of apartments, forcing the imperial couple to move to a "detached" palace, a comfortable villa at Akasaka, a mile away. In 1880, construction began on a magnificent new home for Meiji and Haruko, and within eight years the ruins of the old fortresslike castle had been buried under a luxurious new palace. It was equipped with the West's latest miracle conveniences, including gas, electricity, and hot and cold running water.

In a state procession on January 11, 1889, one that mirrored in miniature his earlier progress from Kyoto to Edo, the emperor and his family drove through the *Mikurumayose,* the "Grand Ceremonial Entrance," and took formal possession of their new home. Unlike the post–World War II main palace structure that replaced the destroyed Meiji building and was erected purely for ceremony, the steam-heated building into which the monarch moved a century ago was both a comfortable home for the emperor and his empress and the capital's locus of the ritual aspects of the monarchy. The imperial couple's personal apartments filled much of the grand structure in the center of the compound's 240 acres, the building a sort of Japanese-Victorian hodgepodge faintly resembling modern Tokyo's Kabuki Theater. The principal throne room was the south-facing *Seiden*, or "State Hall," scene of the most important ceremonies and formal functions. At one end, a Western-style throne-dais covered with a reddish-purple carpet held a pair of matching European-baroque golden chairs, much like those used by Meiji's contemporaries Victoria or Franz Josef; the chair on the left was for the sovereign, its mate for the empress. Covering the throne platform was a canopy embroidered with the golden sixteen-petaled chrysanthemum. A secondary throne room, the Phoenix Room, named for the mythological fire bird whose many representations were artfully worked into every feature of the chamber, primarily served for the presentation of credentials by foreign ambassadors and state ministers. Here the emperor received most of the endless orders of knighthood given him by foreign governments in the then-expected tit-for-tat exchange between heads of state; he was said to most prize the order considered by the fraternity of monarchs the world's greatest, Britain's Garter.

The largest chamber was the *Homeiden*, the "State Dining Room." Here were held the enormous Western-inspired formal dinners in which visiting princes and potentates were entertained. For the less formal audiences she held on her own, the empress used the Paulownia Room, so-called after the flower that made up the imperial consorts' personal crest. A warren of smaller rooms, ones that never figured in the official Court Gazette, housed the many beautiful young women of high rank in front of whose apartments Meiji would play his handkerchief game. All these rooms were separated by sliding wooden doors crafted with superlative native joinery, but instead of common paper, the panes were fitted with ivory- and gold-embossed parchment.

By four of his ladies Meiji sired a total of fourteen children, five sons and nine daughters. (The empress Haruko bore no children.) All the sons except his successor died in infancy, and only four of his daughters lived to survive their father. Meiji's heir—the third of the five sons—was born in 1879, his mother the imperial concubine Naruko Yanagiwara. Perhaps the monarch's genes conspired against male children, for even this sole surviving son was "delicate" from his earliest days. Named Yoshihito, he was nominated crown prince at the age of ten. His father attempted to ameliorate the inevitable apartness the boy would endure by raising him in a way that would downplay the differences between prince and commoner. Enrolled at the school for nobles at eight, Yoshihito was the first imperial prince forced to master the daily necessities of life, including dressing himself and even tying his own shoelaces. As he grew into manhood, the boy developed the manners and much of the outlook of the West, influenced by the new customs that had swept the country in its headlong rush to modernity. Yoshihito's increasingly disgusted father, still in many ways a traditionalist, considered that the son had become "dandified." The prince leapt at the opportunity to demonstrate his germinal and naive ideas of democracy, from pitching in to help a disabled *jinrikisha* driver to courteously rescuing a fellow cavalry officer who had fallen out of his saddle. Contemporary articles in Western publications described such behavior on the part of a prince as "outlandishly democratic."

Yoshihito began to show ominous signs of serious illness by the time he reached his late teens. The problems with which he was overcome were not only physical: strokes sadly left his mental capacity to reason and carry on normal social intercourse greatly diminished. And by the time he reached his young manhood, he had adopted a number of eccentricities that would almost totally incapacitate him from fulfilling his later imperial role. In fact, of the men who have occupied the Japanese throne in historic times, Yoshihito would count as one of the strangest. Devoid of any qualities describable as refined, and lacking a sensitivity for the ancient Japanese esthetic that even the coarsest of his imperial ancestors exhibited in their private lives, he turned dandiness into laughable, then pitiable, foppishness. A slavish admiration of Germany's William II, one of history's most foolish monarchs, was even carried so far that the prince adopted the Wilhelmine waxed-handlebar mustache, which looked as idiotic on the Japanese prince as it did on

William. Yoshihito's libertine manners with the ladies of the court far exceeded the traditional bedding with privileged concubines in which his father engaged, and his temper tantrums combined with a complete personal ineptitude for rule made the crown prince a poor heir to a great father.

The long reign of Meiji was winding down as these melancholy conditions were overtaking his successor, but the last years of his era saw Japan attain the status of a great international power. Wars of aggrandizement had forged Japan's army into an internationally respected force, its navy into the envy of much of the world, and its empire into a far larger entity than that which Meiji had inherited from his own father.

The first of the two Meiji foreign conflicts was the Sino-Japanese War of 1894–1895, a war that grew out of Japan's territorial interests in its old bête noire—Korea. China had already lost to foreign interests principal vassal states, Indochina and Sikkim, and saw that Korea was now strong enough to go the same way. The Chinese government was understandably anxious to preserve its influence on the strategic Korean peninsula against the designs of both Japan and Russia, but put out conflicting signals: If Korea was exploited by Japan, China protested; but if the Koreans themselves were the instigators of troubles, China disclaimed all responsibility. When Japan decided to strike against Korea, it intended to suggest that the sole Japanese motive was the preservation of Korea's independence from Peking's corrupt Manchu government, but the Chinese emperor self-righteously responded: "We have Ourselves always followed the paths of philanthropy and perfect justice, while the pygmies of Japan have [on the other hand] broken all the laws of nations and treaties, which it passes Our patience to bear with. Hence We recommend . . . Our various armies to hasten with all speed to rout the pygmies out of their lairs."

Japan's real motive, of course, was simply to turn Korea into a Japanese colony. The Koreans, against their own best interests but anxious to wriggle free of Chinese hegemony, obstructed China's efforts to stop the Japanese, thus, unwittingly, exchanging one, perhaps lesser, tyranny for another, perhaps greater, one. Military victory also brought Japan spoils in the Chinese province of Taiwan, as well as other minor bits and pieces of China, including land in Manchuria; moreover, 200,000 taels in indemnity was added to the Celestial Empire's humiliation. Korea's independence was to be "guaranteed" by its conqueror, but that beleaguered land soon became a Japanese "protectorate" and in 1910 was annexed outright. The peninsula entered upon a reign of terror emanating from its occupiers that would last the better part of the next half century.

Meiji's personal behavior in the Sino-Japanese War is worth comment. Moving from Tokyo to Hiroshima to take up supreme command of his armed forces, the emperor established his headquarters in a comparatively simple tent that was divided into a conference room, a bedroom, and a small dressing room. Its comforts were, admittedly, worthy of another planet compared to the hardships his soldiers were enduring in the fighting in Korea, but the canvas structure nonetheless roughly equaled those housing his top battlefield commanders. Meiji remained in Hiroshima throughout the conflict, moving the bed out of the center of the room in the morning to make way for a table and chairs, reversing the procedure each evening. When a retainer, taking pity on an emperor living in such "modest" circumstances, insisted that his sovereign at least have a sofa brought in, the monarch replied, "Are battlefields furnished with sofas?" When word of his comments reached his troops, as inevitably such comments do, the effect was powerful.

A decade later the second war was fought. The Russo-Japanese War of 1904–1905 removed any lingering doubts among the nations of the world whether Japan's victory over China had been a fluke. This time the enemy wasn't the decrepit Manchu empire, but one then considered among the strongest in the world. Japan made mincemeat of the pick of Russia's military and naval forces, and did so in very short order.

As Japan had had designs on Korea, so did she have the same aspirations for Manchuria, the great chunk of largely frozen wasteland that formed China's northeastern frontier province, which separated the Celestial Empire from Siberian Russia. Japan, realizing that the czar coveted the enormous and strategically important province of Manchuria, went to war to "guarantee" that Russia respected China's sovereignty there. On the evening before the day hostilities were to begin, a depressed Meiji is reported to have said to his wife, "Diplomatic relations with Russia are to be severed. Although it is against my will, it is inevitable." He then composed a poem giving vent to his sadness: "When people in the four directions over the seas think of one another as brothers, why do billows rise and winds rage?"

It was one of the most straightforward imperialistic wars in history. Of the combatants, 120,000 Japanese and 115,000 Russians died. The climax of the conflict, which had gone against Russia since its outset, was the destruction, in the spring of 1905, of the czar's Baltic fleet in the Sea of Japan by the Japanese armada, which had increased from 6,000 tons at the beginning of Meiji's reign to 380,000 tons by the fall of 1905. Czarist Russia was finished as a top power, as her performance in the Great War a decade later would ineradicably confirm. The victory brought wild jubilation to Meiji's islands. Japan was now, beyond all doubt, a *power*. [15]

Shortly after the conclusion of the Russo-Japanese conflict, the emperor's health rapidly deteriorated. Not only did his usually brisk gait turn into a faltering shuffle, but the uniquely un-Japanese huskiness of his features fell away. On July 20, 1912, the Imperial Household Ministry announced to the shocked nation that its sovereign was seriously ill. Although it wasn't stated, Meiji was suffering from the terminal effects of an incurable stomach cancer compounded by diabetes and a chronic kidney ailment.

A stunned pall fell over the capital as crowds of bereaved subjects gathered each day at the Double Bridge spanning the palace's encircling moat. Streetcars passing the imperial compound slowed, trying not to make any noise that might disturb the dying monarch. During the ten days of his final illness, more than ten thousand men and women—"infants of His Majesty," as the Japa-

---

[15]Fittingly, Japan's first objective in joining the Allied side in World War I would be to relieve Russia of her possessions in China.

nese of that era called themselves—massed daily in the palace plaza, staring over the massive walls into the pine-shrouded sanctum of their "Imperial Father." Hardly a sound arose from this mass of praying people. A few men even committed ritual suicide in the forlorn hope that the gods would accept the offering of a private life for that of the emperor.

Death came on July 30. Japan began a mourning that would last, in three consecutive periods of diminishing depth, for one year. The girl students of the Peeresses' School marked the twelve months with the wearing of black kimono; much of the rest of the country ceased laughing. Even marriages were postponed until the mourning period ended. It was, according to the Japanese calendar, Meiji 45. Crown Prince Yoshihito assumed the throne, and named his era Taisho, "Great Righteousness."

Forty days later, the dead sovereign's resplendent funeral cortege left the palace, crossing the same Double Bridge to which his subjects' attention automatically turned in times of national peril. As one, the entire nation became quiet, except for the cannon that sounded mournfully in the great monarch's memory. The gun carriage bearing Meiji's coffin was pulled to Tokyo Station, where it was entrained for the journey to interment in Kyoto. The train car in which it traveled was made of white unfinished wood, free of blemishes, symbolically representative of the essence and simplicity of the nation's Shinto faith.

Two thousand years of funerary tradition—more than that of any other nation—were imbued in Meiji's funeral and interment. By custom, the ceremonies took place at midnight. Kyoto's streets were swept spotless, pine torchlights substituting for the new and somehow now-inappropriate electric illumination. At each crossing between the palace and the gravesite shrine, bundles of straw were burned and fresh white sand was spread to help the caisson maintain traction as it was slowly pulled by eight carefully selected and trained oxen. The errant high-pitched squeak of its wheels was one of the few sounds that couldn't be controlled.

Although the nation did not know it, the monarch it was burying with such majestic pomp was not only the first modern emperor to take a substantive, if not decisive, role in the workings of his government, he was also the last who would effectively do so. The man for whose glory the Japanese people were coaxed into becoming a modern world power was succeeded by a cipher. His son would be remembered for little other than rolling his Speech from the Throne into a "telescope" at the annual opening of parliament so as to get a better look at the stupefied audience.

CHAPTER VIII

Imperial Icon
1900–1926

At this point in our recounting of the monarchy, the point at which the present emperor enters the picture, a degree of hesitant delicacy is appropriate. The particulars dealing with the union of Meiji's heir, Prince Yoshihito, and the princess who would become that heir's empress, encompass a controversy regarding the present emperor's birth. Two quite different versions exist—the first official, the second not—of the timing of Yoshihito's marriage and the birth of Hirohito.

The official story put abroad in virtually all histories of Japan has Crown Prince Yoshihito taking as his crown princess the sixteen-year-old Sadako, a daughter of the Fujiwara. The noble Lady Sadako, besides being a member of the Kujo branch of that illustrious family, was uncontestably well suited for her destined status: The princess was possessed of a pleasant and intelligent mien, this according to firsthand knowledge on the part of the wife of the Belgian envoy extraordinary to the Japanese court. Sadako's astonishingly young age was for that era considered to be well within the prime marriage and childbearing years.

Following the couple's routine affiancing, the wedding was duly celebrated in a small ceremony at eight o'clock in the morning on May 10, 1900, at the imperial shrine on the palace grounds in Tokyo. Bride and bridegroom were attired in the antique court wedding costume, with only members of their immediate families serving as witnesses to the rites. After changing into modern-style costume, European formal morning clothes for Yoshihito, a silk day costume for his now crown princess, the couple returned to their new home on the grounds of the Akasaka Detached Palace. In the normal fullness of time—a span just short of twelve months—the first of the couple's four male children was born, the baby ceremoniously given the name Hirohito and the title Michi-no-miya, "Prince Michi." It is this infant prince who today reigns over Japan, descended from 123 sovereign predecessors, each of whom had, in turn, descended from the Sun Goddess herself.

A significantly different sequence of events is presented in David Bergamini's book on the role played by Hirohito in World War II, *Japan's Imperial Conspiracy.* Bergamini's recounting is one that the author admits to be based on "court gossip," gossip that he asserts had been substantially corroborated since the 1920s by knowledgeable insiders, including the emperor's one-time personal public relations adviser, Count Yoshinori Futara. Because Bergamini's hypothesis is logical within the context of the Japanese court's then-existing standards of what constituted international propriety, it would be remiss to ignore it. The relevant chronology begins just a year earlier than in the first story.

The Imperial House Law established by Meiji contained a key provision concerning the succession, one to which his son Yoshihito would be the first heir to the throne to be bound. It implicitly mandated that the mother of the heir should be the wife of the sovereign. Since the beginning of the imperial family's known history, princes succeeding to the throne had been routinely born to mothers other than the emperors' wives or chief consorts; the most urgently respected qualification for the female was that whichever mother gave birth to a prospective heir, that mother should herself be a highborn woman of the palace. The reason that the House Law's drafters included the new condition was primarily to bring the rules governing Japan's court into closer harmony with those of the Western monarchies. How the specifics of the rules governing succession in the imperial family were perceived by the Japanese themselves wasn't of the slightest consideration; how these matters were perceived by outsiders was of *major* import.

Accordingly, when it came to the critical matter of an heir to his own son, and thus a future emperor, Meiji had been perfectly willing to let the concerned court officials interpret the House Law in whatever way would be of greatest benefit to the future well-being of the family. Germaine to Yoshihito's marriage, it was thus decided that Sadako should have both her fertility and her ability to deliver a well-formed male child tested *in advance* of the crown prince actually taking the irrevocable step of marrying the girl. Having been duly gotten with child by Yoshihito, the still unmarried fifteen-year-old candidate is said to have uneventfully passed the months of her pregnancy in the secluded beauty of central Tokyo's Aoyama Palace, once the residence of a cadet branch of the Tokugawa family.[1]

As it happened, a healthy son was indeed delivered, the first stout cries of the child rebounding throughout the delicate wooden hall-ways of the Laying-In Pavilion at ten minutes past ten o'clock in the evening on April 29, 1900, the thirty-second year of Meiji. The imperial physician, Dr. T. Hashimoto, who attended the birth, spontaneously rang out with the traditional congratulatory cry of "Banzai" on seeing the child's sex, so great was his joy at a prince to extend the direct line of succession through yet another generation.

Having indisputably passed her test, the baby's mother and its father were married eleven days later, a union whose date no one has ever questioned. The justification for the marriage—young Hirohito—was, so to speak, put in hiding. A year to the day after the crown princess-to-be became a mother, the baby's birth was first announced. Kept out of the limelight for several years, the matter of his real birth date simply never became an issue: As far as the outside world knew, he was born a year after his parents' marriage. And as far as Japan was concerned, what did it matter?—no inviolable Japanese custom had been breached, Western propriety was served, and Yoshihito was already safely guaranteed an heir.

Historian Bergamini's version of events was based on several sources besides the already mentioned "court gossip." Perhaps most

[1]Today the grounds contain the palatial villa housing the present crown prince and princess.

convincing of his evidence was that supplied by the above-mentioned Count Yoshinori Futara. Futara wrote in 1928 that the prince was "born on the night of April 29, 1900," a statement that he was never made to recant by Japan's tough prewar police, according to the count's publisher. Bergamini also pointed out that all Japanese newspapers for the two-week period surrounding April 29, 1901, were removed from the country's libraries in 1945 and still remain unavailable. It seems unlikely today that the controversy will be publicly commented on by those palace officials who might know the truth.

After seclusion at the Aoyama Palace, the new crown princess was at last free to leave her isolation and join her husband in the less etiquette-dominated environment that Yoshihito had, in the face of his father's increasing rancor, carved out for himself at the old Akasaka Palace, one of the many so-called detached residences at the imperial family's disposal. The larger palace, about a mile northwest of the main Imperial Palace, had in prerestoration days been the property of the Kii family and then served as the young Meiji's temporary residence after the 1872 burning of the shogunal castle. What luxuries existed at the original Akasaka Palace were evidently considered by the crown prince to be lacking in the splendor, not to mention the Western comforts, he considered appropriate to his station and his role as the leader of the capital's emerging Edwardian-flavored high society. Accordingly, at the height of Japan's "catching up with the West" period shortly before the turn of the century, Yoshihito commissioned a flashy and utterly un-Japanese structure to replace the old-style mansion that had once adequately served his father.

Designed by one of the nation's leading architects, Toyu Katayama, with construction beginning in 1906, the resulting structure is by a comfortable margin the most European-rococo imperial residence in Japan. Ten years in the building, the immense, two-story, earthquake-reinforced stone building, with its four acres of floor space, looked like the offspring of the mating of the Grand Château at Versailles and Buckingham Palace, leaning more toward the former on the inside, the latter on the outside. Unexplicably, one important Western comfort was almost entirely omitted: A single bathroom—in the basement—was seen adequate for the whole palace, the lavish private living quarters making do with portable tubs and chamber pots. In addition, the imperial couple's bedrooms were placed in opposite wings, which in the colossal building translated to a healthy walk for any conjugal visits between husband and wife.

The grounds of the new Akasaka Palace were lush with oaks, gingko and camphors, cedars and pasanias, the mass of trees in places forming a canopy that almost blotted out the then-clear Tokyo skies. The chrysanthemums, possessing a special status as the imperial symbol, were tended with special care and respect by an army of gardeners, particularly the golden sixteen-petaled variety that replicated the emperor's official crest. But the pink marble facing that lent the building its unique hue caused Meiji to voice publicly his disgust at this un-Japanese monstrosity, and the gaudy knockoffs of barbarian Louis XV furniture helped ensure that the emperor would never visit his son's home, which he contemptuously referred to as "Yoshihito's French house."

Hirohito's earliest years weren't spent in this cosmopolitan environment so repugnant to his more traditionally minded grandfather.[2] Imperial custom had long called for the removal of princes from their families at an early age so they could be brought up in the homes of "appropriate" subjects. Originally, the logic justifying this seemingly cruel behavior had to do with keeping heirs away from scheming at court—usually in the person of ambitious concubines anxious to further the fortunes of their own offspring—but its retention into the twentieth century was more readily justified on the grounds that it gave the future monarch an unbiased glimpse into life as lived by his subjects. Meiji himself had passed his first five years in the home of the Nakayama family, a clan notable for producing generations of high state counselors whose relative impoverishment (the family's income was a comparatively trifling two hundred koku of rice per year) meant that as a child the future emperor tasted life close to that of the subjects over whom he was

[2]In later years, Hirohito would publicly describe the Akasaka Palace as "unlivable."

destined to reign. Yoshihito was, when his turn came around, farmed out to the Hibiya[3] home of the same Nakayama family.

By the time Hirohito was old enough to be subjected to this separation, Meiji was anxious it be carried out if for no other reason than to ensure that the young prince was not contaminated any more than necessary by the behavior of his father. Vice Admiral Count Kawamura, the prince's new foster father and a man deeply cognizant of the responsibility he was undertaking, had tried without success to decline the honor. "Think of the child as one of your own grandchildren and raise it as you like," the crown prince counseled the Kawamuras. Though probably aware of the somewhat disingenuous nature of the imperial heir's advice, the admiral was given the night to think the matter over, and in realizing that refusal to accept little Hirohito could be construed as failure to his sovereign, the next day he acquiesced to the charge, promising only that he would do his "duty."

Accordingly, in July 1901, Hirohito was bundled up in a carriage and driven to the home of Count Sumiyoshi Kawamura in Tokyo's Azabu district. The admiral's wife, Countess Haruko, carried the swaddled infant in the carriage, the three passing under a congratulatory arch erected by the admiral's neighbors in front of his house to honor the child. The pure Japanese atmosphere of the admiral's home, influenced by the primal Shinto forces to which both the imperial family and the nation owed their roots, had been a major factor in the decision to choose this particular subject's household for the prince's critical early formative years.

In the atmosphere both ascetic and homespun that surrounded the prince at the seventy-year-old Kawamura's home, small incidents accumulated that would have a great bearing on the future emperor's personality. When, for example, Hirohito threw his chopsticks from his pudgy hands at the appearance of some dish or another that he didn't like, the grandfatherly foster father agreed he shouldn't have to eat anything he didn't wish to, but neither should he eat anything else. At the inevitable flow of the boy's tears, Count Kawamura turned his own face away, the enormity of disci-

[3]A district of Tokyo near the palace.

plining his future sovereign having momentarily overcome him. Though only a toddler, Hirohito evidently sensed the pain he had caused. As an adult he would never complain about the food he was served or very little else affecting his own personal comforts or tastes.

In 1902, Crown Prince Yoshihito became a father for a second time, another son, thus doubly ensuring the succession. Prince Yasuhito, later titled Chichibu, was also taken to the Kawamura home, there to join his older brother in the protective but spartan family regimen Meiji's advisers deemed so desirable for the imperial offspring. The double responsibility became more than the old admiral and his wife could handle, so the crown prince ordered that two Red Cross Society nurses be sent over to help the elderly Kawamura and his wife with the chores normal to bringing up two rambunctious boys. The count even consulted an English governess resident in Tokyo who had purportedly served one of Europe's royal families as to how she had carried out her duties, and he was said to be "much moved" by her lofty views on royal education. His favored method of disciplining the often mischievous Hirohito was to threaten to declare Prince Chichibu the "senior" prince under the Kawamura roof.

After three years in what for the boys was fortunately a remarkably warm setting, the old admiral died, psychologically orphaning Hirohito and necessitating the princes' return to the Aoyama Palace and the supervision of Takamasa Kido, the son of a samurai and former Meiji oligarch. Kido's own son, the Marquis Kido of World War II fame, would, in the years just before the Pacific conflict, become one of Hirohito's closest personal advisers. In 1906, a kind of kindergarten was set up for Hirohito and his brother Chichibu, with other boys carefully selected from the peerage becoming their classmates. (A year earlier, the crown prince had fathered a third son, Prince Nobuhito, later called Takamatsu.)

In April 1908, the crown prince's eldest son began formal education. Hirohito was enrolled at the Victorian-style red-brick Peers' School, a facility to which his young noble classmates were routinely driven by jinrikisha, wrapped in soft silk quilts in the protective arms of their families' servants as if the parents feared that even the briefest exposure to the city's smoky breezes would injure the little scions. The fifty-nine-year-old principal, General Maresuke Nogi,[4] a popular national hero, was to become one of the major influences on Hirohito's life. During the Russo-Japanese War, the austere army officer had with considerable bloodletting led the victorious Japanese forces against the Russians at Port Arthur, winning his nation's near idolatry for his efforts. Famed for his reverence for the throne and adherence to the ancient ideals of bushido, the principles of loyalty and honor so sacred to the samurai class, Nogi was envisioned by Yoshihito's advisers as the perfect mentor to instill these same attitudes in the prince.

Hirohito was soon introduced to Nogi's soldierly bearing. On his first day at the school, the small and probably frightened boy failed to execute a salute smart enough for the general's satisfaction as he left at the end of the day. Nogi sharply brought the new student to a halt, yelling, "Prince! You must always salute your teachers wholeheartedly." As he snapped to attention and threw a smart salute, just as courtiers had already taught him at home, the general gladdened and beamed, evidently pleased that his newest charge appeared excellent material to be molded for the nation's increasingly military-oriented throne.

Hirohito was thrust into every kind of sport known in Japan. Years later he modestly reminisced on his athletic acumen that "I am not really good at any sport. In swimming, however, I rather think I can hold my own." Nogi made it abundantly clear to his faculty that no special favors were to be extended to Hirohito. As the eight-year-old boy was destined to become commander-in-chief of all branches of the nation's armed forces, his educational goals were to be set with this role always uppermost in mind. Since Hirohito's national military figureheadship—not his station as the high priest of Japan's Shinto faith—would be the function perceived by his subjects as his most important until the end of World War II, Nogi's charge to the school's faculty was anything but trivial.

[4]Nogi, together with his wife, would, in a gesture of respect to the emperor, commit suicide on the day of Meiji's funeral; as the guns marking the departure of the emperor's coffin were fired from the Imperial Palace, the general sliced open his abdomen and his wife plunged a dagger in her throat, killing themselves according to the precepts of seppuku.

The first emperor, Jimmu

The emperor's method of travel
in ancient times

A court noble in ancient Japan

The four classes of society:
military, agricultural, craftsmen,
and mercantile

Daimyo (nobles of feudal times)

A battle between the Minamoto and the Heike clans

Dolls clad in ancient court dress

A royal progress at an enthronement ceremony

Prince Shotoku, regent of Japan, with his two sons

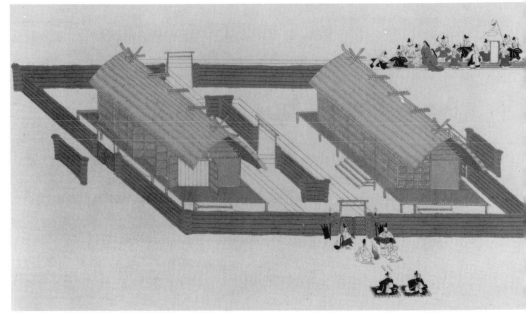

The enthronement ceremony's Daijo-gu

Enthronement ceremony at the Shishinden

The emperor's throne

The empress's throne

Traditional Upper-Class Costumes

Samurai in hunting robe

Court attendant *(Kwanjo)*

Imperial court noble *(Kuje)*

Samurai in court robe

Emperor Meiji and his consort

Emperor Taisho and his consort

Views of the Meiji palace, completed in 1888, destroyed in an air raid in 1945

Views of the Imperial Palace and garden, Kyoto. *Courtesy of the Rockefeller Archive Center.*

Emperor Hirohito

Empress Nagako

Aerial view of the Imperial Palace, Tokyo

Imperial Household Agency headquarters building, Tokyo

The wedding of Crown Prince Akihito and Michiko Shoda

The Crown Prince and Princess with Mr. and Mrs.
John D. Rockefeller III. *Courtesy of the Rockefeller Family Collection.*

The Emperor and Empress at the home of Mr. and Mrs.
John D. Rockefeller III. *Courtesy of the Rockefeller Family Collection.*

A recent photo of the imperial family (front row, left to right):
Princess Sayako, the Emperor, the Empress, Prince Fumihito; (back
row, left to right): Prince Naruhito, the Crown Princess, the Crown
Prince, Prince Hitachi, Princess Hitachi.

When his Peers' School studies began, Prince Hirohito took leave each morning of the Akasaka Palace through its Samegahishi Gate for the walk to Tokyo's Yotsuya district. A year later, the morning journeys included his brother Chichibu; when Takamatsu reached school age, the three of them—with the youngest prince always protectively framed by his two older brothers, the trio's police escort following at a discreet distance—were a daily sight to the respect-fully bowing Tokyoites who lived or worked on the route. The oldest brother soon began to pick up insects and plants along the way, specimens he would later catalog into notes of ordered exactitude in the love of science that became Hirohito's chief personal hall-mark.

The dynastic events of 1912 caused a major dislocation in Hirohito's life. When Meiji died on July 30 and Yoshihito suddenly became emperor, Hirohito's own status was as a consequence im-measurably elevated. Some historians have written that a small segment of the most influential courtiers, including General Nogi, had secretly preferred that the sturdier and more military-minded Prince Chichibu be named crown prince to replace Yoshihito, now the emperor Taisho.[5] Their desire to set aside the strict rule of primogeniture in the new Imperial House Law was partly based, according to David Bergamini, on the shaky premise that since Hirohito was born out of wedlock, Chichibu had, in the view of the courtiers privy to this information, a strong claim to displace Hirohito and stand first in line as Yoshihito's heir. But of more immediate concern than this highly dubious interpretation of the House Law was Hirohito's health. His physical state had become, in fact, of considerably more than minor concern to the court. Osanaga Kanroji, an imperial attendant who for seventy years had served as chamberlain to both Hirohito and his father, relates that young Hirohito's fingers were so clumsy that he had trouble even buttoning the uniforms that were, like those of almost every other schoolboy in the empire, his daily school dress. Chamberlains were instructed never to help him, but to let the young prince manage

[5]For his reign name, Yoshihito chose the name meaning "Great Righteous-ness."

as best he could, the only possible course for one whose future held such an enormously important destiny.

Hirohito also suffered a more than normal lack of coordination in some sports and in calisthenics, and his posture was so bad that he was provided with a special chair that forced him to sit in a position calculated to improve his bearing. In spite of these liabilities, all notions of skipping Hirohito in the line of succession were officially discarded, and he was formally proclaimed crown prince and heir to the throne on September 9, 1912. He was also appointed sublieutenant in the army, second sublieutenant in the navy, and, to serve the needs of imperial etiquette, was awarded the Supreme Order of the Chrysanthemum, his country's highest decoration.

Six years after he first arrived, he passed out of the Peers' School elementary-level classes with academic honors. A special educational institute was then established with Hirohito its sole student. The Crown Prince's Learning Institute, furnished with scientific apparatus, natural history exhibits, and military maps covering its walls, was set up in its own one-story, Western-style building on the grounds of the Takanawa Palace. The only softening of its foursquare features was the potted seasonal plants grown with fond care by the crown prince himself. The school wasn't heated, even during Tokyo's severe winters, the logic being that the discipline would "toughen" Hirohito and provide the kind of self-mastery an emperor would require. Hirohito's own personal living quarters were established next door in a traditionally Japanese-style building contrasting sharply to the Western-influenced schoolhouse.

Admiral Heihachiro Togo, a national hero for his victory at the Battle of Tsushima in which the Russian fleet had, in the 1905 war, been so convincingly defeated, became the institute's president. The prince's individual instructors, carefully vetted for this immensely prestigious duty, were drawn from the highest ranks of both army and navy, the two primal forces in Japanese life then vying with the country's civilian authorities for control of state policy. Courses in the arts and sciences were included, but tutoring in the military arts, including instruction in swordsmanship, was considered the most important part of the curriculum. Hirohito spent much of his classroom time hearing, as an audience of one, lectures from the nation's preeminent scholars and professors, including a special moral philosophy class called *teiogaku*, "learning for the emperor." A remarkable fact emerging from Hirohito's educational immersion into the glories of Japan's military tradition was that as an adult he became neither a martinet nor personally preoccupied with a military mentality, a situation profoundly different from that of many other royal scions, both at home and abroad, of his era.

Hirohito's interests, piqued most sharply by the natural world since his earliest youth, now turned fully toward science, an inclination so deeply felt that it would eventually lead to his becoming a recognized authority in the esoteric study of marine biology and, in his mature years, achieving the rare distinction of respect from the academic world without reference to his official station. In 1917, Hirohito made his first scientific discovery—a hitherto unknown species of marine life—while vacationing at the family villa at Numazu in the peach-growing region two hours southwest of Tokyo. The boy had been collecting shellfish on the beach one morning, when suddenly his eye caught the unfamiliar sight of the shell of a bright red sea animal. After unsuccessfully trying to identify the strange little crustacean in his library of reference books, he found that it was totally unclassified. Carefully wrapping the treasure and taking it to an authority in the field, Dr. Terao Arata, Hirohito learned that it was an unknown species of deep sea prawn, one never before seen. It was given the appropriately regal scientific name *Sympathiphae imperials*.

The life that Hirohito led was, compared with then-existing European standards for its royal families, cloistered in the extreme. Princes in the imperial line of succession were emphatically not expected to be playboys or bon vivants, the Japanese not regarding their monarchy as the public diversion European monarchies were already becoming. In an act traditional for an heir to the throne, Hirohito was established in the Akasaka Palace grounds' Togu Villa, away from his brothers and solely in the company of chamberlains and attendants, men who could hardly be expected to provide any kind of normal companionship for a man they considered a god-to-be. Hirohito spent holidays at one of the string of imperial villas dotting the country's four islands, his favorite being the seaside palace at Hayama. Set on the lovely Miura peninsula that protects Tokyo Bay from the open sea, the imperial enclosure was perched by itself at the end of a small neck of land that jutted out into the surrounding waters. In an area long a holiday resort for Tokyoites, the villa itself was surrounded by private riding grounds for the imperial family's exclusive use. Kanroji was adamant that Hirohito consider his holidays at Hayama not as an opportunity for the pursuit of mere leisure, but primarily as a time to collect marine biology specimens. Also, the seaside days gave the prince a chance to build up his weak physical state, a critical objective in light of what would be expected of him in his adult life.

The privileged world of Hayama still included many of the esoteric elements of a way of life little changed since the days of the feudal emperors. Courtiers would take turns serving as the imperial food tasters, men whose duty it was to eat a small portion of any dish served to the prince to ensure it hadn't been poisoned. Hirohito's father, who had gone through the same experiences, later jokingly reminisced about one particular attendant who, with a bigger than average appetite, always left a rather skimpier meal for its intended recipient than did any of the other official tasters.

In 1918, Hirohito both came of age and was formally engaged. The first circumstance, on May 7, involved the traditional palace ceremony when, before the sacred Kashikodokoro shrine on the palace grounds and in the presence of the assembled court, the crown prince was vested with the special headdress signifying his right to succeed as sovereign without a regency.[6] The next month, Hirohito's betrothal, which was expected to last for some four or five years before the actual marriage, was announced. That the bridegroom was marrying for, of all things, love *and* outside the usual Five Families of great court nobles were, as might be expected, matters of intense interest to the losing families. That the crown prince's choice had, additionally, been approved by the Imperial Household Ministry as, in their opinion, the most appropriate

---

[6]His mother had been designated to serve as regent if he had come to the throne earlier; it was the only exception in the Imperial Household Law permitting such a degree of sovereign authority to a woman.

choice for Hirohito, was immaterial to the offended courtiers. The autocratic adviser to the emperor, the Choshu samurai Prince Yamagata, held center stage of the controversy, the dispute becoming so intense that the young Hirohito was himself unavoidably and bitterly introduced to the world of political intrigue that had been central to the clans' jockeying for power in his grandfather's reign.

Fourteen-year-old Princess Nagako was a daughter of Field Marshal [Imperial] Prince Kuniyoshi Kuni and his wife, the princess Chikako Kuni, collateral branch members of the imperial family. Ominously, the young princess's maternal heritage descended from the Shimazu family of the Satsuma clan, sometimes allies but far longer the hereditary enemies of Prince Yamagata's Choshu family. The sole concrete imperfection that her opponents could come up with in Nagako's otherwise unimpeachable qualifications sprang from this Shimazu connection. It was an imperfection Yamagata jumped on, urging Hirohito's parents to forbid the match and thus sustain the Yamagata and Choshu influence against the day Hirohito would succeed to the throne.

The pitiable weapon used against the girl was color blindness. An article was planted in a Tokyo medical journal in 1920—more than a year after the betrothal—purporting to be a scholarly discussion of the effects of color blindness in the Shimazu family of the Satsuma clan. Nagako's father immediately understood the significance of the magazine's article, a journal received, hardly by coincidence, by the personal physician to Prince Yamagata. Yamagata's opposition to the Satsuma alliance now had a physical justification: There must be absolutely no chance of a defective gene being introduced into the imperial line where it might strike a future emperor, analogous to the way Queen Victoria's hemophilia (admittedly a far more serious condition) was being passed on to so many of her progeny peppering Europe's courts.

Naturally, Prince Yamagata saw a canceling of the engagement as the simple solution to this manufactured crisis. Hirohito himself was in too weak a position to insist on anything, but he made it clear to his family and retainers that he "preferred Nagako" to any alternative fiancée that the Choshu faction might suggest. Finally, Yamagata made his move. He presented his case directly to the emperor and empress, believing they would side with him and wisely demand that Hirohito marry a princess from one of the traditional Five Families. Yamagata had his man at court, Imperial Household Minister Najiro Nakamura, present the case to Their Majesties. After apologizing to the emperor for having "discovered" the color blindness in the Shimazu family, and implying that with this discovery surely His Majesty understood the impossibility of the marriage, Nakamura got the surprise of his life. The ailing Taisho (who had suffered an almost totally disabling stroke in 1919) was still lucid enough to make a personal decision on the matter: The monarch's startling and none-too-subtle reply to the minister—"I hear that even science is fallible"—put an immediate end to further discussion of Nagako's vision "defects." That same night the imperial engagement was officially confirmed from the palace. Yamagata lost the battle, the war, and, very soon, his influence. Incidentally, as matters turned out, Nagako was not herself color blind—in fact, she later developed into a talented painter—and there is no indication that she has passed any such imperfection to her own children.

Soon after this protracted unpleasantness (Nagako's own considerations throughout the entire affair weren't thought to be worth considering, nor, indeed, was her approval of the engagement ever sought), Hirohito set out on an adventure that gave him an entirely new perspective on a world whose rough edges he had never encountered. In March 1921, he left on a precedent-breaking tour of Europe.

Its people today have, of course, become totally blasé where international royal progresses are concerned, but to the Japan of 1921, the idea that the heir to the throne might leave the home islands was both unprecedented and shocking. Some thought it might even be illegal. The planned trip aroused substantial controversy most significantly among the empire's political leadership. Those who considered it disgraceful that the heir to the throne of a "divine land" should find any compelling reason to depart that land for the unknowable dangers of a "barbarian country" were undoubtedly motivated more by the fear of whatever liberalizing influences Hirohito might encounter than by considerations of tradition or precedence. Siding with this conservative faction were groups of radicals willing to throw their bodies across the railway tracks that would be used to take the Imperial Presence from Tokyo to the embarcation port of Yokohama. But Taisho's agreement to the trip proved decisive, forcing the politicians who had opposed it to drop, or at least quiet, their protestations. The grand progress would not only be the first, but it would also be the last time Hirohito was allowed to leave his country until many years after the end of his own divine status.

On the morning of March 3, 1921, to the sound of a twenty-one-gun salute and clad in the uniform of an admiral, Hirohito together with his considerable retinue boarded the twelve-thousand-ton Imperial Navy battleship *Katori* (for security's sake in the company of a second battleship, the *Kashima*) and steamed out of Yokohama harbor and headed for England. The emperor's heir was taken away from his homeland for the most carefree six months of his life. (In the Japanese tradition, because those affianced, especially of noble blood, were to have an absolute minimum of social contact before marriage, Nagako was not allowed to see Hirohito off.) A matter of some needling worry for the basically xenophobic advisers who had legislated against the trip was the very real chance that the twenty-year-old Hirohito might make a fool of himself. Having been shielded from virtually all of the seamier aspects of the world, as well as from the intricacies of European royal social conventions, Hirohito might conceivably get himself involved in some unforeseen question of etiquette, its resolution, if bungled, reflecting badly on the imperial institution.

After a stop in Egypt, where, in Cairo, Field Marshal Lord Allenby gave a garden party for the imperial party (ruined, unfortunately, by an especially nasty sandstorm that blew up out of the desert onto the embassy's grounds), the *Katori* and the *Kashima* arrived in Portsmouth Harbor on May 7. The squadron was met two days later by Hirohito's opposite number in Britain, and a man as different from the Japanese crown prince as buttons are from braces. Edward, the Prince of Wales, was an international media darling whose father, King George V, might by 1921 have gladly traded his increasingly unmanageable and unpredictable son for Taisho's complacent heir.

The British leg of the Grand Tour got off to a euphoric start when the two princes—who were unable to speak directly to each other, Hirohito being too shy to try out his faltering English and his British counterpart unable to utter a single syllable of Japanese—arrived at London's Victoria Station to be met by Hirohito's host, King George. Accommodated for the first three days of his visit with the English royal family at Buckingham Palace and at Windsor Castle, Hirohito was boggled by the apparent relative lack of strictures on European royalty. It must have come as a shock to the prince to see people looking at him as a man rather than deeply bowing before a Divine Presence. King George dealt with the crown prince in his natural, gruff way, slapping him on the back and looking in on him in his palace bedroom before lights out. Hirohito found himself almost dizzy with happiness, a happiness that made him the convinced Anglophile he was to remain for the rest of his life, the tragic events of 1941-1945 notwithstanding.[7]

Following a protracted and eye-opening tour of Britain, Hirohito left for France at the end of May. The studious prince would always keep the Metro ticket he bought while traveling incognito in Paris, and remember the station attendant who rudely pushed him back from boarding a full train. "I had a good scolding," he would tell visitors a half century later, recalling fondly an incident from which his cossetted life in Japan insulated him. After being honored with a state banquet hosted by the French president at Versailles and a private dinner at Paris's famed La Perouse restaurant (one courtier mistook the escargot for worms, and lodged a protest against such lèse-majesté), the entourage moved on to the Netherlands and Italy. The latter stop involved an audience with Pope Benedict XV, in this still pre-Lateran Accord era a "prisoner" (of his own making) in the Vatican Palace. The crown prince arrived back in Tokyo on September 3, 1921, to encounter a deliriously patriotic welcome at the capital's main station. Though the Japanese man-in-the-street

[7]Exactly a half century later, during his 1971 imperial tour of Europe, Hirohito and his empress paid the then-Duke of Windsor and his duchess a short visit at their Paris mansion. The two men, erstwhile friends and erstwhile enemies, were at the meeting able to converse in the by-now less shy Japanese sovereign's serviceable English.

wouldn't have been informed if Hirohito *had* caused any "embarrassment" to the nation or its dynasty, the truth is that the rapidly maturing prince carried off the tour beautifully, conducting himself with dignified, if shy, aplomb throughout and popularizing abroad not only his country but himself.

The trip did not, however, as conservative courtiers and the nation's military leaders feared, convert Hirohito to European political liberalism. Taisho's heir may have enjoyed himself enormously in the freedom of Western society, but it by no means made him stupid: He knew he could no more bring back to Japan the liberal democratic notions with which he had been confronted, even if such had been his wish, than he could have personally taken the reins of government into his own hands. But to the men whose interests would have been ill-served by such a development, even the suggestion that Hirohito intended to reign in a way comparable to the Western forms of constitutional monarchy was frightening. To them, constitutional monarchy equated to democracy, a form of government alien to Japan—even to a not-yet-totalitarian Japan, which was then undergoing its sole experience to date with genuine party government, albeit a limited democracy that would shortly be extinguished by the advocates of undisguised totalitarian rule. In the view of the oligarchs and influential politicians who despised democracy as a weak and unworkable form of government, Hirohito's role as emperor was that of godhead, underwriting their decisions with the divine authority that he received directly from the deities who founded the dynasty and the nation. The real role of the pre-1945 Hirohito, just as it had been with Meiji and Taisho, rested not in his own deeds, but in acting as the foil for the government's political decisions.

If the prospect of a substantive role in the administration of his nation was dim, Hirohito's constitutional status did undergo a major change shortly after his 1921 trip to Europe. The emperor's mental health had degenerated alarmingly, making him incapable of even putting on a pretense of normal behavior. The court decided that as a result he had to be "retired," in respect of which, on November 25, 1921, the crown prince was formally elevated to the position of regent; Taisho was thereafter sequestered completely out of public view at his seaside villa at Hayama. With this enforced retirement of his father, Hirohito was now emperor in all but name.

To give Nagako the opportunity to grow into physical womanhood, the engagement between the new regent and this daughter of the nobility had been put in a state of formal abeyance, but the time for their wedding was now approaching. In June of 1922, formal imperial sanction to the marriage was personally conveyed by Grand Chamberlain Tokugawa, a member of the former shogunal family, to the princess's family, in token of which the grand chamberlain presented nuptial gifts to Nagako's family in the name of the imperial family, including two lacquered wine casks and a pair of sea bream, ancient symbols of good luck. Together with five old and important scrolls, the Japanese equivalent of the Old Masters hanging in Europe's galleries, these symbolized her impending elevation to imperial status. Shortly thereafter a wedding date was finally announced: The couple would end what would amount to a five-year betrothal and be married on November 27, 1923. The announcement was followed by months of fittings for the fabulously intricate wedding clothes each would wear and the rehearsals required so that the major participants could master their roles in the complex Shinto ceremonies. Even Prince Yamagata, the Kuni family's nemesis, got into the picture, taking the occasion to, at long last, die. (In revenge for his opposition to Nagako, Hirohito would eventually do everything he could to eliminate Choshu influence from the affairs of both the court and the army.) The engagement was proceeding apace to its historic and solemn conclusion when a tragedy of unimagined proportions brought a dramatic end to all thought of nuptial festivities.

At one minute before noon on September 1, 1923, the floor of Japan's Kanto plain—the country's largest flatland and the site of the Tokyo metropolitan conurbation, even in that day far-reaching—shook with such a furor that before the earth's movement and the resulting tidal waves and fires had ended, 140,000 people were dead, tens of thousands more injured, and vast stretches of the Tokyo-Yokohama metropolis a fire-blackened wasteland. Author Leonard Mosley described the effect of the quake to be like "a carpet with a draught under it." With but few exceptions, the city was built of insubstantial wooden houses, many of which contained, at the time the quake started, a charcoal-burning fire in the brazier for the noon meal. Combined with the normal dryness of late summer, the conditions seemed to conspire with the earth's convulsions to produce the most destructive combination possible, the quake the worst ever to strike the country.

The imperial family was at the time of the disaster dispersed over far-separated corners of the afflicted region. The emperor and empress had left the villa at Hayama, the hot, sticky air making the invalid sovereign uncomfortable in the seaside humidity, Sadako taking her husband to an alternate imperial villa at Nikko, the mountainous Tokugawa shrine city east of the capital. The town was spared the earth tremors, but from the villa's terrace that evening the couple could see the glow from the blazing city.

Nagako was also out of Tokyo, equally to escape the summer heat. The princess was staying with her family at Akakura, a spa on the slopes of Mount Myoko in the Japanese alps, where newsmen informed the crown princess-designate's father of the extent of the disaster. Able to do little to help, Nagako nonetheless immediately ordered that her own clothes be given to the victims, and then set about organizing collections of goods to be sent to the capital and used as relief officials saw fit.

The prince regent was himself in Tokyo. About to sit down to lunch in the Akasaka Detached Palace, the marble mausoleum that had become his own official residence, he and his guests fled the palace's dining room on sensing the earth's first convulsions. Seeking an open space to ride out the quake, the prince was following the instinctive behavior of all of his countrymen who underwent earthquakes. Because of its massive steel-reinforced concrete construction, the palace was nearly undamaged (as were most of the buildings in the more modern western districts of the city), but Hirohito was nevertheless immediately taken to the safer massive wooden structure on the grounds of the Imperial Palace a mile away, there to wait out the inevitable aftershocks. The monarchy's chief residence held up under the quake with very little damage, the mortarless high stone walls surrounding it remaining completely intact, as did all of the family's private residential villas in the palace grounds.

One of the ancient motivations for imperial abdications had to do with atonement for natural catastrophes. Many Japanese believed, and continued to believe in 1923, that earthquakes were the movement of a giant catfish under the sea, a creature that stirred only when bidden to do so by a Sun Goddess angry or discontent with her descendant on the throne. Since it was obvious that this method of absolving responsibility could no longer be invoked, another excuse for the tragedy had to be found. General Masataro Fukuda, the martial law commander chosen by the prince regent to maintain order in the city, hit on just such a solution with a stroke of evil genius.

In a country as ethnically homogeneous as Japan, racial prejudice—the human affliction that seems to be shared in more or less equal parts by people all over the world—would seemingly have a hard time finding its focus. Although Japan has its own small but dispersed and hard-to-identify outcast class, only one foreign community existed with the necessary qualifications to engender deep and bitter national prejudice. Korea was, in 1923, under the brutally unsubtle thumb of its Japanese overlords, and economic conditions in that beleaguered land were so bad that many of its people emigrated to take low-paying jobs in Japan. There they settled in slum ghettos where the underemployed residents often turned, by necessity, to illegal occupations of unsavory mien. Partly for this reason, and partly out of sheer racial hatred, they became easily the most despised minority in the country. It therefore wasn't difficult for General Fukuda to encourage the homeless Japanese quake victims to mindlessly take their anger and frustration out on the Korean aliens, who had themselves suffered as wretchedly in the quake as the native Japanese. This fury translated into something like four thousand Koreans being tried at mock street trials, after which many were summarily beheaded by their tormentors.

During the period immediately following the disaster, Hirohito was effectively confined to the palace. To stress his personal commiseration, which was said to have been genuinely profound, Hirohito ate only unhulled rice during the weeks following the quake, sharing this then-standard of Japan's poor as a "token of His Majesty's profound sympathy with the victims of the disaster." His advisers and the government's ministers apparently were weighed down by more pressing matters than to think about effectively utilizing the magic of the monarchy to succor the desperate and destitute people. Since the prince regent was unable to assert any initiative himself, he sat unused for days before finally being allowed to tour the devastated city.

When at last he did get out among the people, his drawing power proved to be unprecedented. Though he appeared too late to have any effect on the bloody anti-Korean butchery, the fact that he did venture among his subjects had the effect of turning a respected but remote prince into a popular hero. As gratifying as this may have been to Hirohito, the shadowy powers in the background of palace politics nonetheless menacingly saw even this as a danger to their vision of a proper, inaccessible, and godlike sovereign whose only real purpose was to give authority to the decisions they made.

Because of the savage trial Japan underwent with its Great Kanto quake, the wedding of the prince regent and Princess Nagako had to be temporarily postponed, it being obvious that by the planned date for the ceremony, November 27, such unrelieved misery would still be wracking the Kanto area that it would have been tasteless, as well as unpropitious, to go forward with the planned celebrations. When the union was finally solemnized the following January, the ceremony was, at Hirohito's own request, greatly muted, its scale and color far less impressive than the weddings of his younger brothers or his own enthronement, which would follow a little less than five years later.

Wearing the uniform of a lieutenant colonel in the army, the prince regent left his own palace at Akasaka at ten minutes after nine on the morning of January 24, his destination the Imperial Palace still serving as the residence officially occupied by his father. At the same hour, in the wealthy district of Shibuya in the western part of the city, a parallel procession centered around the about-to-be crown princess, the Lord Chamberlain officially escorting the young bride in a closed carriage borrowed from the imperial stables. After the two corteges came together in front of the Ceremonial Hall of the palace, Hirohito and Nagako left separately for their own pavilions to begin the complicated job of changing into the elaborate robes Japanese royalty wears on great occasions of state. Nagako's scarlet and purple ancient court kimono was covered with a snow white train trailing far behind her high-dressed shiny black hair, the coiffeur pinned with the small golden sunray ornament of a Japanese imperial princess. Hirohito's costume consisted of an orange robe over a wide white split skirt. The crested black lacquered hat symbolizing a Prince of the Blood rested on his head. He carried a paddle scepter. His bride held a delicately decorated folding hinoki-wood court fan of the most exquisite example of this honorable Japanese art.

Some seven hundred witnesses—the imperial family, the court, government officials—crowded the outer precincts of the shrine where the vows were solemnized. Inside the Kashikodokoro, only the Master of Rites, Prince Kujo, witnessed the simple declaration that serves as the marriage vow in Shinto rites. After stating to his enshrined ancestors his intention to take Nagako as his wife, the deed was done, and Hirohito collected the new crown princess and left the shrine to receive the congratulatory felicitations of the high-ranking guests. The battleship *Nagato* sounded a twenty-one-gun salute as it lay at anchor outside the Yokohama Naval Base. The reverberations from an even closer 101-gun army salute rearranged many of the ashes that still formed conspicuous reminders of the late disaster. In the main palace building, a toast from Prince Fushimi, offered in sake, was followed by a wedding dinner, after which the couple finally settled into a horse-drawn carriage to be driven to the Buckingham Palace–like pile at Akasaka that would be their home for the first five years of their life together.

The morning after their nuptial night, an audience had been arranged with the retired emperor at his confinement in the Numazu Palace; the sovereign had been thought too sick to travel to the capital for the ceremony itself. Nearly eighteen months later, the young couple finally honeymooned at the Okinajima Palace of Hirohito's uncle, Prince Takamatsu, in a house romantically located on a little island in the middle of Lake Inawashiro. But the princess's absolute primary duty to her husband—the birth of an heir—would wait considerably longer to be fulfilled, a situation causing increasing anxiety to a court that accounted the birth of an heir as the sole element of any importance in the marriage.

Domestic life for the newlyweds revolved around their apartments in the sprawling pink Akasaka Palace. The prince's suite would have aroused the same sort of disgust from his grandfather Meiji as that of Taisho had a generation earlier. Decorated in an ersatz French motif derived from late-eighteenth-century styles, the rooms were most conspicuous for their great golden chandeliers. A huge mirror shaped like an arch covered the wall of Hirohito's bedroom, while Nagako's ground-floor room on the palace's western side was carpeted in pink, a yellow-spotted marble mantelpiece and walls hung with oil paintings vying with the carpet for attention. The couple shared a second-floor sitting room in the southwest corner of the building; light filtered through the stained glass in the ceiling over the books that filled the teak cases on all four walls of what was Hirohito's favorite room of the palace.

Centered in the midst of an enormous private park encircled by high wrought-iron railings and mature trees, the palace escaped public scrutiny—not that very many people would have had the temerity to try to disturb the private tranquility of the heir to the throne. The Great Lawn, a verdant expanse dappled with the shade of tall pine trees, was the scene of early morning strolls, when the prince would stop to feed the wild ducks and cranes and swans that gathered in the ornamental pond. Hirohito invariably and somewhat unfairly stood in one spot to toss the crumbs to the birds, only to have the food monopolized by a single large and powerful black swan. Chamberlains following at a discreet distance, and taking pity on the smaller birds, would later see that more food was passed around to them.

In June 1925, a special "biological" laboratory was built for Hirohito on the grounds, and Dr. Kataro Hattori,[8] the prince's close friend and natural history tutor from his Takanawa Palace school days, served as its first director. (When he later moved to the main

---

[8]In 1965, at the age of eighty-nine, Dr. Hattori retired from the post of Tutor to the Emperor in Biology.

palace as sovereign, the emperor had a duplicate laboratory constructed there.) Hirohito's love of marine biology was beginning to
absorb more and more of what free hours he had, time that was
severely limited because of the constant formalized engagements he
was expected to attend to as regent for his father. Holidays, when
they could be snatched from the prince's official routine, were often
passed quietly at his traditional Japanese-style seaside villa at
Hayama, where, following the habit established in his bachelor days,
Hirohito would joyously wander the beach, picking out likely looking specimens for his collections. Sometimes he warned Nagako,
who followed behind with a tool her husband could use for prying
the shells out of clefts, if the footing was bad in a particularly craggy
spot. Evenings during these idyllic days often found the couple on
the peculiarly Japanese cantilevered moon-viewing platform overlooking the water, with its vista across the bay to Mount Fuji.

Nagako became pregnant in the spring of 1925, after what the
courtiers thought to be a "frighteningly long wait" since the marriage had been celebrated the prior year. The delay was interpreted
by some as a sign that a possible physical impairment might be
preventing the couple from producing infant princes and (far, far
less desirably) princesses. The more superstitious of the gossipers
implied that Prince Yamagata had put a curse on Nagako to keep
Satsuma blood from an imperial heir. There were even whispers that
one of Nagako's maids had openly told her mistress of the maledic-
tion of Yamagata, and that Nagako should try to do what she could
to break the evil charm. The empress, who was urgently consulted
by concerned courtiers at Numazu, had helpfully given Nagako
some herbal infusions to try to speed matters along. Even Nagako's
mother was worried about what was turning into a "situation";
having given birth to six children in nine years, and with Nagako's
sister already pregnant after only five months of marriage, Princess
Kuni was terrified at the thought that she might have contributed
a barren daughter to this most important marriage in the nation. An
enormous national sigh of relief was breathed at the official announcement of the impending confinement.

When the couple returned to the capital in the fall, a pavilion was
built on the grounds of the Akasaka Palace to serve as a lying-in

hospital for the princess, and tents were placed on the grounds for the reporters who kept a vigil over the pregnant Nagako when the end of her term was nearing. Alas, the birth did not bring the happiness that the increasingly economically depressed nation had hoped for. The child was a girl. What would have been merely unfortunate for parents in a private station was a bitter disappointment for a future emperor who was trying to lead his country by example into Western notions of the sanctity of the monogamous marriage union. Putting the best face on the situation, the girl was given the titular name Teru-no-Miya, "Princess Sunshine" (later named Shigeko), with the wished-for expectation that she might have a sunny effect on a hard-put nation. But the Japanese still wanted an imperial heir.

Within a year of the birth of the baby princess, the health of the virtually unseen emperor began its rapid deterioration. All through 1926, Taisho suffered from cerebral anemia, and in May of that year the state of his health pitched downward when a cold brought on bronchial catarrh. Hirohito canceled his annual military maneuvers in Saga prefecture and left for the villa at Hayama, where his father was being kept alive by a battery of court physicians. Between the endless audiences he was forced to grant as regent, Hirohito would slip away to the special annex where the monarch's bed had been set up, there ministering to the monarch personally. Finally, on Christmas Day, 1926, in the presence of his empress and his heir, the emperor Taisho died. Nearly as cloistered in his last years as had been so many of his ancestors, Taisho left little personal impression on his people. Although national mourning was declared, the difference between the feelings of the Japanese people at the death of this sovereign from those experienced when his father died couldn't have been more pronounced.

At the instant Taisho's spirit was released to join those of his 122 imperial predecessors, the twenty-six-year-old Hirohito ascended the throne as the nation's 124th monarch. For five years he had been his father's surrogate, fully imbued with the constitutional role of an emperor, lacking only the title itself. Now, at last, he, too, had become a God.

The ceremony of accession was a short, formalistic service in which the Grand Master of the Rituals announced to the nation that Hirohito had come into possession of the Three Sacred Treasures, the act that solemnizes and legalizes the assumption of the Japanese throne. Because Hirohito was at the villa at Hayama when he succeeded his father, the ceremony was somewhat makeshift, lacking the ceremonial punch it would have had in the capital. A jury-rigged throne and a pedestal for each of the treasures was quickly put together, and the regalia were brought out and formally placed in Hirohito's presence where he just as formally now claimed them as his own.

One of the first public utterances of a Japanese sovereign is to inform the world of his reign name, the name that will symbolize the span of time that the gods ordain he occupy the throne, and the designation that after his death will become his own name throughout posterity. Considerable thought is unquestionably given to this matter when the heir sees his accession in the foreseeable future.

The two syllables in *Showa* have been variously transliterated, but "Enlightened Peace," or "Harmony," is probably as close to the Japanese meaning as can be had in English. There is little doubt that the young man who chose them prayed for nothing so fervently as that his people would enjoy enlightened peace throughout the years of his reign. In respect of the horrendous trial by fire that Japan would undergo in the next two decades and force so many innocent people to undergo with it, the choice of Showa must rank as one of the saddest ironies in the history of the imperial dynasty.

CHAPTER IX

Showa—The Tempest
1926–1945

"All my subjects, with simpleness of mind and with
all the nation's strength shall do their best to
avoid undesirable consequences in the effort to
attain the goals of the military expeditions."

—HIROHITO, DECEMBER 8, 1941, IMPE-
RIAL RESCRIPT ISSUED AT THE TIME OF
THE ATTACK ON PEARL HARBOR

Among the discontented army officers who watched as their nation's
rightful place in the world seemed to be denied by a conspiracy of
the white nations, the apparent solution to such iniquity was simplicity itself: Shinto—the rock on which the Japanese monarchy had
always found its firmest anchorage—would provide the key to an
invincible Japan. Since the hazy, myth-enshrouded time when the
Son of Heaven's ancestors were simply tribal chieftains raised high
among loyal followers, the paramount justification for the emperors'
existence had been to function as their nation's high priest. Confirm
and strengthen the sovereign in his role as undisputed godhead, let
the nation be governed by the military with the divine imperial
guidance undiluted by constitutional restraints, and the result would
be a clear path to Japan's invulnerability. To these ends, in the
1930s, "State Shinto" became to Japan much as Marxism was to
Soviet Russia.

By definition, State Shinto was the post-1867 official national cult, co-opting as instruments of increasingly fanatical nationalism the traditional state-centered Shinto precepts, especially the emperor's personal authority. Although it was to bring unprecedented grief to Japan, this development oddly never technically nullified the Meiji Constitution's guarantees of freedom of religious belief; even the Vatican's Congregation of the Propagation of the Faith was still able, in 1936, to find it technically possible to accept State Shinto merely as "veneration of departed persons" and not as the worship of false gods.

The empire had emerged from World War I as an indisputably first-class world power, no state having benefited from the conflict to any greater degree than had Japan. Despite their deeply ingrained racial biases, the Western nations controlling the world's sea lanes and sources of vital and strategic supplies in the 1920s could no longer write off Japan's strength as a freakish accident or a temporary aberration, as many had contemptuously done following its victories over the Chinese and Russian empires during Meiji's reign. Having left the war virtually unscathed, a condition sharply contrasting to that of the battered states of Europe, Japan was the single nation represented at the Versailles Peace Conference without any motive whatsoever to give up the kind of big power imperialism that had characterized the preceding century's exploitation of the undeveloped world. Not only did Japan take over Britain's role as the major supplier of textiles to Asia, it also inherited Germany's Pacific possessions. Yet as strong as the new giant of east Asia had obviously grown, the West saw its interests dangerously jeopardized if it were to allow Japan to claim what it reckoned to be a rightful share of the postwar spoils.

Racism was, of course, a major factor at the bottom of the Western attitude, and so undoubtedly was the unalloyed fear that Japan was going to be an increasingly dangerous threat to the European and American political and economic hegemony that then existed in much of Asia. At the London Naval Conference of 1929, Japan's still-civilian government was forced to accept the "10-10-7" formula for capital war ships, a division—regarded as odious by its nationalistic militarists—giving Britain and the United States a proportion of ten tons of ships each for every seven allowed Japan. Japan, not without reason, perceived the equation even more unjustly, as a combined twenty shares for the potentially adversarial allies against only seven for itself. Ominously, there were many elements in Japan's ruling oligarchy who swore they wouldn't allow this threatening situation to cripple the nation's "destiny."[1]

The chain of events that led so inexorably to Hiroshima and Nagasaki saw its first ineradicable link forged in 1931. Through the 1920s and into the 1930s, Japan had experimented with something approaching genuine—if fragile—party democracy, with suffrage eventually extended to virtually the entire male population. But there always remained one fatal flaw in the civilian constitutional system Meiji's young Turks had bequeathed the country: The military—both the army and the navy—retained, in effect, final veto authority over the decisions of the nation's civilian administrations. The ministers of both services were always active duty officers, and cabinet or parliamentary decisions that ran counter to the wishes of the forces they represented could thus be effectively and fatally thwarted.

Had there existed true political power in the throne, Japan's ever-increasing international problems might have found a resolution in a less belligerent direction. Meiji's constitution clearly put formal power into the hands of the sovereign, but the monarch was expected merely to personify the powers of state, not to act in an executive capacity. Meiji, a strong personality in his own right, had to a limited degree participated in Japan's actual political deliberations, but his successors were far different men. Taisho was early on simply too irresponsible and preoccupied with social trivialities, and too sick later, to impose his personality in any practical way on Japan's political process. And Hirohito had been guided by a lifetime of advisers—principally Prince Saionji—in the belief that for

---

[1] In justice to the American point of view, the ratio could be seen as generous to a country with half the United States's population, a tenth of its Gross National Product, and a twentieth of its area—while at the same time being "allowed" within 70 percent of naval equality of its giant Pacific neighbor. Furthermore, Japan built every ton allowed her, while Britain and the United States, with their pared-down defense budgets, fell short of constructing their maximum allowances.

him to initiate orders and then risk having them ignored would be potentially fatal to the throne's sacrosanct standing. Thus, when he ascended the throne, Hirohito's personal wishes were irrelevant to government decisions. His disembodied authority was invoked only when his ministers needed a formal stamp of imperial approval on their decisions. Ironically, while he lived, Saionji was the single major factor standing between the emperor and the extreme right-wing nationalists constantly striving to replace the comparatively less bombastic constitutional monarchists Saionji himself had put into influential court positions.

While Japan abided by the unwritten but understood rules that kept nations in a relatively involatile state via-à-vis their neighbors, the Meiji system worked. But in 1931, the constitutional safeguards broke down, and Japan found itself firmly committed to a course of totalitarianism. One contemporary ultranationalist writer described his vision of a new order: "The meaning of world history is that the august virtue of His Majesty should shine on all the nations of the world. This will indubitably be accomplished as a manifestation of the martial virtues of the Empire." The impact this widely accepted logic would have on Japan was to be enormous. On September 18, 1931, an explosion on the South Manchurian Railway line just outside Mukden lit the kindling of World War II.

Manchuria was a hardscrabble land containing little on her monotonous and bleak landscape. *Under* the soil, however, was another matter. There she possessed enormous supplies of oil, coal, and iron ore that resource-poor Japan lacked. These substances were needed not only to keep Japan's industrial machine going, but were important to guarantee her military strength. Since the 1905 victory over Russia, Japan had been allowed—or "won the right," as she would have preferred to put it—to station troops in Manchuria, presumably to guard vital Japanese interests, among which was her railway monopoly that was being threatened by new Chinese railway building. It was in this setting that the railway bombing occurred, a tragedy whose ripples would eventually reach around the world. Claiming that the explosion was caused by attacking Chinese troops, and that Japan was thereby acting in self-defense, elements of the Japanese army quickly and brutally occupied Mukden, the Manchurian capital.

Japan palmed off the Mukden Incident to the world in the same way Hitler would eight years later baldly try to transfer guilt for the action that was used to justify his own murderous attack on Poland. In reality, the "incident" had been carefully planned by the Japanese General Staff as an excuse to grab Manchuria's oil. The Chinese army was rapidly overwhelmed by its far superior Japanese counterpart, and the soon-conquered Manchuria was transformed into the Japanese puppet state of Manchukuo, with Tokyo handpicking a Chinese Manchu "monarch"—King Pu-Yi—to be installed on its "throne."

For the next five years, Japan's military adventurism remained mostly confined to Manchuria while the generals prepared for their next big move. Hirohito was powerless to do more than ineffectually and mildly question the wisdom of his ministers' actions. When Prime Minister Inukai tried in 1932 to obtain an Imperial Rescript ordering the halt of the army's precipitous advance into China, Saionji advised Hirohito against it on the old and unimpeachable grounds that if the army ignored such an imperial plea, which was likely, the monarch's prestige would inevitably suffer as a result.

Although the throne's authority was frankly manipulated by highranking officials—politicians, advisers, military officers—the emperor's personal attitudes were still of some consequence to his handlers. And because Hirohito's views carried potential symbolic weight, he was paradoxically endangered by those whose protestations of loyalty to the throne were loudest—the army. During the early thirties, influential officers, both high-ranking staff officers as well as young and often aristocratic recent military academy graduates, quietly but with increasing vehemence began criticizing the sovereign for his nonmartial and scholarly attitudes and lack of more obvious support for their strident cries for military aggrandizement. Hirohito was even censored when he voiced "too much" concern for the safety of the troops sent into battle on the Chinese front. The criticism, private and usually discreet though it was, tended to encourage coup-minded cliques of young military hotheads to regard the sovereign as *bon'yo,* "mediocre," a man who should change his mistaken ways and acquiesce in a so-called Showa Restoration that would vest direct political power in the throne—or else allow himself to be replaced by someone more closely resembling their idealized vision of a strong sovereign.

Not only was Hirohito himself a target of the young officers, but these latter-day samurai had long despised the politicians and industrialists for their supposed corruption and "tenuousness." The worldwide depression had struck Japan early and hard, the price of silk, its leading export, dropping drastically during the late twenties and early thirties. Scandal involving the prominent leaders of the *zaibatsu,* the huge cartels controlling a grossly disproportionate share of the nation's wealth, coupled with the government's apparent inability to come up with solutions or easy fixes, combined to fill the young officers with disgust. Their answer to these difficulties lay so tantalizingly close: a "genuine" restoration of imperial rule, a nation under a strong sovereign, and a concomitant return to the people's "basic values."

Such was the political milieu in which Hirohito found himself as his first decade on the throne concluded. During these years his personal, unseen life had been through days nearly as tumultuous as those his nation was undergoing. The central cause of the monarch's private difficulties revolved around dynastic considerations of profound importance to the throne: After nearly ten years of marriage, there was still no direct heir. Following Princess Sunshine's birth in 1925, more girls arrived in fairly rapid succession. Sachiko was born in September 1927, but died the following March of unexplained causes. After getting through the arduous enthronement ceremonies in 1928, during which time a confinement would have been extremely discommoding to the empress, two more girls, Kazuko and Atsuko, were delivered in 1929 and 1931, respectively. But these births in no way fulfilled Nagako's real dynastic duty of giving her husband and her nation an heir, and whispers about the Yamagata "curse" inevitably started to surface again. After the fourth pregnancy brought no son, the advice to Hirohito to do "something" was taking on a disquieting urgency. Even Prince

Saionji was beginning to show signs of agitation, as though it were a problem the couple could voluntarily overcome if only they tried hard enough.

In pre–World War II Japan, female members of the imperial family past their twenties were considered homebodies, not bed partners; as princesses entered their thirties, their husbands generally looked elsewhere for conjugal comforts. Hirohito and Nagako's mutual marital fidelity represented a very major change to this otherwise still generally held dictum. But the rules governing the succession in Meiji's Imperial Household Law demanded that the heir be of the emperor's blood—adoption was specifically outlawed. Although its desirability was implied, the Law made no direct statement that he be "legitimate" as that term is understood in the West. Notwithstanding Hirohito's dismissal of the thirty-nine official concubines who had remained on the palace's payroll at his accession, it was beginning to seem as though it might become necessary for the sovereign to bring one out of mandatory retirement.[2]

Saionji advised the emperor, in the gentlest and most circumspect way, of course, that he must do his duty to his country, and, furthermore, that he must understand this was the proper thing, in no way a rebuke of the empress. After all, she had had four chances already. The emperor categorically rejected the counsel. Not only under pressure on these most intimate matters, Hirohito was also being buffeted by the nation's domestic political situation, which, after 1931, was becoming more violent with each passing month. The influential elite of young army officers who were angry and becoming more so at Hirohito's reluctance to wholeheartedly embrace their plans for overseas adventurism also rebuked the throne for what they held to be the monarch's willingness to "allow" Asia to remain dominated by the white races. The most aggressively fanatical among them were even secretly beginning to formulate plans to topple the emperor from his throne and replace him with his

[2]A concubine bearing an heir to the sovereign under circumstances holding at the time would gain no official position therefrom, not even after her offspring inherited the throne.

more vigorous brother Chichibu, a prince who had recently married and who might have a whole string of sons.

In the summer of 1933, Nagako's fifth pregnancy was announced. Hirohito well understood the importance of the birth: a boy could knock the underpinnings from the malcontents who were daily gaining powerful adherents to their position, a girl could mean the end of his reign—especially if he continued to refuse the possibility of taking a concubine. When at 6:39 A.M. on December 22, 1933, an heir was born, the imperial crisis evaporated.

The birth of Prince Akihito, coming so late in his parents' marriage and after four sisters, caused an enormous outburst of celebrating in the country. The baby was the first in anyone's memory actually born to the position of crown prince, the most recent emperors having arrived in the world while their own fathers were still heirs to the throne. Furthermore, the birth was, not surprisingly, broadly interpreted as a particularly auspicious omen for both dynasty and nation.

On the seventh day after the delivery, Hirohito formally wrote for the first time, on paper made specially for the occasion, the prince's new name: Tsugu-no-Miya Akihito. The titular part, Tsugu-no-Miya, means "The Prince Who Will Succeed to the Throne," his personal name, Akihito, "Clear as the Autumn Sky," or "Enlightened Benevolence," according to the reading. After six years of beseeching the nation's deities to send them a crown prince, the entire country waited with a special fervor for the first rite of the many Akihito would undergo. To ensure that the long-forgotten Gomeimei Shiki, "Name-Bestowing Ceremony for a Crown Prince," conformed precisely to ancient usage, scholars had been busy searching the national archives from the day the prince was born. Having come up with the form they felt would be approved by the imperial family's ancestral gods, the ritual was duly carried out at the palace on December 29 in the presence of the entire court.

The baby was prepared by being bathed in sanctified water in a bathtub hewn of rare and costly woods, newly crafted for the rites. After the emperor formally signified his son's name by signing the handmade-parchment document, the patent was reverently placed in a lacquered casket and wrapped in a cloth of gold; it was then carried to the high altar of the Kashikodokoro to receive the blessings of the gods. All the Princes and Princesses of the Blood, led in the place of honor by the dowager empress, paid their formal respects to the baby. To the strains of ancient music and a twenty-one-gun salute from His Majesty's ships lying-to in the capital's harbor, a great banzai was raised across the islands of Japan. The day of celebration closed with 600,000 school children marching in a torchlit parade through the city while overhead air force fighters buzzed in salute, casting their high-powered lights down in maneuvers precursing the aircraft that would a decade later drop death instead of congratulatory rays of light. For this peaceful interlude, though, the joy of the nation possessing a successor to the Son of Heaven knew only happy things.

In the 1930s, the imperial family reached the zenith of its status and wealth as well as the reverence in which it was popularly held by the nation. Both literally and figuratively heading the dynasty was the dignified emperor and the cozy family, now more firmly than ever enthroned since the momentous addition of an heir. By 1939, Hirohito's family had yet again grown, with two final births filling the imperial nursery: Akihito was followed by another boy in November 1935, Prince Hitachi, and a final child, another daughter, Princess Takako, in March 1939.

The dowager empress, Taisho's widow, played the formidable role of materfamilias when it came to the conduct of family affairs and her all-important influence over her eldest child. A member of the Kujo line of the Fujiwara clan, Empress Sadako followed in the tradition that its daughters be removed to common foster homes for their early years; in her own case, she had been taken from her mother when only seven days old and for five years put in the charge of peasant farmers near Tokyo. Forty-two years old when her son succeeded her husband to the throne, she could claim a special hold on Hirohito's loyalty for having supported his engagement to Nagako against the bitter and truculent Choshu opposition. The widowed Sadako's Tokyo palace (the Omiya Villa on the grounds of the Aoyama Detached Palace) was the home of the new crown prince Akihito during the 1930s, although technically a completely separate Household was maintained for him, distinct from that of his grandmother.

Having gained a comparatively sophisticated sense of state affairs during the years of caring for her invalid husband, Nagako's mother-in-law also controlled the traditional veto authority over most of the domestic matters pertaining to the emperor's personal household. To those not familiar with Japanese custom, such an arrangement would seemingly make life both unbearable and unfair for Nagako. However, for a Japanese daughter-in-law it was a natural and expected course of affairs. Importantly, Sadako's ability to influence her son was utilized by Prince Saionji, who often asked the still-young dowager empress to impress upon the monarch the importance of unswervingly following the advice tendered by his courtiers.[3]

In the thirties, Hirohito's brothers became the nuclei of their own cliques attempting to peddle influence with the emperor. According to established social etiquette, no member of the imperial family was supposed to deal directly in business or politics, instead remaining strictly as prestige-lending figureheads to worthy civic organizations. But the independent spirit and desire on the part of the oldest of Hirohito's brothers to be more than a peripheral prince led, in the 1930s, to his own active, and sometimes messy, immersion into Japan's agitated political waters.

Like all imperial princes, Yasuhito, the second son, was automatically promoted to the headship of his own newly created house of Chichibu-no-Miya, which literally translates to "Prince Chichibu," when he reached his majority. In the same way younger brothers of European royal families were apportioned out over their country's various branches of the armed services, Chichibu became his family's army career officer after graduating from the military academy in 1922.[4] It was while a student at the academy that the prince

[3]Now posthumously known as the empress Teimei, Sadako died on May 17, 1951.

[4]As commander-in-chief, Hirohito was, of course, commissioned in each of Japan's military branches.

contracted long-standing friendships with fellow cadets, officers who would in later years persuade him that the country needed "young" leadership; in the next decade, some would try to put these ideas into motion with a famous but ultimately unsuccessful coup attempt. During an eighteen-month enrollment, beginning in 1925, at Britain's Oxford University, Chichibu remained in close contact with his Japanese classmates, most of whom had by that time graduated to careers as army officers.

Chichibu married into the powerful and historic Matsudaira family in 1928, his wife being Princess Setsuko,[5] the niece of Viscount Matsudaira and daughter of Tsuneo Matsudaira. The couple refrained from having children, it being feared that fathering a male child before his elder brother might constitute a breech of etiquette. Viscount Matsudaira, now his uncle by marriage, adopted the prince at the time of his marriage, a formula by which the viscount's own line would be legally continued. Chichibu and his wife were popular hosts at their huge crenellated and towered Victorian home in Tokyo's fashionable Akasaka district.

Having escaped the most stifling and ponderous of the rigors that Hirohito endured in his cloistered upbringing, Chichibu evolved into a thoroughly modern, popular, and gregarious young man about Tokyo. Most conspicuously, considering his position, the prince was noted for his relatively critical views of the upper classes, who he felt unfairly exploited both the workers, the backbone of Japan's economic strength, and the peasants, whose sons were the primary source of fodder for the nation's military strength. Chichibu, specializing in the infantry, advanced rapidly through the army's lower officer ranks,[6] as befitting the brother of the sovereign. He came to be seen by extremists unhappy with the emperor's timidity about supporting their military plans as a likely ally in their causes. His openness led a clique of officers in one of the prewar period's innumerable groups of plotters—the so-called Young Officers' Move-

[5]She received her title just before the marriage, being formally adopted by a titled cousin so as to give her the rank deemed necessary to marry into the imperial family.

[6]Because of their ages, none of the imperial younger brothers had achieved truly important military positions by the end of World War II.

ment, the most serious of the several that emerged—to propose him as a replacement for the "weak-willed" Hirohito. The group's purported ideals gained the prince's support and respect (after the war, Chichibu said he "always wanted to do something to help the poor farmers," one of the Young Officers' aims), but there is no evidence that he ever collaborated with them in their plans to displace Hirohito on the throne. Chichibu, a colonel by 1940, fell victim to tuberculosis, spending the years of the Pacific War convalescing, with his wife, at Gotemba, near Mount Fuji.

The next brother was Takamatsu-no-Miya (Nobuhito), five years younger than the emperor and the family's representative in the Imperial Navy. Graduated from the naval academy in 1924, Takamatsu had, by the time of the attack on Pearl Harbor, attained the rank of captain. The third son of Taisho received his title in 1913 after succeeding to the headship of the Takamatsu family, a princely house established in 1625 by a son of the emperor Go-Yozei but which had in the interim gone dry. When he received his title as head of his own house, he also personally assumed the special family duty of offering Shinto services to the ancestors of the House of the Imperial Prince Arisugawa, which had also become extinct when it failed to produce an heir. Takamatsu's marriage strengthened this Arisugawa connection; his wife, Kikuko, with whom he maintained a palatial villa in the Shiba area of the capital, was a granddaughter of the last shogun and a sister of Prince Yoshimitsu Tokugawa. Her mother was an Arisugawa princess, thus, the husband's and the wife's grandfathers were, two generations earlier and at the same time, emperor and shogun respectively. Takamatsu's chief distinction during the war would be his advocacy of a strong naval air arm; historians have noted that his association with Admiral Isoroku Yamamoto, chief of Japan's Combined Fleet, led to the adoption of the Pearl Harbor attack plan. Furthermore, the prince was closely associated with the development of *kamikaze* tactics, the country's last substantive attempt to force a military stalemate in the Pacific. Toward the end of the war, while stationed in Tokyo, Takamatsu became involved in a conspiracy to overthrow the failing Tojo cabinet.

The youngest of Hirohito's brothers was Mikasa-no-Miya

(Takahito), born in 1915 and raised in a virtually different generation from his three brothers. Like Chichibu a graduate of the military academy, Mikasa would, in 1938, be commissioned a second lieutenant in the cavalry, his specialty the tank corps. He graduated from the Army Staff College in December 1941. The youngest imperial brother served one year of combat duty in China, reaching the rank of lieutenant colonel by the war's end. Two months before Pearl Harbor, Mikasa married Yuriko Takagi, a daughter of Viscount Takagi. The couple moved into a home on the grounds of the Aoyama Palace in Tokyo.

Taisho had been the father of four officially recognized daughters, all older than Hirohito but none of whom ever gained an independent reputation outside court circles. They included Princess Masako, born in 1888; Princess Fusako, two years younger; Princess Nobuko, born a year after Fusako; and Princess Yoshiko, the youngest, born in 1896. All married distantly related cousins—imperial princes—and settled into lives completely merged into those of their husbands. The eldest son of Princess Fusako, Prince Kitashirakawa, became the first member of the imperial family to bring the war's mortality into the family circle: In 1940, Captain Prince Nagahisa Kitashirakawa was killed in an airplane accident in Inner Mongolia while serving with the army. The death of the strikingly handsome thirty-year-old first cousin to Hirohito, who was promoted posthumously to major and awarded the Grand Cordon of the Order of the Chrysanthemum, caused court functions to be officially suspended for a day of mourning.

The extended imperial family included the uncles and cousins of Hirohito, and formed a group in which several dozen people, divided into eleven collateral branches, were, in 1939, entitled to the style of Imperial Highness. The House of Kan'in was the best known of the corollary imperial branches, having been founded in 1718 by Prince Naohito, a son of the emperor Higashiyama. The elder Prince Kan'in was born an imperial prince, later having the tie doubly reinforced when he was adopted, in 1867, by the emperor Komei; he was the granduncle of Hirohito and the brother of Meiji, as modified by Japan's peculiar adoption rules. Physically distinguished by a heroic waxed mustache, Kan'in was the youngest field marshal in the Japanese army and the chief of the Army General Staff from 1931 to 1940, the period when the General Staff was both directing the China War and planning the attack on the United States. In May 1945, shortly before the final disastrous sowing of the seeds he had helped plant, the prince died of infected hemorrhoids.

Virtually every facet of the life of the emperor and the lives of his immediate family were governed by the Imperial Household Ministry. An official government handbook published in the 1930s required eleven pages to list the Ministry's staff—at the same time the Foreign Office needed only ten. Five thousand of the Ministry's employees worked in the Imperial Palace in Tokyo, in jobs ranging from minister to stable-boy. In the lavish prewar days of the court, each of the 121 imperial mausoleums spread over the country required its own on-site retinue of official keepers to ensure proper maintenance, with little concern to the costs incurred by such lavish staffing.

Few visitors were ever allowed onto the palace grounds, and the majority of those who were went specifically to visit one or another of the officials in what was perhaps the dowdiest official building in Japan, the headquarters of the Imperial Household Ministry. Squatting directly next door to the main palace, the triangular concrete structure had been built in 1936 to house the highest-ranking of the Ministry's civil servants, a function it fulfilled all through the war and continues even to this day. In the era of the Meiji Constitution, from 1889 to 1945, the imperial establishment's structure was considerably different from today's model, most notably in that it constituted a separate government ministry unto itself, contrasting sharply to the postwar establishment's status as a mere subdepartment of the prime minister's office.

In the 1930s, the Ministry was divided into eleven principal offices, including that of the Minister of the Household himself, the Board of Chamberlains, the Board of Ceremonies, the Imperial Family and Peerage Board, the Imperial Mausolea Bureau, the Bureau of the Imperial Table, the Imperial Treasury Bureau, the Maintenance and Works Bureau, the Imperial Stables Bureau, the Imperial Archives Bureau, and the Imperial Physicians Bureau. Aside from these primary divisions, several other separate and important functions existed semiindependently under the minister's direct charge, including the Office of the Empress's Household, another for the dowager empress, the Board of Imperial Auditors, the Imperial Poetry Bureau, and the Kyoto Office of the Imperial Household. Significantly, the entire Ministry was placed outside the control of the normal bureaucratic administrative system, which meant, most importantly, that the person of the minister was not routinely affected by cabinet changes.

Beyond any question, the Imperial Household Ministry was one of the most influential and powerful organizations in the Japan that existed before 1945: Control of the emperor's ear and dispenser of the imperial blessing had since the beginning of the monarchy been crucial prizes in whatever political permutation the country was undergoing, and the throne's publicly enhanced financial position in the 1930s gave an extra dimension to this cachet. Within the agency, the minister himself was one of its two most important officials, the other being the Lord Keeper of the Privy Seal, a personage roughly equal in rank to the minister.

Until his death in 1940, Prince Kimmochi Saionji, the "unofficial" veteran elder statesman, was, however, probably the greatest single influence guiding Hirohito's thinking (Saionji, born in 1849, had twice served as prime minister, the second time in 1912 bridging the death of Meiji and the accession of Taisho). A democrat and liberal by the standards of his times, Saionji ironically gave strict constitutional advice to Hirohito that inhibited the emperor from using his potentially significant powers of personal suasion—powers inherent in his position—to direct a less bellicose course for Japan's foreign policies. Already ancient by the time Hirohito came to the throne, Saionji was the last of the genro, the council of elders who helped make the restoration and who served as unofficial but powerful counselors to the throne. Saionji's influence had begun to wane by the end of the 1930s, but as late as 1937 he still personally approved the choice of Prince Konoye as prime minister.

Household Minister through the tumultuous and tragic years of the late 1930s and early 1940s (he was appointed in 1936) was Prince Chichibu's father-in-law, Tsuneo Matsudaira. A former ambassador to Britain and the United States, and the descendant of a high-ranking shogunate family, he was accounted, like Saionji, a "liberal" in the palace establishment. It was Matsudaira's job as minister to serve as the link between the government and the palace, a position entailing something like the responsibilities of the British monarch's Private Secretary. Alongside the minister in importance was the office of Lord Keeper of the Privy Seal, a position held by Count Kurahei Yuasa during Matsudaira's early years as minister; Yuasa was replaced by Marquess Koichi Kido on June 1, 1940. The primary duty of the Lord Privy Seal was to serve as the sovereign's chief day-to-day civilian political adviser, a role that caused Yuasa, and later Kido, to become as personally close to Hirohito as any men in Japan.

Distinct from the Ministry was the Privy Council, in the late thirties headed by Baron Kiichiro Hiranuma, balancing Matsudaira and Saionji's liberalism with his brand of reactionary chauvinism. Hiranuma was named prime minister in 1939. The Council was a consultative body that had been established in 1888 to clarify for and advise the emperor on issues of "grave importance." Originally nicknamed "the watchdog of the Constitution," the Council included the highest-ranking court, civil, and military personages in Japan (all ministers had the right to attend all meetings). This meant that it was sometimes able to take the upper hand over the cabinet in directing decisions on the most critical issues of national policy.

In the matter of its financial holdings, the imperial family was at the peak of Japan's moneyed establishment. The genesis of the fortune was in the Meiji oligarchs' development of an entirely new financial footing for their postfeudal nation, one firmly anchored to the three great pre-Meiji cartel clans: the Mitsui, the Iwasaki of the Mitsubishi Company, and the Sumitomo. When the monarch personally influenced events so that these three families would be given monopolistic rights to develop the country's emerging industrial base, the reward the throne received was a share of the profits from each. The combined cuts were enough to make Meiji's personal fortune the fourth-largest concentration of capital in the empire, immediately after those of his three benefactors. Because these concerns, forming the lion's share of what became known as the zaibatsu, or "financial clique," were so deeply involved in nearly every significant sector of the nation's rapidly growing economy—from banking to heavy industry to foreign trade—the fortunes amassed were staggering in scope.

The $40 million that Meiji bequeathed his heir in 1912 had grown to a private imperial purse believed to hold about $3.109 million at the 1941 dollar/yen conversion rate.[7] By the time of Pearl Harbor, the imperial family was said by the official publication *The Japanese Empire* to have owned, outright, the Imperial Hotel (although palace officials denied this) and to be heavily involved in some thirty banks and corporations, including the Bank of Japan (47 percent of the shares of Japan's central bank and its most powerful financial institution were reportedly held by the Imperial Household), South Manchurian Railway stock, the enormous Nippon Yusen Kaisha (N.Y.K.) steamship company (Japan's equivalent of France's French Line), as well as vast tracts of the nation's real estate, which will be explored shortly. The sovereign was also the nation's leading single shareholder. Owning some 22 percent of the private Yokohama Specie Bank, the empire's official foreign exchange institution, Hirohito, through his financial managers, was able to exercise direct clout on the European financial markets. Palace spokesmen characterized the official justification for these vast imperial investments not as "profit making," but instead necessary to "assist the development of the nation's financial and industrial activities"; following this reasoning, the N.Y.K. investment was a signal that the Imperial Household regarded as "highly important," from a national security standpoint, the expansion of maritime transportation.

Aside from this private fortune, which grew at a dizzying pace through the efforts and financial skills of the nation's most sophisticated and skilled investment managers, the monarchy was also the recipient of a not inconsiderable Civil List, the family's "official" government appropriation. Significantly, no approval from the Diet

---

[7]In 1945, MacArthur's financial investigators placed a tag of more than $100 million on Hirohito's personal fortune, excluding jewels, art, and gold and silver bullion.

was required when an increase was demanded in the Civil List. At the time the Pacific War began, it stood at ¥4.5 million—something over $4 million, an amount unchanged since it was first set in 1910.[8] Out of this appropriation, the emperor was expected to provide for his immediate family's needs as well as the upkeep of the imperial estates. In 1920, the total valuation placed on the real estate was ¥637 million, but in the fall of 1930, Hirohito ordered twelve of his "superfluous" palaces to be sold, "an example to all in these hard times" of the worldwide economic depression. By 1941, the total amount spent to keep the monarchy running was something on the order of ¥20 million, met by both the Civil List and profits from the imperial forests and other income-producing properties.

A look at these prewar imperial estates makes for interesting reading, it being difficult to conceive the reigning family of another country of comparable size with access to such a vast array of palaces, villas, and estates. The total area of the land owned by the imperial house came to more than 3.5 million acres (1,352,752 hectares), with forests and woodlands taking up most of the total, a situation that made Hirohito the nation's biggest landlord. By far the most valuable of the estates was Tokyo's enormous Imperial Palace complex, a chunk of land to which it had been for decades virtually impossible to affix a meaningful value, so precious was and is land in the center of the Japanese capital. Nearly as priceless was the combined Akasaka-Aoyama Palace grounds a mile from the city's main imperial compound. All three of these complexes housed, in addition to their main palatial structures, numerous luxurious villas and outbuildings, exemplified by the virtual imperial housing estate in the Aoyama grounds. Three other imperial properties existed in Tokyo: the Shinjuku Imperial Gardens, wherein were held the emperor's annual spring and autumn garden parties; the Hama Detached Palace and park on the city's waterfront, a former shogunal castle used by Hirohito for his traditional duck-hunting parties; and the Kasumigaseki Detached Palace, near the Diet Build-

[8]The Japanese government in Korea also provided a Civil List of ¥1.8 million for that country's puppet sovereign.

ing, in which the sovereign could at his discretion put up various relatives.

Functioning primarily as a stage for the ceremonial activities associated with enthronements and funerals, the private park surrounding the Imperial Palace in Kyoto compared to that ancient city much as Central Park in size and relationship does to Manhattan in New York. It is by far the single largest element on the Heian capital's landscape, and is sited virtually in the center of the city. Aside from this palace, Kyoto's suburbs held two of the most elegant of the entire collection of imperial properties, the Katsura and the Shugakuin villas, stunningly beautiful estates known (only from reputation; neither was opened to the public) for their traditionally manicured gardens providing refuge for the retired emperors who had once been their primary occupants.

An accounting of other imperial estates scattered around the country included the Hakone Detached Palace in the mountain region around Lake Ashi; Kobe's Muko Detached Palace; the Hayama Imperial Villa where Hirohito liked to spend summer weekends collecting sea samples; the Ise Detached Palace, built especially for imperial visits to the dynasty's chief shrine; the Numazu Imperial Villa, also a seaside retreat; the Nikko Imperial Villa; the Ikao Imperial Estate, another mountain resort; the Nagara River Preserve; and the Yedo River Preserve, which was generously stocked with wildlife to ensure success for the emperor's weekend shooting guests.

The riches of the Japanese monarchy could have intoxicated Midas at the prospect of sampling them all, but the treasures and estates were, ironically, little coveted by the provident Hirohito. Although his personal surroundings were necessarily made up of only the most superb materials and components elegantly executed by the nation's most skilled craftsmen, they were nonetheless markedly unostentatious in their overall effect. In his preference for simplicity, Hirohito was to the core a Japanese of the old school, of far greater affinity to his like-minded grandfather than to his Westernized father. Leaving his palace perhaps only twice a month on average, Hirohito confined himself to a picturesque but not particularly comfortable house behind the ornate main palace, a small dwelling of the kind based on the imported tropical style first constructed in Japan's ancient days. It was, incidentally, singularly inappropriate to the country's winters, a season not known for severity in the islands where the architectural style had first been developed. The monarch altered the house with the substitution of some Western furniture, and in the tokonoma, or prayer alcove, busts of Napoleon and Darwin were the central treasures instead of the traditional scroll with its standard calligraphic characters. One end of the living room gave onto the private imperial park, the Fukiage Garden, for which the villa itself was named.

In this private world at the epicenter of the Japanese universe, where the loudest sound was the gentle murmurs of the obsequious courtier, sounds still spoken in the traditional Kyoto dialect of the court, Hirohito maintained a rigid daily routine that only the most critical of circumstances would alter. An hour of exercise after arising at six was followed by a Western-style breakfast taken with the empress; the eggs and toast were a tradition he had begun on his European tour and they became a lifelong custom except during the war, when he switched to the unpolished rice eaten by his poorer subjects to symbolize his sharing of the common lot's deprivations. Hirohito was noted for and took pride in his personally temperate habits, refraining from both tobacco and alcohol. He more than once pointed out to visitors the fact that his wristwatch was a domestic model that had cost only ¥17, or about $8. But the normally cozy domesticity of a Japanese father's relationship with his children was dampened by his position: The imperial princes and princesses were never allowed to follow their august father anywhere other than to the family's private suite.

Mornings were routinely devoted to daily briefings of domestic and foreign news and developments, particularly those of Japan's ever-widening war fronts. After scrutinizing the two biggest Tokyo dailies, the *Asahi* and the *Mainichi*, and making a stab at the influential English-language *Japan Advertiser*, Hirohito saw the Lord Privy Seal who apprised him of major political crises, which, in the 1930s, often included some kind of coup-in-gestation. Military aides then arrived with the latest dispatches from General Staff headquarters or directly from whichever front was in the midst of a battle.

The work routine continued after a light Japanese-style lunch at about 12:30. In the afternoon, the Grand Chamberlain would present the sovereign with a list of the day's remaining audiences. Top-ranking advisers with right of direct access seeking an interview were admitted. Many of these encounters were the kind of audiences with which all heads of state have to contend: the reception of new ambassadors, state visitors, ministers delivering formal reports. Even during the years of the Pacific War, Hirohito continued to fill his traditional role as receiver of foreign heads of state. One such visit involved some especially delicate problems in political etiquette: Despite the fact that Manchuria—Japan's Manchukuo— was being ruthlessly exploited by its unwelcome occupiers, the puppet and utterly powerless local "head of state," styled Emperor Kang-te,[9] was personally welcomed by Hirohito at Tokyo's Central Station and treated as though he were a genuine and equal co-sovereign. Kang-te was even prestigiously housed at the Akasaka Palace for the duration of his ceremonial visit.

From about two until four, Hirohito tried to keep a time for some exercise, usually golf, and often played with Prince Konoye, the Fujiwara-descended president of the House of Peers; the scores of Hirohito's golf matches were carefully guarded secrets lest it be learned that he might have been beaten by an opponent. The matches were usually played on the expansive lawn of the Shinjuku Imperial Garden, today a public park but before the war a private imperial property to which the emperor traveled the short distance from his palace in a closed limousine. To his Lord Keeper of the Privy Seal, Lord Makino, Hirohito was quoted as carefully analyzing his pastime, "Golf is very effective in making one calm and self-possessed. One must be absolutely quiet as he is about to hit the ball. Tennis, on the other hand, is very effective in cultivating alertness. One must think and act quickly in that game." Somehow, it was a very Japanese observation. An alternative to golf was a relaxing hour

[9]Kang-te was the former Henry Pu-yi, son of the last Manchu monarch of China.

riding his famous white horse Shirayuki, "White Snow." Occasionally, Hirohito's presence was required at a military review or troop inspection, which he often carried out seated on the magnificent charger.

Following a four o'clock bath—his *ofuro,* the "honorable wind on the backbone"—he returned to his office in the main palace to sign more of the state documents that never ceased to fill his in-basket. The emperor rarely signed with his personal name, using instead a seal signifying imperial review; laws passed by the Diet requiring his assent were marked with a stamp whose two characters meant simply "Honorable Name." Sometimes the monarch used the Japanese characters for "Hirohito," but only on a limited number of papers; even more rarely he would sign in English, but only if the document was a patent accompanying honors to be bestowed on a foreigner.

Dinner, taken in the empress's company, was generally a light three- or four-course meal and always served in their small villa's Western-style dining room fairly early in the evening, soon after his six o'clock return to his private family quarters. Hirohito would end the day either reading, attending to his diary, indulging in his beloved biology studies, or, when some state crisis or other was particularly pressing, seeing to more paperwork. But it was the hobby—indulged in almost on the level of a professional—that was the emperor's chief escape from the structures of his uniquely suffocating position. Soon after moving into the central palace following his accession, the monarch had ordered that a biology laboratory be built near his personal villa in the area of the Fukiage Gardens. Saturday mornings were reserved for studies in this lab, work he carried out as neither a dilettante nor as an exalted front for "real" work performed by underlings. Visiting biologists of international repute or distinction passing through Tokyo were often invited to share the sovereign's company in the imperial laboratory.

In his book, *Japan's Imperial Conspiracy,* David Bergamini implied that a primary motivation for Hirohito's intense interest in pursuing his biology studies sprang from the desire to make the results useful to Japan's military needs. The author asserted Hirohito's pride in the fact that his knowledge of tides and currents, learned during his experiments and research in marine biology, was helpful to the Imperial Navy, and, what was far more potentially sinister, that the findings were even germaine to the military's research in biological warfare. Also suggested was that a number of biologists and physicians who had been his tutors were "encouraged"—by whom it isn't reported—to devote themselves full time to war research. Though this view could as easily and less dramatically be interpreted as the monarch's understandable wish to contribute to his country's defense, it seems far more likely, in light of Hirohito's personality, that had his findings ever been used in such a way it would certainly have been without any direct approval from the sovereign.

In his limited public life—Japan's monarch never mixed with his subjects in any way comparable to European royalty; the Japanese emperor only had to exist to earn his keep—Shinto-centered ceremonials were the sovereign's primary, unshirkable duty. Though the performance of ritual as the justification for the throne would be a misleading simplification in view of the fact that the prewar Japanese monarchy needed no "justification," it was nevertheless beyond question what underlay his extremely important role as the nation's chief priest. Most ceremonies involving the emperor were carried out at the palace in Tokyo, if for no other reason than the fact that moving the monarch *anywhere* was invariably a logistical nightmare.

When he traveled (usually in a private train or in his maroon limousine, a color reserved by law for the imperial family), even when it was for hundreds of miles, every intersecting street was sealed off and all window shades along the planned route had to be lowered so as not to allow any possible "diminution of the sovereign's majesty." The ludicrousness of such behavior in prewar Japan often achieved phenomenal heights, leading one teacher to be killed running into a burning school to rescue the emperor's official portrait. Another example involved a police inspector named Juhei Honda, who detoured the imperial limousine through a street not on the official route, a route that hadn't been properly cleaned for an imperial visit and whose pedestrians were dressed normally, which translated as "too informal" for the sovereign's eyes. What made the simple error unforgiveable was that it resulted in their arrival at the planned destination thirty minutes early. Honda attempted suicide for this "affront" to the sovereign, and the prime minister even offered personal apologies in what turned into a national brouhaha.

After 1931, Hirohito almost always appeared in public in uniform. Most of the photographs of the sovereign that appeared in the press were provided by the Imperial Household Ministry, and press photographers were required to submit their pictures to court censors who approved only those showing a serious mien and stiff military bearing. One famous photo, taken at the Tokyo Station in 1935 and widely circulated in the West, was not published in Japan because it showed the emperor wearing a broad grin, it being deemed "inappropriate" or "frivolous" that the commander-in-chief of the nation's armed forces should be seen "soiling" his sacred image.[10] All portraits of Hirohito were customarily covered with cellophane or tissue, and his face never appeared on the cover of Japanese magazines in case it might be desecrated. When *Time* magazine ran a 1932 cover story on Hirohito, the editors inserted a facetiously worded warning at the end of the article that stated: "Japanese who hope and trust that *Time* readers will show every respect to His Majesty have made the following request: let copies of the present issue lie face upward on all tables; let no object be placed on the likeness of the Emperor, shown in his sacred enthronement regalia." Regardless of *Time*'s jocularity, the matter of imperial prestige was viewed with absolutely no humor within Japan itself. To emphasize the unique and seriously maintained singularity of their sovereign, the Ministry of Foreign Affairs announced in April 1936 that forthwith the only word that could be used by foreign correspondents to describe the emperor would be *tenno*, the distinctive Japanese "Son of Heaven," of which "emperor" is not really a satisfactory translation anyway, the more domestic "king" being a closer approximation.[11]

During the prewar Showa years, twenty-one annual ceremonies required Hirohito's presence as crucial to the rites involved. Virtu-

[10]The picture was finally published in Japan in January 1986.
[11]*Kotei* is the Japanese word used to designate all other monarchs.

ally all of the guests who filled the palace courtyard on these occasions were the privileged and highly placed sliver of the population who held official court rank, which in 1939 included some 327,532 persons classified within sixteen ranks from First Rank Senior to Eighth Rank Junior; the holders were mainly high-ranking civil officials and military and naval officers and peers, persons who had distinguished themselves in service to the state, the whole forming something like Britain's titled and knighted aristocracy. One of the highest honors Hirohito could bestow on a subject was the granting of a long, polished wooden stick, a custom based on a twelfth-century ceremony from the court of the emperor Go-Toba. Only those over the age of eighty who had rendered "extraordinary" service to Japan were so honored; in 1941, ten such stick-holders were alive.

The court rites requiring the emperor's personal participation were divided into two broad categories: Grand Rituals, those conducted by the monarch personally; and the Ordinary Rituals, which he attended as an observer in the company of other members of the imperial family. The most important of the Grand Rituals came at the New Year, when the "auspicious origin" of the imperial throne was celebrated. Always held on January 3, the ritual required Hirohito to worship at the so-called Three Shrines on the grounds of the Imperial Palace, the Kashikodokoro, where the Sacred Mirror was kept, the Koreiden, the shrine of the imperial ancestors, and the Shinden, the chief Shinto shrine. After chamberlains murmured ancient prayers that were nearly as antique in their origins as the language itself, the emperor, uniquely garbed in a heavy, white brocaded-silk court kimono and using the high-pitched stylized monotone reserved for his public utterances, intoned an invocation on the proceedings.

The following month, a ritual marking the accession of the emperor Jimmu, Hirohito's earliest predecessor, was observed with sacred ritualized court dances accompanied by doleful, monochromatic music performed by musicians wearing robes of scarlet, their white hats indistinguishable from those worn at similar services a millennium earlier. On the first day of spring, rites giving special obeisances to all prior emperors and empresses and princes and princesses of the imperial line were celebrated, and in April another Grand Ritual marked the anniversary of the death of Jimmu. Autumn thanksgiving festivals paying tribute to the harvests were followed by the last of the annual Grand Rituals, that commemorating the death of Hirohito's father, the emperor Taisho.

The lesser Ordinary Rituals were basically palace remembrances extolling the lives and eulogizing the deaths of individual emperors somewhat more distantly related to the sovereign, such as Meiji, Komei, and Ninko—Hirohito's grandfather, great-grandfather, and great-great-grandfather. Two rather less austere annual commemorative observances at court honored distinguished persons who might not have attained court rank, who in fact sometimes were ordinary Japanese to whom a moment in the imperial limelight was an honor lasting officially only through the next several generations of their individual families; the observance was partially analogous to the Roman Catholic's continued religious remembrance of saints. The Kosho-hajime, or the New Year ceremony of delivering lectures in the court, enacted in the palace's primary throne room, the Phoenix Hall, gave scholars notable for their erudition (as well as their political correctness) in the areas of Japanese and Chinese classics and Western learning the unique opportunity to lecture not only the emperor and empress but the entire court at the same time. A week or two later came the Utakai-hajime, the Imperial New Year Poetry Party first performed in 1869 and, in the public's mind, the best known of the annual palace rituals. Anyone in the country was allowed to submit a waka, a highly stylized poem consisting of precisely thirty-one syllables. Of the thousands who entered each year, the creators of the winning submissions became overnight national celebrities. From the twelve thousand presented for consideration in 1940, only thirteen survived the winnowing process. In that ultramilitaristic time, it was perhaps inevitable that among the winners was the following, typical of the majority if undoubtedly rather more elegant in its murmured Japanese cadences:

> Listen! Happy voices of praise and gladness
> From the lips of the people proud of living
> This year of Imperial glory exalted

Resound all over the country
Echoing the voices from time immemorial.

A decade and a half into his reign, the political situation over which Hirohito austerely presided had taken Japan to the edge of what would soon prove to be a bottomless abyss. After 1936 and an aborted coup d'état—really a mutiny—by officers disgruntled by their seniors' policies, the nation's foreign policy was unequivocally set by the military, who had held the prime ministership (but not necessarily the balance of power) almost without interruption since 1932. Then, a full-scale, few-holds-barred war with China erupted in 1937 when a small force of Japanese troops clashed with the local Chinese garrison at the Marco Polo Bridge near Peking, both sides firing in the dark and allowing the incident to get out of control. The Chinese government viewed this latest outrage as a mortal threat to its continued sovereignty and reacted forcefully. The Japanese mobilized, the Chinese followed suit, and the bloodiest, most savage war Asia had ever seen was well and truly underway.

The military's authority in domestic political affairs had become so entrenched throughout the period of the war with China that anything resembling civilian constitutional government virtually ceased to exist in Japan by the beginning of the decade. In February 1940, a member of the Diet, Takao Saito, made a final effort to brand publicly the China war as aggression, regardless of how the government cloaked the fighting in patriotic platitudes of hypocritical self-righteousness. Before the nation's legislative body Saito said, "If we miss a chance for peace, the politicians of today will be unable to erase their crimes, even by their deaths"—prophetic words but nonetheless heresy that led the military government to force Saito's resignation. Six months later, all political parties in Japan were banned. Hirohito, as the ultimate embodiment of the nation's values and the commander-in-chief of the empire's armed forces, was placed squarely at the center of the storm that would rage in his name.

A still deeply emotional question confronting the Japanese to this day was to what degree Hirohito should be held morally accountable for the cataclysm. Had he been powerless to control the actions of his government? Could he have used his unique authority in any effective way to curb the nationalists' abuses? Did the emperor himself actively promote the aims espoused in the throne's name by Japan's military leadership?

However true it was that Hirohito managed to carve out for himself a modicum of independence in his private life, in all matters related to his state role he adhered rigidly to the principles and conventions that had been inculcated in him by the endless stream of tutors and advisers who had been his constant companions since childhood. However much one may look for guile in his actions, the evidence is that he was simply too trusting for his own and for his country's good. The position of sovereign was perhaps not entirely without resources for its incumbent to have altered the course of the nation's destiny, but Hirohito was, tragically, not the monarch to fulfill such a role. In the abstract, he was in a position to force his views on the government, whether or not the government was bound to abide by them. Yet throughout the oncoming war he almost always faithfully adhered to the strictures of "constitutional" monarchy, particularly as Saionji had laid them out to him. Until the final days of the undefeated Japan, Hirohito handed down hardly a single decision for which he had truly been the originating party, complaining in quiet despair that the army was "using silk floss to suffocate [him]." Even if the monarch had wished to reverse the clearly dangerous militarization and its ensuing adventures leading to Pearl Harbor, the stakes were so high to the ultranationalistic adherents of that course that Hirohito could have been, without insuperable damage, "retired" or even deposed with a regency in Akihito's name, a situation that would have deprived the government of whatever utility an adult monarch at the head of state would bring.

How much, then, should a man be held responsible for such shortcomings, deficiencies that would attach to his name international opprobrium? If Hirohito had been a stronger personality, and conceding a pacific cast to that personality, could he, as his nation's ultimate living symbol, have at least pointedly denounced the worst of the Japanese armed forces' excesses—the Rape of Nanking, the

Bataan Death March, the lurid maltreatment of war prisoners and of Asians in the areas "liberated" by the Japanese from the European colonialists? Or would such actions have negated the chance he had to make his final, supreme contribution to his people, a decision permitting the actual physical continuation of his nation, when he finally spoke out in 1945 for an end to the war? These are not questions that make for easy or glib answers, and the lack of such a satisfactory conclusion was perhaps the most nagging domestic postwar conundrum imperiling the monarchy.

The closely related issue of the extent of the emperor's active encouragement of the militarists in their countdown to world war is another question to which no generally agreed conclusion has been reached. It should be kept in mind that, for all its wartime butchery and effrontery to principles of civilization, crimes that because of their sheer scope were unimaginably devastating to China, Japan was nonetheless not in the same uniquely barbaric league as Nazi Germany. It did not espouse a national creed mandating the utter destruction of any racial group, nor did it possess an evil skein of death camps in any way comparable to the hell on earth Germany created in occupied Europe. Until 1940, remnants of constitutional government existed, even though Japan was slowly coming to emulate some of the most horrific of its ally's excesses; one such was the War Office's 1942 bill calling for the sterilization of the mentally unfit, an act taken "in cooperation" with the Japan Eugenics Society. Perhaps most difficult for its wartime enemies to understand, Japan was a nation that, with some degree of justification on its side, felt victimized by the white imperialism so much a part of the prewar world order, an order very different from the one prevailing today. That it so utterly diminished whatever right it had on its side by its attack on Pearl Harbor and its savage treatment of fellow Asiatics was, of course, Japan's tragedy and the true measure of its own imperialistic misdeeds.

During the fateful period just preceding Pearl Harbor, Hirohito made one small gesture in an attempt to gain time to resolve differences, a gesture that reflects his own antihawkishness in a country whipped to fever pitch to exact retribution on the white men who had "stolen" East Asia from them. When the decision for war with the United States was made at a cabinet meeting in September 1941,[12] the emperor broke the custom of silent approbation of his ministers' deliberations and quoted a poem, written by his grandfather, that asked, "Though I consider the surrounding seas as my brothers, Why is it that the waves should rise so high?" Reports are that the cabinet was "awed" by their sovereign's words, but even this unprecedented utterance was to absolutely no avail, the emperor's person and mystique being held in considerably greater thrall by his ministers than were his political opinions. The awe that accompanied his words should have demonstrated to Hirohito the immense moral authority he possessed; tragically, his failure to meaningfully employ such authority against their designs was a boon to the men who took Japan down the road to total war.[13]

The throne was torn between two opposing forces during the war. The liberal agenda called for the emperor to stay above and out of politics, making him appear the model constitutional monarch but effectively crippling his ability to have any real influence in the direction of the nation's affairs. The militarists and ultranationalists, on the other hand, wanted Hirohito to appear the compleat ruler-by-divine-right, all the state's power and prestige wrapped in the cloak of the throne—with the new oligarchs calling every shot, of course. In the end, the monarch was inevitably the loser: He had lost his constitutional footing by having been used by the militarists, and he lost equally his totem of divinity by acquiescing to the liberals' model of constitutionality.

[12]At an earlier meeting in July, Hirohito first concretely moved toward war by giving approval in principle to the broad strategy that a strike should be made south—against the Philippines and the Dutch East Indies—for the oil and other vital commodities the empire would gain; any strike north, toward the Soviets, was ruled out.

[13]Historian and journalist Paul Manning wrote in his book *Hirohito—The War Years* that the emperor's behavior at this meeting rather than being dovish was decidedly hawkish, that he in fact searchingly interrogated his top generals about the nation's readiness to take on the United States if circumstances would require it. Such an interrogation might also, of course, be interpreted as a precautionary warning against war.

After the attack on Pearl Harbor, Hirohito became a virtual prisoner in his palace, emerging rarely and then usually only to celebrate a particularly important military or naval victory. As the war's tide irreversibly turned after Midway, the outings were more likely to have the purpose of personally inspecting the destruction visited on the nation's cities by the bombers that came to control the skies over Japan. Like the vast majority of their subjects, the imperial couple also shared the hardships and deprivations that became ever more onerous as the war's fortunes turned against the empire. The already thin monarch dropped twenty pounds from his normal weight of 143, but he refused to accept the extra rations that would have appeared instantly at the slightest word. One of the first sacrifices Hirohito made was his beloved biology studies. The emperor's advisers decided the country needed a highly conspicuous personal relinquishment from the sovereign as propaganda, and thus "advised" that the palace laboratory was a "self-indulgence inappropriate to wartime." Courtiers were aware of how the bad news from the fronts was distressing Hirohito, and after 1942 they conspired to keep the worst of it from him.

The years immediately prior to Pearl Harbor saw an enormous upturn in the state-sponsored deification of the sovereign. The chauvinism extended all the way down to such fripperies as the government's insistence that English-language periodicals[14] always capitalize personal pronouns referring to the emperor in the same way pronouns referring to Christ are generally capitalized in English. While the Japanese penchant for sloganeering went into high gear—"Fight Onward Till Asia Is Asia's Own" and "The Front Line Wins When the Home Front Endures"—the sovereign kept up his visits to the imperial shrines to report for the benefit of his imperial ancestors the war's progress.

Following the disastrous Battle of Midway, the balance of power shifted inexorably to the Allies, and by late 1943 any chance of a

---

[14]Of which the *Nippon Times*, incidentally, continued publication through to March 1945; the paper had been jingoistically renamed from the *Japan Times* a year earlier.

Japanese victory was clearly eliminated—clear, at least, to the war's managers if not to the Japanese people. To perk up the home front, the government turned the crown prince's tenth birthday into a jubileelike national celebration. Newspapers reported that the boy, whose father refused his ministers' wishes to let him become symbolically commissioned in the armed forces, was paying "close attention to the developments of the war situation . . ." and that "His Imperial Highness is extremely satisfied with the series of glorious victories scored by the Imperial Forces. It is learned that His Imperial Highness is glad to hear of the superior strategy and bravery of the Japanese officers and men on the front line." The boy was at that time living away from his family in the safety of the Japanese alps.

Nagako passed the dreary days putting together first-aid kits for the troops and making farewell gifts for the military commanders of units that were being decimated faster than replacements could be thrown into the breech. When Nagako heard of some general being assigned a cold-weather post, she would set about knitting a scarf for him; if a top commander drew a tropical assignment the imperial gift was likely to be a wall-hanging made precious by the fact that it had been directly fashioned by the empress's own hand. By 1944, she was making several such gifts each day, refusing the assistance of helpers. As food became first scarce and then obtainable only in virtual starvation quantities for Japan's noncombatants, Hirohito and Nagako asked the palace cooks to replace the high-quality white polished rice they were served with an inferior Siamese one. As soon as the extreme rightists heard of this melancholy bit of symbolic identification with the rest of the nation, they stormed the Imperial Household Ministry with protests, demanding to know why palace officials were "giving hog's feed to the One and Only god."

One of the few occasions that might have provided the imperial couple with some personal joy during these onerous years turned out to be more a source of aggravation than of the pleasure. Their daughter Shigeko, Princess "Sunshine," had come of marriageable age shortly before the attack on Pearl Harbor, and it was arranged that she should wed the imperial prince Morihiro of the House of Higashikuni. As was custom, the feelings of the prospective bride and bridegroom—she was still a child at fourteen—weren't given the slightest consideration. But Shigeko was an unusually outspoken young girl for her time, even more so for a girl of her position, and she made her unhappiness at the prospective marriage well known to both her parents, a source of worry not needed as the war got underway. However, the wedding was finally celebrated in October 1943, by which time the princess had grown into a beautiful and willowy young woman of seventeen; for the ceremony, she was dressed in the same marriage robes her mother had worn twenty years earlier. After the rites, the couple visited the Yasukuni Shrine—Japan's principal place where its warriors killed in battle are honored—during which the newlyweds' car was mobbed by bereaved families of some of the thousands who were dying each day on Japan's farflung fronts. The new Princess Morihiro was said to have started loving the stranger who was her husband as she watched his kindness in personally soothing the distraught families.

Through MacArthur's stepping-stone strategy, the United States had by November 1944 won the islands that finally enabled its air forces to bomb Japan itself, to which end eventually 40 percent of urban Japan would be destroyed. The biggest target was Tokyo, affording the greatest symbolic and psychic damage that they could possibly inflict on the enemy. American strategists had given the air force clear and unequivocable instructions to avoid dropping their bomb on the easily recognized Imperial Palace compound, but the remainder of the immense city was soon turned into a moonscape of gutted buildings, burned-out trolleys, scorched trees, and rotting corpses. The raid of March 9, 1945, by far the heaviest the city endured in the entire war, reduced to ashes 158 square miles, razed 267,171 buildings, killed 83,793 people, and injured another 41,000; a million more were made homeless.

Household Minister Matsudaira assured the emperor that the Americans had no intentions of destroying the palace, asserting that the enemy realized such a move would only "fan enmity" among the Japanese people. But on May 25, even this one last unburned island in the center of the metropolis went up in flames. Postwar American claims were that the burning of the palace wasn't the result of a direct bomb hit from the attacking B-29s, but was caused by flaming bond certificates wafting in the superheated air currents from the burning Stock Exchange a few hundred yards across the moat from the imperial compound. Whatever the origin, nearly all of the main buildings forming the so-called Outer Palace were razed, including the largest structure containing Meiji's central ceremonial chambers; twenty-eight members of the palace staff died in the blaze, including a dozen firemen who perished trying to contain the fires in the Imperial Household Ministry's building. Burned on the same evening were the imperial villas housing the dowager empress, the absent crown prince, Prince Chichibu, Prince Mikasa, and Prince Kan'in. Hirohito was said to have exclaimed, "We have been bombed at last," taking some comfort in that at least he could now share his subjects' agony in a more personal way. Though the sovereign was not bombed in the technical sense, the end results made the point depressingly moot.

On March 19, Hirohito embarked on an inspection tour of areas of Tokyo that had been devastated by the fire raids. The *Nippon Times* reported that "His Imperial Majesty's personal inspection has profoundly impressed the officials and people with the boundless Imperial benevolence." It added that "we cannot but be profoundly moved by the benevolent Imperial Mind of taking compassion on the privation and hardships of the people. We, the 100,000,000 people, must pledge ourselves to safeguard the noble fundamental character of the Japanese empire with the best of our strength, thereby placating the Imperial Mind at ease." Such was the official stance regarding the role of the nation's throne in its "war of Asian liberation."

Shortly before the raid that destroyed his palace, Hirohito and his wife had been moved into the palace outbuilding called the *obunko*, originally constructed to serve as the imperial library and archives. Built on the side of a hill in the Fukiage Gardens, it was a sturdy concrete affair containing a number of anterooms in addition to the chambers that served as the main living suite for the emperor and empress. Buried sixty feet under the obunko was an air raid shelter hurriedly put together for the imperial couple by the army in the fall of 1944; a massive twenty-foot-thick, concrete-walled series of rooms vied in a sort of spare *luxe* with the famous Berlin bunker that Hitler had constructed for his own Götterdämerung. Besides comfortable, cedar-lined bedrooms for Hirohito and Nagako, the shelter held a conference room that would serve as the stage for the last angst-filled acts of Japan's imperial gamble.

Despite the fact that the Japanese armed forces were still a formidable threat, and one that would have been capable of inflicting incalculable casualties on any invasion force, by 1945 Hirohito could plainly see that Japan's chances for a military stand-off, let alone any kind of victory, had ceased to exist. One hundred and nineteen of the nation's cities had been or were being systematically bombed into charcoal. Only Kyoto, alone of towns of any appreciable size, escaped this conflagration visited from the skies, and then evidently only because of cultural considerations on the part of the U.S. war planners.

On June 22, the monarch finally called for a conference with the leading members of his government, clearly telling them that a way had to be found to end his people's suffering. In the presence of the prime minister (by now Kantaro Suzuki; General Hideki Tojo had been forced out of office nearly a year earlier), the foreign minister, the war and navy ministers, and the chiefs of staff of the army and navy, he gently but unequivocally asked his top war leaders, "Isn't it time for you to consider ways to bring the war to an end?" It was the first time the sovereign had officially voiced such feelings to the war cabinet. As a result, plans were set in motion to send Prince Konoye to Moscow, where he was to ask Stalin to serve as an intermediary between the Allies and Japan. On receiving the envoy's message, Stalin transmitted it to the then-meeting Potsdam conferees, leaders who with such knowledge realized beyond any further question that they need offer no concessions whatever to the Japanese, thus unhesitatingly promulgating their demand that Japan's surrender be unconditional and immediate.

The undreamt-of horrors visited on Hiroshima and Nagasaki in early August made the emperor and his advisers aware of the pointless futility of prolonging the war in the hope of gaining less-onerous surrender terms. The demands presented by the Allies were clearly understood as "nonnegotiable." Still, extremists who preferred to see the nation and its people destroyed in a final act of immolation attempted to sway events, knowing that if the enemy couldn't be stopped altogether, then considerable pain could still be inflicted on invaders who were only a few short weeks or months away from a full-scale landing on the Japanese home islands. It was these die-hard members of the army who threw up the minefield Hirohito spent the last few days before surrender delicately and dangerously feeling his way through.

With events closing in on the nation, on August 9, 1945, the emperor at last took personal charge of the political decision-making process. The second atomic bomb had just been loosed that day on Nagasaki, and Prime Minister Suzuki knew that Japan had to act quickly in order to avoid a third being dropped (which is how the Americans hoped he would react; in reality, no third bomb was available). But Suzuki by himself was not able to convince the war cabinet that accepting the provisions of the Potsdam Declaration was of critical importance to the very future of the island nation. Into the fray, the forty-five-year-old emperor finally invoked the powers that had been his only in theory since his accession, and by doing so became the sword that cut through the knot of wrangling and deadlocked ministers.

In the dimly lit, coffer-ceilinged room in the shelter under the obunko, unventilated and thus stiflingly hot in Tokyo's August heat, the exhausted monarch met with his frazzled cabinet, all sweating equally, their formal attire so much at odds with the surrealistic twilight-world a few feet above their heads. When it became clear that the men could still not agree on surrender, Suzuki, in an act approaching sacrilege, turned to face the emperor. He said simply and quietly that the monarch's wishes must now be made manifest. The stunned assemblage heard their sovereign state that "we must bear the unbearable" and accede to the Allied demands. Following their sovereign's bidding, the cabinet agreed, with the single stipulation that the institution of the monarchy should not be abolished, a scenario that would have, for the Japanese, equated to the loss of the polity of their race and nation, a burden considered beyond the merely unbearable.

The American government seemed to accept the provision: Its response, written by Secretary of State James Byrnes, stipulated that the final form of government in Japan would be decided by the popular will of the Japanese people. When the reply was received in Tokyo, Hirohito bowed to this proviso, face-savingly stating that he felt he would be "useless if the people did not want an emperor." For the next two days, desperate maneuvers on the part of the extremist army officers, fearing that the concept of a Japanese nation under its god-emperor would be lost forever if the country surrendered, tried to coerce the cabinet into continuing the fight. Concerned that another atomic bomb would irrevocably remove matters from his hands, Hirohito called a final cabinet meeting for August 14. Without resorting to histrionics—which would have been unimaginable for a man of his character and position—he left no doubts that he expected the war to be stopped immediately. To that end he recorded a surrender speech to be played on the state radio the following day, words that would make it crystal clear that the conflict was over, that to continue was no longer possible.

Never before had their monarch's voice been heard on the radio, and to virtually all the listeners the reality of the situation was almost unspeakably poignant. As the few undamaged factory whistles blew the noon hour, Japan came to a dead halt. The exhausted Hirohito stopped his own duties to listen to the prerecorded message over the old RCA radio outside the bunker's conference room. The audience—millions of people ranging from soldiers and sailors to students to factory workers and housewives—were instructed by the announcer to rise. All did, unhesitatingly. As the measures of the "Kimigayo," the national anthem, died out, the strained first words of the "Voice of the Crane," the euphemism for a sovereign, began. Because of the high singsong of the court intonations and the remote linguistic phrasings reserved for the use of the monarch alone, his listeners found they were nearly unable to understand the words of the formal language in which the historic message was composed, but they nonetheless instinctively understood they were being ordered to lay down their arms and accept what must be: "Should we continue to fight, it would not only result in an ultimate collapse and obliteration of the Japanese nation, but it would also lead to the total extinction of human civilization." The power of the new bomb was not lost on its victims. "This is the reason why We have ordered the acceptance of the provisions of the Joint Declaration of the Powers . . . Submit, ye, to Our Will!"

With those words one kind of monarchy was dead. The concept of the emperor as a God at the head of a sacred polity was now history, the reality of it destroyed on beaches all over the Pacific, in fields across China and Southeast Asia, and in the still-smoking ruins of scores of Japanese cities—especially in the deadly radioactive ashes of Hiroshima and Nagasaki. An era was dead. A new, unimaginably different future loomed on the horizon.

In 1986, several letters that were written by and between members of the imperial family in 1945 were made public, copies having been kept by a member of the Imperial Household Ministry, the government department whose existence ended with the war. The documents, the first personal imperial letters ever released, showed both a concern and a brave face put on by Hirohito for his family's sake, and are probably little different from those of any of his hard-pressed subjects. Writing to the crown prince soon after the capitulation, the emperor told the boy, "Although the nation is facing difficulties, I am all right. So there is no need for you to worry about me." Trying to explain to his son his nation's first defeat in its recorded history, Hirohito listed what he thought were the causes of the Allied victory. "For one thing, we Japanese overestimated the power of *kokoku* [the national polity—i.e., Imperial Japan] and held Britain and the U.S. in contempt. Another cause is that our armed forces put too much emphasis on the spiritual side and forgot science." Placing some of the blame on incompetent military leadership, Hirohito continued, "At the time of the emperor Meiji, there were great army and navy commanders . . . but in this war, military men were overbearing and failed to take a wide view of the matter. . . . They only knew advancement but did not know retreat."

The empress also wrote to Akihito, wanting him to understand his father's difficulty in reaching the surrender decision. "Your father was worried every day. Although it was regrettable, Japan has been saved for good through the decision." In an aside referring to the horrors of the American air raids, Nagako added, "I have to admit that B-29s are well-built airplanes."

CHAPTER X

Showa—Enlightened Peace

1945 TO THE PRESENT

"The pine tree bears the weight of snow,
but how green is the spring."

—HIROHITO, JANUARY 1946

We stand by the people and we wish always to share with them in their moments of joys and sorrows. The ties between us and our people have always stood upon mutual trust and affection. They do not depend upon mere legends and myths. They are not predicated on the false conception that the Emperor is divine and that the Japanese people are superior to other races and fated to rule the world.

So it came about that on the first day of the year Showa 20—January 1, 1946—Hirohito canceled his own quality of godliness. The common belief holding the monarch as divine had been integral to Japanese life for nearly two thousand years, and the first shock of its sudden repudiation came as a blow to a nation still convulsed in the unprecedented agony of military defeat. But a great deal more than purported divinity was lost to the monarchy following this new barbarian invasion. The victors' scornful abrogation of the Meiji Constitution nullified with it the emperor's status as supreme ruler and holder of final responsibility for his nation's administration. With the new constitution, in its planning stages

299

since the surrender, Japan's sovereignty would rest solely in its people, not in a man who would stand only as its "living symbol of nationhood." No longer would the monarch be the state itself.[1]

What was left were the two functions the country's monarchs had clung to even during the centuries when the throne's very existence threatened to succumb to inertia. As the embodiment of the national culture and as his people's high priest, Hirohito's role remains unchanged. In its religion, Japan has experienced a complete turnaround from the excesses of the emperor-centered personality cult of State Shinto, but Hirohito's position as the ultimate authority in its traditional religious beliefs is nearly as firmly accepted as it was before the war.

Hirohito knew, as his advisers certainly did, that the emperor's postwar status would have to be radically revised. Both the image and the functions of a politically authoritative emperor-as-godhead were dead, and a suitable *and* desirable replacement was urgently needed. The change would necessarily be extreme in magnitude, but because of the disaster of war and foreign occupation the country's institutions of government were a virtual tabula rasa ready to be reborn in a vastly changed mold. If the monarchy was to take any kind of meaningful place in the new state beyond that of mere existence, it required a substantive transforming. The answer lay, quite simply, in turning the sovereign into a father-figure, not an infinitely remote recluse, but a comparatively accessible, thoroughly politically disenfranchised symbol of the nation's essential familyhood.

With the help of the surviving core of old-school liberals, Hirohito began the process of democratizing the throne within weeks after the September surrender formalities had taken place on the deck of the American battleship *Missouri*. The unpleasant possibility still existed in the emperor's mind that the Allied pro-consul for Japan, General Douglas MacArthur, might add him to the list

---

[1]Not only did the monarch lose his ultimate political status as sovereign, but the emperor's role as commander-in-chief of the nation's armed forces was abolished; even the wearing of uniforms-as-costume in the manner of the British queen has, since 1946, been denied the Japanese monarch.

of former military and government leaders about to be indicted for war crimes,[2] the uncertainty putting a large question mark on what actions might best be taken by Hirohito and his advisers in the monarch's rebirth as a constitutional figurehead. The issue of possible charges against him was settled early in the Occupation, when Hirohito asked to see MacArthur. In their famous encounter at the general's residence on September 17, 1945,[3] MacArthur was surprisingly impressed when he found that Hirohito had come not to plead his own innocence ("to beg for his own life," as one of MacArthur's biographers described the general's preconception of the emperor's reason for the visit), but rather out of a desire to personally assume the entire burden of responsibility, if not of guilt, for the war itself. The encounter was a factor in prompting the general to convince the still-undecided American government—to convey a fait accompli is perhaps a more accurate way of putting it—that under no circumstances should further consideration be given to trying Hirohito as a war criminal. MacArthur clearly recognized the emperor to be of far greater importance to America's essential interests in Japan than would be achieved by simple revenge. With characteristic perspicacity, the greatest genius in American military history understood that in Hirohito there existed a rallying point around which the devastated Japanese people could regroup and emerge whole once again, a nation no longer a threat to the West but instead a strong ally in the strategic dike even then being built against the red tide.

Shortly thereafter, a succession of profound institutional changes

[2]Hirohito's cousin, Prince Higashikuni, thought this would be a good time for Hirohito to abdicate in favor of Crown Prince Akihito, the reasoning being that "the captain of the ship must take responsibility for its going aground."

[3]For the interview, MacArthur chose his personal quarters in the former U.S. embassy over the forbidding occupation headquarters, the famous Dai Ichi building across the moat from the palace. His apparent purpose was to avoid any suggestion that the sovereign had been "summoned to a meeting," thus contributing to the monarch's martyrdom in the eyes of the Japanese people. Although imperial officials wanted the general to pay a return call to the palace to "maintain the emperor's dignity," the U.S. State Department vetoed the suggestion as an "inappropriate" visit to the monarch of a defeated nation.

in the way Japan was governed began to issue forth, an unending flood of directives and demands of the Occupation authorities transposed into law by the tethered Japanese government. The earliest ordinances removed restrictions on the freedom of speech and released political prisoners; equal rights for women, the encouragement of labor unions, liberalization of education, and divestment and democratization of the country's economy followed in rapid succession. The General Staff and Naval High Command were abolished. Zaibatsu holdings were first frozen and later dispersed. Land reform, turning vast numbers of tenant farms into owner-cultivated property, was instituted. A new law guaranteed the separation of Shinto from state control. And, closer to the throne, 7,500 retainers attached to the Imperial Household were fired, an act carried out at the personal order of General Courtney Whitney, MacArthur's chief aide, in an effort to "cut the Emperor down to size."

In November 1945, the assets of the Imperial Household were seized; Hirohito's personal wealth, estimated at roughly $100 million in 1945, was overnight decimated by an SCAP-ordered[4] capital levy. MacArthur's new constitution contained the provision that income from imperial estates and investments was to be paid into the national treasury, rapidly ending the almost uncontrolled prewar growth of the sovereign's private fortune; six years later the emperor's liquid assets had dwindled to a reported $70,000. As to his illiquid assets, little concrete evidence is available to accurately estimate the imperial treasure, but speculation continues to circulate that sizable portions of the monarch's prewar fortune were transferred out of the country before SCAP auditors could reach it, rumors most recently discussed in Paul Manning's book *Hirohito— The War Years*. Manning asserts that shortly before the end of the war a large part of Hirohito's wealth was sent through the Yokohama Specie Bank—seized by occupation authorities within days after the surrender—to neutral foreign countries for safekeeping. Furthermore, the writer states that the imperial gold reserves were likewise shifted out of the country, probably to Switzerland or

[4]Supreme Commander Allied Powers, MacArthur's headquarters.

South America, with Lord Privy Seal Marquis Kido most likely responsible for the transfer.

On New Year's Day, 1946, the most historically significant act reflecting on the monarchy occurred. Hirohito issued the Imperial Rescript denying both his own purported divinity and any presumed innate superiority of the Japanese people over other nations, purging the throne as well as the nation of much of their prewar theoretical underpinnings. (Ironically, the right of the sovereign to issue rescripts was shortly thereafter permanently proscribed.) The New Year's Rescript was not, as it is commonly supposed, forced on Hirohito by the Occupation authorities, but was instead initiated at his own free will. MacArthur received the declaration with surprised satisfaction, and it eventually came to be regarded as one of the most consequential documents to come out of the Pacific War's aftermath. Hirohito's rescript by no means destroyed the entire fabric of the emperor-as-divine mythology, but, once digested, its effect was both electric and liberating on his subjects and the nation's will to start anew.

To codify the changes that were transforming both the monarchy and the nation, the Allied High Command ordered a new basic law to replace the discredited Meiji Constitution, a document that had proven to be the perfect recipe for despotism. In light of the earlier constitution's manifest failure, a replacement, one with a democratic framework on which the new state was to be built, was assigned a high priority by the country's occupiers.

In abstract terms, the constitution that became effective on May 3, 1947, was not an entirely new ground law, instead supposedly only a "revision" of the Meiji document,[5] but the revised version nonetheless embraced radically new notions of the state and its relationship to the people it served. First and most fundamental, sovereignty was irrevocably transferred from the emperor to the people, with the Diet—the national legislature—now the highest organ of state. The cabinet would be responsible to the Diet, not to the monarch. The most stunning provision was embodied in

---

[5]Whose underlying democratic constitutional guarantees were, as we've seen, easily subverted.

Article Nine, the famous renunciation of war. It denies Japan the right to maintain armed forces and the state's right of belligerency, the first—and so far the only—time in history any government has specifically constitutionally denied itself the right to take up arms to settle disputes with other nations. In respect to its monarchy, the new constitution's most basic change was to shift the theoretical basis of the state from one in which the people were granted limited rights by a sovereign who reserved ultimate authority to himself, to one in which this ultimate sovereign authority was the people themselves; the throne would now serve officially only as the highest voice of legitimacy for the Japanese people.

The first eight articles of the MacArthur-imposed constitution dealt exclusively with the emperor and the monarchy. The shrunken government agency responsible for the monarch and the court was demoted from a full Ministry of State to a mere "agency" in the prime minister's office, that office in turn responsible to the cabinet; the Executive Branch was made co-equal with the other two branches of government, the legislative (the Diet) and the judicial (the Supreme Court); and, finally, the Privy Council was abolished. Another provision held that because all his acts were considered to be taken only with the consent and approval of the government, the emperor could not be held personally accountable and thus would remain guilt-free in any decision taken by the government. Further, to help ensure that the monarchy would never again become an independent economic power, the eighth article prohibited the imperial house from receiving any "gifts" without the express authorization of the Diet. Finally, in the tenth chapter of the document, the emperor was declared to have the "obligation to respect and uphold this Constitution." As before, an Imperial House Law (see Appendix D) was maintained as an adjunct to the constitution, and in the revised version the downgrading of the institution of the throne in relative importance to the people was even further delineated. Thus, insofar as being compatible with the retention of the throne at all, the imperial institution's official role was decisively demoted to little more than the ceremonial, its lofty status brought in line with those of other democratic constitutional monarchies.

The end of the war and the constitutional change in his status gave Hirohito, for the first time in his life, something that began to approximate the ordinary freedoms the new constitution guaranteed his countrymen. As emperor he still could never entirely share the freedoms of the ordinary Japanese, but at least now he was able to escape the most stifling of the etiquette-decreed strictures of the prewar court. Advised by his astutest courtiers to publicly show himself, the monarch took the first small steps out of the palace's claustrophobic confines, soon finding that his initial trepidation was being replaced with curiosity. Before the war, forays beyond the moat-girt safety of the imperial fortress involved such oppressive security precautions and symbolic impediments that these occasions were inevitably logistical nightmares and ordeals to be endured. In that era, onlookers weren't permitted to approach within a hundred yards of his limousine, a realistic precaution considering the frequent terrorist attacks on high-ranking government officials in the 1930s. As a consequence, Hirohito, who endured such outings without so much as a wave of the hand or even the suggestion of a smile that might indicate awareness of the bystanders, experienced virtually no close contact with his ordinary subjects or the broader perspective such contacts might have brought him. With the war's end, the need for this kind of protection and pomp largely evaporated.

Hirohito's post-1945 metamorphosis was far-reaching. In part, it took the form of a series of visits eventually extending to every part of his now starkly reduced empire—an empire again consisting almost entirely of the four islands that had constituted the same lands over which his grandfather once reigned as boy-emperor. The visits represented an accomplishment not achieved by a single one of his predecessors, even the relatively widely traveled Meiji. Sometimes the entire imperial entourage consisted of only four persons: two chamberlains, a physician, and the emperor himself—the latter having permanently forsaken the modified black field marshal's uniform that he wore in the immediate postwar period for a plain, even ill-cut business suit topped by a felt hat, its front brim turned up to give the emperor what became his well-known signature "look." Wherever the desanctified monarch traveled, the crowds would greet him with respectful friendliness, not quite sure what to make of this cosmic change in Japan's history. But most people generously saw him as a precious symbol of continuity to their ravaged nation, and in time much of the ice if not broke, at least softened.

In some cases, Hirohito was almost mobbed by the increasingly familiar crowds, as when one day at the still-half-destroyed Osaka prefectural office he literally disappeared inside a happy throng, completely separated from his protectors for the first time in his life. Occasionally there were insults. One day a placard appeared with a derisive inscription under the headline of "Imperial Rescript: The [throne] has been safeguarded. We [the imperial family] are filling our bellies while you, our subjects, starve and die—signed with the seal of Hirohito." This sort of insolence was ignored by its target, who, incidentally, had given orders that the palace and every one of its occupants share the average citizen's near-starvation regimen, even seeing to it that the Imperial Household donated food to his beleaguered countrymen.

The emperor's visits were nearly always prosaic affairs—walks through bombed-out factories or to newly rebuilt industrial installations, tours of coal mines from Hokkaido to Kyushu, and the like. Even though he still looked embarrassingly uncomfortable in news photos recording the events, the discomfort was the result of a lifetime of elevation and isolation. On one trip through a dye-making factory in 1949, Hirohito was unexpectedly greeted by a sea of fluttering *hinomaru* flags, the national emblem of the Rising Sun that had just been reauthorized by the Occupation authorities for public display. Afterward he mentioned that he had found this particular visit "an especially enjoyable" one, the specialness perhaps heightened by seeing, after four stressful years, the symbol of what had at his accession been an unconquered realm. The habitual comment of the shy emperor to the lucky few who were allowed to speak to him—*Ah, so desuka*, "Yes, I see"—led these trips to be called the Ah, So Desuka Tours in commemoration of the nonloquacious sovereign. But sometimes Hirohito's growing self-assurance allowed him to ask more meaningful questions out of a very real concern for the people of his ravaged nation: "Are you hungry?" or "Have your children come back from the front?" Early on, a nervous worker reached out to shake his hand, to which Hirohito instinctively responded with the more Japanese gesture of bowing. (Even today, Hirohito shakes hands only with foreigners, never with Japanese.[6])

The deeper meaning of the trips was anything but curiosity-assuaging or mere ceremony: Hirohito wanted to make it understood both to his people and to the Occupation authorities that he would do whatever was necessary to counter the increasing tendency in the newly democratic country to regard his position as completely without substance, a doll on top of a monarchic wedding cake. The newly emboldened leftists took the opportunity to mock the monarchy and even begrudge simple courtesy to the emperor himself, but such insults were generally albeit politely ignored. The placard incident, a highly publicized contretemps in which demonstrators paraded around the palace carrying signs slandering the emperor, revulsed the overwhelming majority of Japanese, but with the legal abrogation of the prewar lèse-majesté laws, little could be done to stop such behavior. Despite such needling, when the new constitution and rapidly improving conditions of the late 1940s finally vouchsafed the throne's probable continuation, Hirohito felt able to retreat back behind his ancient chrysanthemum curtain, allowing a decade to pass before letting it rise again for a new generation.

A predictable sprinkling of demands for the emperor's abdication arose in the immediate postwar years—usually from Communists who held him accountable for war crimes and who couched their cries in the logic that such an act would "refresh the public mind." Hirohito himself squelched them on May 3, 1952 (five days after the treaty officially ending World War II went into effect), when he declared that after reflecting on the past and appraising public opinion, and after "serious and profound deliberation," he would "exert [himself] to bear the heavy burden." The statement, making

---

[6]He would eventually learn to relax. Years later, on chatting with a judo champion, the emperor remarked, "I see you are doing very well, but with the training matches you must have a backbreaking schedule." The wrestler replied, "Actually, I broke my leg two years ago." Everyone burst into laughter, including Hirohito.

clear Hirohito's intention to continue on the throne despite any feelings of self-guilt, put an end to further substantive public discussion of the matter.

Hirohito's redefined status and the new activities associated with the throne did not, to keep these events in their proper perspective, turn Japan's imperial institution into anything like Scandinavia's so-called bicycle monarchies, their monarchs scooting around just like ordinary folk. Its head became neither a glamour figure—snipping ribbons, opening new hospital wards, or constantly being put on view at "command" performances—nor did he effect the kind of semidemocratization associated with "walkabouts" and society racing meets. The monarchy had no experience as an entertainment, and even though its newly de-deified paterfamilias admitted he was a mere mortal like everyone else, he was still far removed from the level of his countrymen. After the relatively brief period of public flurry in the first few years after the war, he willingly fell more and more into the shadows, becoming to his people simply Ohoribata, the "Honorable Across-the-Moat." Inevitably, much of the public scrutiny of the throne began to refocus on the person of the crown prince, the attractive young heir whom the emperor purposely urged into the limelight during the late fifties. To the Japanese, this period would become known as the "Michi Boom," a time characterized by wildly enthusiastic popular interest in the throne stemming from the crown prince's engagement to the commoner Michiko Shoda.

Akihito, who prior to the surrender had been sent out of Tokyo to escape the bombing raids, was, in the first postwar years, enrolled in his own establishment about forty minutes outside Tokyo called the Kokaden, "the Palace of Glorious Light." With the more liberal social atmosphere brought about with the war's end, the still chubby teenager was irreverently called Chabuta, "Brown Pig," by his classmates, the nickname later familiarized to Chabuta Chan, and finally shortened to Chabu Chan, a kind of democratic informality that would once have been an unthinkable breech of etiquette. With the ancient court strictures loosened, the younger members of Hirohito's family were allowed to experience friendships and a degree of camaraderie unknown to Akihito's father in his own youth.

(However, the new freedoms did not alter the time-honored imperial custom whereby the sovereign's children lived away from their parents, and Akihito only visited the palace on weekends, when the whole family would share dinners together.[7]) Later, instead of having a separate segregated "institute" set up for his middle education, as had been the case with Taisho and Hirohito, Akihito attended a public school: the Gakushuin (enrolled in its Faculty of Politics and Economics), the postwar reorganization of the Peers' School and still very much an elitist and socially influential institution. The prince also received individually tailored lectures, including discourses on the constitution from the Chief Justice of the Supreme Court.

In the spring of 1951, Hirohito was chief mourner at one of the saddest state ceremonies of his reign, the funeral of his mother. Often called by Westerners the Queen Mary of Japan, the immensely dignified Dowager Empress Sadako had in spite of her "retirement" from an official social life in 1925 remained in the postwar years a strong influence on her family, especially in the molding of Akihito's character. In his youth the crown prince frequently visited his grandmother's Omiya Palace, the empress and the boy forming a close rapport. Three weeks after Sadako's death in May 1951, the emperor, in the Rite of Informing Her Spirit of the Posthumous Title, bestowed on his mother the name by which she would be known to posterity: Teimei, "Enlightened Constancy." The empress was buried near her husband, Taisho, in his mausoleum at Tamagorio, in Tokyo's western suburbs.

A year and a half later, on November 10, 1952, the traditional state ceremony marking Akihito's coming-of-age was celebrated in the palace with due pomp, the heir's formal installation as crown prince emblematic of the right to inherit the throne on his father's death without an intermediary regency. The rites were also the occasion that prompted the court to start in earnest its search for

---

[7]His three unmarried sisters had their own residential quarters on the palace grounds called the Kuretake-ryo, the "House of Bamboo," so named in hopes all three would grow "as straight as bamboo." A separate house was also maintained near the Imperial Household Agency headquarters for Akihito's brother Hitachi.

a suitable crown princess. Shortly after his majority solemnities, Akihito was offered the same opportunity his father was given thirty years earlier when Hirohito was allowed to undertake his controversial European Grand Tour. The crown prince was named to officially represent the emperor at the June 1953 coronation of England's Queen Elizabeth II, a duty he fulfilled with dignity among a people who had not in the prior eight years forgiven Japan or its imperial family their wartime transgresses.

By the time Akihito returned from Britain in October to continue his schooling, the subject of matrimony for the twenty-year-old scion of the imperial house had grown into a heatedly discussed national concern. With the prince's own comparatively emancipated views taken into account by his family and the court, a decision was taken not to limit eligible matrimonial candidates to the extended imperial family itself or the five Fujiwara branches that had supplied Japan's imperial consorts for centuries. The only limitations publicly known to be placed on Akihito's choice were that his bride be, first, a daughter of one of the formerly noble families (the nobility had been formally abolished on the promulgation of MacArthur's constitution) or at least of an "old family of good name," and second, that she had been educated at the Peeresses' School or its successor, the now-coeducational Gakushuin.

While most of the country's press was busy comparing one candidate's qualifications with those of another, each impeccably within the palace's purported eligibility guidelines, the court was methodically carrying out its own search for the perfect young woman to carry forward another generation the Sun Goddess's seed. The press's speculation over eligible "candidates" finally managed to ruffle the court's otherwise almost unrufflableness. "It is not a public office one can run for," as one palace statement put it in an attempt to cool speculation a bit. But to give the journalists their due, the eventual winner had been the inside settled favorite for three months before she was eventually announced as the new crown princess–designate.

The young woman who was so obviously eligible had first met Akihito on the tennis courts of Kuruizawa, an exclusive and expensive resort in the Japanese alps that conjures up for the Japanese much the same tone that Aspen does for Americans or St. Moritz for Europeans. Ten months younger than the prince, Michiko Shoda was the eldest daughter of an indisputably rich industrialist, the president of his own flour milling company, albeit a commoner even by prewar standards. Shortly after Akihito first saw her at Karuizawa, a woman private detective received a request from an unidentified client to run a thorough background check on Miss Shoda, the results of which confirmed an unflawed, perfect empress candidate, and one whom the smitten crown prince irreversibly decided would be his bride.

Less carried by storm, Miss Shoda wasn't so sure that marriage into the imperial institution was what she wanted for her life. And she wrote her concerns to her family: "I believe the Imperial Household after all is no place for a person of our status to enter. . . . I am afraid the Crown Prince would be the one to suffer most." The letter found its way to the press, its sentiments of modesty widely quoted in papers all over the country. Having been a physics and English literature student at Tokyo's tony Sacred Heart Women's University (not a Gakushuin alumna, as had been thought a primary requirement), she could have married comfortably into Japan's plutocracy, settling into a life of comfort and pleasure unknown a generation earlier even to women of the upper stratum of the nation's society. The inevitable loss of personal freedom that would accompany an imperial marriage was not necessarily a desirable prospect for this bright example of Japan's first generation of emancipated women.

But Akihito won the day, and official announcement of the engagement was released on November 27, 1958, when the prospective bride and bridegroom were each twenty-four years old. Michiko San, meaning something like "Miss Michiko" in Japan's respect language, was immediately upgraded to the far more deferential Michiko Sama, "Lady Michiko," and her life, every minute of it, became the eagerly sought-after daily fare of Japan's tabloid-reading public. No one, incidentally, was able to come up with even the minutest trace of anything shocking in Michiko Sama's past or pedigree—not even color blindness.

Though the marriage rites were Japan's premier imperial extravaganza since Hirohito's enthronement more than three decades earlier, a Japanese imperial wedding in no way resembles the sort of state spectacle one associates with the confabulations involving Europe's—especially Britain's—royal families. Set for April 10, 1959, the wedding, as with most rites pertaining to the imperial family's affairs, was witnessed by only a handful of people. Akihito's spectacular costume was the same one he had worn at his coming-of-age ceremony: Not priestly robes, which he wears occasionally as official observer at palace religious ceremonies, the costume was instead an ancient-style court dress now used nearly exclusively by the male members of the emperor's immediate family. Michiko's kimono was borrowed, having been worn by Princess Shigeko at her 1943 wedding to Prince Morihiro, and even earlier by Nagako at her marriage vows; the twelve-layered dress, called the *juni-hitoe,* was modeled on the costume used for imperial brides since the eighth century. The couple was formally joined in the imperial palace's special family shrine, outside of whose blossom-bowered courtyard gathered a large invited throng. In accordance with tradition, neither the emperor nor the empress was present, but both watched the solemnities on television in their concrete villa a few hundred yards away.

After the wedding, the imperial family went into another palace "hibernation" away from the public limelight, not retaking the public stage again for five years. In 1964, Japan was to convincingly demonstrate to the world that it was a nation reborn, an industrial power that would soon be the third mightiest on earth. The occasion was the XVth Summer Olympics, awarded to Japan by the International Olympic Committee as a replacement for the aborted Tokyo games that had been scheduled for the summer of 1940. To observers with even a modest appreciation of political realities, it was clear that Japan had, with the 1964 games, finally shed its postwar shroud of contrition. Proudly hosting the opening ceremonies in the enormous new Tokyo stadium was the man who less than two decades earlier had had to counsel his people to "endure the unendurable." With his empress, Hirohito was greeted by thunderous applause as he entered the stadium, leaving no doubt as to his own popularity and to his people's pride in their democratic monarchy. Surrounded by his sons and daughter-in-law, his two surviving brothers and his sisters-in-law, the emperor appeared a man in secure possession of his throne and his dynasty's well-being. When the white-jacketed ranks of waving and cheering Japanese athletes marched past the front of the imperial box, Hirohito laughed and waved right back at them. For once in his public life, the strictures of court traditions wouldn't prevent the emperor from openly sharing the pleasure he felt at the remarkable accomplishments of his people.

On December 25, 1986, Hirohito reached a milestone. The man who was by far the world's longest reigning monarch quietly passed the day that marked his Diamond Jubilee, an anniversary signifying precisely six decades as the unifying symbol of his nation. Over the years, he had witnessed from a position of unique privilege a kaleidoscopic host of great events. He saw China, his nation's great neighbor and rival, wrenchingly converted from a collection of warlord-ruled fiefdoms into a monolithic Marxist superstate; he watched as Stalin systematically collectivized and ravaged Russia and its captive fiefdoms; he saw Hitler seize his nation and then turn it and Europe into a charnel house. He saw one world organization wither and ignominiously die of impotence, and its replacement immobilized by Big Power politics and an ironic tyranny of the majority. At closer quarters, he looked on as a renascent Japan squandered millions of lives and nearly the entirety of the nation's physical infrastructure on a militaristic dream gone berserk, only to be miraculously reborn into a country far stronger than the one that had perished in flames. He himself had gone from being a God to being his nation's First Gentleman, from having his name invoked to goad armies to having his person serve primarily as a living link between his peoples' fabled past and their exciting present. For all the complexity of the Japanese imperial tradition, the monarch was still, at the purest distillation, the incarnate symbol of his nation.

The Imperial Palace, together with its extensive surrounding park, is like a great mysterious hole smack in the middle of one of the world's most overinhabited pales of settlement. Yet a metropolitan conglomeration of 15 million people swirls around this eye in the urban hurricane without ever seriously compromising its essential solitude. Smog-generating exhaust fumes and a headache-inducing din arising out of the city's traffic, endless and endlessly animated construction sites, even the ubiquitous streetcorner loudspeakers, all intrude on the solitude of the green, moat-girt oasis, but the gaze of human eyes has been kept from the innermost recesses of the imperial sanctuary with almost seamless success. Typical of how convincingly off-limits the palace is to the Japanese is that instructions to a taxi driver to be taken to the Sakuradamon Gate, the palace entrance reserved for Imperial Household Agency visitors, were met with the response that he had never in his years of negotiating Tokyo's mazelike streets and hair-raising traffic delivered anyone to that location. The palace is truly a place apart in this city.

Hidden from view inside the carefully guarded perimeter of the imperial compound, the two-story headquarters building of the Kunaicho, foursquare and obviously aged by the heavy trials it suffered in the half century since its construction, sits in the lee of the nearby ceremonial palace. Visitors approaching the building pass a protective cordon of Metropolitan Tokyo police and military sentries—members of the ultra-smart Imperial Guard, the official Household regiment of Japan's Self-Defense Forces—praetorians equipped with the most modern walkie-talkies and computer terminals, the indispensable necessities of modern security and the fruits of the country's electronics genius.

The office of a high echelon member of the imperial court, while not gilded, at least has the merit of spaciousness. With its large seating area for guests, comfortable sofas, and a low coffee table, it looks much like executive quarters anywhere, but the view through the tall windows to the forestlike park on the far side of the gravel driveway reminds the visitor of the uniqueness of the building's setting. Occupying the larger rooms on the two marble-floored stories are Hirohito's top courtiers, the few dozen men who stand at the peak of the 1,135 employees—the 1985 figure—comprising the staff of the Imperial Household Agency, civil servants about whom almost nothing is ever written in English, and not all that much in Japanese.

At the top of the Household's organization chart is the Board of Chamberlains, the highest-ranking office in the imperial retinue, which is headed by the Grand Chamberlain, who is in turn assisted by a Deputy Grand Chamberlain and six chamberlains, some of the latter nowadays the same age as the emperor's grandchildren. The six assistants detailed for this prestigious duty come from various government departments, while the Grand Chamberlain and his assistant represent permanent, usually long-term positions. The Grand Chamberlain is responsible for many of the same functions carried out by the British sovereign's Private Secretary. All of the chamberlains are routinely physically close to the sovereign in his entourage, following Hirohito anywhere his duties take him and assuming responsibility even for some of the more private aspects of his life.

On New Year's Day and the emperor's birthday, former members of the bureau gather at the palace for reunions, where they swap memories of their years of unique service to the imperial institution. The one who for many years had the most stories to tell was Sukemasa Irie, five years younger than the emperor, who had been an imperial chamberlain from 1934 to 1985, the last sixteen years as Grand Chamberlain. Irie's father had served Hirohito when he was still crown prince. A professor at the Peers' University when he joined the imperial service in 1934, Irie, over the course of his palace years, wrote twenty books, most of them about the emperor, coming to be known as the "Emperor's storyteller." In a country where the general civil service retirement age is sixty, Irie, at eighty, finally told Hirohito he felt it wasn't "good to still be serving" the monarch at such an advanced age. Hirohito's understated reply was, according to Irie, "Mmmmm, you've become eighty!" Toward the end of his career, Irie gracefully summed up his employer in the following words: "I have served His Majesty for fifty years, and throughout the whole period, I have felt as if I were being perpetually caressed by a soft spring breeze." In the fall of 1985, two days before his scheduled retirement, the poet, calligrapher, and faithful servant and friend to his master died unexpectedly of a heart attack.

Seventy-eight-year-old Vice Grand Chamberlain Yoshihiro Tokugawa succeeded Irie to the higher position. A chamberlain since 1936 and a descendant of Japan's last shogunal family, Tokugawa is also an uncle of Hirohito's younger son's wife, Princess

Hitachi. That Hirohito would want comrades of such long standing as his closest advisers is understandable. On August 14, 1945, while the rubble of the nearly destroyed city above the palace's air raid shelter was still being rearranged by the American Superfortresses, Irie and Tokugawa were witnesses to the historic recording of Hirohito's surrender speech, Tokugawa personally responsible for guarding the precious wax disc until it could be played over nation-wide radio the following day. When desperate army officers intent on preventing surrender tried to find and destroy the record, Tokugawa guarded its hiding place with his life, even suffering the indignity of a blow to the face from a rebelling army officer outraged at the prospect of capitulation.

The imperial institution is directly represented in the cabinet, of which the Imperial Household Agency is a suboffice within the prime minister's office, by a Director General, today the closest equivalent to the powerful prewar Imperial Household Minister. (The Director General is not, incidentally, a member of the cabinet, as was his pre-1945 counterpart.) The major responsibilities of this diminished functionary have mostly to do with the imperial family as it relates to foreign affairs, which often translates into arranging the details of state visits both to and from Japan, the majority of such overseas visits now being carried out by the crown prince and his wife in the name of a monarch no longer physically up to taking them on himself. (Prince Hitachi, Hirohito's second son, is also occasionally asked to carry out state visits abroad.) Immediately under the Director General comes the Grand Steward, a position roughly analogous to a ministry's vice minister. The emperor's *official* "private secretary" (although the Grand Chamberlain also serves as a kind of private secretary), the Grand Steward represents the monarch to the government, and in turn explains state affairs to the emperor.

Aside from the Chamberlains' Bureau and the Grand Steward's Secretariat, four other major divisions and two minor offices share in the responsibility for the over-all functioning of the monarchy. Like the Chamberlains' Bureau, the Board of Ceremonies is headed by a Grand Master of Ceremonies, under whom two Vice Grand Masters—one for domestic ceremonies, the other for "external affairs" (meaning visits outside the palace)—and a number of assistants report. The separate Crown Prince's Household is responsible for Akihito, his wife, and their three children; the crown prince's younger brother does not come under its aegis. Hirohito's married daughters are not, incidentally, in any way a part of the imperial establishment, even when widowed. The Archives and Mausolea Department, whose purview is thinly spread out over the entire country in both the responsibility for burial places as well as for the various imperial libraries to which ancient documents are sent for storage, has been a function of the imperial establishment for centuries; its headquarters are on the grounds of the Kyoto Palace. A Maintenance and Works Department, sometimes referred to as the Administration Department, oversees repairs to the palaces and their gardens, the catering arrangements for the Imperial Household, and the garages in which are stored the emperor's limousines and antique carriages, the latter still publicly displayed on rare occasions of state. The final two minor offices are the Treasury House and the Kyoto Bureau, the latter primarily dealing with tourists visiting the ceremonial palace in the pre-Meiji capital, to which, incidentally, foreigners have a far easier time gaining access than do native Japanese.

Even in pre-1945 Japan, political power never resided in the Household Ministry in a general way, but came instead as a result of the direct access to the emperor enjoyed by its few highest-ranking officials. To the extremely limited degree that the imperial institution retains any political influence today, the same is true. A man like Grand Chamberlain Yoshihiro Tokugawa has seen a dozen cabinets rise and fall during his tenure as an imperial retainer, and his counsel regarding his own and the emperor's views will still occasionally be sought by the government on important basic issues affecting the national polity. But the monarch is no longer directly involved in any part of the normal policy-making process, not even to the extent of being solicited for his official blessing. Like the Queen of England, he automatically signs acts of the legislature without even considering the alternative; were he to regard this responsibility any differently, he could not and would not survive as monarch under Japan's present constitution.

To a people that views, despite the lessons taught by the war and its aftermath, its genesis as sacred and membership in the Japanese race as a uniquely superior matter, issues related to the mythology and history of the nation take on a deep importance not readily grasped by foreigners. It is in this aspect of Japanese life that the monarchy still maintains a measurable, sometimes significant, role by influencing popular perceptions of what is, for lack of a better word, right. As an official put it to me, the Household tries to "mediate opposing views" on controversies related to the nation's history, particularly the role of the throne. It sees itself as a kind of umpire between the convictions of those on the conservative side who believe the founding mythology contains historical elements of the way things really happened, however highly colored, against those on the left willing, sometimes even eager, to denigrate virtually every facet of the traditional imperial story. As would be expected, the right looks to the palace for official support for its views, but such is the prestige of the monarchy that the left also solicits the throne's tacit agreement. When the palace does occasionally let its views become subtly known on how it perceives elements of the dynasty's and the nation's history, there is little doubt that Hirohito's personal thoughts on the matter have been given much weight.

Today, the imperial institution is held by probably a majority of the emperor's countrymen to be the single most important source of the national culture, the strongest link to all that is still undilutedly *Japanese* in the nation. Much of that culture is directly related to the country's overlapping religions, with the monarchy something like a Japanese papacy; palace officials stressed that the court regarded these religious duties as by far the most important of the monarch's work. And in the uncompromisingly secular state that Japan has become since the war, it is perhaps appropriate that this religious role is also one completely divorced from the control of the Imperial Household Agency. In fact, the government is constitutionally barred from spending a single yen on the traditional religious activities of the emperor, self-imposed duties that take up a large part of his time and most of his ceremonial life. Neither the agency's officials nor even its salaried staff are permitted to do one thing to assist Hirohito in his religious activities; when courtiers are present at such functions, officially they are there only as observers. Furthermore, the cost of funding these rites is underwritten from the sovereign's private purse, not by his official government allowance, such being the legacy left by the abuses of State Shinto as it was constituted prior to 1945.

Another cost to the monarchy resulting from the war was a major reduction in what was defined as "imperial family." Before 1945, the extended clan—nearly a dozen separate households made up the families of Meiji's siblings and descendants—formed all by itself a social superstratum above the peerage, its dozens of imperial princes and princesses of the imperial satellite branches bearing names like Kan'in, Higashi-Fushimi, Fushimi, Yamashina, Kaya, Kuni, Nashimoto, Asaka, Higashi-Kuni, and Kitashirakawa. Although Hirohito disapproved of the plan by which, at the war's end, all the imperial princely houses were forced to descend to the level of ordinary taxpaying subjects,[8] the new boundary of imperial status nevertheless ended with the families of Hirohito's brothers, who might be thought of as the ducal Gloucesters and Kents of Japan.

Of the three younger sons of the emperor Taisho, only one has become the founder of his own line. Meiji's House Law specifically barred the practice of adoption on the part of the sons of sovereigns who might be childless, a rule that has effectively ended the lines of Princes Chichibu and Takamatsu, the brothers being, in formal courtly terminology, "without issue." Prince Chichibu, who died of tuberculosis on January 4, 1953, was survived by his widow, the elegant and charming Princess Chichibu (Setsuko). Born in Britain where her father was ambassador, the imperial sister-in-law today lives in a villa tucked into the easternmost corner of the stone-walled garden behind the Akasaka Palace, protected by an electrified fence and within a few feet of the expresswaylike Aoyama Boulevard; police officers stationed every few yards around the perimeter ensure

[8]Though their Civil Lists were discontinued, each received a lump-sum "gift" as a kind of personal apology from the emperor for their loss of royal status.

the compound's privacy and security. Prince Takamatsu, the war-time "navy brother," was until his death (of lung cancer) in February 1987 a well-established public personality in Japan, having served as president of a number of "friendship" societies, including the Franco-Japanese Society and the Italian-Japanese Society. His widow, Kikuko, like her fellow princesses, acts as honorary chairman of a variety of philanthropic organizations.

The last and youngest of the imperial sons of Taisho is Prince Mikasa, who has earned accolades as a historian on a scale approaching his eldest brother's credentials in biology. Specializing in Middle Eastern history, particularly that of the early Hebrews (he is president of the Japan Society of Orientology, and has directed the Society for Middle Eastern Studies in Japan since 1954), he was, in 1985, appointed guest professor in the Department of Oriental Arts History at Tokyo National University of Fine Arts and Music. The prince has also sat on the guest faculties of the University of London and the Tokyo Christian Women's University and was a lecturer at the universities of Hokkaido and Shizuoka. He and his wife, Princess Yuriko, live a few hundred yards from Princess Chichibu in a villa on the Aoyama Palace grounds. As with the princesses Chichibu and Takamatsu, the Mikasas are almost unknown outside Japan, their primary duties being the sort of royal public appearances at the heart of most modern monarchies, work that officially justifies the Civil List allowances they receive from Japan's taxpayers.

The Mikasa line (the prince was named Takahito at birth; "Mikasa" was the title bestowed on him) appears to be firmly established, and when it ceases to be "imperial" after the third generation descendent from the sovereign, the lines of its male members who start their own branches will constitute Japan's first nonimperial princely houses of the postwar era. As it happens, Prince Mikasa has three sons, all of whom officially bear their father's title; thus, at present there is one Prince Mikasa in the first generation and three in the second (of the family's two daughters, one automatically lost both title and imperial status when she married; the second will lose her's if she too marries). The goateed Tomohito is the oldest second-generation Prince Mikasa. Born in

1946, he is an Oxford graduate in English history and an author, having written a book entitled *Tomohito's Lovely English Life.* He and his wife, Princess Nobuko, the daughter of a cement company chairman from Kyushu, are the parents of two daughters, Princess Akiko, born in 1981, and two years younger, Princess Yohko. The Mikasas' home is in the Akasaka-Aoyama Palace complex between that of his parents and his aunt Chichibu. The second Mikasa prince, Yoshihito, is still unmarried; his younger brother, Norihito (now titled and known as Prince Takamado), is married to Hisako Tottori and the father of one daughter, Princess Tsuguko.

The emperor's three surviving daughters are, if anything, even less known to Westerners than were his brothers; it is not generally realized outside Japan that Hirohito even has daughters. Although details of the lives of the former princesses don't constitute anything like the sort of daily grist-for-the-press that European royalties endure, their identity inside Japan is no secret, and their lives are the subject of continuing national curiosity—observers have reported the phenomenon of crowded restaurants suddenly quieting as an imperial daughter is shown to her table. Each woman maintains normal familial relationships with her parents, but the Imperial House Law unequivocally mandates that a princess lose her rank, title, and official standing as a member of the imperial family on marriage, leaving her completely excluded from assuming any official public function in the monarchy.

Over a period of thirteen years, from 1925 to 1939, Nagako bore her husband five daughters. The second, Princess Sachiko, died within six months of her birth in 1927. Princess Shigeko (Princess Sunshine)—the eldest and reputedly her father's closest child—died in 1961 at the age of thirty-five; her wartime marriage to Prince Morihiro Higashikuni (also deceased) produced five children. Today, the remaining former princesses are Kazuko Takatsukasa, fifty-eight in 1987 and a Shinto priestess since her husband, a member of the Fujiwara clan, died in 1966—the ex-princess and her husband had adopted a son from the famous Matsudaira family; Atsuko Ikeda, fifty-six, wife of businessman Takamasa Ikeda (the son of a former marquis); and Takako

Shimazu, forty-eight, an English literature graduate of the Gakushuin University married to a banker who, like Mrs. Ikeda's husband, is descended from Japan's old feudal class of daimyo lords.
Living in Washington, D.C., during the sixties, Mrs. Shimazu accompanied her husband, who was stationed in the American capital, as an official of his Japanese bank.

When Princess Takako's engagement was announced, gossips
reported that she was going to marry a "commoner bank clerk." In
reality, of the emperor's three living sons-in-law, Hisanaga
Shimazu's lineage is probably the most aristocratic, his family ties
such that he would have qualified as an acceptable marriage alliance
for an emperor's daughter even in prewar days. The couple's son,
Tadahisa, is like his cousins, the children of the late ex-Princess
Shigeko, an imperial grandchild without a title of any kind to denote
his close relationship to Hirohito.

The only titled offspring of the present emperor besides the
crown prince is Hirohito's second son, Prince Hitachi, whose
princely title is apparently not destined to survive beyond his own
generation. Given the personal name Masahito at his birth in 1935,
this younger son was considered "insurance" for the imperial line's
direct descent through Hirohito, and was second in line to the
succession until the birth in 1960 of his older brother's first son.
Hitachi—the title was bestowed at his coming-of-age—is a graduate
of the science department's chemical school at the Gakushuin University. He furthered his education with graduate study at Tokyo
University.

Besides assuming an appreciable part of the imperial family's
ceremonial load, the fifty-year-old Hitachi shares his father's and his
brother's love of marine biology, choosing the arcane subject of fish
tumors as his own special area of scientific pursuit. His wife, the
former Hanako Tsugaru, is like her aunt by marriage, Princess Takamatsu, descended from the Tokugawa clan. Prince and Princess
Hitachi, who have no children, live in the Aoyama district of
Tokyo's fashionable west end, near Sacred Heart University.

In the absence of the current emperor passing the century mark,
it is highly probable that the monarch reigning over the Sun God-

dess's islands as they enter their third imperial millennium will be Hirohito's eldest son, Crown Prince Akihito. The fifty-three-year-old heir to the throne,[9] described by William H. Forbis in his book *Japan Today* as "utterly suave compared to his father," is looked upon by many Japanese as likely to give the throne's stature a needed refurbishing, freed of the pre-1945 ghosts that inevitably still encumber Hirohito. It comes as a shock to those who remember only the perennially baby-faced Akihito that he is today a gray-haired man whose own grown sons have all but usurped their father as the most ubiquitous symbols of their country's monarchy in Japan's popular press. As understudy to the monarch since he was first deputized to represent Japan at Queen Elizabeth II's 1953 coronation, the introverted Akihito has over the succeeding years gained a comparative sophistication and polish the far shyer Hirohito never achieved. Reported to have a greater interest in the day-to-day political workings of his country than his father, Akihito may take a more visible role for the throne after his accession. Though the realities of Japan's constitution uncompromisingly prohibit imperial involvement in the nation's governance, the monarch's still-unique position assures that an astute emperor can wield subtle but measurable moral influence, particularly if the Japanese public were to perceive strong imperial feelings on an especially controversial policy.

Akihito and his extraordinarily chic princess—besides being an accomplished harpist who sometimes provides piano accompaniment for her husband's cello and her eldest son's viola, Michiko is a walking advertisement for Japanese haute couture—live in a substantial mansion called the Togu Palace ("Togu" is an ancient name for the crown prince's household), secluded deep within the grounds behind the Akasaka Palace. The forestlike setting is insulated from the surrounding city by a heavily patrolled stone glacis, and a chain of four small lakes separates the crown prince's compound from the

---

[9]His official title is kotaishi, "imperial heir"; he has no additional title corresponding to that of Prince of Wales held by the heir apparent to the British throne.

smaller residences housing various of Akihito's uncles, aunts, and cousins.[10]

Akihito's private pursuits are very much in line with the family preoccupation with marine biology; his own subspecialty is fish genetics and he has had twenty-four papers published in the *Japanese Journal of Ichthyology*. Over the last years he has with increasing frequency stood in for his aging and ailing father on state visits; Hirohito's last venture out of Japan was a state visit to the United States in 1975. The monarch's chief understudy also occasionally attends, in an official capacity, the funerals of prominent countrymen.

The heir to the throne and his wife are the parents of two adult sons, Prince Naruhito and Prince Fumihito, as well as a high school–age daughter, Princess Sayako, also titled Princess Nori. Princess Sayako, eighteen (in 1987), is still a student at the Gakushuin School, and will, as a married ex-princess, most likely lead a completely nonpublic life. The middle child, twenty-two-year-old Prince Fumihito (formally titled Prince Aya), is now a political science student at Gakushuin University, where the tall—he towers over his stockier elder brother—and good-looking undergraduate began studies in Chinese after a 1985 visit to Thailand piqued an interest in Japan's Asian neighbors. In late 1985, Fumihito played the central role in the traditional palace ceremonial in which the robes of manhood (a costume costing ¥7 million—about $50,000) and their phallic-inspired headdress, called the *enbi-no-ei*, were bestowed on him by the emperor. The rites formally marked his coming-of-age, a ceremony whose significance lies in the fact that the prince could now succeed to the throne without a regency—although as a second son it is, of course, unlikely he would ever inherit his grandfather's throne.

The first grandson of a reigning sovereign ever to have celebrated the same rite is Prince Fumihito's elder brother, Prince Naruhito

[10]The huge Akasaka Palace a few hundred yards to the east of the Togu Palace now serves as Japan's official guest house for visiting heads of state, and was refurbished in the early 1970s at a cost of $334 million. A Japanese-style wing was added to relieve the relentless "Westernness" of the palace, considered an eyesore by at least some officials of the Imperial Household Agency.

(officially called Prince Hiro[11]), and, barring disaster, the man who will someday be the 126th emperor of Japan. The young (now twenty-seven) and popular Naruhito is today probably the most visible member of the family, even having appeared on television as both a violinist and a cellist in a string quartet.

After the Gakushuin University education that all imperial offspring receive (his field of study was Japanese medieval history), Naruhito spent two and half years at Oxford University's Merton College surveying eighteenth-century British river commodity traffic, an episode the prince called "a very precious experience in life." A facet of his Oxford days that particularly impressed Naruhito was the relative freedom with which his counterparts in Britain's royal family were able to live their lives, leading him to express the wish that the Japanese imperial family might emulate its Western equivalents—especially in the matter of broadening its still very limited contacts with the emperor's subjects. Following his return to Japan in the fall of 1985, Naruhito's eventual marriage immediately became an intensely discussed object of national interest, exactly as his father's had been when Akihito returned from his own European experience. The list of the prince's personal bridal requirements, duly published in the Japanese press, included the proviso that a woman "who shops right and left at Tiffany's would not be appropriate." The palace interjected with the information that three generations of a successful candidate's background would have to check out satisfactorily, her family "should not have been involved in politics," and she must be no taller than the prospective bridegroom (meaning a maximum height of five feet five inches).

Some of the Oxford-induced liberalization of Naruhito's thinking seems to have rubbed off on his own parents when he returned to Japan. The recent graduate convinced the crown prince and princess that dancing in public, a freedom Japan's royalty had never been free to indulge, might constitute a convincing breakthrough in lowering some of the psychological barriers between palace and

[11]"Hiro" is more in the nature of a title; he will most likely be known in English as "Emperor Naruhito."

public. Akihito and Michiko were subsequently photographed engaging in a sedate fox trot. Another imperial prerogative eliminated at their son's suggestion was the police traffic clearance on the official trips through town, an annoyance capable of bringing Tokyo's always-snarled traffic to a state of paralysis.

If Japan's empress were to stand as a representation of a single idealized facet of the nation's life, it would be for the classical and intensely admired Japanese model of a wife's devotion to her husband. Nagako is to the Japanese what Britain's Queen Mother is to that island: a human face on the nation's most mysterious and etiquette-bound institution.[12] Japan's empress-consort is the most endearing public figure in a country that treats all family life—and especially that of the emperor—very much more privately than does the West. What particularly distinguishes Nagako is that she has successfully overcome the extraordinarily ritualized isolation of her position to achieve stature as a distinguished artist. Under her "art name" To-en,[13] Nagako's strikingly polychromatic paintings, splashes of primary tints executed in the traditional Japanese style and often incorporating a representation of the *kiri* flower, whose leaves and flowers form the distinctive elements of the empress's personal crest, have been widely exhibited and published in Japan.

Accomplishment in painting has gone hand in hand with a variety of less publicized attributes: skill as a poet; public approval as a patron of music who has sponsored performances by a broad spectrum of international artists; a much appreciated helpmeet to her husband in collecting specimens for his biological collections, which she then sketches for him; service as the nation's most distinguished sponsor of philanthropic causes, including holding the honorary presidency of the Japanese Red Cross Society. Nagako conducts her public life (now markedly limited due to her age) with charm, even occasionally lending genuine warmth to deadly dull imperial cere-

[12]Taking its lead from European usage, the 1947 Imperial House Law allows the honorific style of "Majesty," *heika,* for the sovereign and his consort; the consort also retains it in widowhood. "Imperial Royal Highness," *denka,* is used by all imperial princes and princesses.

[13]Pseudonyms are commonly assumed by Japanese artists; To-en means "peach garden," which to Japanese ears is said to convey a very soft and gentle impression.

monial: A conspiratorial wink has taken the edge off many cases of understandable jitteriness in the imperial presence.

When Nagako's husband was asked by a palace correspondent to comment on the secret of their long and happy life together, the emperor's reply was appropriately enigmatic. "I don't know what you consider a secret. We have followed morals of ancient times and kept the spirit of harmony at all times. They may be the secrets, if you can call them secrets."

The emperor and the citizens of Japan are bound in a relationship incomparably stronger than that of the world's other surviving monarchies. These ties are similar to those shared in the physical relationship of an extended family. The concept does not imply anything like equality or familiarity; instead it can be understood as the kind of relationship that ties a remote family patriarch to the least of his kin. The doctrine of placing the imperial institution at the center of the national community is founded on millennia of belief on the part of the Japanese people that the emperor's prerogatives are tantamount to those of the state, that they are omnipotent and supreme. Especially so since the war, the monarch is a kind of superfather, a concept not unimportantly fortified by the fact that the present emperor has reigned longer than the overwhelming majority of his subjects have been alive.

Physically, Japan's emperor is indistinguishable from his fellow Japanese. His physiognomy has none of the kind of magisterial, inbred characteristics that often caricature an English duke or a Spanish grandee, or, for that matter, a highborn Japanese. At five feet four inches, neither fat nor thin, and temperate in habits, Hirohito has remarkable health for a man approaching his tenth decade. His habitual workaday dress is a slightly ill-fitting suit, the glint of a gold watch chain usually draped across the matching vest. If the occasion is a formal one, his suitcoat will be decorated with the Order of the Chrysanthemum, Japan's highest distinction of merit.

The emperor's daily life flows with the rhythmical constancy it has known since his accession, a routine broken only by social occasions of state or divine commemoration over which he is obligated to officiate. The singularity of his station combined with a natural reticence, instilled in him since his earliest training as a quality befitting a god, have all of his adult life made social intercourse a hurdle more to be endured than savored. He still murmurs little more than the impassive "ah so desuka" in response to the often stiff and self-conscious conversation of those presented to him, and only his family and his scientific studies have ever elicited from him much obvious joy. He has, at the sixty-year mark in his reign, become more an idea than a flesh-and-blood man.

Despite his years, Hirohito maintains, with few curtailments, a schedule honed over a lifetime bound to duty—the delegation to the crown prince of state visits abroad is one of the few obvious retrenchments. At 9:30 every morning the monarch is driven to the ceremonial main palace from the Fukiage Imperial Villa, his home for the last quarter of a century, set a few hundred yards away in the beauty of the palace's pine forest; in former years he walked the short distance, often stopping to thank the volunteer gardeners tending the palace's manicured grounds. Transport is a glistening Nissan President limousine, a muscular and unmistakable symbol of his nation's international economic ascendancy.[14]

Official duties in the Omote-gozasho Hall of the palace consume the morning hours. Among the first chores will be signing a stack of Diet bills, only a few of the twelve hundred or so that each year become law only after he has affixed his brushed signature or personal chop—the latter, a Japanese-style stamp, is moistened on an ink pad and then carefully applied to the formally worded state documents. When specially demanded, two imperial seals, weighing nearly eight pounds each, are pressed onto imperial documents; one reads "The Seal of His Majesty the Emperor," the other "The Seal of the Great State of Japan." On the days when the paperwork is temporarily put aside for some function outside the palace walls, the visit will, like all such official visits wherever royalty still exists, prompt from the hosts major renovations: new carpets wherever the emperor will walk, repapered walls, even fresh light bulbs—everything checked against the

[14]The limousine has no license number; instead, it is distinguished by a placat marked with a golden chrysanthemum.

minutest chance that some malfunction might occur that would embarrass the hosts or the honored guest.

As in his prewar routine, the emperor still leaves his palace office around noon to return to the villa for lunch with the empress. The meal might be either Western or Japanese; both husband and wife have in recent years tended to forsake highly caloric foods for the lighter traditional Japanese vegetable dishes. Since an unfortunate episode involving overindulgence with sake in his youth, Hirohito has avoided alcohol; he customarily sips boiled water served in a specially sterilized glass, one of the subtle indications of his unique rank. If events or backlogged paperwork require it, a return trip to the palace office will replace or delay personal pleasures in the afternoon. When needed, the emperor's barber, Ishii-Yukiie, arrives from his shop on the twelfth floor of the Kasumigaseki Building just across the moat. After Hirohito's bath, dinner[15] will be served, usually between five and six, after which the couple spend the remainder of the evening watching a television schedule largely made up of soap operas and sumo wrestling.

What constitutes "personal pleasures" for the emperor usually translates to work in his cherished and well-equipped biology laboratory. Monday and Thursday afternoons are, if at all possible, reserved for his research pursuits, as are the entirety of Saturdays. To receive an invitation to join the sovereign in his lab is an almost unmeasurable honor for Japanese scientists. For a week each year, the monarch isolates himself at his seaside villa at Suzaki, there to study living sea life, the specialty in which he has become a recognized international authority. Some twenty-six of his scientific monographs have been published (although not all over his signature; a few have been collaborations or else based on data collected by the emperor), including such esoteric titles as "Some Hydrozoans of the Bonin Islands" and "Five Hydroid Species from the Gulf of Aqaba, Red Sea." The author's name is shown simply as "Hirohito, Biological Laboratory, Imperial Household, Tokyo" (see Appendix

[15]It has been reported that the emperor has never been served fugu fish, the famous and potentially lethal delicacy (the fish's poisonous liver and ovaries must be carefully and professionally removed); any pleasure involved is not considered to outweigh the risk.

F). Although generally imperturbable by nature, Hirohito is said to have once flashed a sharp bit of ire when his sense of scientific priorities was disturbed: After it came to his attention that the palace gardeners had removed some weeds from his gardens, he remonstrated to a surprised chamberlain, "They are not weeds. Every plant has a name, every plant lives where it chooses. It's man's one-sided view to assume that they are weeds."

What his countrymen primarily see of the Japanese monarch is, of course, a carefully orchestrated ceremonial facade. In carrying out the venerable rites of monarchy and the nation's priesthood, Hirohito has for six decades remained consistently stoic and aloof, as if still believing the ancient notion that his role is more divine than human. The complex skein of traditions that he has inherited from his six score of predecessors normally take the form today of religious ritual intended not only to venerate the imperial family's personal gods, but also to elicit special protection and prosperity for the whole of the Japanese people. In historic terms, the ceremonies can be defined as rites in which he assumes the role of a classic divine king reaffirming the basic cosmic order in traditional ceremonies passed down remarkably unchanged in their essentials.

Three especially sacred sites are still reserved in the palace grounds for the major part of Hirohito's ritualistic observances; all take place behind the main palace in the far more secluded privacy of the woods surrounding the emperor's private residence. The Koreiden, the Shinden, and the Kashikodokoro Shrine—the structure that played such a central part in his enthronement rites—are to the Japanese what to some degree St. Peter's is to Roman Catholics. With bronze-tiled roofs, their simple cypress-wood walls sheltered by a dense thicket of old and gnarled pines and graceful Japanese elms, the trio is far removed from the impurities of mean things and common eyes. In the Koreiden, the spirits of every one of Hirohito's predecessors dwell, enshrined where the sovereign can seek their advice; the larger pantheon of the entire Japanese universe rests in the Shinden; and, most sacred of all, the Kashikodokoro is where Amaterasu, the mother of the imperial line, is enshrined. The latter also contains the Sacred Mirror.

Seven principal religious observances punctuate the emperor's liturgical year, starting on New Year's Day with the shiho-hai, said to have originated in the ninth century reign of the emperor Uda. Celebrated at the Hour of the Tiger—from three to five A.M.—the ritual is a communion with the gods for the nation's health and happiness and to beseech preservation from calamities during the coming year. Sitting on a thick tatami mat and dressed in traditional Heian-court costume, Hirohito prays in front of each of the four points of the compass, hoping to attract the attention of each spirit no matter in which direction it may dwell. No one but the emperor has the authority to perform this sacred rite; if he is ill, even the crown prince is not allowed to substitute for him. The harvest rite, going two centuries further back than the New Year's ceremony, is solemnized on February 17. The monarch offers up his country's staple crop of rice, grain that has been cultivated with his own hands, to the hoped-for propitiation of the spiritual world. The equinoxes—vernal and autumnal, both national holidays—are commemorated in the Koreiden with a special ceremonial held in the presence of Japan's highest elected officials; emperors and empresses who preceded him on the throne are the principal recipients of veneration.

Twice a year, at the end of June and at the end of December, the yo-ori, a purification ritual, is painstakingly carried out in the hope of exorcising any evil spirits that may have entered the imperial body; switches of bamboo are wielded by an attendant to urge the evil spirits to leave the emperor's body in favor of an earthenware urn into which the monarch exhales his impurities. Following His Majesty's exorcism comes a matching ceremony to provide the same service for the rest of the imperial family and members of the court. On October 17, at the kanname-sai, the emperor makes an offering of the crops to Amaterasu; held only since Meiji's reign, this rite is the newest of the modern-day grand ceremonials.

The most sacred and important of the solemnities over which Hirohito officiates is the niiname-sai, the ritual banquet in which, every November 27, the monarch invites the goddess Amaterasu to join him in a meal prepared from the newly collected fruits of the nation's harvest. It is essentially the same rite as that performed at an enthronement, when it is called the Daijo-sai. Reputedly the oldest of all the rituals the emperor performs, it is thought to have a provenance that stretches back to the country's prehistoric period. Thick silk pillows surround the emperor's throne, luxurious cushions on which the invisible gods are invited to be seated while they observe and record the monarch dining with their chief deity. Dressed in the purity of a brilliant white silk robe, the emperor appears in the hall holding the Necklace and the Sword, the crown prince close on his father's heels, Akihito in turn followed by high court attendants. The emperor alone enters the sacred, dimly lit site where the meal is taken. The food is identical to the holy supper he shared with Amaterasu at his enthronement: boiled rice, boiled millet, and white and dark sake are consumed by the monarch while symbolically internalizing the sacred powers of the gods to help him carry out his duties as emperor. After a night of prayerful communion with his otherworldly benefactress, one final meal—a sacred breakfast—is shared with the spirit. When the lonely night ends, Hirohito returns in solemn procession to his palace, the orange flames from the bonfires lit to mark his way reflecting off his glistening white robes.

Though these momentous observations form the chief sacramental rites of the monarchy, the temporal ceremonial life of the emperor is more widely known by his countrymen. Like his secular duties, the essentially social events are defined by a routine that closely follows the calendar, varying only imperceptibly from decade to decade. To the Japanese, the turn of the year is the time of renewal and the most important national holiday, and it is, appropriately, when the most famous of the palace's social gatherings occurs. Since the reign of Hirohito's grandfather, the Utakai-hajime, the renowned New Year's Poetry Party, has been famous as the occasion when the monarch's own attitudes and feelings on matters affecting the nation can often be discerned—though his expression is always cloaked in exquisite subtlety. In the form of a celebration to the nationally admired poems called waka (also known as *tanka*), this quintessentially Japanese happening merits a close look. (The waka is distinct from *haiku*, the seventeen-syllable poems more familiar to Westerners.)

The waka is a rigidly constructed poetic form, invariably composed of thirty-one syllables arranged in five lines as follows: five-seven-five-seven-seven. It doesn't use Western-style rhyming words, but is nevertheless judged on its musicality as well as the sentiment it must ever-so-subtly suggest. Some Japanese consider these poems "frivolous" because they do not reflect solemn or "important" issues of moral values or relations between individuals. Instead, the traditional waka composer uses his or her skill simply to record, as artfully as possible, fleeting emotions. No one knows exactly when the custom of formalized poetry gatherings first took root, but the waka style of poetry has for centuries played a major part in Japan's literary history, especially at court, where readings were necessarily confined to the most aristocratic stratum of society. From early days, waka became a necessary and often passionate component in the education of the nation's princes.

Just as he modernized and began the democratization of so much else in Japan, Meiji also turned the palace's poetry readings from an exclusively court pursuit into something approaching a public, almost democratic event. Himself the proud author of ninety thousand waka, Meiji held the first formal New Year's Poetry Party at the palace in Kyoto shortly after his enthronement, within six years accepting offerings from any of his subjects—from prince to untouchable—to be considered for inclusion in the readings. A formal Imperial Poetry Bureau was even made an official part of the Household.[16]

When the end of the Pacific War allowed for a much broadened concept of what was held to be a fitting relationship between the palace and common people, the authors of the poems selected to be read at court were themselves invited to attend the ceremony, a revolutionary form of recognition verging on the scale of winning a knighthood in Britain or the Kennedy Center Honors in the United States. The contest judges are today the nation's preeminent poets (before the war, the officials of the Poetry Bureau were responsible for the judging), and the winning entries have more to do with such "democratic" subjects as nature and the human condition than did their pre-1945 counterparts, many then patriotically rife with

---

[16]The bureau was abolished in the postwar scaling-down of the Household.

implied praise for the nation's chauvinism and military expansionism. In 1959, for the first time, a poem was even based on human love.

Waka can today be submitted by anyone (nearly thirty thousand efforts were received for the 1987 contest), but applicants are limited to a single entry and will be disqualified if more than one are proffered. The blind are now allowed to submit in braille. In a society as closed to outsiders as is Japan, it is remarkable that non-Japanese are eligible for the contest; even more remarkable is the fact that in 1957 Lucille Nixon of California, an American fluent in Japanese, became the first such foreign winner. The personal efforts submitted by the members of the imperial family do not, of course, compete with those tendered by the public.

Today a major media event throughout Japan—its annual nationwide televising on the NHK network, something like the American Oscar ceremonies, is widely viewed—the New Year's Day ceremonies are a formal ritual bearing little relationship to anything in the Western experience, literary or otherwise. The officials responsible for the competition point out that the event stresses the place of meritocracy over birth in the new Japan, a goal that hasn't quite yet permeated all aspects of the nation's still class-sensitive populace.

Held in the palace's gymnasiumlike Room of the Pines, a high chamber with pitched ceiling already stark and made starker by the light reflecting off the mirrored surface of a glistening wooden floor, the ceremony has as its focal point the double-throne dais. In front of a three-part screen, scallop-topped and decorated with waves of golden bamboo, sits a matching pair of thrones, facing which are boxy tables wrapped in brocade, the tailing flaps tied with thongs. The awards to be presented to the winning entrants are placed on top of the tables. Flanking the seats for the imperial couple are chairs for their family, males according to rank on the emperor's side, females in the same order on the empress's side. In front of the imperial grouping a table seats the contest officials and readers; invited guests—seventy at the 1987 party—line either side of the striking but severe chamber. In such a setting the extraordinary ingredient distinguishing this gathering from nearly all other palace functions is the humble rank of so many of the guests.

The recitation of the winning poems is not carried out by their authors; instead, they are read by *Koji,* an experienced group of highly skilled readers, each of whom has a precise and unvarying role in the proceedings. The *dokuji* is a sort of master of ceremonies, quiet himself throughout but directing the others with subtle hand signals. In a relatively normal way the koji reads the winning poems aloud, the successful entries being read in order of their authors' ascending ages, each of whom stands, stiff and unsmiling, as his or hers is presented. The koji then hands them off to the *hassei* and four *kosho* who add highly formalized vocal stress to the waka, making them sound almost like music. The hassei and the kosho finally chant in unison, this last effect designed to give the audience one last appreciation of the poems' musical qualities.

Following the winning efforts and one traditionally written by some preeminent national figure at special invitation of the court, the poems of the imperial family itself are read. This is when the ceremony gets interesting. The traditional routine is for each junior member of the family who is over twenty to write a waka, and the best one is selected to be read aloud. Each poem is presented on handmade paper, and for those entered by the princesses and the empress two sheets of special colored paper are used, one for the waka itself and another contrasting shaded sheet in which to wrap the document. Following the junior family offerings, entries from both crown prince and crown princess are recited, which then give way to the empress's poem. This more important work is read twice, in chorus. After everything is finished, the really important part of the service is reached, when the emperor's own poem, called the *gyosei,* is, with extreme care in its pronunciation and timing, read through three times. The first recitation is deliberately intoned at the lowest possible pitch, the second somewhat higher. The third and ultimate reading breaks through like the climax of a Bach chorale. With this poem's concluding notes, the festivities end.

Imperial poems have over the years given important clues to the emperor's attitudes regarding his government's policies or even his own aspirations, clues that have not been constitutionally possible for him to air in plain voice but which he can express guardedly in

335

the age-old rhythms of poetry. Hirohito's first public effort after his accession was a poignant question mark: "The colors of mountain and stream appear fresh to my eye—and what, I wonder, of my reign? What lies up ahead?" A decade later, with the country deeply involved in its war with China and making plans for a far wider conflict with the United States and Britain, the sovereign wrote: "Stopping by Cape Shio on the Kii Peninsula I looked out far across the sea, and saw clouds trailing o'er the waves," a statement taken by many to express the author's sorrow at the increasingly gloomy outlook of his nation's foreign policies. And in 1940, with less than two years before his still-whole empire would begin the gamble that would end in its near-annihilation, the monarch voiced a hope that efforts for peace would continue, writing: "The east and west in harmony may mingle, and in prosperity grow—this is my earnest prayer at the start of the New Year." Hirohito's wartime poems, arduous years during which the ceremony continued unbroken (since Meiji's reign it has been canceled only when the court has been in personal mourning), spoke not to the lost cause of peace, but were attempts to address moral succor to his troops dying in appalling numbers in battlefields from Mongolia to Borneo. In his first postwar waka, Hirohito wrote: "Man should be like the manly pine that does not change its color, though bearing the fallen snow," a tacit acceptance of his own responsibility for the war. The emperor's postwar trend has been to messages expressing his love for beauty and nature, the same subjects that comprise the themes of the entries from thousands of his fellow Japanese. But a vaguely economic theme marked his 1987 effort: "Year by year, as our country has recovered from the war, the dawn redwood has grown taller."

Although few others of Hirohito's social-ceremonial tasks compare in elegiac uniqueness to the Poetry Party, most are nonetheless graceful evocations of the nation's imperial heritage, rites whose annual repetition help tie the modern country to its increasingly unreachable past. In May, Hirohito takes the central role in the annual rice-planting ceremony, a rite closely tied to the religious kinen-sai observation and whose real justification today is to promote the slipping labor ethic. The monarch carries out, in a small symbolic measure at least, the actual physical labor involved in planting Japan's indispensable crop; in autumn, the other end of this cycle is reached when he harvests his own planting and dedicates the small yield to the gods. The Imperial Household Agency has made an effort to subtly publicize this ceremonial labor in other Asian countries, on the principle that if it is seen that the Japanese monarch dirties his own hands on planting and harvesting, however much a token effort, it only adds luster to a labor ethic that flourishes far less healthily in many of Japan's underdeveloped neighbors.

A large part of the emperor's day-to-day work has its source in Hirohito's constitutional status as Japan's chief diplomat, a role nearly universally assumed by heads of state. Legally, an ambassador becomes the personal representative of one head of state to another, and because the monarch is the highest officer of state in Japan, it falls on Hirohito to preside at the ceremonies in which chiefs of diplomatic missions are both dispatched and received. It is this job that amounts to his single most substantive public relations effort.

An unending stream of foreign envoys representing almost two hundred nations and sovereign entities with which Japan maintains diplomatic relations have to be presented to the monarch and hand him their formal credentials. Through interpreters, Hirohito greets and chats with each in a few well-measured phrases of diplomatic niceties. Until recent years, new ambassadors were brought to the palace from their embassies in one of the horse-drawn carriages maintained for these court occasions, but their effect on Tokyo traffic is today thought too calamitous to continue such risk to horse, driver, and ambassador. Now, the carriage is merely used to bring the envoy from a hotel located near the imperial compound. Japanese ambassadors departing for foreign postings are also allowed a few precious minutes in their monarch's presence to receive his best wishes.

Whenever a foreign head of state visits Japan in an official capacity, a state dinner is extended as a normal diplomatic courtesy.[17]

[17]Hirohito is not legally Japan's head of state, but he is the living "symbol of the state and the unity of the people," according to the 1946 constitution. Technically, Japan has no head of state, the prime minister being only head of government.

Held in the State Dining Room of the new Imperial Palace, these dinners are regarded as opportunities for Japan to use the prestige of its monarchy to strengthen ties with foreign states, ties most importantly resulting in trade agreements to further the absolutely vital trade lifeblood of the Japanese nation. These glittering affairs today equate to the imperial family's primary opportunity to gather in white tie and tiaras; here, Hirohito and most of his near kin greet the visiting president or king or people's chairman with all the modern dress spectacle and ceremony the monarchy can muster. The emperor's white tie and tails ensemble is carefully assembled by his five dressers, the jacket hung on a tailor's dummy so the evening's medals and decorations can be properly placed according to the rules of precedence. Kimono are not usually worn at such functions by the women of the imperial family, if for no other reason than that the foreign stars and sashes that are expected to be displayed simply don't work very well on the traditional Japanese dress. The gold and silver plates that sparkle on the tables, chosen from among the twenty thousand pieces available from the palace vaults, are each marked with the sovereign's unique emblem, the sixteen-petaled chrysanthemum. Timing is planned to the second, the orchestra having been rehearsed so that its playing will stop precisely as the last guest sits down. The banquets require speeches from the two principals, little homilies dressed in the diplomatic garb of toasts; Ambassador Hideki Masaki, chief interpreter of the Japanese Foreign Office, often stands behind Hirohito to translate the toast/speech of the emperor's principal guest.

Aside from the emperor's social gatherings, the Imperial Household Agency also stages an annual round of traditional entertainments for foreign ambassadors, old-fashioned stag gatherings that have their foundations in Meiji-era court hospitality. Among the more esoteric of these are the traditional cormorant fishing parties. Small groups of high-ranking envoys are invited in two annual groups to the Gifu imperial estate on the Nagara River to look on as tame cormorants, pelicanlike water fowl known for their hearty appetites, are set out to catch little river fish called *ayu*. In this sport, first mentioned twelve and a half centuries ago in the *Kojiki,* the cormorants are fitted with wire loops around their necks, and when one of the hungry creatures snares a fish, a handler quickly tightens the loop to keep the fowl from swallowing its prey. The emperor, who doesn't attend these parties, is known to find the whole affair rather cruel, but tradition dictates the parties' continuance, and for the diplomatic guests the honor of an imperial invitation evidently makes the occasion palatable.

More genteel, and of a slightly higher rating on the protocol scale for the simple reason that the emperor wishes it so, are the imperial garden parties that have as their central feature duck netting. Groups of diplomats are taken to the imperial duck preserves at either Chiba or Saitama. One of the family princes is always in attendance. An outing in late May to the Imperial Livestock Farm is put on for the ambassadors together with some of their lower-ranking staff members, the latter chosen on a "pro-rata" basis, according to a Household official. The Spring Garden Party is for top-ranked Japanese; the Autumn Garden Party is for the diplomatic corps.

A prominent observance that has in recent years elicited increasing notoriety is the biannual visit by an imperial messenger to Tokyo's Yasukuni Shrine. The striking memorial just across the moat from the Imperial Palace is where, in the emperor's name, the emissary reads the *gosaimon,* a prayer addressed to the spirits of the men who inhabit this chief resting place of warriors who have died in Japan's modern armed conflicts. The vast majority are there, of course, as a result of the Great Pacific War, and for this reason the shrine has taken on a somewhat sinister political significance. The projected upgrading into official obeisances of the prime minister's private visits had brought out stinging criticism both at home, principally from the political left, and from the Peking government, justifiably sensitive to the least suggestion that Japan might be ameliorating its sense of war guilt. Besides the 8 million commoners who visit the Yasukuni each year, every member of the imperial family has at least once paid his or her personal respects at the Shinto memorial.

Lastly, there are two now-traditional annual occasions when the monarch shows himself and his family to all comers, at least to those who can make it either to Tokyo or to a television set. The New

Year's and birthday appearances on the palace balcony impart something of the flavor of the British royal family's periodic balcony viewings at Buckingham Palace. Thousands of Hirohito's countrymen troop to the palace forecourt, directly over the place where the underground parking lot has been sunk into the historic shogunal castle hill, there to wish their monarch felicitations on these two auspicious days in his life; both, by the way, are national holidays. Since a mentally disturbed attendee tossed a few pachinko balls at the emperor a few years ago, the mostly immobile imperial family is now safely positioned behind glass. The family members—lighted, as if on a stage, by a series of overhead spotlights—line up in careful order of seniority, the monarch at the center, with relatives of descending rank to either side. The crowd is today too great to be allowed in all at once, so five or six shifts of about thirty thousand each are let up the steep driveway in successive waves from 9:30 A.M. to 3:00 P.M., which also gives needed breaks to the family members on view. Numerous Imperial Guards stand on raised platforms facing the throng, trying to make sure that any potential troublemakers are spotted before harm is done. Countless fluttering hinomaru flags give the gatherings a nationalistic flavor (although a surprising number of the attendees are foreigners evidently anxious to glimpse royalty). The historic cry of banzai is shouted as the sovereign hesitantly acknowledges the fervent commotion.

The cost of all this court-centered ceremony isn't a question that is debated with much seriousness in Japan today—except perhaps by a few cranky Communists. On November 20, 1945, as mentioned, Allied Headquarters blocked and froze all Imperial Household fiscal transactions. MacArthur took the action primarily to reduce the influence of the Imperial Household in Japan's economic and industrial life, not to personally punish the already frugal Hirohito, who, in any event, later gave away much of his remaining property as grants, including the palaces at Hakone, Hama, and Muko. In spite of the tremendous diminution of the imperial family's pre-1945 holdings, the emperor today still lives in a manner none of his subjects would be able to match.

In the first place, Hirohito's Tokyo residence sits on a piece of land that ranks as possibly the most valuable parcel of single residential real estate in the world. If in the demise of the monarchy the 284 acres were put on the market, they would carry a collective price tag conservatively marked in the billions of dollars, although nothing on the land is in any way as valuable as the land itself. The Japanese Imperial Palace and its outbuildings are not historically irreplaceable structures in the same way as are the White House or Windsor Castle. It is primarily the privacy his compound affords the emperor that is unmatched by the homes of any of Hirohito's tightly packed subjects, either in Tokyo or anywhere else in the island nation.

In return for the duties Hirohito has for seventy years so faithfully carried out for the state, the Diet annually turns over to the Imperial Household Agency a stipend of just over ¥10 billion, or about $70 million (the 1985 figure)—a sum the legislature can raise—or, presumably, lower—as it sees fit. The appropriation is divided into two parts: About ¥7.5 billion represents the operating expenses of the Imperial Household Agency; the remainder (¥2.959 billion) is divided into allowances to cover the upkeep of the main palace in Tokyo as well as the imperial estates spread out over the country and the families of the emperor's extended clan—his younger son, brother, and widowed sisters-in-law, each of whom receives something in the neighborhood of ¥22 million annually. Finally, ¥239 million is appropriated for the emperor himself. (The crown prince receives his own Civil List.)

These figures say little of the personal financial holdings of the emperor, just as their Civil Lists and Privy Purses don't begin to encompass the vast income and personal wealth of the sovereigns of Britain or of the Netherlands. The monarch's private fortune, held in trust by loyal brokers, has grown sufficiently since its postwar decimation (MacArthur's seizure represented about two-thirds of the emperor's liquid assets) to once again establish Hirohito in the select company of the world's dollar billionaires. His proxies, advised by the country's most astute financial advisers, have openly acquired some $50 million in stock—most heavily in hotel and electronic issues—to replenish the imperial purse. The stocks have, of course, soared in value as a result of the nation's phenomenal economic rebirth. Paul Manning asserts that the $3 billion hidden in secret Swiss accounts in the midst of the 1945 Götterdämerung has been the principal factor in this purported rejuvenation of the imperial coffers, and that for lending bits of the Swiss horde to commercial enterprises in Japan, the emperor has been handsomely repaid with "remarkable investment opportunities."

Whatever the extent of the imperial assets, it must be stated that Hirohito has not squandered them personally, nor allowed his family to do so. None has embarked on any kind of irresponsibly lavish life-style. Although he never particularly cared for perambulating between one and another of the palaces and villas he owned in his prewar life, Hirohito nonetheless had them at his disposal. They are now whittled down to a precious few, "precious" being the operative word. The paradox of his existence today is its simplicity in a setting of such priceless grandeur.

For the first decade and a half after the war's end, when Tokyo's future shape was to a degree still open to rearrangement because of its recent destruction, there was some agitation to remove the emperor's residence from its location in the center of the city. The argument was advanced that the city's hopelessly congested traffic patterns might be improved by simply eliminating the acreage around which everything in central Tokyo was unavoidably forced to detour. Although the site (which represents only a small fraction of the gigantic Edo castle complex that it replaced) has been designated a "cultural property of the nation," there was a nagging logic to the plan, especially in a city that has preserved little more than a fraction of the architectural cultural heritage remaining after the bombing. The spot on which the Meiji Palace had squatted in its Victorian dowdiness before destruction in the 1945 fire raids sat starkly empty as a little-used lawn for years after the war. The emperor's personal residence was none other than the damp and poorly fenestrated library/bunker that had figured so importantly in the war's final deliberations. Through the 1950s, Hirohito steadfastly refused to allow a more fitting residence to be built, symbolically but nobly sharing in the discomforts his subjects were having to endure. Without a formal facility on the grounds in which to hold court entertainments and ceremonial affairs—the emperor's villa was barely big enough for his own family's use—the Imperial Household Agency building, the dour office building that unfortunately survived the firestorms, was pressed into service. The smallish rooms of the gussied-up third floor became the scene of hundreds of imperial functions from audiences to state dinners.

With the rebirth of the country through its rip-roaring 1950s economic miracle, Hirohito, at the end of the decade, agreed to let plans for a new palace go forward, the first stage of which was to be a residence for himself. Although Meiji had his own apartments in a private residential building a few steps from the adjacent ceremonial palace, the decision was made to build Hirohito's residence in the more secluded area of the Fukiage Garden, the 4.6 million square feet of private forest that covers much of the palace compound's grounds. The new home, which still serves as such for the emperor and empress today, was completed in 1961, and in December of that year Hirohito and Nagako took possession. Three stories—two above ground, one below, all connected by elevator—with a flat roof and fifteen rooms, the house is an utterly private haven for the imperial couple; no official functions take place in it. The thoroughly undistinguished house is essentially a box, its walls made of milk-white brick. It contains a living room, a library, a dining room, and a traditional Japanese-style room for the empress's use on the first floor, with bedrooms and baths above.

Whatever scattered objections there were to a new ceremonial palace had evaporated by the time the private home for the emperor was built. Immediately following the completion of the Fukiage residence, initial plans were drawn up for the successor palace to the lost Meiji structures. "Since the palace is a building for holding national functions, it must be a building having symbolic significance both internally and externally . . . new techniques and materials should be used in such a manner as to express Japan's traditional beauty, while basic accent should be on familiarity rather than dignity, upon plainness rather than solemnity, so that the palace may endear itself to the people." Thus read the guiding principle of the national committee formed to bring into existence the most important new structure in the nation, the ultimate architectural affirmation that the postwar period was over and Japan whole again.

Seven years and $44 million went into converting the building committee's goal into a finished palace. The first significant decision was to place the structure directly on the spot where the Victorian-era Meiji palace had stood, although the orientation of the modern building's principal facade would be turned slightly off its predecessor's axis. Responsible for the basic architecture, Professor Junzo Yoshimura of the Tokyo University of Arts saw his design—exquisite in detail but severely plain in its overall appearance—begin to rise in July 1964. So great was the honor of participating in the building of Japan's most distinguished address that subcontractors for dozens of the different structural and design elements that would go into the palace submitted bids tantamount to these companies giving away their labor and materials. Unsurprisingly, the five leading construction companies involved in the building all gained immeasurable prestige for their association with the project.

Enormous care was lavished on the 133,000 square feet of the structure, down to and including the minutest details. Entirely new construction techniques and building elements had to be developed. An example was the planned bronze roof, which if built with existing material and technology would have eventually turned an ugly black from the corrosion caused by Tokyo's near-permanent smog. Ideally, such a prominent roof should achieve its patina gracefully, rusting to the greenish tint much desired by the Japanese on buildings of consequence. To remedy the problem, a complex technique was developed that artificially turned the bronze to the proper hue before the city's pollution was able to permanently blacken it. Even ordinary trees would be inadequate for supplying the necessary timbers, and giant eight-hundred-year-old cedars and three-hundred-year-old cypresses were tracked down to provide the expanses of clear, rare woods needed for the floors and ceilings of the palace's enormous reception rooms.

In 1968, the seven structures that together made up the ceremonial palace were completed. Connected to one another by cloisters and corridors, each of the halls is reserved for different kinds of state functions and private family uses, from the imperial proclamations in the Hall of Pine, the palace's formal "throne room," to the *Homeiden,* the "State Dining Room"—the complex's largest chamber and the scene of banquets in honor of visiting heads of state—to the *Chowa Den,* a suite of four rooms set aside for imperial soirées. The Omote-gozasho houses not only the emperor's offices, but also a lecture room and smaller dining and social rooms used by the imperial family for official business. The palace's interiors neither resemble the usual European notions of royal architectural splendor nor are they related to the heavily embellished Meiji/Victorian chambers they replaced. Vast empty spaces, essentially Japanese in their basic form but written on a gigantic scale, were finished with the finest materials: mirror-finished floors, ultramodern glass and chrome chandeliers, billboard-size tapestries meant to evoke nature, and, scattered artfully and economically throughout the whole, the most ethereal and precious of Japanese arts and crafts.

In some areas, the results came up short, as in the Homeiden, which looks something like a high school combination cafeteria-gymnasium. On the other hand, the *Seiden,* the beautiful "State Hall," was notably successful in meeting the tricky requirement of expanding the delicate Japanese interior to a scale for which it was never intended. There are small surprises here and there that delight and amaze: What look like slender columns supporting the wide overhang of the buildings' traditional-style roofs are really drainpipes made of chains of bottomless buckets connected one to the other with little supports, objects whose artfulness accomplishes the mundane task of drawing rainwater off the roof in an eminently practical yet thoroughly beautiful way. Set on plinths around the buildings are lovely sculptures, some representing stylized distillations of Japan's traditionally "lucky" pine tree.

The remainder of the palace grounds exclusively reserved for the emperor and his family are the site of a variety of outbuildings; many are used for mundane workaday purposes, others are small pleasure pavilions. A hospital maintained for members of Hirohito's family sits near a guest residence kept for the empress's ladies-in-waiting. It is, in turn, close to a villa where the ex-princesses and their husbands are put up on family visits. Hirohito has converted the old library into his research laboratory. The former stables house Rolls-Royces, Daimlers, Mercedes-Benzes, Cadillacs, limousine-sized Toyotas and Nissans, and eleven state coaches copied decades ago from those used by the British royal family. A greenhouse, paddocks for the horses used for the imperial carriages, and a silkworm farm—sericulture is one of the most fundamentally Japanese (if no longer so economically important) of the nation's skills—take up a few of the compound's precious acres. What is beyond question the world's most exclusive golf course provides the emperor and crown prince with a carefully clipped nine-hole course—unused and untended at Hirohito's order during the war. One day he found a single pink wild dianthus, a kind of carnation, on an overgrown fairway; so pleased was the monarch with the serendipitous discovery that he became firmly attached to wildflowers, one of the factors that caused him to change the Fukiage Gardens from their formal prewar state to the natural wooded acres they are today.

The greater palace complex—the whole five-kilometer circumference can be negotiated by a reasonably fit jogger in about three-quarters of an hour—is divided into four unequal parts. The quadrant we've just described, the personal compound of the emperor and empress and the Imperial Household Agency, is the only part still wholly off-limits to the general public. Fronting these private palace grounds at their southeast corner is an immense square—the "Concourse in Front of the Palace," as it translates from the Japanese—divided into two sections: the Imperial Palace Plaza and the Imperial Palace Outer Garden. An empty and lifeless former drill-grounds turned formal esplanade, it served as the initial refuge of the thousands of burned-out victims of both the 1923 earthquake and the 1945 fire raids. The square was also witness to the macabre ritual disembowelings of so many officers as propitiation for the disgrace suffered by the loss of the war. The busy Uchibori Avenue—on whose passing tramlines passengers were obliged in prewar times to rise and bow in the Son of Heaven's august direction—bisects the vast plaza, this part of the old Edo castle having been accessible to the public since Meiji times. Its black pine thickets and graveled plazas are today the chief marshaling yards for clouds of black-and-white uniformed schoolchildren who come here every day to be photographed in rigid squadrons against the backdrop of the famed Double Bridge, the palace's ceremonial entrance.

The northernmost grounds, today a public park, were the prewar domain of the Imperial Guard. Cut off from the emperor's acres by a half-elevated, half-buried freeway, the area now called the Kitanomaru Park is home to the National Museum of Modern Art and the Nippon Budokan, a performing arts hall built in the form of a huge Buddhist temple.

By far the most interesting and historic section of the former castle enclosure is the East Garden, the verdant acres that cover the site of the principal shogunal *maru*, or "fortified castle," before it gave way to Meiji's Imperial Palace built to the west. The latter was reconstructed on the site of a less important shogunal residence— the *Nishi no Maru*, or "western fortress"—that was primarily intended for use during the frequent periods when the *Hon Maru*, the "principal fortress," was undergoing reconstruction following one of its many fires. All that remains of the East Garden's Hon Maru today are the stark boulder-hewn foundations of the shogunal castle, a romantic reminder of the power of this office during the years when the Tokugawa capital ranked as the world's largest city.

Opened to the public to commemorate the 1968 completion of the new palace, the East Garden is somehow a sylvan enigma, a little-used mystery park that is probably the most beautiful public place in the entire Tokyo metropolitan area. Visitors are handed a little numbered plastic placat on entering, a token that has to be returned on exiting the garden and a clever way to make sure no one accidentally gets locked in at night. Although entry is free, on most days the place is nearly deserted, a delightful discovery for those, most of whom appear foreign, trying to escape the crowding that is Tokyo's depressingly chief characteristic. Though the sweeping lawns blanketing the hillocks and meadows contribute to the beauty of this sumptuous sylvan isle, the edges of the preserve are still lined with barrackslike structures that house Japan's Self-Defense Forces's Imperial Guards and from whose interiors one sometimes hears the low grunts and curdling yells emanating from the military judo classes.

Around the combined whole of the four quadrants, sworls of riverlike moats flow in and out of the forested acres, passages that are the remnants of the protective liquid barriers of the shoguns' centuries. Only the birds are free to pass without hindrance across

347

the forbidden waters encircling the emperor's sacred living place, although common eyes can see into the palace's arbored acres from the skyscrapers on the encircling avenues. The swans and doves and pigeons that have since the time of the great Ieyasu watched men carry word of great exploits across the bridges today coo and chirp mostly for the tourists—and for the white-aproned volunteers, senior citizens who have the unbounded honor of weeding and policing the grounds and for which their sole material reward is a chrysanthemum-encrested packet of cigarettes, few of which treasures will ever be consumed. Though divorced from the processes that govern the modern state, this sacred heart of Japan is still, for most of its citizens, the place from which the nation's heartbeat continues, thankfully, to be regulated.

Wherever the ancient form of governance called monarchy still exists, mystery plays an important part—and nowhere more so than in Japan. The quiet appreciation of subtle beauty that is central to the Japanese character also applies to the attitudes of the people toward the monarchy. By its lack of empty pomp and showy circumstance, the throne is rendered more beautiful, more revered, more essentially Japanese, and any move to abolish it would most certainly be met with mass incredulity.

Shortly before Hirohito was to celebrate the 1986 Diamond Jubilee marking the sixtieth anniversary of his reign, the *Asahi Shimbun*—one of his country's leading newspapers—commissioned a poll whose results showed that 84 percent of the respondents thought the monarchy ought to be preserved, that the emperor should remain the symbol of the state. But a concurrent survey, one by the Kyodo News Service, indicated that the percentage of Japanese with a "friendly feeling" toward Hirohito himself had declined from around half the population in 1975 to about a third a decade later. The figures tend to confirm what has been evident in Japan since the war: Whatever doubts surround the monarchy appear not to concern the institution but rather the present occupant of the throne. The single negative attitude toward the monarchy, strongly evidenced from this cross section of the emperor's subjects, concerns Hirohito personally: namely, his responsibility for the

Great Pacific War in which 3 million Japanese died in his name.

This controversy was recently illuminated when a jubilee coin with Hirohito's image was planned. Although imperial loyalists objected to it on the grounds that the monarch's minted portrait would almost certainly be defiled if the coin were dropped or scratched, as would surely happen, far more people objected to the minting because of the sad memories it raised of the police-state years when the emperor's portrait was an object of reverence.

There are many in Japan who think, albeit ever so quietly, that it would be wise for Hirohito to abdicate. Though abdication is generally contrary to the notions of kingship as practiced in the West, notions the Japanese throne has tried to emulate since Meiji's days, there is ample precedence for the practice. Akihito is already well into middle age with two adult sons of his own, and the throne could be, many Japanese reason, at a single stroke cleared of any personal association with the war by the crown prince's accession. It is evident, however, that Hirohito simply will not countenance abdication, so immersed has he been all his life in what he considers to be an unbreakable duty to his people. Though time will likely soon obviate the issue, the question continues to simmer as long as Hirohito remains monarch.

The Japanese people have undergone quantum changes in two great periods of metamorphosis since Meiji's accession, but that experienced since 1945 has altered the nation's essential spirit above all that went before in its entire history. The throne, however, more than any other agency, remains the link between modern Japan and the country's distant past. So important was that symbol to the government's leadership in the summer of 1945 that the monarch's continued existence at the head of the nation became the overriding issue standing between surrender and a continued struggle that could well have ended in the near-annihilation of the Japanese race. Above any other token of nationhood, the monarch represents to the Japanese their uniqueness.

The function of Japan's monarch is no longer to be a symbol of government, not really even to be a public man. It is simply to be, and by being to remind his people of all that has gone before.

349

 APPENDIX A

Japan's Emperors and Reigning Empresses

(latter marked*)

POSTHUMOUS NAME	BIRTH/DEATH	REIGN DATES
1 Jimmu	Legendary	
2 Suizei	"	
3 Annei	"	
4 Itoku	"	
5 Kosho	"	
6 Koan	"	
7 Korei	"	
8 Kogen	"	
9 Kaika	"	
10 Sujin	"	
11 Suinin	"	
12 Keiko	"	
13 Seimu	"	
14 Chuai	"	
15 Ojin	late 4th/early 5th century	
16 Nintoku	1st half 5th century	
17 Richu	"	
18 Hanzei	"	
19 Ingyo	mid 5th century	
20 Anko	"	
21 Yuryaku	latter half 5th century	
22 Seinei	"	
23 Kenzo	"	
24 Ninken	"	

POSTHUMOUS NAME	BIRTH/DEATH	REIGN DATES
25 Buretsu		"
26 Keitai	1st half 6th century	
27 Ankan		"
28 Senka		"
29 Kimmei	509–571	531 or 539–571
30 Bidatsu	538–585	572–585
31 Yomei	?–587	585–587
32 Sushun	?–592	587–592
33 Suiko*	554–628	593–628
34 Jomei	593–641	629–641
35 Kogyoku*	594–661	642–645
36 Kotoku	597–654	645–654
37 Saimei* (same as 35)	594–661	655–661
38 Tenji	626–672	661–672
39 Kobun	648–652	672
40 Temmu	?–686	672–686
41 Jito*	645–703	686–697
42 Mommu	683–707	697–707
43 Gemmei*	661–722	707–715
44 Gensho*	680–748	715–724
45 Shomu	701–756	724–749
46 Koken*	718–770	749–758
47 Junnin	733–765	758–764
48 Shotoku* (same as 46)	718–770	764–770
49 Konin	709–782	770–781
50 Kammu	737–806	781–806
51 Heizei	774–824	806–809
52 Saga	786–842	809–823
53 Junna	786–840	823–833
54 Nimmyo	810–850	833–850
55 Montoku	827–858	850–858
56 Seiwa	850–881	858–876
57 Yozei	869–949	876–884
58 Koko	830–887	884–887
59 Uda	867–931	887–897
60 Daigo	885–930	897–930
61 Suzaku	923–952	930–946
62 Murakami	926–967	946–967

POSTHUMOUS NAME	BIRTH/DEATH	REIGN DATES
63 Reizei	950–1011	967–969
64 Enyu	959–991	969–984
65 Kazan	968–1008	984–986
66 Ichijo	980–1011	986–1011
67 Sanjo	976–1017	1011–1016
68 Go-Ichijo	1008–1036	1016–1036
69 Go-Suzaku	1009–1045	1036–1045
70 Go-Reizei	1035–1068	1045–1068
71 Go-Sanjo	1034–1073	1068–1073
72 Shirakawa	1053–1129	1073–1087
73 Horikawa	1079–1107	1087–1107
74 Toba	1103–1156	1107–1123
75 Sutoku	1119–1164	1123–1142
76 Konoe	1139–1155	1142–1155
77 Go-Shirakawa	1127–1192	1155–1158
78 Nijo	1143–1165	1158–1165
79 Rokujo	1164–1176	1165–1168
80 Takakura	1161–1181	1168–1180
81 Antoku[1]	1178–1185	1180–1185
82 Go-Toba	1180–1239	1183–1198
83 Tsuchimikado	1195–1231	1198–1210
84 Juntoku	1197–1242	1210–1221
85 Chukyo	1218–1234	1221
86 Go-Horikawa	1212–1234	1221–1232
87 Shijo	1231–1242	1232–1242
88 Go-Saga	1221–1272	1242–1246
89 Go-Fukakusa	1243–1304	1246–1260
90 Kameyama	1249–1305	1260–1274
91 Go-Uda	1267–1324	1274–1287
92 Fushimi	1265–1317	1287–1298
93 Go-Fushimi	1288–1336	1298–1301
94 Go-Nijo	1285–1308	1301–1308
95 Hanazono	1297–1348	1308–1318
96 Go-Daigo	1288–1339	1318–1339
97 Go-Murakami	1328–1368	1339–1368

[1]Reign dates overlap because Antoku fled the capital with the Taira and Go-Toba was put in as rival emperor by the Minamoto.

POSTHUMOUS NAME	BIRTH/DEATH	REIGN DATES
98 Chokei	1343–1394	1368–1383
99 Go-Kameyama	?–1424	1383–1392
A Kogon—Northern[2]	1313–1363	1331–1333
A Komyo "	1322–1380	1336–1348
C Suko "	1334–1398	1348–1351
D Go-Kogon "	1338–1374	1351–1371
E Go-Enyu "	1359–1393	1371–1382
100 Go-Komatsu	1377–1433	1382–1412
101 Shoko	1401–1428	1412–1428
102 Go-Hanazono	1419–1471	1428–1464
103 Go-Tsuchimikado	1442–1500	1464–1500
104 Go-Kashiwabara	1464–1526	1500–1526
105 Go-Nara	1497–1557	1526–1557
106 Ogimachi	1517–1593	1557–1586
107 Go-Yozei	1572–1617	1586–1611
108 Go-Mizunoo	1598–1680	1611–1629
109 Meisho*	1624–1696	1629–1643
110 Go-Komyo	1633–1654	1643–1654
111 Gosai	1637–1685	1655–1663
112 Reigen	1654–1732	1663–1687
113 Higashiyama	1675–1709	1687–1709
114 Nakamikado	1702–1737	1709–1735
115 Sakuramachi	1720–1750	1735–1747
116 Momozono	1741–1762	1747–1762
117 Go-Sakuramachi*	1740–1813	1762–1771
118 Go-Momozono	1758–1779	1771–1779
119 Kokaku	1771–1840	1780–1817
120 Ninko	1800–1846	1817–1846
121 Komei	1831–1867	1846–1867
122 Meiji	1852–1912	1867–1912
123 Taisho	1879–1926	1912–1926
124 Showa (Hirohito)	1900 or 1901–	1926–

[2]99A thru E represent "emperors" of the Northern Court.

APPENDIX B

Descendants of the Emperor Taisho

Emperor Hirohito   1900 (or 1901)–
   m. Princess Nagako   1903–
      Princess Shigeko*   1926–1961
         m. Morihiro Higashikuni   1916–1969
      Princess Sachiko   1927–1928
      Princess Kazuko*   1929–
         m. Toshimichi Takatsukasa   1923–1966
      Princess Atsuko*   1931–
         m. Takamasa Ikeda   1926–
      Crown Prince Akihito   1933–
         m. Michiko Shoda   1934–
            Prince Naruhito (Hito)   1960–
            Prince Fumihito (Aya)   1965–
            Princess Sayako (Nori)   1969–
      Prince Hitachi (Masahito)   1935–
         m. Hanako Tsugaru   1940–
      Princess Takako*   1939–
         m. Hisanaga Shimazu   1934–

Prince Chichibu (Yasuhito)   1902–1953
   m. Setsuko Matsudaira   1909–

Prince Takamatsu (Nobuhito)   1905–1987
   m. Kikuko Tokugawa   1911–

355

Prince Mikasa (Takahito) 1915–
  m. Yuriko Takagi 1923–
    Princess Yasuko* 1944–
      m. Tadateru Konoe 1939–
    Prince Tomohito of Mikasa 1946–
      m. Nobuko Aso 1955–
        Princess Akiko 1981–
        Princess Yohko 1983–
    Prince Yoshihito of Mikasa 1948–
    Princess Masako* 1951–
      m. Masayuki Sen 1956–
    Prince Takamado (Norihito) 1954–
      m. Hisako Tottori 1953–
        Princess Tsuguko 1986–

*Lost status as imperial family member on marriage.

APPENDIX C

The Imperial Rescript
on Education

Know ye, Our subjects:

Our Imperial Ancestors have founded Our Empire on a broad basis and everlasting and have deeply and firmly implanted virtue; Our subjects ever united in loyalty and filial piety have from generation to generation illustrated the beauty thereof. This is the glory of the fundamental character of Our Empire, and herein also lies the source of Our education. Ye, Our subjects, be filial to your parents, affectionate to your brothers and sisters; as husbands and wives be harmonious, as friends true; bear yourselves in modesty and moderation; extend your benevolence to all; pursue learning and cultivate arts, and thereby develop intellectual faculties and perfect moral powers; furthermore, advance public good and promote common interests; always respect the Constitution and observe the laws; should emergency arise, offer yourselves courageously to the State; and thus guard and maintain the prosperity of Our Imperial Throne coeval with heaven and earth. So shall ye not only be Our good and faithful subjects, but render illustrious the best traditions of your forefathers.

The Way here set forth is indeed the teaching bequeathed by Our Imperial Ancestors, to be observed alike by Their Descendants and the subjects, infallible for all ages and true in all places. It is Our wish to lay it to heart in all reverence, in common with you, Our subjects, that we may all thus attain to the same virtue.

The 30th day of the 10th month
of the 23rd year of Meiji.
[October 30, 1890]

(IMPERIAL SIGN MANUAL.   IMPERIAL SEAL.)

 APPENDIX D

The Imperial House Law

OFFICIAL GAZETTE
ENGLISH EDITION

Thursday, January 16, 1947
GOVERNMENT PRINTING BUREAU, TOKYO

I hereby give My sanction, with the advice of the Privy Council, to the Imperial House Law, for which the concurrence of the Imperial Diet had been obtained, and cause the same to be promulgated.

Signed: HIROHITO, Seal of the Emperor

This fifteenth day of the first month of the twenty-second year of Showa (January 15, 1947)

Countersigned:
Prime Minister and concurrently Minister for Foreign Affairs— YOSHIDA Shigeru
Minister of State—Baron SHIDEHARA Kijuro
Minister of Justice—KIMURA Tokutaro
Minister for Home Affairs—OMURA Seiichi
Minister of Education—TANAKA Kotaro
Minister of Agriculture and Forestry—WADO Hiroo
Minister of State—SAITO Takao
Minister of Communications—HITOTSUMATSU Sadayoshi
Minister of Commerce and Industry—HOSHIJIMA Niro
Minister of Welfare—KAWAI Yoshinari
Minister of State—UEHARA Etsujiro
Minister of Transportation—HIRATSUKA Tsunejiro
Minister of Finance—ISHIBASHI Tanzan

Minister of State—KANAMORI Tokujiro
Minister of State—ZEN Keinosuke

Law No. 3

THE IMPERIAL HOUSE LAW

Chapter I. Succession to the Imperial Throne

Article 1. The Imperial Throne shall be succeeded to by a male offspring in the male line belonging to the Imperial Lineage.

Article 2. The Imperial Throne shall be passed to the members of the Imperial Family according to the following order:

1. The eldest son of the Emperor.
2. The eldest son of the Emperor's eldest son.
3. Other descendants of the eldest son of the Emperor.
4. The second son of the Emperor, and his descendants.
5. Other descendants of the Emperor.
6. Brothers of the Emperor and their descendants.
7. Uncles of the Emperor and their descendants.

In case there is no member of the Imperial Family as under the numbers of the preceding paragraph, the Throne shall be passed to the member of the Imperial Family next nearest in lineage.

In the cases of the two preceding paragraphs, precedence shall be given to the senior line, and in the same degree, to the senior member.

Article 3. In case the Imperial Heir is affected with an incurable and serious disease, mentally or physically, or there is a serious hindrance, the order of succession may be changed by decision of the Imperial House Council and in accordance with the order stipulated in the preceding Article.

Article 4. Upon the demise of the Emperor the Imperial Heir shall immediately accede to the Throne.

Chapter II. The Imperial Family

Article 5. The Empress, the Grand Dowager Empress, the Empress Dowager, Shinno, the consorts of Shinno, Naishinno, O, the consorts of O, and Jo-o shall be members of the Imperial Family.

Article 6. The legitimate children of an Emperor, and the legitimate grandchildren of an Emperor in the legitimate male line shall be Shinno in the case of a male, and Naishinno in the case of a female. The legitimate descendants of an Emperor in the third and later generations in the legitimate male line shall be O in the case of a male and Jo-o in the case of a female.

Article 7. In case an O succeeds to the Throne, his brothers and sisters who are O and Jo-o shall specially become Shinno and Naishinno.

Article 8. The son of the Emperor who is the Imperial Heir is called "Kotaishi" and in case there is no Kotaishi, the grandson of the Emperor, who is the Imperial Heir, is called "Kotaison."

Article 9. The Emperor and the members of the Imperial Family may not adopt children.

Article 10. The institution of Empress, and the marriage of any male member of the Imperial Family shall be passed by the Imperial House Council.

Article 11. A Naishinno, O, or Jo-o, of fifteen years of age or more, shall leave the status of the Imperial Family member according to her or his own desire and by decision of the Imperial House Council.

Beside the case as mentioned in the preceding paragraph, a Shinno (excepting the Kotaishi and the Kotaison), Naishinno, O, or Jo-o, shall in the case of special and unavoidable circumstances, leave the status of the Imperial Family member by decision of the Imperial House Council.

Article 12. In case a female of the Imperial Family marries a person other than the Emperor or the members of the Imperial Family, she shall lose the status of the Imperial Family member.

Article 13. The consorts of a Shinno or O who leaves the status of the Imperial Family member, and his direct descendants and their consorts, excepting those females who are married to other members of the Imperial Family and their direct descendants, shall lose simultaneously the status of the Imperial Family member. However, as regards his direct descendants and their consorts, it may be so decided by the Imperial House Council that they do not lose the status of the Imperial Family member.

Article 14. A female, not of the Imperial Family, who is married to a Shinno or O, may, upon the loss of her husband, leave the status of the Imperial Family member according to her own desire.

When a female mentioned in the preceding paragraph has lost her husband, she shall, in case of special and unavoidable circumstances beside the case as under the same paragraph, leave the status of the Imperial Family member by decision of the Imperial House Council.

In case a female mentioned in the first paragraph is divorced, she shall lose the status of the Imperial Family.

The provisions of the first paragraph and the preceding paragraph shall apply to the females married to other members of the Imperial Family mentioned in the preceding Article.

Article 15. Any person outside the Imperial Family and his or her descendants shall not become a member thereof except in the cases where a female becomes Empress or marries a member of the Imperial Family.

Chapter III. Regency

Article 16. In case the Emperor has not come of age, a Regency shall be established.

In case the Emperor is affected with a serious disease, mentally or physically, or there is a serious hindrance and is unable to perform his acts in matters of state, a Regency shall be instituted by decision of the Imperial House Council.

Article 17. The Regency shall be assumed by a member of the Imperial Family of age according to the following order:

1. The Kotaishi, or Kotaison.
2. A Shinno or an O.
3. The Empress.
4. The Empress Dowager.
5. The Grand Empress Dowager.
6. A Naishinno and a Jo-o.

In the case of No. 2 in the preceding paragraph the order of succession to the Throne shall apply; and in the case of No. 6 in the same paragraph, the order of succession to the Throne shall apply mutatis mutandis.

Article 18. In case the Regent, or a person falling in the order of assumption of Regency, is affected with a serious disease, mentally or physically, or there is a serious hindrance, the Imperial House Council may decide to change the Regent or the order of assumption of Regency, according to the order stipulated in the preceding Article.

Article 19. When, because of minority of the person falling in the order of assumption of Regency or because of the obstacles mentioned in the preceding paragraph, another member of the Imperial Family has become Regent, he shall not yield his post of Regent to the said member of the Imperial Family who has the precedence on the ground of his attainment to majority or the removal of those obstacles, except in the case such person happens to be Kotaishi or Kotaison.

Article 20. In case the obstacles mentioned in Article 16, paragraph 2 have been removed, the Regency shall be abolished by decision of the Imperial House Council.

Article 21. The Regent, while in office, shall not be subject to legal action. However, the right to take that action is not impaired hereby.

Chapter IV. Majority; Honorific Titles; Ceremony of Accession; Imperial Funeral; Record of Imperial Lineage; and Imperial Mausoleums

Article 22. The majority age for the Emperor, the Kotaishi and the Kotaison shall be eighteen.

Article 23. The honorific title for the Emperor, the Empress, the Grand Empress, the Grand Empress Dowager and the Empress Dowager shall be "Heika."

The honorific title for the members of the Imperial Family other than those mentioned in the preceding paragraph shall be "Denka."

Article 24. When the Throne is succeeded to, the ceremony of Accession shall be held.

Article 25. When the Emperor dies, the Rites of Imperial Funeral shall be held.

Article 26. The matters relating to the family status of the Emperor and the members of the Imperial Family shall be registered in the Record of Imperial Lineage.

Article 27. The graves of the Emperor, the Empress, the Grand Empress Dowager, and the Empress Dowager, shall be called "Ryo," and those of all other members of the Imperial Family shall be called "Bo"; the matters relating to Ryo and Bo shall be entered respectively in the Ryo Register and the Bo Register.

Chapter V. The Imperial House Council

Article 28. The Imperial House Council shall be composed of ten members.

These members shall consist of two Imperial Family members, the Presidents and Vice-Presidents of the House of Representatives and of the House of Councillors, the Prime Minister, the head of the Imperial House Office, the Chief Judge, and one other judge of the Supreme Court.

The members of the Imperial Family and the judge other than the Chief Judge of the Supreme Court, who are to become members of the Council, shall be chosen by mutual election respectively from among the members of the Imperial Family of age and from among the judges other than the Chief Judge of the Supreme Court.

Article 29. The member of the Imperial House Council, who is the Prime Minister, shall preside over its meeting.

Article 30. There shall be appointed ten reserve members in the Imperial House Council.

As regards the reserve members for the Imperial Family members and the judge of the Supreme Court in the Council, the provision of Article 28, paragraph 3, shall apply mutatis mutandis. The reserve members for the Presidents and the Vice-Presidents of the House of Representatives and of the House of Councillors in the Council shall be selected by mutual election from among the members of the House of Representatives and of the House of Councillors.

The number of the reserve members mentioned in the two preceding paragraphs shall be the same as the numbers of the members in the Council, and the order of assuming their functions shall be determined at the time of the mutual election.

The reserve member for the Prime Minister in the Council shall be the Minister of State who has been designated as the one to perform temporarily the functions of Prime Minister under the provisions of the Cabinet Law.

The reserve member for the head of the Imperial House Office in the Council shall be designated by the Prime Minister from among the officials of the Imperial House Office.

In case there is a hindrance with regard to a member of the Council, or he is missing, the reserve member for him shall perform his functions.

Article 31. As regards the President, the Vice-President and members of the House of Representatives mentioned in Article 28 and the preceding paragraph, they shall be, in case the house has been dissolved and pending the selection of the successors, those persons who were respectively the President, the Vice-President, and members of the House at the time of its dissolution.

Article 32. Term of office for the members of the Council, who are members of the Imperial Family and a judge other than the Chief Judge of the Supreme Court and their reserve members shall be four years.

Article 33. The Imperial House Council shall be convened by the President of the Council.

The Imperial House Council must be convoked, if demanded by four members or more, in the cases as under Article 3; Article 16, paragraph 2; Article 18; and Article 20.

Article 34. The Imperial House Council, unless attended by six members or more, may not open deliberations and make decisions.

Article 35. The deliberations of the Imperial House Council shall be decided by a majority vote of two-thirds or more of the members present, in the cases of Article 3; Article 16, paragraph 2; Article 18; and Article 20; and by a majority in all other cases.

In case of a tie in the case of the latter clause of the preceding paragraph, the President shall make the decision.

Article 36. A member may not participate in the deliberation of any matter in which he has a special interest.

Article 37. The Imperial House Council shall exercise only those powers which are provided for by this and other laws.

Supplementary Provisions:

The present law shall come into force from the day of the enforcement of the Constitution of Japan.

The present members of the Imperial Family shall be considered as the members of the Imperial Family under this law; and with regard to the application of the provisions of Article 6, they shall be considered the legitimate offspring in the legitimate male line.

The present Ryo and Bo shall be considered as the Ryo and Bo as under Article 27.

Law No. 4

THE IMPERIAL HOUSE ECONOMY LAW

Article 1. State property which is assigned, or which has been determined to be assigned, to the official use of the Imperial House (called the Imperial House Use Property hereafter) shall be treated as government use property under the State Property Law, and matters pertaining to it will be handled by the Imperial House Office.

In case an item of state property is assigned, or is determined to be assigned to the official use of the Imperial House, the matter must be passed by the Imperial House Economy Council. So shall it be also in case the use of any Imperial House Use Property is discontinued or altered.

The Imperial House Use Property shall not be property intended for revenue.

The Imperial House Economy Council shall make the necessary survey concerning the Imperial House Use Property at an interval of not more than five years and will make a report to the Cabinet.

When the report of the preceding paragraph has been made, the Cabinet shall report to the Diet the content thereof.

Article 2. In the cases of sale or purchase for reasonable price and of other ordinary private economic transactions, and in any of the cases specified below, a property may be alienated to, or received by, the Imperial House, or a gift can be made therefrom without authorization by the Diet each time:

1. Giving or receiving of properties not exceeding a certain amount in value as fixed by law separately.

2. Giving or receiving of properties exceeding the amount of the preceding subparagraph, but not exceeding a certain amount in value as fixed by law separately, which has been passed by the Imperial House Economy Council.

When the giving and receiving of property takes place more than once one year between the same parties, the provisions of the subparagraphs of the preceding paragraph shall apply to the aggregate amount of such transactions.

In case the amount in value of the properties given by or to a member belonging to the Imperial House under the provisions of 1 or 2 of paragraph 1 in a period less than one year has reached the amount as fixed separately by law, the above provisions do not apply to the giving or receiving of property by such member during the remainder of the year.

Article 3. The appropriation for the expenditures of the Imperial House to be made in the budget shall be divided into the Inner Court Appropriation, the Imperial Court Appropriation, and the Imperial Family Appropriations.

Article 4. The Inner Court Appropriation shall apply to the daily expenditures of the Emperor and Empress, the Grand Empress Dowager, the Empress Dowager, the Kotaishi and his consort, the Kotaison and his consort, and other Imperial Family members belonging to the Inner Court, and to other miscellaneous expenditures of the Inner Court; a fixed sum shall be appropriated annually as is determined by law separately.

The sums provided by the Inner Court Appropriation shall constitute the Privy Purse and shall not be treated as public money to be administered by the Imperial House Office.

In case the Imperial House Economy Council deems it necessary to change the fixed sum of paragraph 1, it must submit to the Cabinet its opinion thereon.

When the opinion of the Council has been submitted, as under the preceding paragraph, the Cabinet shall report to the Diet the content thereof at the earliest opportunity.

Article 5. The Imperial Court Appropriation shall apply to all the expenditures of the Imperial Court other than those of the Inner Court and shall be administered by the Imperial House Office.

Article 6. The Imperial Family Appropriations shall apply to the sums which are provided as annuities for the maintenance of the dignity of the members of the Imperial Family and those which are provided by the persons who leave the status of the Imperial Family member for the maintenance of dignity as persons who have been members of the Imperial Family, in one-time payment to be made at the time when they leave their status. The sums of such annuities or one-time payments shall be calculated on the basis of a fixed sum as will be determined by law separately.

The annuities shall be calculated according to the stipulations set forth under the following numbers and in paragraphs 3 to 5; and they shall be paid annually to the members of the Imperial Family other than those specified in Article 4.

1. Shinno shall receive: Married—the whole of the fixed sum; of age and unmarried—one-half of the fixed sum; underage and unmarried—one-quarter of the fixed sum.

2. The consort of a Shinno shall receive one-half of the fixed sum.

3. Naishinno shall receive: of age—one-half of the fixed sum; underage—one-quarter of the fixed sum.

4. O, the consort of an O, and Jo-o shall receive sums corresponding to 70 percent of the amount of the annuities calculated respectively on the basis of Shinno, the consort of a Shinno, and Naishinno.

A married Shinno or O, even after the cessation of marital relationship, shall receive the same amount as before.

A member of the Imperial Family who is the Regent, shall receive five times the fixed sum during the term of his office.

A person, possessing more than one status, shall be paid according to the status commanding the highest annuity.

A person who leaves the status of member of the Imperial Family according to the provisions of the Imperial House Law shall receive a sum in one-time payment, as determined by the Imperial House Economy Council, and within the limits of not exceeding the amount corresponding to fifteen times the amount of the annuity due to the said person to be calculated according to the provisions of paragraphs 2 and 3 and the preceding paragraph.

In calculating the sum for one-time payment, as under the preceding paragraph, an unmarried or underage Shinno or O shall be considered as a married Shinno or O; and Naishinno or Jo-o underage as a Naishinno or Jo-o of age.

The provisions of Article 4, paragraphs 3 and 4 shall apply to the fixed sum of paragraph 1.

Article 7. The Imperial Heir upon his accession to the Throne shall receive such traditional properties as are to be handed down with the Throne.

Article 8. The Imperial House Economy Council shall be composed of eight members.

The members shall be the Presidents and Vice-Presidents of the House of Representatives and of the House of Councillors, the Prime Minister, the Minister of Finance, the head of the Imperial House Office, and the head of the Board of Audit.

Article 9. There shall be appointed eight reserve members in the Imperial House Economy Council.

Article 10. The Imperial House Economy Council unless there are five members present or more may not open deliberations and make decisions.

The deliberations shall be decided by a majority vote. In case of a tie, the chairman shall make the decision.

Article 11. The provisions of Article 29; Article 30, paragraphs 3–7; Article 31; Article 33, paragraph 1; Article 36; and Article 37 of the Imperial House Law shall apply to the Imperial House Economy Council mutatis mutandis.

The post of the reserve member of the Minister of Finance in the Council shall be filled by the Vice Minister of Finance; and that of the reserve member of the head of the Board of Audit by an official of the Board of Audit, who shall be designated by the Prime Minister.

Supplementary Provisions:

The present Law shall come into force as from the day of the enforcement of the Constitution of Japan.

Those items of the former Imperial Household Property which are in the use of the Imperial House at the time of the enforcement of the present Law and which have become State Property under the State Property Law shall be considered, without a decision of the Imperial House Economy Council, as the Imperial House Use Property, regardless of the provisions of Article 1, paragraph 2.

The necessary matters relating to the transitional disposition of the rights and obligations which belong to the former Imperial House Account at the time of the enforcement of the present Law, and which are to be carried over by the State, shall be provided for by cabinet order.

The Inner Court Appropriation and the sum of the annuities under the Imperial Family Appropriations for the fiscal year in which the present Law takes effect shall be provided for on the basis of monthly quotas.

 APPENDIX E

World War II Surrender Documents

I

Accepting the terms set forth in Declaration issued by the heads of the Governments of the United States, Great Britain, and China on July 26th, 1945, at Potsdam and subsequently adhered to by the Union of the Soviet Socialist Republics, We have commanded the Japanese Imperial Government and the Japanese Imperial General Headquarters to sign on Our behalf the Instrument of Surrender presented by the Supreme Commander for the Allied Powers and to issue General Orders to the Military and Naval Forces in accordance with the direction of the Supreme Commander of the Allied Powers. We command all Our people forthwith to cease hostilities, to lay down their arms, and faithfully to carry out all the provisions of Instrument of Surrender and the General Orders issued by the Japanese Imperial Government and the Japanese Imperial General Headquarters hereunder.

This second day of the ninth month of the twentieth year of Syowa.*

SEAL   Signed: HIROHITO

                                  Countersigned: Nuruhiko-o
                                                 Prime Minister
                                                 et alia

*Japanese-English transliteration system in effect at time.

II

HIROHITO

By the Grace of Heaven, Emperor of Japan, seated on the Throne occupied by the same Dynasty changeless through ages eternal,

To all to whom these Presents shall come, Greeting!

We do hereby authorise Yoshijiro Umezu, Zyosanmi, First Class of the Imperial Order of the Rising Sun, Second Class of the Imperial Military Order of the Golden Kite, to attach his signature by command and in behalf of Ourselves and Our Imperial General Headquarters unto the Instrument of Surrender which is required by the Supreme Commander for the Allied Powers to be signed.

In witness whereof, We have hereunto set Our signature and caused the Great Seal of the Empire to be affixed.

Given at Our Palace in Tokyo, this first day of the ninth month of the twentieth year of Syowa, being the two thousand six hundred and fifth year from the Accession of the Emperor Zinmu.

Seal of the Empire

Signed: HIROHITO

Countersigned: Yoshijiro Umezu
Chief of the General
Staff of the
Imperial Japanese
Army

Soemu Toyoda
Chief of the General
Staff of the
Imperial Japanese
Navy

APPENDIX F

Foreword to Scientific Paper by Hirohito

Five Hydroid Species from the Gulf of Aqaba, Red Sea

by: Hirohito

BIOLOGICAL LABORATORY, IMPERIAL HOUSEHOLD,
TOKYO, 1977

Over the past fifty years or more, I, availing myself of the leisure hours from my official duties, have been continuing my studies of biology, first under the guidance of the late Dr. Hirotaro Hattori and then with the help of Dr. Itiro Tomiyama. I am hoping to pursue further studies as heretofore in the future so far as my spare time permits.

His Royal Highness Crown Prince Hassan bin Talal visited this country in 1974 on a goodwill mission, and on May the 9th I had the pleasure of receiving him at my Palace. Later in the same year, His Royal Highness was so good as to send me eight biological specimens, which I received on December the 11th. I am most grateful to him for his kindest thought.

The specimens are those of five species, viz., *Halocordyle disticha* (Goldfuss), *Cytaeis nassa* (Millard), *Eudendrium temellum* Allman, *Clytia linearis* (Thornely), and *Dynamena crisiodes* Lamouroux, all of which were collected in the Gulf of Aqaba during the period between June the 25th and August the 19th in the same year. I have got on with the study of these hydroid species, and now have decided to bring out the results of my study as a report entitled "Five Hydroid Species of the Gulf of Aqaba, Red Sea."

All the specimens used for the purpose of this present study of mine belong to the Biological Laboratory, Imperial Household.

It is to be added that, to supplement the study of these five hydroid species, I also have used specimens collected in the sea area of Japan and other places. As for the enumeration of synonyms, I have tried to search and mention as many as possible of them. In conducting my present study, Drs. Tohru Uchida and Itiro Tomiyama have given me useful hints and suggestions, and Mr. Hatsuki Tsujimura has cooperated with me in the research work.

I have taken advice from Dr. Tadashige Habe of the National Science Museum regarding the generic name *Halocordyle* and also asked him to identify two kinds of shells to which *Cytaeis nassa* (Millard) is attached, while requesting Dr. Takeo Ito, Professor of the Ehime University, for the Japanese translation of "stenotele" and Dr. Mayumi Yamada, Professor of the Hokkaido University, for that of "blastostyle" respectively.

I was presented by Dr. F. M. Bayer, Curator of the Department of Invertebrate Zoology, National Museum of Natural History, Smithsonian Institution, with a copy each of parts of the works by L. Oken (1815) and G. A. Goldfuss (1920) respectively and several colonies of *Halocordyle* collected by Dr. Bayer himself at Miami, and also with the sketches of the type specimen of *Pennaria pacifica* Clarke belonging to the Museum. Moreover, through his kindness, I was given several representatives of the colonies obtained at three different localities and kept as *Pennaria tiarella* (Ayres) in the Museum.

Dr. James D. Ebert, ex-Director of the Marine Biological Laboratory, Woods Hole, also presented me with a copy of John McCrady's thesis of 1859.

It was a great pleasure for me to be able to broaden my views and advance a step further in my study, thanks to the kindness of the two scholars mentioned above.

I feel indeed very grateful to all these scholars and parties concerned in arranging for me to have such lucky chances, recollecting my good fortune to be able personally to meet many scientists and exchange with them views and knowledge in the field of biology at various places during my visit to the United States in autumn, 1975.

I am indebted to Mr. Tatsuya Shimizu for making permanent slides, and to Mrs. Hiroko Daba for drawing sketches.

Grateful acknowledgments are due to Dr. Jean Dan, ex-Professor of the Ochanomizu University, who has taken the trouble to look over the English translation, as well as to all those who have cooperated with me in conducting the present study and otherwise.

My best thanks are due to the Hoikusha Publishing Co. for the trouble taken about printing and binding for this publication.

HIROHITO

June, 1977

Glossary

AMATERASU: the Sun Goddess; progenitrix of the imperial family.

BAKUFU: literally "tent government"; name given Yoritomo's Kamakura shogunal government in the late twelfth century; came to stand for shogun's military administration until the end of the shogunate in the late nineteenth century.

BANZAI: literally "Ten Thousand Years"; a cry of congratulations or rejoicing.

BUSHIDO: literally "the way of the samurai"; the principles of loyalty and honor samurai always follow.

DAIDAIRI: literally "Great Inner Enclosure"; original Heian palace; present Kyoto imperial palace built to south of the original structure.

DAIJO-SAI: literally "Great New Food Festival"; the part of the enthronement ceremonies in which the emperor shares a symbolic meal with the Sun Goddess.

DAIMYO: literally "great name"; a noble, or lord, in feudal times; from Ieyasu's time, it included those 262 nobles whose incomes exceeded ten thousand koku of rice per year.

DAJO TENNO: literally "Great Abdicated Sovereign"; honorific title for abdicated monarchs; Jito (a regnant empress) was the first to receive the title on retirement.

DENKA: equivalent of "Imperial Royal Highness."

GENRO: the "Elder Statesmen"; extraconstitutional group of high-ranking advisers to Meiji.

GO-: when applied before the posthumous name of an emperor it means "the Second"; no emperor's posthumous name was used a third time.

GOSHO: the Imperial Palace.

GO-TAIREI: literally "Great Etiquette," meaning the Great Ceremonies; a term embracing the entirety of the enthronement ceremonies from beginning to end.

HEIAN: ancient name for Kyoto; also Heian Period (794–1185), from establishment of the city to the beginning of the military government (shogunate).

HEIKA: literally "Lord"; equivalent of "Majesty."

IMINA: the personal name of the emperors; almost never used by the Japanese to refer to the sovereigns.

INSEI: the "cloister government" of abdicated sovereigns as practiced from the late eleventh to the late twelfth century; ex-sovereign retained final authority in practice.

KAMPAKU: chancellor; from 882 to 1868 the highest dignity at the imperial court.

KASHIKODOKORO: the portable sanctuary of the Sacred Mirror, always kept near the emperor; the shrine of the same name on the grounds of Tokyo's Imperial Palace is the palace's chief place of worship.

KIMIGAYO: the Japanese national anthem; the entire lyrics are "May our Sovereign reign for thousands of ages until pebbles become rocks overgrown with moss."

KINSEI SOVEREIGNS: the emperors of "modern times," meaning since the establishment of the Tokugawa shogunate at the beginning of the seventeenth century.

KOJIKI: "Record of Ancient Matters"; the first Japanese history, written by imperial command 711–712, it disagrees in many specifics with the slightly later *Nihongi*.

KOKU: a unit of rice equaling about five bushels or forty gallons; from the sixteenth century a daimyo's revenue was measured in koku.

KOTAISHI: literally "Imperial Eldest Son"; heir apparent if the son of an emperor.

KOTAISON: literally "Imperial Eldest Grandson"; heir apparent if the son of a deceased kotaishi.

KUGE: hereditary nobles of the imperial court, from families such as the Fujiwara; they held precedence at court over the military nobles (daimyo).

MICHODAI: literally "Curtained Throne"; empress's throne platform at enthronement ceremony.

NIHONGI: a collection of the ancient chronicles of Japan, from its origins to the end of the reign of Jito in 696; written in 720; also called the *Nihonshoki*.

OKURINA: a posthumous name given to a person of rank; the names by which deceased emperors are known; Hirohito's okurina will be Showa.

RITSU-RYO: the two parts of the Taiho Codes, namely the Taiho Ritsu, the penal code, and the Taiho Ryo, the civil code.

RONIN: masterless, or unemployed, samurai.

SAMURAI: until the Meiji Restoration a military man or warrior; also stood for his class, and thus the wives and children of samurai shared this title.

SESSHO: regent for underaged emperors; fulfilled virtually same duties as the kampaku; when there was a kampaku, there was no sessho, and vice-versa.

SHIMBETSU: literally "descendants of the gods"; the second-ranking class of citizens in ancient imperial Japan; it comprised the bulk of freeborn society.

SHOGUNATE: throughout most of its history (late twelfth to late nineteenth century) this office retained final political authority, either in the person of the shogun himself or in his regent.

SOKUI-REI: literally "Ascend Throne Ceremony"; the part of the enthronement ceremony in which the monarch makes the formal announcement of his accession.

SONNO JOI: literally "reverence the emperor" and "reject the foreigners"; renewed interest in the position of the throne and attendant criticism of the shogunate in nineteenth-century Japanese politics.

TAIHO CODES: the civil and penal codes of the early eighth century; an encoding of the principles of the Taika Reform.

TAIKA REFORM: the adoption of Chinese governmental practices in the late seventh century whose effect was to strengthen the position of the emperor in the state.

TAKAMIKURA: literally "High August Seat"; emperor's throne platform at enthronement ceremony.

TENNO: literally "Son of Heaven"; reigning emperor (either male or female).

TOKAIDO: literally "Eastern Seaway Road"; beginning in Kyoto it traversed fifteen old provinces to Edo (Tokyo); the most traveled of the seven primary roads of feudal Japan.

UJI: clan; largest kinship unit, such as the Fujiwara or the Minamoto; o-uji was the senior family within the clan, ko-uji the branches.

ZAIBATSU: the financial and industrial cartels, or conglomerates, that largely controlled Japan's wealth in the modern era.

Bibliography

Akimoto, Shunkichi. *The Lure of Japan.* Tokyo: Hokuseido Press, 1934.

Asakawa, K. *The Early Institutional Life of Japan—A Study in the Reform of 645 A.D.* New York: Paragon Book Reprint Corp., 1963 (first published 1873).

———. *Japan.* Philadelphia: John D. Morris & Co., 1906.

Aston, W. G., trans. *Nihongi, Chronicles of Japan from the Earliest Times to A.D. 697.* Rutland, Vt.: Tuttle, 1972.

Bayrd, Edwin. *Kyoto—Japan's Ancient Capital.* New York: *Newsweek,* 1974.

Benedict, Ruth. *The Chrysanthemum and the Sword.* Rutland, Vt.: Tuttle, 1946.

Bergamini, David. *Japan's Imperial Conspiracy.* New York: Wm. Morrow & Co., 1971.

Brewster, Jennifer, trans. *The Emperor Horikawa Diary.* Honolulu: University Press of Hawaii, 1977.

Brinkley, Capt. F. *A History of the Japanese People—From the Earliest Times to the End of the Meiji Era.* New York: Encyclopedia Company, 1915.

Buchan, John, ed. *Japan.* Boston: Houghton Mifflin, 1923.

Chamberlain, Basil Hall. *A Handbook for Travellers in Japan.* London: Murray, 1913.

———. *Things Japanese.* London: John Murray, 1905.

———, trans. *The Kojiki—Records of Ancient Matters.* Rutland, Vt.: Tuttle, 1981.

Clement, Ernest W. *A Handbook of Modern Japan.* Chicago: A. C. McClurg & Co., 1904.

Clyde, Paul H., and Burton F. Beers. *A History of the Far East.* Englewood Cliffs, N.J.: Prentice-Hall, 1948.

Coffey, Thomas M. *Imperial Tragedy—Japan in World War II—The First Days and the Last.* New York: World Publishing Co., 1970.

Courdy, Jean-Claude. *The Japanese—Everyday Life in the Empire of the Rising Sun.* New York: Harper & Row, 1984.

De Garis, Frederic. *We Japanese.* Miyanoshita, Japan: Fujiya Hotel, Ltd., 1934.

De Mente, Boye. *The Whole Japan Book.* Phoenix, Ariz.: Phoenix Books, 1983.

Devos, George A. *Japan's Invisible Race—Caste in Culture & Personality.* Berkeley: University of California Press, 1972.

Dickson, Walter. *Japan.* New York: Peter Fenelon Collier & Son, 1901.

Dilts, Marion May. *The Pageant of Japanese History.* New York: David McKay Co., 1938.

Dower, John W. *The Elements of Japanese Design—A Handbook of Family Crests, Heraldry and Symbolism.* New York: Weatherhill, 1971.

Dunn, Charles J. *Everyday Life in Traditional Japan.* Tokyo: Tuttle, 1969.

Enthronement Edition, *The Japan Advertiser.* Tokyo: Japan Advertiser Press, 1928.

Farsari, A. *Keeling's Guide to Japan.* Yokohama: A. Farsari, 1890.

Fleisher, Benjamin W., pub. and ed. *Enthronement of the One Hundred Twenty-Fourth Emperor of Japan.* Tokyo: *Japan Advertiser,* November 1928.

Forbis, William H. *Japan Today—People, Places, Power.* New York: Harper & Row, 1975.

Foreign Affairs Association of Japan. *The Japan Year Book—1934.* Tokyo: Kenkyusha Press, 1934.

Fortune Magazine. June, July 1933; September 1936; February 1942; April 1944.

Fraser, Mary Crawford. *A Diplomat's Wife in Japan—Sketches at the Turn of the Century.* Tokyo: Weatherhill, 1982.

Frederic, Louis. *Daily Life in Japan at the Time of the Samurai, 1185–1603.* Tokyo: Tuttle, 1972.

Futara, Count Yoshinori, and Setsuzo Sawada. *The Crown Prince's European Tour.* Osaka: Osaka Mainichi Publishing Co., Ltd., 1926.

Gauntlett, John Owen, trans. *Kokutai No Hongi—Cardinal Principles of the National Entity of Japan.* Cambridge, Mass.: Harvard University Press, 1949.

Gibney, Frank. *Five Gentlemen of Japan.* Tokyo: Tuttle, 1953.

Griffis, Wm. Elliot. *The Mikado: Institution & Person.* Princeton, N.J.: Princeton University Press, 1915.

———. *The Mikado's Empire.* New York: Harper & Bros., 1883.

Gunther, John. *Inside Asia.* New York: Harper & Bros., 1938.

Hall, John Whitney, ed. *Japan Before Tokugawa—Political Coordination and Economic Growth, 1500–1650.* Princeton, N.J.: Princeton University Press, 1981.

———. *Japan from Prehistory to Modern Times.* New York: Delta, 1970.

——— and Richard Beardsley. *Twelve Doors to Japan.* New York: McGraw-Hill, 1965.

Hane, Mikiso. *Peasants, Rebels & Outcastes—The Underside of Modern Japan.* New York: Pantheon, 1982.

———, trans. and intro. *Emperor Hirohito and His Chief Aide-de-Camp—The Honjo Diary, 1933–1936.* Tokyo: University of Tokyo Press, 1967, 1982.

Hawley, Willis M. *The Japanese Family Crest.* Hollywood, Calif.: privately published, 1976.

Hirai, Kiyoshi. *Feudal Architecture of Japan.* New York: Weatherhill, 1973.

Hirohito, Emperor—A Pictorial History. Tokyo: Kodansha, 1975.

Holton, D. C. *The Japanese Enthronement Ceremonies with an Account of the Imperial Regalia.* Tokyo: Kyo Bun Kwan, 1928.

Hunter, Janet, comp. *Concise Dictionary of Modern Japanese History.* Berkeley: University of California Press, 1984.

Hurst, G. Cameron, III. *Insei—Abdicated Sovereigns in the Politics of Late Heian Japan 1086–1185.* New York: Columbia University Press, 1976.

Hyde, Murakami, and J. Harper, eds. *Great Historical Figures of Japan.* Tokyo: Japan Culture Institute, 1978.

Ienaga, Saburo. *The Pacific War, 1931–1945.* New York: Pantheon, 1978.

"Imperial Court of Japan," *Japan Illustrated.* Tokyo: Nippon Dempo Tsushinsha, 1938.

Imperial Palace, The. Tokyo: Mainichi Editional Center, n.d.

Inouye, Jukichi. *Home Life in Tokyo.* London: KPI Ltd., 1985 (first published 1910).

Irie, Sukemasa. "My 50 Years with the Emperor," *Japan Quarterly.* Tokyo: Asahi Shimbun, Jan.–Mar. 1983.

Irita-Seizo. "On the Three Imperial Treasures," *Cultural Nippon.* Tokyo: Nippon Bunka Chuo Renmei, 1941.

Ishimoto, Baroness Shidzue. *Facing Two Ways—The Story of My Life.* New York: Farrar & Rinehart, 1935.

Iwai-Hirosato. "A Study of the Varied Names for Japan," *Cultural Nippon.* Tokyo: Nippon Bunka Chuo Renmei, 1940.

Japan National Commission for UNESCO. *Japan—Its Land, People & Culture.* Tokyo: Printing Bureau, 1964.

Japan Times Photo Book of the Imperial Palace. Tokyo: Japan Times, Ltd., 1971.

Japanese Government Railways. *Japan—The Official Guide.* Tokyo: Board of Tourist Industry, 1941.

Kanroji, Osanaga. *Hirohito—An Intimate Portrait of the Japanese Emperor.* Los Angeles: Gateway Publishers, 1975.

Kennedy, Malcolm D. *A Short History of Japan.* New York: Mentor Books, 1963.

Kishida, Hideo. "Utakai-Hajime: The New Year's Poetry Party," *Japan Quarterly.* Tokyo: Asahi Shimbun, Jan.–Mar. 1983.

Koyama, Itoko. *Nagako—Empress of Japan.* New York: John Day Co., 1958.

Kurzman, Dan. *Kishi & Japan: The Search for the Sun.* New York: Obolensky, 1960.

Lehmann, Jean-Pierre. *The Roots of Modern Japan.* New York: St. Martin's Press, 1982.

Leonard, Johnathan Norton. *Early Japan* (Great Ages of Man Series). New York: Time-Life Books, 1968.

Macintyre, Michael. *The Shogun Inheritance—Japan and the Legacy of the Samurai.* New York: A & W Publishers, 1981.

Mainichi Newspapers. *Japan Almanac 1975.* Tokyo: Mainichi Newspapers, 1975.

Manning, Paul. *Hirohito—The War Years.* New York: Dodd, Mead & Co., 1986.

Maraini, Fosco. *Meeting with Japan.* New York: Viking Press, 1959.

Mass, Jeffrey P., ed. *Court & Bakufu in Japan—Essays in Kamakura History.* New Haven: Yale University Press, 1982.

Matsumura, Gentaro. *The Emperor's Islands—The Story of Japan.* Tokyo: Lotus Press, 1977.

Minnich, Helen Benton. *Japanese Costume and the Makers of Its Elegant Tradition.* Tokyo: Tuttle, 1963.

Mitford, A. B. (Lord Redesdale). *Tales of Old Japan.* Rutland, Vt.: Tuttle, 1966 (first published in 1871).

Morris, Ivan. *The World of the Shining Prince—Court Life in Ancient Japan.* Baltimore, Md.: Penguin Books, 1964.

————, trans. and ed. *The Pillow Book of Sei Shonagon.* New York: Penguin, 1967.

Morton, W. Scott. *Japan—Its History and Culture.* New York: McGraw-Hill, 1970.

Morton-Cameron, W. H. *Present Day Impressions of Japan.* Yokohama: Globe Encyclopedia Co., 1919.

Mosley, Leonard. *Hirohito—Emperor of Japan.* Englewood Cliffs, N.J.: Prentice-Hall, 1966.

Munro, Neil Gordon. *Prehistoric Japan.* New York: Johnson Reprint, 1971.

Murray, David. *Japan.* New York: G. P. Putnam's Sons, 1894.

Nishi, Kazuo, and Kazuo Hozumi. *What Is Japanese Architecture?* Tokyo: Kodansha, 1983.

Nourse, Mary A. *Kodo—The Way of the Emperor.* Indianapolis, Ind.: Bobbs-Merrill, 1940.

Omori, Annie Shepley, and Kochi Doi, trans. *Diaries of Court Ladies of Old Japan.* Boston: Houghton Mifflin, 1920.

Omura, Bunji. *The Last Genro—Prince Saionji.* Philadelphia: J. B. Lippincott Co., 1938.

Pacific War Research Society, comp. *Japan's Longest Day.* Tokyo: Kodansha, 1980.

Papinot, E. *Historical and Geographical Dictionary of Japan.* Rutland, Vt.: Tuttle, 1982 (originally published 1910).

Peerage of Japan. Yokohama: *Japan Gazette,* 1912.

Peterson, James W. *Orders and Medals of Japan and Associated States.* Chicago: Orders and Medals Society of America, n.d.

Pine, L. G. *The Story of Titles.* Newton Abbot, England: David & Charles, 1969.

Ponsonby-Fane, Richard. *Imperial Cities: The Capitals of Japan from Oldest Times Until 1229.* Washington, D.C.: University Publishers of America, 1979.

————. *The Imperial Family of Japan.* Kobe: Japan Chronicle, Taisho Era.

Price, Willard. *Japan and the Son of Heaven.* New York: Duell, Sloan and Pearce, 1945.

Reischauer, Edwin O. *The Japanese.* Cambridge, Mass.: Harvard University Press, 1977.

————. *The Emperor of Japan—A Profile on the Occasion of the Visit by the Emperor and Empress to the United States.* New York: Japan Society, Inc., 1975.

————, ed. *The Great Contemporary Issues: Japan.* New York: Arno Press, 1974.

Richardson, Bradley M., and Scott C. Flanagan. *Politics in Japan.* Boston: Little Brown, 1984.

Richie, Donald. *A Taste of Japan.* Tokyo: Kodansha International Ltd., 1985.

Sadler, A. L. *The Maker of Modern Japan—The Life of Tokugawa Ieyasu.* London: Allen & Unwin, 1937.

Sakaiya, Taichi. "Hirohito and the Imperial Tradition," *PHP Intersect* Magazine. Tokyo: Dec. 1985.

Sakamoto, Taro. *The Japanese Emperor Through History.* Tokyo: International Society for Educational Information, 1984.

Scherer, James A. B. *The Romance of Japan Through the Ages.* Tokyo: Hokuseido Press, 1933.

————. *Manchukuo: A Bird's-Eye View.* Tokyo: Hokuseido Press, 1933.

Scidmore, Eliza Ruhamah. *Jinrikisha Days in Japan.* New York: Harper & Bros., 1891.

Scott-Stokes, Henry. "Behind Closed Doors—A Reassessment of the Emperor," *PHP Intersect* Magazine. Tokyo: Dec. 1985.

Seidensticker, Edward G. *Low City, High City.* Tokyo: Tuttle, 1983.

————, trans. *The Tale of the Genji by Murasaki Shikibu.* New York: Alfred A. Knopf, 1985.

Seward, Jack. *Hara-Kiri—Japanese Ritual Suicide.* Tokyo: Tuttle, 1968.

Shillony, Ben-Ami. *Revolt in Japan—The Young Officers of the February 26, 1936, Incident.* Princeton, N.J.: Princeton University Press, 1973.

Shogun Age Exhibition Executive Committee. *The Shogun Age Exhibition* (Catalog). Tokyo: 1983.

Sladen, Douglas B. *Queer Things About Japan.* New York: Kegan Paul, 1912.

Smith, Bradley. *Japan—A History in Art.* Garden City, N.Y.: Doubleday, 1964.

Smith, Robert J. *Japanese Society—Tradition, Self, and the Social Order.* Cambridge, England: Cambridge University Press, 1983.

Sugawara, Makoto. "The Cloistered Emperor and Yoritomo," *The East* Magazine. Tokyo.

Taguchi-Shota. "His Majesty the Present Emperor in His Early Age," *Cultural Nippon* Magazine Vol. III, No. 2 (June 1940).

Terry, T. Philip. *Terry's Guide to the Japanese Empire.* Boston: Houghton Mifflin, 1914 and 1930 editions.

Tiedemann, Arthur E. *Modern Japan—A Brief History.* Princeton, N.J.: D. Van Nostrand, 1955.

Togashi, Junji. *Koshitsu Jiten* (Encyclopedia of Imperial Household). Tokyo: Meigenshobo Bookstore, 1976.

———. "The Emperor's Daily Life Revolves Around Nature," *The East* Magazine. Tokyo: Jul.–Aug. 1975.

Trewartha, Glenn Thomas. *Japan—A Physical, Cultural & Regional Geography.* Madison: University of Wisconsin Press, 1945.

Turnbull, Stephen R. *The Book of the Samurai—The Warrior Class of Japan.* New York: Arco, 1982.

Varley, H. Paul, trans. *A Chronicle of Gods and Sovereigns.* New York: Columbia University Press, 1980.

Vining, Elizabeth Gray. *Return to Japan.* Philadelphia: J. B. Lippincott, 1960.

———. *Windows for the Crown Prince.* Philadelphia: J. B. Lippincott, 1952.

Waley, Arthur, trans. *The Tale of the Genji by Lady Murasaki.* New York: Modern Library, 1960.

Waley, Paul. *Tokyo Then & Now.* Tokyo: Weatherhill, 1984.

Ward, Robert E. *Japan's Political System.* Englewood Cliffs, N.J.: Prentice-Hall, 1967.

Webb, Herschel. *Japanese Imperial Tradition in the Tokugawa Period.* New York: Columbia University Press, 1968.

Wiencek, Henry. *The Lords of Japan* (Treasures of the World series). Chicago: Stonehenge Press, 1982.

Yonekura, Isamu. "The History of the Imperial Family," *The East* Magazine. Tokyo: Jul.–Aug. 1975 to Jan. 1976.

———. "The Yamato—The Establishment of the First Unified Government in Japan," *The East* Magazine. Tokyo: Nov. 1974.

———. "Kanmu . . . The Emperor Afflicted with Ghosts," *The East* Magazine Vol. 9, No. 8.

Young, A. Morgan. *Japan Under Taisho Tenno 1912–1926.* London: Allen & Unwin, 1928.

Index

393

ETHS Central Library

Sons of heaven

101023343   952 pa